Alberta Church of Christ
1110 Twenty-Sixth Avenue, East
Tuscaloosa, Alabama

GOD SPEAKS TO MODERN MAN

 Harry Anderson, Artist

There is no human experience that affords so much joy and peace of heart as that which comes to a sinner when he finds his Saviour, who is "the way, the truth, and the life."

GOD SPEAKS to MODERN MAN

Also Published Under the Title "Highways to Truth"

By ARTHUR E. LICKEY

REVIEW AND HERALD PUBLISHING ASSN.
Washington, D.C.

OFFSET IN U.S.A.

Introduction

THE world today is troubled. Men everywhere are seeking the solution to their problems, personal, social, national, and international. And underneath it all is a longing to know what is the real meaning of life, and the destiny to which it leads.

Where did the world come from, and how did life begin? Who arranged the earth as we see it today, peopled by races of varying tastes and talents, of conflicting interests and ambitions? Why are men continually at war? Is there no chance for peace? Why is human nature torn between ideals and actions, between hope for something better and perverse inclination to do something worse?

Unaided by some power outside himself, man has never been able to find a satisfactory answer to these questions. But there is hope, for implanted in every heart is a desire to worship some higher power, a desire after God. And God has the answers.

This book is intended to lead men to God and the Book that is His message to His earthborn children. Listen as God speaks to modern man in these distraught times.

MERWIN R. THURBER.

Contents

SECTION 1—Man's Questions About God

SECTION 2—Man's Questions About Evil

SECTION 3—Man's Questions About the Bible

SECTION 4—God Speaks to Man About Christ

SECTION 5—God Speaks Through the Prophecy of Daniel

SECTION 6—God Speaks Concerning Heaven's Government for Man

SECTION 7—God Speaks Concerning Heaven's Trademark and Sign

SECTION 8—God Speaks Concerning Divine Healing and Healthful Living

SECTION 9—God Speaks Concerning Death and Immortality

SECTION 10—God Speaks Concerning the Prophecies of Revelation

SECTION 11—God Speaks Concerning the Church, Civilization, and Happiness

H. A. Roberts

The world is full of interesting books for the pleasure and development of the mind. But none is so potent a force for building character as the Holy Scriptures.

SECTION ONE

MAN'S QUESTIONS ABOUT GOD

Combine Photos

War and flood and tornado have no favorites. Good and bad suffer alike when in their destructive paths. This wrecked church in London is typical of war's destruction.

CHAPTER 1

Where Is God?

IT WAS another day of modern life and modern war. In a small church a handful of devout men and women were gathered to worship God.

From an airplane, high above, a great bomb was released. Like a diabolical contraption concocted in some unearthly, infernal region afar, it whined its fiendish way earthward, bent on its violent business of destruction.

It was not an atom bomb, with its surpassing explosive power and its alarming aftereffects, which might show up in generations yet unborn. It was not an unheralded rocket bomb descending faster than the speed of sound. It was not a gas bomb, which on explosion would release deadly poisonous gases to make deep burns in the flesh, choke its victims to death, and linger for days to lure tardy, unsuspecting souls to suffering. Nor was it a biological bomb packed with germs of disease and terrifying plagues.

It was only a plain, ordinary, old-fashioned blockbuster. People knew just about how much damage it would do. When it struck the little church square on and went off in a thunderous explosion, the house of worship was obliterated. Experienced salvage workers knew that no ambulances would need to be called, and no burial arrangements made for the erstwhile worshipers. The bomb had taken care of everything.

Crowds of people gathered as near to the scene as officers would permit. Among them was a young man who seemed deeply disturbed but said nothing until he turned to leave. Then half to himself and half aloud he whispered, "Where is God?"

This man was not an atheist, who disbelieved in the existence of God. He was not an infidel, who had hardened himself in unbelief. He was not an agnostic, who could happily or unhappily teeter between belief and unbelief. He did not consider himself justly to be classed as even slightly skeptical. And when there stirred within his soul a strange mixture of fear and disappointment and rebellion at what he had seen, he gave but a spontaneous expression to that question which has come to the minds of unnumbered millions, who, though sincere, are troubled to know, "Where is God?" Why does He not do something about the horrors attending life on this earth? Why does He not manifest Himself and "destroy them which destroy the earth"? Why does He not destroy all evil?

The Universal Cry of Distress

To Adam in Eden, God said, "Where art thou?" Modern man has turned about to ask, "God, where art Thou?"

Since the days of Adam probably no human being ever reached the age of responsibility without being plagued with the question: "Where is the hand of a loving God in my life?"

The bride of a few months, with her babe yet unborn, may weep in bitterness at the graveside of the man she loved more than life itself.

An invalid mother of a large family of small children may suddenly be left alone to battle in apparent futility the brutal forces of life arrayed against her.

Small children are rudely shorn of parental love and care, sometimes by cruel fate and sometimes by sordid sin.

Lives are snuffed out by the powers of nature. Lightning strikes like a flaming sword. Winds sweep in fury as though bent on wreaking vengeance. Floods mock the helpless. Flaming fires leave but bits of bones and heaps of ashes. Earthquakes make the earth reel to and fro like a drunkard.

In a hundred ways man dies by the machines of his own invention. Thousands perish in the wrecks of trains, airplanes, ships, and automobiles; by accident in the home, in the factory, and on the farm; and millions die or are mutilated in the ghastly and seemingly endless business of satanic, scientific modern war in earth and sea and sky.

A strong man traveling the sunlit path of success sees his way turn sharply into deep shadows he scarcely dreamed existed. There in the darkness a torturous load of almost unbearable sorrow is fastened upon his struggling soul. Heavier than the sand of the sea is the sorrow that would seek to crush out the very spirit of life itself. In the agony of his calamity the man cries out, "Let the day perish wherein I was born," "my soul chooseth . . . death rather than my life." Job 3:3; 7:15.

Job and Elijah, two of the greatest and most fearless men who ever lived, sought death as an escape from life. He who has not known such depths of distress may yet find sudden and intimate acquaintance with this unwelcome stranger, and cringe under both the crude and the refined forms of his pain and torture.

Does the world have no compensating joys? Indeed! Yet in this abode of sin, sickness, suffering, and death; in this place of fear, hatred, and suspicion; of crime, war, and bloodshed; in this land of thorn and thistle, storm and earthquake, famine and disaster, man's problems are as numberless as time is endless. Invention of the atom bomb and advancing discovery in the realm of destruction but extend the limits of disaster and make more universal and pitiful man's cry of distress. One is sharply reminded of the prediction made by the Jewish Messiah concerning men of our time: "Men swooning with panic and foreboding of what is to befall the universe." Luke 21:26, Moffatt.

The Universal Cry for God

There is no question about man's cry of distress. The growing ranks of those whose troubles drive them to insanity, or to the psychiatrist because of the fear of insanity, are like a mighty army. Thousands seek to escape their troubles by committing suicide. The majority meet their problems and solve them, or live with them to the accompaniment of much complaining, or seek happiness through one or more of a thousand cults.

Man's cry for God is just as universal as life and trouble. Somewhere down under the burden of business and the load of care, beneath the lusts of pleasure and sin, beyond the seeking for gold and power and glory, there is a lowly, hidden spot in the soul of every man, whence go forth eternal longings for the eternal God. Like a hidden transmitter, this inner, sacred station seeks to beam through to God.

This desire for God has been called the "God-ache." Without question it is universal among all races, whether white, black, yellow, red, or brown, or any of the shades between. Rich and poor, high and low, educated and uneducated, civilized and uncivilized—all know, or have known, this desire after God, the God-ache. If there is a blank space in the heart of a modern man, it is, as Julian Huxley has said, "a God-shaped blank."

"God hath dealt to every man the measure of faith." Romans 12:3. This faith is not only like a transmitter, trying to break through to contact God, but like a delicate receiver, sensitive to messages from God.

Charles Kellogg, the noted naturalist, and a musician friend were walking together on Sixth Avenue in New York City, amid the aftertheater throng and the rumbling, honking, clanging babel of noise and confusion.

Suddenly Mr. Kellogg stopped and unceremoniously brought his friend to a halt. "Listen," he said. "Do you hear that?"

"Hear what?"

"That cricket!"

The musician drew up in doubt and amazement. "Cricket!" he replied. "How could anybody hear the song of a cricket in all this bedlam?"

"Come with me," said Kellogg, and he led his friend down a basement stairs, and there in a niche of the wall sat a small black cricket singing its bedtime song.

"How ever could a man have ears sharp enough to tune in a cricket, and at the same time dull enough to tune out all that street noise?" asked the musician.

"I'll show you," replied Kellogg. "Let us return to the street."

There he took from his pocket a dime and tossed it onto the sidewalk. Scores of people in both directions stopped in their tracks as if they had heard a pistol shot, and looked toward the spot where the dime had fallen.

"You see," explained Kellogg, "the people have their ears tuned to dimes and dollars. I have mine tuned to the sounds of nature."

It is more than a mere sanctimonious platitude to say that the hour is growing late, five minutes to twelve some say, and it is time that modern man began tuning his ears to sounds that, to him, have grown dangerously indistinct. Some healing balm of Heaven needs to touch the calloused ear drums of this generation. The heart of man needs contact with God.

If God should speak to puzzled, bewildered modern man, what would be His first words?

CHAPTER 2

God's First Answer to Modern Man

WHAT IS the first and most fundamental answer for the man uncertain in a fog of fearful doubt? What does God say to one struggling with the skepticism born of disappointment and disillusionment? What word does He have for him who has reached the outposts of unbelief, or who may stand on the verge of open rebellion, or who may have the floodgates of sorrow and disaster opened upon him? What is God's answer to any man who says sincerely, "God, where art Thou?"

Is it that oft-quoted statement: "The fool hath said in his heart, There is no God"? Psalms 14:1. True as this statement is, it scarcely is the answer for the troubled mind of a sincere man. It was not given for that purpose. It might easily prove to be the push that would send a harassed soul over the precipice to utter ruin. This is not God's way.

God's answer is simple. It is a strange challenge to a kind of action that seems almost like no action at all. He who disregards it will be utterly inexcusable. He who heeds it in sincerity will discover life's priceless pearl. Here it is: "Be still, and know that I am God." Psalms 46:10.

What a challenge! If these be the words of God, they place Him under simple test by every sincere person.

Would God disappoint a man at the very first door He asked the man to open?

These words, "Be still, and know that I am God," give the one piece of vital counsel in that entire memorable and beloved refuge psalm, which has been the source of hope to millions for millenniums. It is found in the next to the last verse, in fact. The remainder of the psalm is given over almost entirely to a description of the eternal refuge. The path to that refuge begins at the point where man's confidence in himself ends, and where God can get him to be still and listen.

The Din of the Now

Never has it been so hard to listen. Never in the history of the world has there been such widespread din and confusion, rush and hustle and bustle. Though the pace was never swifter, the end is not yet. Man's genius is harnessed to plans to give the world more leisure to live faster—faster motorcars, ships, planes, and trains; faster tanks, bullets, and bombs; faster education, transportation, and communication—faster everything!

The story is told of an earthly visitor at the gate of heaven. Said the attending angel, "How did you enjoy God's beautiful world during your days on earth?" The man replied, "I didn't get a chance to see much of it; I was too busy telephoning and everything."

The Friend at the Modern Roadside

Alongside this modern, roaring speedway of life on which civilization is rolling at ever-increasing speed stands man's best friend, God. He knows that man's machine is hurtling on toward utter tragedy, because man's faith is burning up and his morals are burning out.

To every traveler God says, "Be still, and know that I am God."

Every truly great man who ever lived took time out to listen to God. Abraham listened, and God said, "I will . . . bless thee." Genesis 26:3. Jacob, fleeing for his life, listened in the lonely night under the stars, and heard a voice from the top of the mystic ladder saying, "I am with thee, and will keep thee in all places whither thou goest." Genesis 28:15. That was just the message he needed. George Washington listened at Valley Forge and heard that "still small voice." Lincoln listened in the White House chambers, and God sent hope in hours of darkness and despair. God is man's best friend at every roadside and lane of every life.

A Sick Man Argues

One of the sickest men who ever got well was a man named Job. He was sick from the sole of his foot to the crown of his head, sick all over outside and all through inside, sick physically and spiritually. In the time of this illness Job had visits from four earthly friends, Eliphaz, Bildad, Zophar, and Elihu.

These prominent citizens of their day fell into a long, and it would seem at times bitter, argument over the meaning of trouble and the question of God's dealings with men.

Job contended that inasmuch as he had been a just and kind man, therefore God was unfair and unjust in allowing him to suffer dread sickness that was now nigh unto death. Furthermore, he insisted that God no longer would hear his prayers, and he pleaded for an opportunity to speak with God. Said he, "I would order my cause before him, and fill my mouth with arguments. I would know the words which he would answer me." Job 23:4, 5. So desperate was Job that he was ready to debate with God, and was fully convinced that before his array of arguments God would stand speechless. How easy it is for man to become wiser than the God in whom he actually believes!

Eliphaz the Temanite got at the matter something like this: "Job, you have been noted for your earnest admonition to others in their time of trouble, but when you get down flat on your own back, you cannot take your own medicine. The fact is, God is punishing you because of some wickedness. Do not despise His chastening. And remember, too, we are wiser in these matters than you because our hair is gray. You yet have much to learn." (See Job 4:3-5, 7-9; 5:17; 15:10.)

Bildad the Shuhite took this positive approach: "Job, if you would only do right you would prosper." (Job 8:6.) The inference was, of course, that Job had been doing things in secret of which the world knew not. Having sores on his body from head to foot, he was open to considerable suspicion.

Zophar the Naamathite pushed the probe a little deeper with the idea: "You really deserve more punishment than you are receiving. Such sins as you evidently have committed ought to bring down upon you a greater wrath." "Know therefore that God exacteth of thee less than thine iniquity deserveth." Job 11:6.

Poor Job. He fought back, embittered by their insinuations, flinging in their teeth such statements as, "No doubt but ye are the people, and wisdom shall die with you. . . . I am not inferior to you." Job 12:2, 3.

It remained for young Elihu the Buzite to finish off the argument in a burst of wrath against both Job and the three friends—against Job because he had sought to justify himself rather than God, and against the three old men because they had failed to answer Job wisely. It may be said that Elihu's lengthy speech, which stopped his elders in their tracks, had considerable wisdom. Among other things he said, "He [God] looketh upon men, and if any say, I have sinned, and perverted that which was right, . . . he will deliver his soul . . . , and his life shall see the light." Job 33:27, 28. Also he added, "If they obey and serve him, they shall spend their days in prosperity." Job 36:11.

Wherein All These Men Failed

In the total words spoken by all these men there was both truth and untruth. Job's friends were wrong when they insisted that his disease came upon him as a punishment for his personal wickedness, and that prosperity is a sign of righteousness. Disease may be the result of one's own sin or it may not be. Job made the mistake of charging God with injustice, and probably of overestimating his own attainments. He did not have all the facts nor did he fully understand any of them. He did not have the long view or the whole view.

But all these searchers for truth made a yet greater mistake. It was much greater in practical significance than were their theological errors and differences of opinion. After all, these men were good moral characters, as men go, contending for what they thought to be right.

What was their real mistake? They had been more ready to express their opinions about God than to let God express His opinions to them. In their zeal to outtalk one another, they had talked God out.

God's Turn Comes

All contenders finally run out of argument, and the greatest filibuster collapses. So it was with these men discussing God and man's troubles. They finally gave God a chance above argument, complaint, suffering, and bitterness.

Addressing His message particularly to Job God said, "Who is this that darkeneth counsel by words without knowledge? Gird up now thy loins like a man; for I will demand of thee, and answer thou me." Job 38:2, 3. God then spoke of creation; the earth, air, and sky; day and night; snow, hail, light, thunder, lightning, rain, ice, and frost; stars and clouds; lions, wild goats, deer; horses going forth into battle; peacocks, hawks, eagles, whales, elephants, et cetera, concerning which the high school boy and girl of today knows more than God revealed to Job.

Yet, when God gave Job a chance to answer, this sick, spent, and bitter man replied, "I will lay mine hand upon my mouth." Job 40:4. Forgotten were his labored arguments and all his planned speeches. Long before Jesus was to say, "He that hath ears to hear, let him hear" (Matthew 11:15), Job discovered his ears, and he listened to the voice of God.

When God had finally finished, it was with these words: "He [God] is a king over all the children of pride." Job 41:34. It was then that Job answered, "I know that thou canst do every thing, and that no thought can be withholden from thee." "Wherefore I abhor myself, and repent in dust and ashes." Job 42:2, 6.

The first thing to remember is that when Job stopped arguing and complaining, either verbally or inwardly, and listened to the voice of God, even as revealed in nature, *he found his God again.*

The second thing to remember is that, according to the record, God gave to Job no explanation concerning the matter of the relationship of his disease to punishment, nor did Job ask for any information. Job had closed his mouth in silence, opened his heart to Heaven, and found his personal God. This God Himself became the personal answer to his distressing personal problems. There is no other satisfactory solution. It is not so much theology about God as it is fellowship with God—knowing God. "This is life eternal, that they might know thee the only true God, and Jesus Christ, whom thou hast sent." John 17:3.

THE MAN WHO HAD IT STRAIGHT

The apostle Paul might well have asked: "Where is God? Why does He not shield me from false friends? Why does He not safeguard me from religious enemies? Why does He not keep me from prison, protect me from floggings, heal my diseases, and reverse the decisions of Emperor Nero? Why does He not hold back from my neck the headsman's hatchet?"

Three times did he beseech God to take away physical affliction. His God answered, "No," but added, "my grace is sufficient for thee: for my strength is made perfect in weakness." Paul approached God no more on this matter, but wrote, "Most gladly therefore will I rather glory in my infirmities, that the power of Christ may rest upon me." 2 Corinthians 12:9.

Back of this submission in affliction, and interwoven with it like the shuttle thread through the warp and woof of the woven cloth, was a golden thread of faith, expressed in his mature manhood thus: "Nevertheless I am not ashamed: for I *know whom I have believed.*" 2 Timothy 1:12. It is one thing to believe in God. It is another thing to know God. Paul knew God. When God spoke he listened and heeded.

That is why, standing in the very shadow of his executioner, he could say, "I am now ready. . . . I have fought . . . , I have finished . . . , I have kept the faith: henceforth there is . . . a crown." 2 Timothy 4:6-8. Here was a man powerful in pulpit or prison, victorious in life or death.

THE PHILOSOPHER AND THE MECHANIC

The richest man in the world of his day is said to have asked the wisest man of his times for an explanation of God. For days and days the philosopher studied, but the more he thought, the more confused he became. Said he, "I cannot frame an answer." He had the frame, but he did not have the picture.

The religious leader Tertullian is reported to have said, "There is the wisest man in the world, and he cannot tell you who God is. But the most ignorant mechanic among the Christians knows God, and is able to make Him known unto others."

What God Asks

God does not ask a man to find Him only by deep study of His nature and plans. "Canst thou by searching find out God?" Job 11:7.

God does ask men to "be still." To them He says, "Still thy words. Still thy prejudices. Still thy preconceived opinions. For a moment still thy pride, thy arrogancy, thy rebellion, and I will speak with thee."

"Look unto me, and be ye saved." Isaiah 45:22.

"Come unto me, . . . I will give you rest." Matthew 11:28.

"Commit thy way unto the Lord." Psalms 37:5.

"Lo, I am with you alway." Matthew 28:20.

This simple approach does not settle all questions or bring complete understanding, but it is God's beginning for every man.

The night that Aaron Burr flung open the shutters of his window at Princeton University and shouted, "Good-by, God," he closed the door of his soul. He who today will open wide the shutters of his soul to God will find the light of God's presence shining in.

"Still, still with Thee, when purple morning breaketh,
When the bird waketh, and the shadows flee;
Fairer than morning, lovelier than the daylight,
Dawns the sweet consciousness, I am with Thee!

. . . . .

"When sinks the soul, subdued by toil, to slumber,
Its closing eye looks up to Thee in prayer;
Sweet the repose beneath Thy wings o'ershading,
But sweeter still, to wake and find Thee there.

"So shall it be at last, in that bright morning,
When the soul waketh, and life's shadows flee;
Oh, in that glad hour, fairer than day dawning,
Shall rise the glorious thought, I am with Thee!"

CHAPTER 3

What Kind of God Can Modern Man Worship?

A SMALL BOY watched in dismay as a cat played with a mouse, finally killed it, and then ate it. Having been taught by his parents that God made everything, the boy was now prepared to ask a few more questions about life. So at the opportune time he inquired of his father, "Did God make everything?"

"Yes, son, God made all things."

"Did He make the birds and the bees?"

"Of course, son."

"Did He make the little mice?"

"Certainly, my boy."

After a fairly long pause the boy, with puckered brow, exclaimed, "Well, then, why did God make the cat too?"

Many persons have found considerable difficulty in exercising belief in God because of the problem posed by cats and mice, to say nothing of man and modern war. The second section of this book will treat more fully the basic problem here presented.

Other people find it perfectly normal to experience a simple and profound faith in God despite all the long and ugly catalog of strife, conflict, and apparent contradictions.

It is wise to remember that all thinking people have had some doubts. We think there never lived an atheist who did not at times, and frequently, doubt his unbelief. Let no believer think that the unbeliever has no struggles with his unbelief. It was Young who wrote, "By night an atheist half-believes a God."

The question that we seriously approach here is, What kind of god can an intelligent, modern person worship? Man is created with a deeply implanted instinct to worship some intelligent power greater than himself and all men. Whom shall he worship?

Scientist Pierre Lecomte du Nouy is quoted as follows:

"Man would accept the hardest disciplines if he could be convinced that there is no conflict between religion and science; if his intellectual, rational self did not always enter into collision with his sentimental, intuitive self."—*Time,* Feb. 24, 1947. Courtesy of *Time,* copyright Time Inc., 1947.

This is indicative of the intelligent man's longing for God and for something definite to be believed and practiced. We cannot fully share the confidence of our French friend that man would obey God if only there were no conflict between faith in Him and some scientific dogma. We remember that there have always been millions who believe but do not obey. "The devils also believe, and tremble." James 2:19. They do not yield to the discipline of obedience. The simple truth must be faced that a large segment of modern Christianity seeks a religious experience of ecstasy and feeling which is divorced from the rigors of discipline and subjection to the laws of God. What Scientist Du Nouy is really saying is that there are intelligent men today who crave an experience of certainty. This we truly believe.

Nevertheless, belief needs to be made doubly certain, for surely there is much so-called faith which is unfounded, and confusion abounds on every hand. To the sincere seeker for truth are the words written: "That I might make thee know the *certainty* of the words of truth." Proverbs 22:21.

We have here to consider five qualities, or attributes, which God must needs have if He is to be sincerely worshiped by modern, intelligent man.

A GOD OF POWER

"There is one thing God has said;
Ay, twice have I heard him say it:
that power belongs to God."

Psalms 62:11, Moffatt.

It would be safe to say that a thousand times in a thousand ways has every man seen the manifestations of power. Power is everywhere. Watch the fiery ball of the setting sun as it slides down beyond a hill or mountain range, disappears on the far horizon of a prairie wheatfield, descends at the yonder edge of plain or desert, or seems silently to sink into the great sea.

That giant atomic power plant is a sort of center about which our earth swings at a distance of more than ninety million miles. We travel around this gigantic solar race track at a speed of more than eleven hundred miles a minute. Men talk of flying planes one thousand miles an hour—faster than the speed of sound. The simple fact is that we are all flying about seventy times that fast in our journey around the sun.

What keeps this earth, traveling 1,140 miles a minute, going peacefully on its path around the sun instead of heading off into space and possible collision and oblivion?

The answer is *Power.* Take a piece of string and tie it to a spool. Hold the end of the string and whirl the spool in a circle about your head. Now let go the string. Does the spool keep traveling round and round? Every child has learned by experience that the spool will strike off in some direction of its own, and he is fortunate if a windowpane is not broken or other damage done.

What kind of string would it take to hold the earth to its path around the sun? "The total attraction between the earth and sun amounts to the amazing pull of 3,600,-000 millions of millions of tons. This would be the breaking strain of a steel rod more than 3,000 miles in diameter—a force inexplicably exerted through, or transmitted by, apparently empty space."—CHARLES A. YOUNG, *Manual of Astronomy* (Ginn and Company), p. 199. That cable, 3,000 miles in diameter, would be more than 90,000,000 miles long, holding the earth in place for its silent race of over 560,000,000 miles every year.

Men have called this invisible cable gravitation. It is strong enough to hold a great planet in its course, yet a chirping sparrow can fly through it with the utmost ease. In fact, while the sun exercises this tremendous pull on the earth, people, objects, et cetera are not drawn off the earth by it, but on the contrary are held on the earth by the operation of the very same kind of power pulling the other way, believe it or not. That may sound like two minus two equals four, but it is the way of power—the power that controls the universe.

With interest we read this from the Bible: "By him all things *consist* [hold together]." Colossians 1:17. "Upholding all things by the word of his power." Hebrews 1:3.

Join the more than two million visitors who annually journey to gaze in awe and wonder at the surging, plunging power of Niagara Falls. Watch 200,000 cubic feet of water per second throw themselves in thunderous, foaming glee over a sheer drop of 150 feet to the river bed and rocks below. You too will understand why men have harnessed only a small fraction of this giant's capacity, producing but a mere million horsepower in hydroelectric plants, lest they mar the glory of this marvelous spectacle of nature.

"NIAGARA

"Flow on for ever, in thy glorious robe
Of terror and of beauty. Yea, flow on
Unfathom'd and resistless. God hath set
His rainbow on thy forehead, and the cloud
Mantled around thy feet. And He doth give
Thy voice of thunder power to speak of Him
Eternally—bidding the lip of man
Keep silence—and upon thine altar pour
Incense of awe-struck praise."

—LYDIA HOWARD SIGOURNEY.

We are thrilled by the magnificent throbbing power of steam. We pale at the ravaging power of unquenchable fire. We are mystified by the lighting, burning, shocking, uncanny power of electricity. We tremble before tornadoes and flee before floods. We feel galvanized, half thrilled and half frightened by the fantastic play and crackle of lightning. We look aghast at the destructive power of terrific explosives. We stand in silent awe before the yet unharnessed power of ceaseless ocean tides. And when we look into the vast dome of night's starlit sky, floods of gentle wonder sweep over the soul, and unresisting, the heart bows in a humility that borders the realm of worship.

At Sagamore Hill, Theodore Roosevelt and William Beebe used to play a little game together. As Beebe tells it: "After an evening of talk . . . we would go out on the lawn and search the skies until we found the faint spot of light-mist beyond the lower left-hand corner of the Great Square of Pegasus. Then one or the other of us would recite:

" 'This is the Spiral Galaxy in Andromeda.
It is as large as our Milky Way.
It is one of a hundred million galaxies.
It consists of one hundred billion suns, each
larger than our own.'

"Then Roosevelt would grin at me and say: 'Now I think we are small enough! Let's go to bed.' "—WILLIAM BEEBE, *The Book of Naturalists* (Alfred A. Knopf, Inc.), p. 234.

"When I heard the learn'd astronomer,
When the proofs, the figures, were
ranged in columns before me,
When I was shown the charts and the
diagrams, to add, divide, and
measure them,
When I sitting heard the astronomer
where he lectured with much applause in the lecture-room,
How soon unaccountable I became tired
and sick,
Till rising and gliding out I wander'd
off by myself,
In the mystical moist night-air, and from
time to time,
Look'd up in perfect silence at the stars."

—WALT WHITMAN.

He who would worship God will of necessity worship a God of power. Power is everywhere. "Power belongeth unto God"—the God of the Bible.

Created beings who never sleep by day or night chant in heavenly rhythm before the throne of God: "Holy, holy, holy, Lord God Almighty." Revelation 4:8.

Of tremendous personal significance to each one of us is this question and its answer: "Who is this that cometh . . . , travelling in the greatness of his strength? I that speak in righteousness, mighty to save." Isaiah 63:1.

God is a mighty reservoir of saving grace for the

needs of all men everywhere. He has literally surrounded this earth with the atmosphere of His grace and power. Breathe it. Receive it.

A God of Wisdom

When one reflects on the total information contained in all the books that men have written, he marvels at the tremendous amount of sheer knowledge possessed today by the human race. Add to this the total achievements of the race, and one stands in no small amazement.

Look at a linotype machine. Could you make one? Do you understand one? Watch a giant newspaper press with paper rolling through it at fifty miles an hour, coming out printed, folded, and ready to go. Can you get through your mind the intricacies of that marvel of engineering skill? Add to these, watches, radios, telephones, automobiles, jet and rocket engines, dynamos, radar, and television.

Then think of the sciences of astronomy, botany, zoology, chemistry, mathematics, medicine, and music. Consider the fields of philosophy, history, literature, and religion. Do not overlook everyday cooking, farming, building, and manufacturing of every kind.

A man spends his lifetime in one field of knowledge. He has all the advantage of accumulated knowledge from the past. He grows old and gets ready to die. What does he say? "I feel like a child playing with pebbles on the seashore, with the vast ocean of knowledge yet undiscovered."

Of Solomon it was said, "He was wiser than all men." 1 Kings 4:31. He studied plant life, bird life, fish life, insect life, everything he saw or thought of. When the queen of Sheba visited him she exclaimed, "The half was not told me." 1 Kings 10:7. Solomon wrote three thousand proverbs—wise, terse sayings. If anyone thinks a proverb is easy to write, let him try writing one that will be quoted by people three thousand years from now. Then write 2,999 more.

Whence cometh wisdom?

"God gave Solomon wisdom." 1 Kings 4:29.

God's wisdom is seen everywhere in the commonest things. Pumpkins do not grow on trees, though someone wrote of a man who thought that they should. Elephants do not have wings and whiz through the air to perch on your roof top. Even the prickly sandbur, hated by every barefooted boy, grows best where soil needs to be kept from drifting.

The yucca moth lays her eggs in the seed pod of the yucca plant. Pollen fertilization is accomplished for the plant by the action of the moth. When the eggs hatch, the larvae feed on the seeds of the plant. Thus the continued existence of each type of life is dependent on the other. The moth dies before her eggs are hatched, so she never could have learned by observation. Whence came her wisdom? God asked Job, "Doth the hawk fly by thy wisdom, and stretch her wings toward the south?" Job 39:26.

Man is finite. Wisdom is infinite. He who would worship God will of necessity worship a God of wisdom—wisdom seen on every hand. "Blessing, and glory, and *wisdom,* . . . be unto our God for ever and ever. Amen." Revelation 7:12.

Here are five gems for memory:

"The price of wisdom is above rubies." Job 28:18.

"The fear of the Lord, that is wisdom." Verse 28.

"Teach us to number our days, that we may apply our hearts unto wisdom." Psalms 90:12.

"The wisdom of this world is foolishness with God." 1 Corinthians 3:19.

"Let not the wise man glory in his wisdom, neither

let the mighty man glory in his might, let not the rich man glory in his riches: but let him that glorieth glory in this, that he understandeth and knoweth me, that I am the Lord which exercise lovingkindness, judgment, and righteousness, in the earth: for in these things I delight, saith the Lord." Jeremiah 9:23, 24.

When the great astronomer Kepler gazed into the skies through the giant telescope he said, "O God, I am thinking Thy thoughts after Thee."

> "Acquaint thyself with God, if thou wouldst taste
> His works. Admitted once to His embrace,
> Thou shalt perceive that thou wast blind before:
> Thine eye shall be instructed, and thine heart,
> Made pure, shall relish with divine delight
> Till then unfelt, what hands divine have wrought."
>
> —COWPER, *Task,* book 5.

A God of Beauty

Volumes might be written about beauty. There are the sunlit sky by day, the starlit sky by night, earth's carpet of green, the wild profusion of tinted flowers perfuming the air, lofty trees, enchanting lakes, peaceful rivers, lofty mountains, and mighty seas. From the twittering bird on a lowly branch to the rainbow that spans the sky beauty abounds in fantastic profusion.

We symbolize it with a story. An old Scottish shepherd tended his flock in the springtime pastures. He fell in with a gentleman examining wild flowers through a magnifying glass. The old man's new friend plucked a tiny flower, placed it under the glass, and invited the shepherd to take a look. He did. He kept on looking. His lips quivered. A tear stole down his weather-beaten face.

"Why are you troubled?" inquired his friend.

"I was just thinking," was the old man's wistful answer, "as I looked at the gorgeous beauty of that little flower, how many thousands of them I have trampled under my heavy shepherd boots, and never paid any heed to them."

Many times we are like the New England farmer who picked up a youthful hitchhiker. As they rode along in the wagon the young man showed him some beautiful pictures he had taken in the neighborhood. One of them especially pleased the farmer.

"Where was that taken?" he inquired.

"I don't recall, for I am a stranger in these parts," answered the youth.

Reaching the farmer's gate the young man suddenly smiled and said, "This is the very gateway in the picture."

"And to think I never before noticed how beautiful the place really is," was the farmer's warm answer.

Man is called to appreciate beauty and to worship the God of beauty. It is true that "eye hath not seen, nor ear heard, neither have entered into the heart of man, the things which God hath prepared for them that love him" (1 Corinthians 2:9), yet even now beauty and loveliness meet the eye at a thousand angles, and someday "thine eyes shall see the king in his beauty" (Isaiah 33:17).

Even to the child the beauties of the now speak of our Father God, who gave them, and stir imagination to grasp the picture of that "land mine eye hath seen in visions of enraptured thought, so bright that all which spreads between is with its radiant glories fraught."

"And Nature, the old nurse, took
The child upon her knee,
Saying: 'Here is a story-book
Thy Father has written for thee.'
'Come, wander with me,' she said,
'Into regions yet untrod;
And read what is still unread
In the manuscripts of God.' "

—LONGFELLOW, "Fiftieth Birthday of Agassiz."

A God of Law

Our fourth consideration is of the attribute of law. From the day a man is born to the day he dies, on every hand he beholds the operation of law, and is himself subject to law.

Twenty stories above the street a woman stood on the window ledge of a skyscraper hotel. While street watchers gazed in frozen amazement she leaped from the ledge and plummeted to the pavement and death.

Why did the body fall downward? Why not upward? Or why could it not descend more slowly? The answer is that there is a power which attracts mass weight downward, and this is the law that governed the speed of that falling body. The boy who drops his marble and sees it fall to the floor observes the same law. It is the selfsame law that operates in the whole universe, from marbles to moons and moon systems, to sun and solar systems, to greater group systems, to billions of gigantic suns in still greater cluster systems, to yet more enormous island universe systems of suns and their families.

"Lift up your eyes on high, and behold who hath created these things, that bringeth out their host by number: he calleth them all by names by the greatness of his might, for that he is strong in power; not one faileth." Isaiah 40:26.

From the mote dancing in the sunbeam to the most giant sun and systems, so far away that light traveling at the rate of 186,000 miles a second would take millions of years to reach them, law reigns.

"Through Him the universe is one harmonious whole." Colossians 1:17, Weymouth.

Law governs fire. Law governs heat. Law governs pressure. Law governs motion. Law governs all physics, all chemistry, all science, all art, all life—everything. Law reigns. God reigns.

"From the very creation of the world, His invisible perfections—namely, His eternal power and divine nature—have been perceptible and clearly visible from His works." Romans 1:20, Weymouth.

"*There is a God!* the sky his presence shares,
His hand upheaves the billows in their mirth,
Destroys the mighty, yet the humble spares
And with contentment crowns the thought of worth!"

—CHARLOTTE CUSHMAN.

As law reigns in the physical realm, so does it also reign in the moral and spiritual realm. "Let us hear the conclusion of the whole matter: Fear God, and keep his commandments: for this is the whole duty of man." Ecclesiastes 12:13.

"If thou wilt enter into life, keep the commandments." Matthew 19:17.

"All his commandments are sure. They stand fast for ever and ever." Psalms 111:7, 8.

THE CROWNING ATTRIBUTE OF GOD

If an intelligent, modern man is to worship God, he will conceive of Him as a God of power, wisdom, beauty, and law. The things he sees and knows give him no other choice.

Yet these four attributes—power, wisdom, beauty, and law—are not sufficient. A forceful human ruler may wield immense power, possess a keen mind, admire beauty and art, and forge a great system of law, yet fail in drawing to himself the love and willing obedience of his people.

If, in addition to these four considered qualities, he holds in his heart a great, constant, and sacred love for his subjects, then a happy realm may be his, provided his followers are sincere.

Despite the curse of evil which lies heavy on the earth, love is also present.

There, down the street, a house was in flames. A crowd quickly gathered. The screaming siren sounded, and a fire engine was soon playing great streams of water on the burning home.

Suddenly a woman came running, tearing and forcing her way through the crowd.

"Let me through," she cried. "My baby is in the house."

Escaping from the grasp of firemen, she plunged through the door into the inferno of smoke, heat, fumes, and flames. Snatching her child from its cradle, she battled her way out to safety.

The price? Burns and scars that destroyed her physical beauty for life.

There is much hate, but there is also much love. Love of children and parents. Love of brothers and sisters. All the varied and ramifying phases of filial and racial love. Love of community, love of country, love of good causes—and love of God.

"Love is of God." 1 John 4:7.

"God is love." Verse 8.

"Like as a father pitieth his children, so the Lord pitieth them that fear him." Psalms 103:13.

"Can a woman forget her sucking child . . . ? Yea, they may forget, yet will I not forget thee." Isaiah 49:15.

"I have loved thee with an everlasting love." Jeremiah 31:3.

Modern man, with his world falling apart, needs what man has always needed. And God is the same as He always was. Nothing can ever be so important to a man as for God and him to get together.

Before a God of power, wisdom, beauty, law, and holy love, man may truly worship. This is the God of the Bible.

The experience is told of a skeptical French general who said, "I cannot form the slightest conception of that mysterious Being which men call the good God." Dumas, the novelist, is said to have replied, "General, I have in my house four dogs, two apes, and a parrot, and their opinions are absolutely identical with yours."

Someone reported a conversation with that esteemed woman Evangeline Booth, general of the Salvation Army. She had passed the age of fourscore years.

She was asked, "Have you always been sure of your faith?"

Her answer was on this wise: "I have had my dark moments. Why did my mother die of cancer? Why did my father go blind? Why is the world so filled with sorrow and suffering?"

Then she added these significant words: "God would not be much of a God if I could understand Him perfectly. The universe would be trifling if I could perceive of it all clearly."

This remarkable woman, with her father and grandfather, threw the forces of her consecrated service against the mighty bulwarks of sin and suffering, and won the plaudits of the world.

The ugly specter of sickness and sorrow thrust itself squarely before them for three quarters of a century. Notwithstanding, they believed fervently in a God of love, and they themselves became channels and living emissaries of that saving love to millions of disheartened men, women, and children. The greatest thing in the world is love, and God is love.

"Could we with ink the ocean fill
  And were the skies of parchment made;
Were every stalk on earth a quill,
  And every man a scribe by trade:
To write the love of God above
  Would drain the ocean dry,

Nor could the scroll contain the whole
Though stretch'd from sky to sky."
—MEIR BEN ISAAC NEHORAI.

A translation of a Chaldean ode, sung in Jewish synagogues during the service of the first day of the Feast of Pentecost.

CHAPTER 4

What Would God Do?

"SHALL MORTAL man be more just than God? shall a man be more pure than his maker?" Job 4:17.

Did you ever have a friend come to you, present some personal problem, and say, "Tell me, what would you do if you were in my place?"

Suppose that the great God would come to you and ask, "If you were in My place, what would you do?"

In this closing chapter of the first section of this book we are to inquire as to what a God of power, wisdom, beauty, law, and love would do regarding three things.

What Kind of World Would He Make?

What kind of world would you expect to be created by a God who has the power to make any kind of world He chooses to make, possesses all the wisdom and know-how to make it, is a God who deeply appreciates beauty, is a believer in law and order, and is a God of love?

What is the Bible answer? The first verse and the last verse of the first chapter of the first book of the Bible read as follows: "In the beginning God created the heaven and the earth." Genesis 1:1. "And God saw every thing that he had made, and, behold, it was very good." Verse 31.

According to the record, when God had finished His six days of step-by-step orderly creation, He looked at His

Franklin Booth, Artist

The earth, perfect in every respect as it came from the hand of the Creator, was an expression of God's character. It was a world of peace, beauty, and love.

work and pronounced it to be "very good." The entire teaching of the Bible harmonizes with this statement.

What is the answer of reason? Since God is love and a lover of beauty, He would desire to create a lovely and beautiful world. And having the power and wisdom to make any kind of world He might desire to make, He would, therefore, create a good and beautiful world. Reason and the Bible agree. It is reasonable to have faith in the Word of God. "Come now, and let us reason together," says God. Isaiah 1:18.

A good god might desire to create a good world, and be unable to do so. A god of power might have ability to make a good world, but choose to create an evil or imperfect world. But the God of love and wisdom and power would wish to make a good world, and could make such a world. According to the Scriptures, He did that very thing.

Tampion, one of the most skilled watchmakers who ever lived, was at his workbench. A customer came in and handed him a watch to be repaired. Mr. Tampion looked at it a moment, saw that his name had been forged on the case, and to the utter astonishment of the owner, picked up a hammer and smashed the watch to pieces. Then to the further bewilderment of the customer, he selected a beautiful, fine watch from the showcase and said, "Sir, take this. Here is a watch of my own making."

With Tampion his name stood for his character, and he wanted his name only on a watch that stood for his character.

It is just so with God. His character and reputation are involved in this matter of the world that He made. If God would be pleased to create an evil and imperfect world when it was in His power to create a good and beautiful world, He could not be a God of love, wisdom, and power. And we know that He was pleased with creation, for we read, "Thou hast created all things, and for thy pleasure they are and were created." Revelation 4:11.

The brilliant Frenchman Voltaire, although considerably troubled with skepticism, said, "The world embarrasses me, and I cannot dream that this world exists and has no watchmaker."

And Voltaire would have been much wiser and happier had he believed that when this world came forth from the hand of its Creator, it was a good world. But he did say, "If there were no God, it would be necessary to invent Him."

What is the answer of science? Is there evidence indicating that the climate, vegetation, and animal life of the earth in its primeval beauty were superior to that of the present world? The answer is Yes.

Animals existed that make anything alive today appear dwarfs by comparison. Plant life was the same. Lepidodendrons grew to a height of over a hundred feet. Treelike ferns grew seeds as large as eggs. Ferns and forest trees grew within fifteen degrees of the North Pole, indicating a more or less worldwide uniform climate.

There is abundant evidence to support this quotation from one prominent writer: "As the earth came forth from the hand of its Maker, it was exceedingly beautiful. . . . The hills and mountains were not abrupt and rugged . . . ; the sharp, ragged edges of earth's rocky frame-work were buried beneath the fruitful soil. . . . The heights were crowned with trees more majestic than any that now exist. The air, untainted by foul miasm, was clear and healthful. The entire landscape outvied in beauty the decorated grounds of the proudest palace."—*Patriarchs and Prophets,* p. 44.

We repeat, "God saw everything that he had made, and, behold, it was very good."

WHAT KIND OF PEOPLE WOULD GOD CREATE?

What is the Bible answer? "God said, Let us make man in our image." Genesis 1:26. "God hath made man upright; but they have sought out many inventions." Ecclesiastes 7:29.

The entire array of Biblical doctrines, presenting every phase of gospel truth, hinges upon the assertion that God made man upright. If this be not so, then the Bible is a farce, the cross folly, the gospel a fallacy, and its preaching foolishness.

What is the answer of reason? God had the power to create a good man. He had the wisdom to do it. He was a God of love, and could not retain His righteous character and create man otherwise than upright. Reason demands the creation of a good and intelligent man, capable of worshiping a God of power, wisdom, beauty, law, and love.

"Had I been present at the creation, I would have given some useful hints for the better ordering of the universe," so spake Alfonso the Wise. In the first place Alfonso was not there; and in the second place, we think that if he had been there, he would never have uttered those words.

What is the answer of science? Has science discovered a missing link, proving man to have ascended from the beast creation rather than to have descended from Adam? The answer is No.

Dr. Austin H. Clark, noted biologist of the Smithsonian Institution, is quoted as follows:

"There is no evidence which would show man developing step by step from lower forms of life. There is nothing to show that man was in any way connected with monkeys. . . .

"He [man] appeared suddenly and in substantially

the same form as he is in today. There is not the slightest evidence of his existence before that time.

"He appeared able to walk, able to think and able to defend himself.

"There are no such things as missing links. Missing links are misinterpretations."—*Rocky Mountain News* (Denver), Jan. 21, 1929, p. 1.

Wasmann is quoted thus: " 'The whole hypothetical pedigree of man is not supported by a single fossil genus or a single fossil species.' "—ALFRED W. MCCANN, *God —or Gorilla,* p. 41.

By the Associated Press, December 13, 1926, Prof. Edwin Grant Conklin, head of Princeton's department of biology, was quoted as follows: "Since the beginning of recorded history there have been few and wholly minor evolutionary changes in the body of man, but what changes have taken place have been retrogressive." That means backward, not forward.

The famous paleontologist Branco said, " 'The man-ape has no existence and the missing link remains a phantom.' "—Cited in MCCANN, *God—or Gorilla,* p. 18.

The Piltdown man, or the Dawn man, was manufactured from a few bones discovered in a gravel pit in England about 1912. Some human skull fragments, plus a jawbone and canine tooth of a chimpanzee, plus the fond imagination of a missing-link lover, produced a theoretical ape man which, as the great scientist Sir Arthur Keith said, " 'could neither breathe nor eat.' "—*Ibid.* Yet this ape man poses as "fact" in the Hall of the Age of Man, American Museum of Natural History, and is accepted as such by unknowing millions who visit this famous place.

The Java ape man, called also the Trinil ape man and Pithecanthropus, has been reconstructed by artists and placed in the Hall of the Age of Man.

A small section of the skull brainpan, a piece of thigh bone (found sixteen yards away), and two molar teeth were discovered in Java in 1891. From these bones, which scientists were not allowed to see, comes the Java ape man, so commonly accepted by an uninformed public. Great scientists like Virchow, Schwalbe, Klaatsch, and Alsberge rejected the theoretical Java man.

In *The American Weekly,* magazine section of the New York *Sunday American,* August 7, 1921, page 2, W. H. Ballou wrote:

"It [this Trinil man, or Pithecanthropus Erectus] stood erect, had a well-shaped human head and was tailed. Science deduced from the skeleton our evolution into the smooth-skinned, tailless creatures that we are today." What a twentieth-century miracle! All that from a piece of skull, a piece of thigh bone, and two teeth, with no proof that they even belonged to one animal, or one man!

You may be assured of one thing. The outstanding fact about the mythical, missing link between man and beast is that he is still missing. He is not alive today. None of his descendants of his likeness are alive. Not a bone or a fossil of any of them has ever been found. Not a trace of the fabricated, so-called original ancestor—supposed common ancestor of the gorilla, the orangutan, the gibbon, the chimpanzee, and the missing link—has ever been discovered.

Strange indeed! The gorilla still lives. The orangutan abides with us. The gibbon stays on, this interesting tailless ape. And the chimpanzee creates amusement at every zoo and circus. Why do we not see their hypothetical brother, this missing link, this wise ape man, from which modern man is supposed to have sprung? Since he was wiser and more cunning than his brothers, how does it happen that he and all his children died? Why cannot we find his bones or fossil imprints, or those of his ancestors?

The answer is simply here: He is a hypothesis, a theory, a figment of the fertile imagination of both learned and unlearned men. They make themselves greater than God. He took of the dust of the ground and made Adam, but these modern men-gods create an ape man out of nothing. To what lengths will modern man go to push the hand of God out of His universe!

"Men are so intent upon excluding God from the sovereignty of the universe, that they degrade man, and defraud him of the dignity of his origin. He who set the starry worlds on high, and tinted with delicate skill the flowers of the field, who filled the earth and the heavens with the wonders of his power, when he came to crown his glorious work, to place one in the midst to stand as ruler of the fair earth, did not fail to create a being worthy of the hand that gave him life. The genealogy of our race, as given by inspiration, traces back its origin, not to a line of developing germs, mollusks, and quadrupeds, but to the great Creator. Though formed from the dust, Adam was 'the son of God.'"—*Patriarchs and Prophets,* p. 45.

Let every man remember two things:

1. All posing specimens of ape men and missing links are mere pretensions. They are the fruitage of faith in evolution.

2. The ancient Cro-Magnon cave dwellers are recognized by scientists to have been possessed of more natural, latent ability than any living race of men today.

Of this race Sir Arthur Keith said, "'The finest the world has ever seen.'"—GEORGE MCCREADY PRICE, *Phantom of Organic Evolution,* p. 110.

Henry Fairfield Osborn, prominent leader in the effort to find the missing link, said:

"'I have every reason to believe that the Cro-Magnon "cave-man" could enter any branch of the intellectual life of this university [Columbia] on equal, if not on superior terms with any of the 30,000 students here.'"—*Ibid.*

The God of power, wisdom, beauty, law, and love said, "Let us make man in our image." Genesis 1:26. The Bible teaches it. Reason demands it. Science cannot refute it. Why then should modern man forsake the truth of God's Word for ghosts of ape ancestors who never existed?

What Would God Do With a Rebellious World?

God as a God of power would be able to crush rebellion. As a God of wisdom He would know what to do. As a God of justice He could not set aside His law of justice and close His eyes to the situation. As a God of love He would make extraordinary effort to solve the problem. These things are inherent in the very character of God.

Subtract love from the character of God, and a sinner might be eternally exterminated instantly. Add love to God's character, and man's failure is met with John 3:16: "For God so loved the world, that he gave his only begotten Son, that whosoever believeth in him should not perish, but have everlasting life."

Human sinners often love sin and yet hate sinners. God always hates sin and loves sinners.

I once hired a strong, hard-muscled sawmill worker to do some stake driving for me. As he rested between stakes he told me why he was in town.

A young man employed at the mill and rooming at my friend's home had suddenly departed for places unknown, taking with him two pairs of shoes belonging to my stake driver. The wielder of the sledge hammer set forth to me in strong and vivid language his deep and abiding aversion to stealing. In his catalog of sins there seemed to be nothing quite so bad, nothing so intrinsically evil, nothing so unthinkable and utterly inexcusable in any normal human being as stealing, especially stealing shoes, and more especially his shoes.

"What are you going to do with the young man if and when you find him?" I queried.

"I'll tell you exactly what I'm going to do," he said, wiping the streaming sweat from his face; "I'm going to kill him."

Here was a man obsessed with hatred for a sinner who had stolen his shoes, yet he proposed the audacious and greater sin of stealing the man's life. The shoes that the young man stole were at least useful for wear, sale, or trade. But what would our friend have done with the young man's life after he had stolen it?

God is not as sinful man is.

In the cool of the day, when the chilling shadows of sin had fallen across the beauty of Eden, God walked in the garden. He too was looking for one who had sinned. His voice was heard calling, "Adam, where art thou?"

In the deep recesses of Paradise He found the man and his mate, trembling in fear, and clothed only with a few fig leaves and the nakedness of flimsy, transparent excuses. As the chill and cold of sin's dark night settled down upon them, God clothed their bodies and lighted a lamp for their souls. To the serpent He said, in their hearing, "And I will put enmity between thee and the woman, and between thy seed and her seed; it shall bruise thy head, and thou shalt bruise his heel." Genesis 3:15.

The seed of the woman was Christ. He was bruised upon Calvary. Someday He will bruise the head of the serpent of sin, and evil will be crushed forever.

In the midst of a world confused and lost, stumbling in the darkness and destruction of its own making, God set the redeeming cross of Jesus. Upon the cross there is a glow of light illuminating Heaven's invitation: "Him that cometh to me I will in no wise cast out." John 6:37.

It has been told that when Dan Poling's son was shipwrecked at sea he took off his life belt and gave it to a soldier who had none. How many millions of soldiers, the cream of youth, have given their lives that others might live! God gave His only Son that all men might live, if they would but choose eternal life.

On the hill of Golgotha there were three crosses. Jesus was nailed to the center one, and the two thieves on the right and on the left respectively.

The one thief raved on with rebellious words to God and man. His was a cross of rejection.

The other thief sought salvation through confession of his sins, and faith that somehow, through Christ, he might make heaven at last. His cross was a cross of repentance.

All the world is represented by those two crosses. Those who repent and accept salvation are represented by the one cross. Those who neglect and reject are represented by the other.

The central cross of redemption represents the God of power, wisdom, beauty, law, and love. He had made a good world. He had made a good man. Sin had marred the plan. The justice of law must be maintained. Love said that man must be offered salvation. God "spared not his own Son, but delivered him up for us all." Romans 8:32. He could do no more for man. He would do no less.

"O Rock of Israel, Rock of Salvation, Rock struck and cleft for me, let those two streams of blood and water which once gushed out of thy side . . . bring down with them salvation and holiness into my soul."—BREVINT.

SECTION TWO

MAN'S QUESTIONS ABOUT EVIL

 Vernon Nye, Artist

Through His prophet God said of the talented Lucifer, "Thou wast perfect in thy ways from the day that thou wast created, till iniquity was found in thee."

CHAPTER 5

Did God Create Evil?

"THE WHOLE world lieth in wickedness." 1 John 5:19.

Optimistic as any man may be by nature bent, he still concedes to himself that this is not the kind of world he would make if he possessed the power to make one according to his desire.

With all our churches, our social and governmental organizations, we still have sin, sorrow, poverty, and woe. Despite the ever-increasing marvels of modern medical science and countless hospitals, the world remains a vast lazar house of sickness, suffering, and death. Fear, hatred, and distrust within the hearts of men bring forth the outward deeds of crime, war, and bloodshed. Storms, earthquakes, famines, and disaster multiply on every hand.

It was Masefield who wrote:

> "The Lord who gave us Earth and Heaven
> Takes that as thanks for all He's given.
> The book He lent is given back
> All blotted red and smutted black."
>
> "Everlasting Mercy." Copyright 1912. Used
> by permission of The Macmillan Co.

The clean, white pages of God's original nature book have been smutted black by evil fingers and blotted red by the blood of agelong strife.

Solomon sent an arrow of truth straight to the target when he wrote, "Lo, this only have I found, that God hath made man upright; but they have sought out many inventions." Ecclesiastes 7:29.

Today we watch tremendous tides of evil sweep over mankind and wreck the most precious things of a world that has had a long time to suffer and learn. Despair grips the hearts of millions. Leaders of men labor in confusion and bewilderment. There is "upon the earth distress of nations, with perplexity." Luke 21:25.

Pastor Martin Knolle, preaching to his congregation in occupied Germany after Hitler's fall, tells a typical story of an educated and pious German. The man said something like this: "My son was killed in action. My daughter is missing. I have lost my wife. My home is gone. The clothes on my back are my total possessions, and they were given to me. I can't pray any more. I can't think any more. I don't want to think any more, neither backward nor forward. After all that I have experienced it is no longer possible."—Reported in *Pulpit Digest,* 1946.

DID GOD CREATE EVIL?

Is there not a verse in the Bible which states that God created evil? Here is that oft-mentioned passage: "I make peace, and create evil." Isaiah 45:7.

Does this scripture say that God created evil in the beginning, that He is the originator of evil? If not, what, then, does it mean?

A simple reading of the preceding six verses will make instantly clear that these words were spoken as prophetic language addressed to Cyrus the Great, king of the Medes and Persians, who was yet unborn.

The ancient kingdom of Babylon had spread its conquests to Palestine. Jerusalem had been taken. The land was subjugated. Thousands of selected Jews were carried away to the golden city of Babylon on the Euphrates River.

The arrogancy of Babylon was to reach a limited height; then God would permit the rising power of the Medes and Persians to bring it down. Cyrus was general of their army. In Isaiah 13:17-19 the Lord forecast this work of the Medes: "Behold, I will stir up the Medes against them. . . . And Babylon . . . shall be as when God overthrew Sodom and Gomorrah."

This bringing of one evil power against another for the purpose of removing from control a nation whose cup of iniquity is running over—this is what God had in mind when He said, "I . . . create evil." To the king of Babylon, God sent the message: "The most High ruleth in the kingdom of men, and giveth it to whomsoever he will, and setteth up over it the basest of men." Daniel 4:17.

> "God is abroad, and wondrous in his ways
> The rise of empires, and their fall surveys."
>
> —DRYDEN.

The age-old, insistent, persistent question of the skeptic has always been, "Why would God create a world like this and let it continue?" This question has doubtless come to every thinking man and woman at some time. The Bible answer is that "God saw every thing that he had made, and, behold, it was very good." Genesis 1:31. God is love. His law is love. All His dealings with all His creatures are, when properly understood, a demonstration of unchanging love. God did not create an evil world, but He does have something to do with things here and has most definite plans for the future.

WHAT IS THE BASIC CAUSE OF EVIL AND TROUBLE?

No human reasoning concerning the cause of evil is offered. The Bible puts it this way:

"Wherefore, as by one man sin entered into the world, and death by sin; and so death passed upon all men, for that all have sinned." Romans 5:12.

"Cursed is the ground for thy sake; in sorrow shalt thou eat of it all the days of thy life; thorns also and thistles shall it bring forth to thee; and thou shalt eat the herb of the field; in the sweat of thy face shalt thou eat bread, till thou return unto the ground; for out of it wast thou taken: for dust thou art, and unto dust shalt thou return." Genesis 3:17-19.

Yes, sin is the basic cause of all our ills. It is the tap-root nourishing the vine that bears sour grapes to set on edge the teeth of all mankind.

In these latter decades millions have been listening to the spiritual deceptions. They have been told that there is nothing but God and good, that nothing is evil except as one thinks it is evil, that sin is something to be eliminated by just believing that there is no sin, and that the only real sin is believing in its reality.

Modern men with ideas of inevitable progress stand aghast at the developments of these latter days and the utter inadequacy of their puny notions. The Holy Spirit of God is doing its utmost to call them back to His holy and eternal Word that says, "Sin is the transgression of the law," and "The wages of sin is death." 1 John 3:4; Romans 6:23.

"There is a way which seemeth right unto a man, but the end thereof are the ways of death." Proverbs 14:12. Sin begins in a way and ends in a thousand ways, which all lead to one place marked *DEATH!*

Dr. Harry Emerson Fosdick, noted liberal thinker, says in his book *Living Under Tension:* "Today we and our hopes and all our efforts after goodness are up against a powerful antagonism, something demonic, tragic, terrific, in human nature, that turns our loveliest qualities to evil and our finest endeavors into failure. Our fathers called that sin."—Page 113.

And it is high time that modern men, above the din of their own conflicts, should hear the voice of God speaking forth His holy commandments, the transgression of which is sin.

No preaching of the Fatherhood of God and the brotherhood of man, no social schemes or church meddling in politics, no giant federations of religious organizations, can ever save a people or a world when the sense of sin is gone. When the spiritual sensory nerves are dead to the touch of sin, we shall burn and sear our very souls and never know it. Our God-given protection is gone.

What Is Sin?

Sin has one comprehensive definition. "Whosoever committeth sin transgresseth also the law: for sin is the transgression of the law." 1 John 3:4. The violation of that law is sin. Be not deceived into believing that the unchanging God will ever set aside His holy law in any plan for saving man. This would destroy the very foundation of His government. The Ten Commandments are the fundamental law of God for man.

"All unrighteousness is sin." 1 John 5:17. The line of demarcation between sin and righteousness should be sharply drawn in our minds. It will include all sins—the breaking of any or all of God's commandments.

"Whatsoever is not of faith is sin." Romans 14:23. If a man violates his conscience, to him it is sin. His conscience must be open to education, but he surely should sacredly guard it. If he does not, it will become seared as with a hot iron. (1 Timothy 4:2.) "To him that knoweth to do good, and doeth it not, to him it is sin." James 4:17.

The only man who possibly may be held unaccountable for his wrongdoing is the man who does not know that he is sinning. Said Jesus, "If ye were blind, ye should have no sin: but now ye say, We see; therefore your sin remaineth." John 9:41.

If we close our eyes that we may not see, our ears that we may not hear, then we shall be responsible for what we might have known. (Matthew 13:15.)

In a fruit warehouse was a sign for those engaged in sorting apples. It read, "A spot today means rot tomorrow."

"A sin is a small and delicate thing
At first; it scarcely raises its head;
It creeps where the dust and shadows cling;
It fears the heel that may bruise and tread.

"And then the swift metamorphosis,
Out of sound, out of sight,
From larva to hard, cold chrysalis—
And then the winged, silent thing bold in the light!

"The great soft moth that doth confound—
So fair and delicate to see!
And in corruption brings to ground
Strength, wisdom, and integrity."

—*Pulpit Digest.*

CHAPTER 6

Who Was the First Sinner?

GOD IS the Creator of all things. He did not create evil in the beginning. There was a time, therefore, when there was no sin.

There can be no sin without a sinner. Sin is not something that God created and sent forth as a foul miasma to taint the atmosphere which men breathe, causing them to turn from goodness to wickedness. Sin is not a sinister germ that a good man "catches" as one would a contagious disease. Sin is connected with the seat of the conscience—the will. Somebody, sometime, somewhere, willed to sin. Evidence of this is everywhere. Who was it?

When and With Whom Did Sin Originate?

To the Bible we turn for the answer: "He that committeth sin is of the devil; for the devil sinneth from the beginning." 1 John 3:8.

Here we have the name of the original sinner and the time of his original sin. His name is the "devil." In Revelation 12:9 he is referred to as "the great dragon . . . that old serpent, called the Devil, and Satan." Isaiah refers to him as "Lucifer, son of the morning." Isaiah 14:12. The time of his original sin was "in the beginning." This we understand to be relatively near the time of the creation, as recorded in the first chapter of the book of Genesis.

 Vernon Nye, Artist

Jealous with pride, the brilliant Lucifer sought the overthrow of God's throne. "I will exalt my throne above the stars of God: . . . I will be like the most High."

How Did Lucifer Originate?

Lucifer was created. The prophet Ezekiel, presenting Satan under the symbol of the king of Tyrus, represents God as speaking to him of "the day that thou wast created." Ezekiel 28:13.

It is well here to recall that God "created all things by Jesus Christ." Ephesians 3:9. This includes all things in heaven as well as in earth; "for by him [Christ] were all things created, that are in heaven, and that are in earth, visible and invisible, whether they be thrones, or dominions, or principalities, or powers: all things were created by him, and for him." Colossians 1:16.

To make this matter of the place and position of Christ beyond all question, the apostle Paul adds, "And he is before all things." Verse 17.

Thus Christ was the active agent of His Father in the creation of Lucifer.

Where Was Lucifer Created?

That Lucifer was created in heaven and that heaven was his abode are beyond all reasonable question. Said Jesus, "I beheld Satan as lightning fall from heaven." Luke 10:18.

God said to Satan, "Thou wast upon the holy mountain of God; thou hast walked up and down in the midst of the *stones of fire.*" Ezekiel 28:14.

That this is a picture of Lucifer in the magnificent glory at the throne of God admits of little doubt. The prophet Daniel, in describing the throne of the Ancient of days, wrote, "His throne was like the *fiery flame,* and his wheels as burning fire." Daniel 7:9.

John the revelator looked into heaven, and there he saw the "Son of man. . . . And his eyes were as a flame of *fire;* and his feet like unto fine brass, as if they *burned in a furnace.*" Revelation 1:13-15.

Thus it is that we see Lucifer in the presence of the great Creator and His Christ, and the ceaseless beams of undimmed glory play upon his elegant form. He seems to be walking on "stones of fire."

What Three Great Gifts Did He Possess?

"Thou sealest up the sum, full of *wisdom,* and perfect in *beauty.*" Ezekiel 28:12.

It seems certain that Lucifer was the wisest of all the angelic host. More than any other created being, outside the inner circle of the Godhead itself, he was able to penetrate and to appreciate the thoughts, plans, and principles of God.

Furthermore, he was "perfect in beauty." Here on earth we have all heard of beauty contests where fair maidens from here and there compete for the beauty crown. But in heaven they held no beauty contests. One and all agreed without a murmur of contention that Lucifer was the one with perfect form, perfect face, perfect movement, and perfect grace, entitled without runner-up competition, to heaven's crown of perfect beauty.

His dazzling garments are described as follows: "Every precious stone was thy covering, the sardius, topaz, and the diamond, the beryl, the onyx, and the jasper, the sapphire, the emerald, and the carbuncle, and gold." Verse 13. Moffatt's translation reads, "Their setting wrought in gold."

Lucifer's third glorious gift seemed to lie in the realm of song. One can scarcely conceive of heaven without the accompaniment of its matchless music. Of Lucifer it is said, "The workmanship of thy tabrets and of thy pipes was prepared in thee in the day that thou wast created."

"Tabret" is derived from Arabic, *tanbur,* the name of a stringed instrument similar to a mandolin, according to *The International Standard Bible Encyclopaedia,* article

Balkin, From Monkmeyer

The Holy Scriptures are uniquely designed to meet all man's spiritual needs, and they are in harmony with the best findings of true science.

 Vernon Nye, Artist

Christ is our living Saviour today. His desire to save men is unchanged. He says, "I am come that they might have life

"Music." This would indicate that Lucifer's vocal bands, or "strings," were of some special and unusual construction.

The "pipes" would naturally refer to some sort of tubes connected with the production of sounds. They were something extraordinary, even in heaven. Some have thought that Lucifer may have been able to sing several parts at the same time. At any rate, we may believe that he was possessed of very special musical ability. Who knows but that he may have led the "innumerable" hosts of angels in the great oratorios of heaven!

What Position Did He Occupy in Heaven?

"Thou art the anointed cherub that covereth; and I have set thee so." Ezekiel 28:14.

Who is an anointed cherub, and what did he cover? To get the true answer, we turn to the sanctuary of God in ancient Israel. It was a type, or shadow, of the heavenly sanctuary, or dwelling place of God, the latter being a pattern for the former. (See Hebrews 8:5; 9:24.)

In the sanctuary or tabernacle of Israel a gorgeous veil separated the holy and most holy apartments. (Exodus 26:31-33.) In the most holy place of that sanctuary we find what we are looking for.

Here was the ark of the testament, containing the eternal Ten Commandments. (Hebrews 9:3, 4; Deuteronomy 10:4, 5.) Over the ark, as a lid, or cover, was the mercy seat. (Exodus 25:21.) Above the mercy seat was the manifestation of God's presence. (Verse 22.)

Now we come to the cherubim. There were two of them, hammered out of pure gold. We read, "And the cherubims shall stretch forth their wings on high, covering the mercy seat with their wings." Verse 20.

They stood upon the mercy seat, which was the cover of the ark of the testament, wherein lay the tables of stone upon which God had inscribed the everlasting words of His holy law. Their wings arched above the mercy seat, and they stood in the immediate presence of God.

John the revelator was given a view of the temple, or sanctuary, of God in heaven, concerning which he wrote, "And the temple of God was opened in heaven, and there was seen in his temple the ark of his testament." Revelation 11:19.

The picture is now clear. Lucifer, full of wisdom and perfect in beauty, was anointed to be a covering cherub of the mercy seat and of the ark containing the law of God. In heaven he was a special guardian of the basic principles of divine government—justice and mercy. He had been elevated to a position of sacred trust and responsibility above his fellows. In the far-reaching plans of the universe he stood next to the Son of God. His allegiance was sworn to the law of God, and his loyalty pledged to God, and to His Son, and to His Holy Spirit, and to their government.

The Picture of Peace

God sat enthroned from the days of His long eternity. Unnumbered worlds and systems of suns and planets, swinging about Him, wafted the sweet music of the spheres from distances far beyond all finite comprehension. The praise and adoration of the upright in heart swept into the throne of God from every point of habitation. On the vast ocean of God's eternity there was not a ripple of discontent. Happiness and joy was universal. God was glad.

"Thou art worthy, O Lord, to receive glory and honour and power: for thou hast created all things, and for thy pleasure they are and were created." Revelation 4:11.

God is love; His law is love. His heart is merciful.

Obedience of His intelligent creatures was an act of responsive love to a God whose law was designed to bring to them the utmost in happiness.

Transgression against the law of God would be sin. Sin would bring unhappiness. Disloyalty could be nothing short of treason, not only to God, but also to the loyal subjects of His government. There had been no instance of sin. God's mercy had never been called into exercise.

Would this universal peace and happiness last forever? We shall see.

CHAPTER 7

The First Sin and the First War

THERE WAS a time when there was no sin. We live in a time when there is not only sin but sin with compound interest. The wind has brought the whirlwind. The first fire has kindled a vast conflagration. There must have been a time, an occasion, when the first sin was committed, the first flame lighted.

The Shadow of Sin

God had two ways in which He might create the higher orders of His creatures. He could make them with the power of choice or without the power of choice.

If He had decided to create them without the power of deliberation and choice, they would have been mere automatons—automatic creatures. As a train on its track follows the rails, so they would have mechanically followed the laid-out plans of God, or, like the lower animal kingdom, have operated by the processes of mere instinct.

A highly intelligent physician friend of mine explained to me about two kinds of nerve cells.

One kind is found in the frog. This cell, when stimulated, has but two outlets for action. One connects with the frog's croaking mechanism; the other, with his legs. So he either croaks, or jumps, or both. He has no other choices. He cannot sit and deliberate with himself, saying, "Now, I wonder what is the wisest thing to do."

In man's higher order of nerve cells there are many outlets. These permit of many choices. Reason and deliberation are made possible. Moral responsibility is sensed. Obedience may come as a result of intelligent decision. Worship is not only possible but may be rendered on a voluntary basis. Frogs cannot do these things.

God chose to create beings with the power of choice, beings whose service and worship would spring from an appreciation of His character. They would serve Him because they loved Him and knew His laws to be just.

Bible religion is based on persuasion and choice, not on force. This is a lesson many religionists and religious organizations have been slow to learn and practice.

"If any man *will* do his will." John 7:17.

"Whosoever *will*, let him take the water of life freely." Revelation 22:17.

"*Choose* you this day whom ye will serve." Joshua 24:15.

Since man was made a "little lower than the angels" (Psalms 8:5), and he was given the power of choice, it is certain that these higher beings are also free moral agents with the power of choice.

Consider these two things:

1. The power of choice makes possible the choosing of either good or evil. Good angels had the power to choose disobedience.

2. Since this is true, the rise of sin and rebellion was a possibility from the time of the creation of the very first angel. Furthermore, because of the infinite number of intelligent beings in God's universe, it may be said that sin was not only a possibility but a probability. Sin, as it were, was always lurking in the shadows. This was a risk God had to take in creating intelligent beings with the power of choice. And He had to be prepared beforehand

to meet such a dire emergency as sin. Sin was not necessary. It was not wise. But it was possible.

Sin Takes Shape

Yes, the shadow took form. Sin took shape. Somebody chose to sin, to question the authority of God, His Son, and His law. Who was this someone? It was Lucifer.

"Thou wast perfect in thy ways from the day that thou wast created, till iniquity was found in thee." Ezekiel 28: 15.

Consider these five steps in Lucifer's fall from the most exalted position God could give to him.

1. *"Thine heart was lifted up because of thy beauty."* Verse 17.

Every gift of God is a gift of love. He who receives the gift may give glory to the Giver, or take honor to himself. The choice is his. The more numerous the gifts, the greater the number of choices. The more the gifts, the more the responsibility. "For unto whomsoever much is given, of him shall be much required." Luke 12:48.

Elizabeth Barrett Browning said, "The essence of all beauty, I call love." Had Lucifer chosen to continue his unfeigned love of God, he would have appreciated God more and more, loved Him more and more, and increased more and more in beauty of countenance.

But he chose the way of pride. How black and evil did this sin appear against the background of his God-given loveliness!

"In beauty, faults conspicuous grow;
The smallest speck is seen on snow."

—Gay.

Said Solomon, "Pride goeth before destruction, and an haughty spirit before a fall." Proverbs 16:18. Lucifer sought to lift himself by pride, but it proved to be his first step on his way down.

2. *"Thou hast corrupted thy wisdom by reason of thy brightness."* Ezekiel 28:17. Although God had given Lucifer more wisdom than any of His other creatures, he came to consider it as pertaining to himself.

> "Knowledge is proud that he has learned so much;
> Wisdom is humble that he knows no more."
>
> —COWPER.

Lucifer's wisdom became corrupted with pride.

> "Wisdom is ofttimes nearer when we stoop
> Than when we soar."
>
> —WORDSWORTH.

Lucifer set out to soar, but instead he took step number two downward.

3. *"For thou hast said in thine heart, . . . I will exalt my throne above the stars of God: . . . I will be like the most High."* Isaiah 14:13, 14.

From time to time Lucifer must have observed the Father and the Son in deep counsel concerning the plans of the great universe, including the creation of the worlds.

Now that he had become lifted up because of his beauty, and was keenly aware of his great wisdom, how easy to become jealous because he was not taken into the inner counsels of the Godhead.

Rancor began to fill his soul. The joy and happiness which he had always known in praising God was strangely absent. He felt restless under the restrictions of God's law of love, over which he was a pledged guardian.

Did God and His Son and the angels seek to stay this deadly evil and save Lucifer from ruin? To ask such a question is to answer it. They could not have done otherwise.

But Lucifer said in his heart: "I will exalt my throne. I will have a government of my own. I will rebel against God." He ignored the law that "whosoever exalteth himself shall be abased." Luke 14:11. This was step number three on his downward way.

4. *"He was a murderer from the beginning, and abode not in the truth."* John 8:44.

These are the words of Jesus, who taught the disciple John that "whosoever hateth his brother is a murderer." 1 John 3:15. Lucifer's heart was slowly but surely being filled with hatred against heaven's leadership and government. He was a murderer. Planning to exalt himself by force, he took step number four on his way down.

5. *"He is a liar, and the father of it."* John 8:44.

That Lucifer at first told the angels of heaven all that was in his heart is highly improbable. Like many other extreme reformers, he doubtless had much to say about freedom and democracy. Cloaking himself under a guise of great interest for the well-being of all, he injected doubt concerning God, His Son, and His law.

He was a liar. He was the first liar, but not the last. He told the first lie and has been steadily at it for thousands of years. He could use methods that God could not employ. Lucifer, "the light bearer," became Satan, "the adversary." And a wily foe was he. He had taken step number five downward. He would soon be out.

War in Heaven

"There was war in heaven: Michael and his angels fought against the dragon; and the dragon fought and his angels." Revelation 12:7.

Michael (Christ) and the loyal angels engaged in battle with the dragon (Satan) and his angels. Read Jude 9; 1 Thessalonians 4:16; and John 5:25-29 for indication that Michael is Christ.

Thus heaven itself became the scene of the first sin, and the first battleground of the first war. Treason arose in the highest bracket of entrusted leadership. It spread from thence to heaven's populace. How much of this world's history stems from that same plan of operation. Those who do not understand are led by those of keen minds and wicked spirits.

Lucifer and Rebels Cast Out

There was only one possible outcome for such a conflict in heaven. Satan and the hosts of angels who had joined him were doomed to defeat in this first battle of a war that still rages on.

"The great dragon was cast out, that old serpent, called the Devil, and Satan, which deceiveth the whole world: he was cast out into the earth, and his angels were cast out with him." Revelation 12:9.

Jude stated it in these mild words when he wrote, "And the angels which kept not their first estate, but left their own habitation, he hath reserved . . . unto the judgment of the great day." Jude 6.

Yes, Lucifer and his angels fell from their high estate, and left their beautiful home in heaven. They left by request. They sought to take over heaven by force, and they left heaven by force. Christ and His angels cast them out. It is well to remember that with Christ victory is certain.

Why Did God Create Lucifer?

God created Lucifer for the same reason that He created any other intelligent being to whom He gave the power of choice. Sin might have arisen with any one of the innumerable hosts of the universe. Any one of the angels of heaven could now sin if he chose to do so.

God receives no satisfaction from an enforced service. He never has. He never can. He never will. When Lucifer served God he chose to serve Him. When he sinned he chose to sin. When the angels followed Lucifer in rebellion they chose to believe what he said rather than what God said.

There was no reason for sin. To give a reason would be to justify the deed. To offer an excuse would be inexcusable. Lucifer had everything that God could give him except the Godhead itself. Seeking this, he entered upon the long conflict with the government of heaven.

"Once to every man and nation comes the
moment to decide,
In the strife of Truth with Falsehood, for
the good or evil side."

—JAMES RUSSELL LOWELL.

Lucifer had his moment. He made his decision. He took the wrong road.

WHY DID NOT GOD DESTROY LUCIFER?

Would it not have simplified matters if God had destroyed Lucifer instantly? Would not this have stopped the spread of sin, and made unnecessary the untold misery and multiplied millions of deaths that have followed?

On the contrary, it would have made matters more complex. Fear would have spread to the utmost limits of the universe. There would have loomed the possibility of the entire creation living in doubt as to whether God was a God of love, and His law a law of love. Why?

Lucifer had questioned the wisdom, love, and justice of the divine administration. God's created beings had never lived under any other form of government. The fact that a great host of the angels followed Lucifer into rebellion is full proof of what terrible possibilities lay ahead.

Had God completely crushed the rebellion, there could easily have arisen a question, even with the loyal subjects of God, as to whether Lucifer might not be correct in holding that improvements could be made in God's government.

God had but one wise choice. The stability of the universe for ceaseless ages was at stake. He must permit Satan to demonstrate his kind of government. There was no possible short cut. It would take time. It would take patience. It would take sacrifice.

"He that ruleth in the heavens is the one who sees the end from the beginning,—the one before whom the mysteries of the past and the future are alike outspread, and who, beyond the woe and darkness and ruin that sin has wrought, beholds the accomplishment of his own purposes of love and blessing. Though 'clouds and darkness are round about him, righteousness and judgment are the foundation of his throne.' Psalms 97:2, R.V. And this the inhabitants of the universe, both loyal and disloyal, will one day understand. 'His work is perfect; for all his ways are judgment: a God of truth, and without iniquity, just and right is he.' Deuteronomy 32:4."—*Patriarchs and Prophets,* p. 43.

"What in me is dark,
Illumine; what is low, raise and support;
That to the height of this great argument
I may assert eternal Providence,
And justify the ways of God to men."

—MILTON.

"GOD IS LOVE

"God is love. How do you know?
What proof have you that this is so?
Do you not see on every hand
Despair and crime in every land?

"Is not this great world full of woe,
Of pain and death, where'er you go?
If God is love and all-wise too,
And knows just what's the best to do,

"Why did He let the devil live
And come to earth man to deceive,
And fill the earth with sin and crime,
And rule for such a length of time?

"Who has the right to judge the One
Who made the worlds and stars and sun
And made us with the power to choose
To do His will or to refuse,

"To say to such a God of might,
'To make us thus you had no right;
Why did you not make us so good,
To disobey we never could?'

"Did you not know a man made so
Could never love or praise bestow
Upon His God, or honor give,
Though through eternity he'd live?

" 'Twas in the providence of Him
Who made the worlds and all therein
That sin should have a time to prove
That it is vile and God is love.

"But Jesus died to conquer him
Who had the power of death and sin,
And bring to naught his wicked reign,
And woo man back to God again.

"All evidence we need to know
Is that our God has loved us so
He gave His Son upon the cross
To save us from eternal loss."

—J. B. THAYER.

CHAPTER 8

What Position Does Satan Hold on Earth?

SATAN SINNED from the beginning. (1 John 3:8.) "In the beginning God created the heaven and the earth." Genesis 1:1. Satan and his angels were cast out into the earth. (Revelation 12:9.) It is therefore clear that Adam and Eve, our first parents, were in the same world with the outcasts of heaven. What would be the end of this arrangement?

The Contest Over the Dominion

The veriest child and the greatest philosopher could agree on one thing. Since Satan sought by force to overthrow the dominion of God in heaven, he most certainly would make it his first and last business to take over and hold dominion of this one little world into which he had been cast. His methods of work will be discussed in the succeeding chapter.

Let it be written in letters of fire and burned deeply into our memory forever, that God did not choose to give Satan the dominion of this world. He chose to give it to man.

"God said, Let us make man in our image, after our likeness: and *let them have dominion* over the fish of the sea, and over the fowl of the air, and over the cattle, and over all the earth, and over every creeping thing that creepeth upon the earth." Genesis 1:26.

This is what God proposed to His Son and to His Holy Spirit. They would create man and give to him dominion over this world. "So God created man in his own image, in the image of God created he him." Verse 27.

Christ, the active agent in creation, took of the dust of the earth and formed man. Then He breathed into his nostrils the breath of life. (Genesis 2:7.) Taking a portion of man, He formed woman.

When He was through there stood before Him a strong, handsome, intelligent, and perfect man. By the side of the man, beautiful of face and form, keen of mind and pure of heart, stood the woman, perfect in all the glory of her primeval loveliness.

Then in the hush and peace and freshnesss of that delightful dawn of creation's morning, amid the indescribable beauty of their home in the garden of Paradise, Heaven joined their hearts in the first marriage of earth. They were one. God stretched forth His hands in divine blessing and said unto them, "Be fruitful, and multiply, and replenish the earth, and subdue it: and have dominion." Genesis 1:28.

Before the creation of Adam and Eve, Heaven had agreed that they were to be given dominion over the earth and all it contained. This plan had now been announced to them.

Together they were to worship. Together they were to enjoy fellowship with Heaven. Together they were to share all the temporal blessings which the senses of sight, hearing, taste, touch, and smell would make possible. Together they were to live, labor, rejoice, and reign. It was mutual love, mutual joy, mutual responsibility.

What an outlook! Life with abundant health, a righteous character, a home in a beautiful, sinless world, and dominion over the created works of God! What more could man desire? Just one thing—that this happy state might last forever!

And that depended upon man. Man was a steward. Man was a regent under God. God placed him under obedience to law as an "indispensable condition of his very existence. He was a subject of the divine government, and there can be no government without law."—*Patriarchs and Prophets,* p. 49.

Man had perfect freedom of choice. Only in this way could he be a morally responsible being. Only thus could character develop or be tested. "Obedience, perfect and perpetual, was the condition of eternal happiness."—*Ibid.* In God's order obedience springs from love, and is rendered by choice. But it is, nonetheless, imperative.

THE PLACE OF TESTING

As Satan viewed Adam and Eve in their unfeigned love and perfect joy, he laid plans to lead them into distrust and rebellion. That God told Adam of His problem with Satan, and warned him of his wiles, is in keeping with the character of God. It could not have been otherwise.

A special command was given with reference to a special tree. Every commandment of God is, of course, a test, whether it be a command to do a certain thing, or not to do it. And since God's law is a law of love, the willful violation of any one command of God violates our love and loyalty to the God who gave the whole law. That is what the apostle James meant when he said, "Whosoever shall keep the whole law, and yet offend in one point, he is guilty of all." James 2:10.

If I ask my child to bring in the newspaper from the front porch, and he says, "I won't do it," he has violated the principle of obedience, though he heeds the call to eat his breakfast cereal. Mankind is prone to choose obedience on a basis of his own desire and caprice. This kind of Christianity is counterfeit. Genuine Christianity obeys all the genuine commands of God.

Now, God chose to place His special tree of testing in the midst of the garden. (Genesis 3:3.) He gave this distinct instruction and warning: "But of the tree of the knowledge of good and evil, thou shalt not eat of it: for in the day that thou eatest thereof thou shalt surely die." Genesis 2:17. The marginal reading is, "Dying thou shalt die"; that is, the sentence of death would be pronounced, and the processes of deterioration and death would set in. A disobedient life would end in certain death.

By this simple device man's faith, love, loyalty, and obedience were to be tested. God was in reality saying to man, "As long as you love Me, as long as you believe in Me, as long as you are happy in obeying Me, just leave that one tree alone. Then I will understand. On the other hand, if you choose to distrust My love, disbelieve My Word, and disobey My laws, just eat of that tree, and I will understand."

Had God given to man a difficult test, His plan might be questioned. But how easy was the test! No great deed, work, or sacrifice was required. There could be no possible reason for transgression. The very lightness of the prohibition would make the sin great. It could not result from inability to do something, for no action whatever was required.

Adam and Eve Fail the Test

Adam and Eve failed in the test. Acceptable reasons for the failure cannot be given, but the matter will be studied in the next chapter. The record reads thus:

"When the woman saw that the tree was good for food, and that it was pleasant to the eyes, and a tree to be desired to make one wise, she took of the fruit thereof, and did eat, and gave also unto her husband with her; and he did eat." Genesis 3:6.

What had they done? Before they were through with the ordeal, they had coveted and stolen that which did not belong to them. They had dishonored their Maker, taken His name in vain, borne false witness, and in principle violated every commandment of the Decalogue. They had lost their righteous character, forfeited their lives, cast away their beautiful home, and parted with the power of dominion. The floodgates of woe, suffering, and death were opened up on the world.

To get a close-up of what sin will do, we listen to the once lordly Adam. He blames his lovely wife. He blames God for giving her to him. In turn she blames the devil. Once that first ill-fated choice had been made, how quickly did the gold of character tarnish under the biting acid of sin.

To the unhappy pair God said:

"Cursed is the ground for thy sake; in sorrow shalt thou eat of it all the days of thy life; thorns also and thistles shall it bring forth to thee; and thou shalt eat the herb of the field; in the sweat of thy face shalt thou eat bread, till thou return unto the ground; for out of it wast thou taken: for dust thou art, and unto dust shalt thou return." Verses 17-19.

Dismissed From Eden

There were two special trees in Eden. One was the tree of the knowledge of good and evil. The other was the tree of life. What would God do about sinners' having access to the tree of life?

"And now, lest he put forth his hand, and take also of the *tree of life,* and eat, and *live for ever:* therefore the Lord God sent him forth from the garden of Eden, to till the ground from whence he was taken. So he drove out the man; and he placed at the east of the garden of Eden Cherubims, and a flaming sword which turned every way, to keep the way of the tree of life." Verses 22-24.

"No funeral march e'er moved
With slower pace bearing the dead than walked
Adam and Eve beyond the walls. Behind—
Creation's glorious morn, the dawn of time,
All bliss and joy and happiness, and God.
Before—the unknown, and sin and death and hell.
Untried the years to come, mysterious.
Unknown the way, and as they passed the gate,
They turned their faces toward the garden, lost,
And saw the tree of life, their Eden home,
The paths beside the waters clear, the place
Where first they met—then God swung shut the gate
And closed Himself the Paradise from man.
Eve gave one long, one bitter wail, a cry
Of agony that reached to Calvary."

—I. H. Evans.

Satan Takes Over

When man cast off the dominion that God had placed over him, he lost the dominion God had put under him. To whom did man lose this dominion? The answer is here: "For of whom a man is overcome, of the same is he brought into bondage." 2 Peter 2:19.

How plain it is, then, that Satan usurped the dominion that God had given to man. That is why—

1. Paul called him "the god of this world." 2 Corinthians 4:4.

2. Jesus called him "the prince of this world." John 12:31; 14:30.

3. Paul called him "the prince of the power of the air." Ephesians 2:2.

4. Jesus called him "the prince of devils." Matthew 12:24.

To a degree God seemed to recognize this dominion of Satan, permitting him to gather with the "sons of God." (Job 1:6.) Satan claimed this dominion when he showed Christ the kingdoms of this world, saying, "All this power will I give thee, and the glory of them: for that is delivered unto me; and to whomsoever I will I give it." Luke 4:6. Jesus did not dispute the claim. Three and a half years later He died on Calvary to purchase the dominion with His precious blood.

It is said that a young soldier carried the flag far in advance of the regiment into the territory of the enemy and face to face with the opposing battle line. The captain cried, "Bring back the flag, you fool!"

When the regiment of soldiers at last reached the flag, which was under heavy shellfire, they found the young man dead, but the flag was waving triumphantly in the breeze.

Jesus invaded the domain of the enemy and carried the flag up the face of Golgotha, "that is to say, a place of a skull." Matthew 27:33. There He died that we might live. By His vicarious sacrifice He made possible the restoration of all that man had lost:

1. The restoration of life. (John 3:16.)

2. The restoration of character. (2 Corinthians 5:17.)

3. The restoration of a beautiful world. (Acts 3:19-21.)

4. The restoration of dominion. (Matthew 25:21.)

"For the Son of man is come to seek and to save that which was lost." Luke 19:10.

What shall we do, then, with Jesus which is called Christ?

We may accept Him, neglect Him, reject Him, or misrepresent Him.

"INDIFFERENCE

"When Jesus came to Golgotha they hanged Him on a tree,
They drave great nails through hands and feet, and made a Calvary;
They crowned Him with a crown of thorns, red were His wounds and deep,
For those were crude and cruel days, and human flesh was cheap.

"When Jesus came to Birmingham,* they simply passed Him by,
They never hurt a hair of Him, they only let Him die;
For men had grown more tender, and they would not give Him pain,
They only just passed down the street, and left Him in the rain.

"Still Jesus cried, 'Forgive them for they know not what they do,'
And still it rained the winter rain that drenched Him through and through;
The crowds went home and left the street without a soul to see,
And Jesus crouched against the wall and cried for Calvary."

—From *Unutterable Beauty* by G. A. STUDDERT KENNEDY.
Used by permission of Harper & Brothers.

---

* Birmingham, England.

CHAPTER 9

Why Did Adam and Eve Sin?

THE SCRIPTURES declare that in the fall of our first parents Eve was deceived but Adam was not. "Adam was not deceived, but the woman being deceived was in the transgression." 1 Timothy 2:14. Eve herself admitted to the same when she said, "The serpent beguiled me, and I did eat." Genesis 3:13.

The serpent was, of course, Satan. (Revelation 12:9.) He did not approach Eve as an angel, but took possession of what was in all likelihood the flying serpent, dazzling in color and brightness, and very wise. Using this medium, he deceived Eve through a definite series of three steps.

The first one had to do with *God's love.* Eve had apparently wandered away from her husband and stood gazing in curiosity and admiration at the forbidden tree. She may have wondered why God had denied them its fruit.

From the serpent in the tree came a voice in questioning, satirical tone, "Yea, hath God said, Ye shall not eat of every tree of the garden?" Genesis 3:1. In other words, "Is that the kind of God you serve—one who receives pleasure in denying to you free access to all the beautiful and wholesome fruit of this lovely garden?"

We sometimes say, "One cannot help it if birds fly over his head, but he can keep them from nesting in his

 Vernon Nye, Artist

The wily Satan, speaking to Eve through a serpent, introduced sin into this world b
raising a doubt in her mind about the plain command of God.

hair." The thought, "Why should God deny us the fruit of this beautiful tree?" was flashed through the mind of Eve. This was not in itself a sin on her part. But she lingered at the tree, and the thought was permitted to remain in her mind, and the talking serpent may well have passed pleasing compliments concerning the beauty and personality of this first fair woman of our world.

Eve took the first step into the deceptive net of Satan. *She doubted the love of God.* Because she could not fully penetrate the purposes of God in certain restrictions, she began to distrust the goodness of God, just as Lucifer had done in heaven when he was not permitted in the innermost circle of Heaven's plans. When the wedge of doubt goes in, the affinity of love is driven apart.

From the time I was nine years old I was busy evenings after school and under full-time employment in my father's mill during the summer vacations. There were times—when I watched the boys in droves go to the old swimming hole, and enjoy many other carefree sports—that I was tempted to distrust the goodness of my father in holding me steadily to my task. There was a straining at the father-and-boy relationship. But as I look back upon those years I can say, without reservation, that work was my salvation. My father demonstrated his love to me in the requirements he made. Eve began to doubt her Father's love in a restriction which He had made.

The next step was perfectly natural. *Eve doubted the word of God.* She remembered that God had said, "Ye shall not eat of it, neither shall ye touch it, lest ye die." Verse 3. The serpent replied, "Ye shall not surely die." Verse 4. It seems certain that the serpent ate of the fruit in the presence of Eve, since in verse 6 we read, "And when the woman saw that the tree was good for food, . . . she took of the fruit thereof." The serpent did not die; why should she die?

Eve was further flattered by the thought of rising to a higher plane, for Satan had asserted, "For God doth know that in the day ye eat thereof, then your eyes shall be opened, and ye shall be as gods." Verse 5.

Our first mother believed that by eating of this fruit she not only would not die but would advance to new wisdom and higher experience. By taking this second step of disbelieving the word of God, she further strengthened her conviction in her first step of departure in distrusting the love of God. For why, after all, would a good God deny a good woman advancement to a higher plane? There are times when restless modern Eves are deceived as to what are the first and best and highest things in a woman's life.

There are three things to be remembered in connection with this second step of doubting God's word.

1. It was impossible for Eve to believe what the devil said without first doubting the words of God.

2. "In the Judgment, men will not be condemned because they conscientiously believed a lie, but because they did not believe the truth, because they neglected the opportunity of learning what is truth."—*Patriarchs and Prophets,* p. 55.

3. Safety lies only in love of the truth. "And with all deceivableness of unrighteousness in them that perish; because they received not the *love of the truth,* that they might be saved." 2 Thessalonians 2:10. It is considerably easier for even a religious person to love his own opinion, or tradition, more than the truth. If we do not love the truth, we shall believe a lie and be damned. (Verses 11, 12.)

Eve's third step into Satan's net came as a result of the first two. Having distrusted God's love, and doubted His word, *she was now ready to transgress His law.* She disobeyed. She looked, coveted, touched, tasted, and then ate of the forbidden fruit. She sinned. She was first in the transgression.

It did not take one sinner long to make it two. Sin works that way. "She took of the fruit thereof, and did eat, and gave also unto her husband with her; and he did eat." Genesis 3:6.

Why did Adam sin? Was he deceived also? The Bible says No. But it is well to remember that he was breathing the very atmosphere of deception. Eve had now sinned, yet as she stood before him, flushed with the unnatural excitement of it all, she seemed to him more beautiful than ever before. His brain was dizzy with flashing thoughts, "How can I live without her! She is more beautiful than ever! Perhaps she will not die! Might not the words of the serpent be true?"

Then, without doubt, there fell upon his ears the lovely music of Eve's voice, saying, "Adam, I love you more than I have ever loved you before. Come! Eat of the fruit with me." Sin is often an exciting, dazzling, tingling, tempting thing. In his heart the decision was made, when to himself he said, "If she must die, I will die with her." Seizing the fruit, he ate.

Eve became a sinner by deception. Adam walked in with excited and trembling heart, but with his eyes wide open. Both sinned because of wrong choice. Both were responsible; both lost. Both might have made the right choice, saved themselves, and saved the world from the disastrous flood of sin and woe. "Notwithstanding the sophistry of Satan to the contrary, it is always disastrous to disobey God."—*Ibid.,* p. 55.

On the Great Continental Divide some fifty miles from Denver, Colorado, the celebrated Moffat Tunnel was bored through James Peak, rising 13,000 feet above sea level.

A drop of rain falling on the eastern slope of James

Peak enters the south fork of Boulder Creek, and makes its way to the Atlantic Ocean by way of the Gulf of Mexico, upon the bosom of whose waters giant hurricanes whirl and dance and destroy.

A drop of rain falling on the western slope of James Peak enters Fraser Creek, and makes its way to the peaceful waters of that vast ocean which Balboa, the discoverer, named the Pacific, the ocean of peace.

So it is with each one of us. We stand at the great divide. Two ways lie in view. To the left is the way of sin and death. To the right is the way that leads to righteousness, peace, and Paradise.

"O that thou hadst hearkened to my commandments! then had thy peace been as a river, and thy righteousness as the waves of the sea." Isaiah 48:18.

"ONLY TWO WAYS

"There are two ways for trav'lers, only two ways:
One's a hill pathway of battle and praise;
The other leads downward; tho' flow'ry it seem,
Its joy is a phantom, its love is a dream.

"There are two guides for trav'lers, only two guides:
One's the Good Shepherd, e'en thro' the death tides;
The other,—the serpent, beguiling with sin
Whose beauty external hides poison within.

"There are two homes for trav'lers, only two homes:
One's the fair city where evil ne'er comes;
The other,—sin's wages, eternal and dread,
The fate of the lost ones, the doom of the dead.

"Quickly enter the strait way, leading to life;
Shun the wide gateway of folly and strife.
The Spirit invites you this moment to come;
The Saviour is waiting to welcome you home."

—F. E. BELDEN.

CHAPTER 10

Satan's Five-Point Method of Attack

AT MADISON SQUARE GARDEN in New York City people paid more than a million dollars to witness a conflict that was to determine who would wear the crown of physical might and skill. Thousands of eyes saw it. Millions of ears listened to the round-by-round description as it was brought to them by radio. It was the advertised, spotlighted arena of a nation.

The critical conflict between Christ and Satan is no mere side show. This world has become the announced arena, the central stage, whereon is being enacted the great, unfolding drama of the ages, in which love and sin compete for lasting supremacy. Christ is the hero. Satan is the villain. We are all actors. The vast universe is the audience. Men also watch each other in action.

"For we are made a spectacle unto the world, and to angels, and to men." 1 Corinthians 4:9. The marginal reading for the word "spectacle" is "theatre." Moffatt's translation speaks of "gladiators in the arena." Weymouth says, "For we have become a spectacle to all creation."

Generations have come and gone. Centuries have grown into millenniums. Countless millions have appeared upon the stage, played their parts, and disappeared. Yet the show goes on. Someday it will end. Before the curtain rings down on the longest of all plays, every morally responsible being in God's world and universe will have settled his eternal destiny by his choice of sides in the conflict. The issue is clear. The stakes are high. There is no neutral ground. Said Christ, "He that is not with me is against me." Matthew 12:30.

We are now to consider five main methods by which Satan, the archenemy of Christ, seeks to overcome man.

He Works by Deception

Everyone thinks that he hates deception. A widow, bereft of her husband, operated a small grocery as a means of livelihood for herself and her children. A motorcar pulled up, and a man emerged. Entering the store he made a 50-cent purchase, gave the woman a $20 bill, received $19.50 change, and drove away. When the storekeeper made her bank deposit she was informed that the $20 bill was a counterfeit. The impostor had taken 50 cents' worth of the widow's merchandise, and $19.50 of her money.

> "Hateful to me as are the gates of hell,
> Is he who, hiding one thing in his heart,
> Utters another."
>
> —Homer.

Christ, the leader of heaven's forces, makes clear the deceptive character of Satan.

"He is a liar, and the father of it." John 8:44. The purpose of every liar is to deceive. When a person lies he seeks to do one of two things—either to lead someone to believe a thing is true when it is not, or to make one think something is not true when it is. A deceived person believes that he is right when he is wrong, or thinks a thing is wrong when it is right.

Satan deceives by making himself a messenger of light and truth. "And no marvel; for Satan himself is transformed into an angel of light." 2 Corinthians 11:14. Although an apostle of darkness he appears as an angel of light. Weymouth puts it, "Satan himself assumes the garb of an angel of light." In order to lead men to accept error he clothes it with light. He mingles the good and the evil, the true and the false.

"The instruments of darkness tell us truths,
Win us with honest trifles, to betray 's
In deepest consequence."
—*Macbeth,* Act I, Scene 3.

Like a fish in the sea, man takes the bait and gets the hook.

Satan deceives men by using even ministers of righteousness. It is an appalling thought that a man set apart as a preacher of truth should become a tool of the devil to deceive men. Yet that is what the Word of God declares: "Therefore it is no great thing if his ministers also be transformed as ministers of righteousness; whose end shall be according to their works." 2 Corinthians 11:15. Weymouth says that they "assume the garb." Moffatt translates it, "His ministers also masquerade as ministers of righteousness."

Since Lucifer led into deception great hosts of angels who had never sinned, and led our first parents into sin, is it unreasonable to suppose that he would be highly successful in deceiving religious leaders and using them to teach error from the pulpit itself? And certainly, if he could do it, he would do it. What a short-cut method to broadcast the seeds of untruth! Such a man, himself having made shipwreck of true faith, in his delusion "kindles on the coast false fires, that others may be lost."

Jesus lifted His voice in warning, "Take heed that no man deceive you." Matthew 24:4.

Satan sometimes deceives men by the use of organizations. The devil can deceive one man. One man can deceive another man. How natural for an entire organization to grow up, engaged in teaching not only truth, but error as well. With the passing of time, lo, one may behold great ecclesiastical organizations possessed of the idea that they have the truth and fired with a zeal to make its application universal, sometimes even by force of civil law. When such organizations become great enough and strong enough, they may become a problem to the humble Christian in his spiritual warfare.

"For we wrestle not against flesh and blood, but against principalities, against powers, against the rulers of the darkness of this world, against spiritual wickedness in high places." Ephesians 6:12.

Satan and his fallen angels make it their greatest work to capture and control great movements of religion, to the end that Christ and His pure truth shall not prevail.

We dare not judge truth by numbers. We may not rightly gauge the depth of holiness by the height of cathedral spires, or the glory of gilded altars, or the grandeur of the matchless music of great organs and celestiallike choirs. We do well to remember that he who leads the entire procession of deception was once full of wisdom, perfect in beauty, skilled in music, specially anointed to be guardian of the golden mercy seat at the very throne of God. He knows how to use good things to bad ends.

> "The world is still deceiv'd with ornament,
> In law, what plea so tainted and corrupt,
> But, being season'd with a gracious voice,
> Obscures the show of evil? In religion,
> What damned error, but some sober brow
> Will bless it and approve it with a text,
> Hiding the grossness with fair ornament?"
> —*Merchant of Venice,* Act III, Scene 2.

The banker detects a counterfeit note by knowing the genuine. The searcher for truth may also test all specimens by the genuine. "To the law and to the testimony: if they speak not according to this word, it is because there is no light in them." Isaiah 8:20.

One may test his own personal genuineness by whether he loves truth enough to choose it above counterfeit, especially when the counterfeit is popular and is passing for the genuine.

The devil deceives by flattery. Human beings tend to love flattery. "We sometimes think that we hate flattery, but we only hate the manner in which it is done."

"Preach the word. . . . For the time will come when they will not endure sound doctrine; but after their own lusts shall they heap to themselves teachers, having itching ears; and they shall turn away their ears from the truth, and shall be turned to fables." 2 Timothy 4:2-4. Moffatt translates a portion thus: "They will accumulate teachers to suit themselves and tickle their own fancies."

The Bible thus predicted a time would come when people would prefer teachers who would tickle their ears with things they wanted to hear. They would desire smooth, flattering messages. The ministry may be blamed for some things, but the Bible says that the preachers would preach what the people desired to hear. The people are always highly responsible, in the long run, for what they continue to hear. "Like people, like priest," saith the Scriptures. (Hosea 4:9.)

"The days are at hand, and the effect of every vision. For there shall be no more any vain vision nor flattering divination within the house of Israel." Ezekiel 12:23, 24. Moffatt gives it as follows: "The time is coming for the truth of every vision. No more vain visions and smooth oracles in Israel!"

It was Hannah More who wrote:

> "Who flatters, is of all mankind the lowest
> Save he who courts the flattery."

Satan deceives by miracles. There are always those who are readily influenced by signs and wonders. Even religious leaders may substitute such for more important matters.

In the days of Christ certain scribes and Pharisees came and said, "Master, we would see a sign." To which the Saviour answered, "An evil and adulterous generation seeketh after a sign." Matthew 12:38, 39.

Well might Jesus have said to them, "You are more interested in seeing a miracle than in being a miracle. I am interested in the miracle of transformed character, made possible through the acceptance of My words." "The words that I speak unto you, they are spirit, and they are life." John 6:63.

In Luke 13:16 Jesus spoke of a woman "whom Satan hath bound, lo, these eighteen years." And He healed, or loosed, her. Could it not be that if Satan had bound a woman in sickness eighteen years, he might also loose her? I believe that Satan is limited in the healing art, but I think that he is almost unlimited in the deceptive art.

In the latter days of this world's history those who do not truly love the truth will be deceived by signs and wonders, "even him, whose coming is after the working of Satan with all power and signs and lying wonders, and with all deceivableness of unrighteousness in them that perish; because they received not the love of the truth, that they might be saved." 2 Thessalonians 2:9, 10.

How clearly this paints the picture! Those who are drawn into Satan's net of signs and wonders are led into the "deceivableness of unrighteousness." They confuse unrighteousness with righteousness. What God calls sin they say is not sin. It seems safe to say that any person who decides what is truth on a basis of signs and wonders and miracles will be led into confusion and disobedience. To such this warning is given: "Woe unto them that call

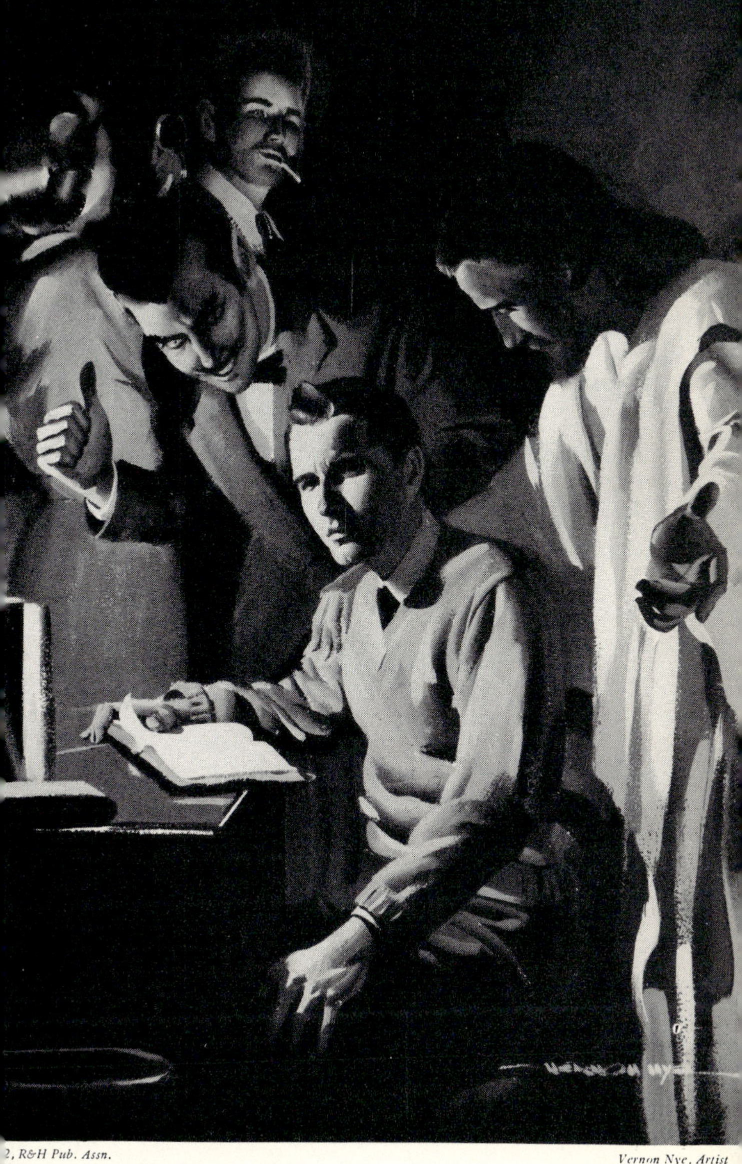

 Vernon Nye, Artist

he forces of good and evil are ever in conflict in the human heart. Our Lord offers
eace and eternal life; Satan offers thrills and eternal death. The choice is ours.

Russ Harlan, A

"Sin is the transgression of the law." 1 John 3:4. Only through Calvary may we see the unchangeable nature of God's law and the terrible penalty for disobedience

evil good, and good evil; that put darkness for light, and light for darkness." Isaiah 5:20.

The leaders of the nations are to be incited to the great battle of Armageddon by "the spirits of devils." (Revelation 16:14.)

"Going to and fro in the earth, and . . . walking up and down in it" (Job 1:7), Satan plies his business of deception. A thousand admixtures of truth and error he dispenses as potions of pleasure, peace of mind, and happiness. He selects just the mixture to suit each customer. He is a quack and a deceiver. All his prescriptions should carry the inscription: "P.D.Q. Pretender! Deceiver! Quack!" The time will come when he will be proved to be just that.

There are two things to be well remembered. One is that we are easily deceived by any person, thing, cause, or organization which we love.

The great Elihu Root is reported to have said in effect, "People do not love truth. They love personalities." He was perturbed as to the future of America because of this. If a man loves money, he will be deceived by it into a thousand paths of wrong. That is why the Saviour spoke of the "deceitfulness of riches." (Matthew 13:22.) Others love a cause, a church, an organization of some kind. There is nothing essentially wrong in such things. But they may blind the eyes of their lovers to truth. All do well to recall the words of Jesus: "And ye shall know the *truth,* and the *truth* shall make you free." John 8:32. And again, "Thy word is truth." John 17:17.

Cardinal Carlo Caraffa, legate of Paul IV, is said to have used the following expression in reference to the devout Parisians: "The people wish to be deceived; let them be deceived."

The other thing to remember is that we may deceive ourselves, and we may even love to do so.

It was Schopenhauer who said, "We deceive and flatter no one by such delicate artifices as we do our own selves."

The brilliant Goethe went so far as to write, "We are never deceived; we deceive ourselves." This was doubtless an overstatement or made with certain reservations in his mind. At any rate, it is interesting in the light of 1 Corinthians 3:18: "Let no man deceive himself." And again in 1 John 1:8: "If we say that we have no sin, we deceive ourselves, and the truth is not in us."

The devil is bad, very bad. He is a deceiver, an artful deceiver. But in all fairness we ought not to blame him when we deceive ourselves.

Satan Attacks by Accusation

When talking to Eve, Satan accused God of two things. By intimation he accused God of denying to her that which would yield great wisdom and personal advancement. Then he charged God with falsehood when he disputed the statement: "Thou shalt surely die." Genesis 2:17; 3:4.

Over against the first charge that God was not love, Jesus Christ put the arresting assertion: "God so loved the world, that he gave his only begotten Son." John 3:16.

Over against the second charge that God had not told the truth about sin and death, Jesus said of Satan, "When he speaketh a lie, he speaketh of his own: for he is a liar, and the father of it." John 8:44.

This is indeed plain calling of names and titles. It represents a sharp and decisive conflict. Someone is a liar, that much is plain. Saith the Scriptures again, "It was impossible for God to lie." Hebrews 6:18. This is because God's very character is truth. "A God of truth . . . is he." Deuteronomy 32:4.

So it is that Jesus said, "And this is life eternal, that

they might know thee the only true God, and Jesus Christ, whom thou hast sent." John 17:3.

When we cast our lot on God's side we shall not be spared accusation, but we shall be on the right side, and on the winning side.

When talking to Eve, Satan accused God to her. When talking to God, he accused Job to God. This is the old trick of the devil, which he has taught to many of us. He suits his speech to the occasion. He is as crooked as a serpent.

Consider the experience of God and Job and Satan. "Then Satan answered the Lord, and said, Doth Job fear God for nought? Hast not thou made an hedge about him, and about his house, and about all that he hath on every side? thou hast blessed the work of his hands, and his substance is increased in the land. But put forth thine hand now, and touch all that he hath, and he will curse thee to thy face." Job 1:9-11.

In short, Satan charged Job with serving God for reward only, and predicted that he would backslide and turn traitor if temporal blessings were withdrawn.

God said, in effect, "Try him out, but spare his life. We shall test the matter." (Verse 12.)

So the prince of this world went forth. In a period of twenty-four hours Job lost five hundred yoke of oxen and five hundred she-asses to the Sabeans, seven thousand sheep to lightning, three thousand camels to the Chaldeans, and seven sons and three daughters in a violent windstorm. Four servants, one from each disaster, were left to bear the sensational and tragic news. In one day his estate was swept clean of livestock, and his home bereft of children, leaving him a wife who was a cynic. What of Satan's accusation? Would it prove true? What would Job do?

"Then Job arose, and rent his mantle, and shaved his

head, and fell down upon the ground, and worshipped, and said, Naked came I out of my mother's womb, and naked shall I return thither: the Lord gave, and the Lord hath taken away; blessed be the name of the Lord. In all this Job sinned not, nor charged God foolishly." Verses 20-22.

Satan had charged Job falsely, but he could not lead Job to charge God foolishly. Job had stood the test, even though he did not understand the background or purpose of it.

God may permit Satan to bring trial and trouble upon you. Satan may suggest to you that your sins are too great for God to forgive, that your backslidings have been too many, that you are too unworthy, and that you can never succeed.

An old man, selling books and Bibles in order to win men to Christ, slumped down in the seat of his buggy as he rode along through the rain and the sticky mud of the Texas blackland country.

Taking advantage of the dark and gloomy day, the devil whispered to the aged saint: "Look at all the black and ugly sins of your yesterdays. Think of all the broken resolutions, the failures, and the foolish things you've done. You might as well give up. You can never make heaven."

The old man sat bolt upright. Half aloud he said, "Devil, be gone! Go talk to Jesus Christ about me. He is my representative. I've turned my life completely over to Him." The devil left, and the old saint rode triumphantly on through the rain.

Satan Attacks by Personal Affliction

Satan is persistent. Driven back on one line of attack, he approaches on another.

Job's faith could not be moved to the degree of a

hairsbreadth by the enormous blows of disaster, which Satan had delivered. But when the devil attacked Job with bodily affliction so terrible that his wife gave up, and his kinsfolk forsook him, his faith was jarred until its teeth fairly chattered, and the light of its life almost flickered out in the darkness of utter despair. Put an ambitious man flat on his back and drag his sickness out over a period of time, and you have one of life's most trying problems.

Even Job's fainting exclamations were filled with abject despondency:

"My soul chooseth . . . death rather than my life. I loathe it; I would not live alway: let me alone; for my days are vanity." Job 7:15, 16.

Yet up through the gloom of despondency and darkness he thrust a hand of hope, and said: "Though he slay me, yet will I trust in him. . . . He also shall be my salvation." "I know that my redeemer liveth, and that he shall stand at the latter day upon the earth: and though after my skin worms destroy this body, yet in my flesh shall I see God." Job 13:15, 16; 19:25, 26.

Here was a faith that met the utmost Satan could do. It was a faith that would be true to death, and could see beyond death to life. Satan and all the cohorts of hell can never vanquish a man who will in simplicity maintain such a faith, though the devil contest every inch of ground.

"O could we know the love that bendeth o'er us,
O could we understand the Father's heart,
Hear how the angels chant their loving chorus
While down our cheeks the bitter teardrops start,
See how all Heaven is moved to consolation,
And all the mysteries of Calvary mark,
We should not doubt the coming of salvation,
Nor think all hope is lost when it is dark."

—FANNIE BOLTON.

SATAN ATTACKS BY PERSECUTION

If Satan cannot lead a man astray by deception, if he cannot discourage him by accusation and bodily affliction, he will endeavor to incite other men to persecute him. He persecutes true religion through the forces of false religion. Sometimes the false uses the power of civil law in crushing the saints of God.

When the three Hebrews refused to bow down to the golden image that the king of Babylon had set up on the plains of Dura in the long ago, they were cast into a burning furnace. (Daniel 3.)

The prophet Daniel found himself faced with a law that prohibited prayer to his God, and then found himself thrust into a den of lions. (Daniel 6.)

The birth of Christ was near at hand. Satan stood ready through the power of Herod, a subruler of ancient Rome, to destroy the Saviour as soon as He was born. (Revelation 12:3-5, 9; Matthew 2:7-16.) The angry, confused, religious leaders of His home town church, stung with the simple sermon announcing His mission, led Him to the brow of a hill to cast Him down headlong. (Luke 4:16-30.)

Both religious and government men were sent to "catch him in his words." Mark 12:13. The chief priests and Pharisees sent officers to arrest Him, but they returned saying, "Never man spake like this man." John 7:46.

Many who believed feared to confess Him because "the Jews had agreed already, that if any man did confess that he was Christ, he should be put out of the synagogue." John 9:22.

Even "among the chief rulers also many believed on him; but because of the Pharisees they did not confess him, lest they should be put out of the synagogue: for they loved the praise of men more than the praise of God." John 12:42, 43.

The organized religion of that day, actuated by Satan, never ceased its persecution of Christ until He was nailed fast to the cross—yea, not until He lay in a rock-hewn tomb, closed with a great stone, sealed with the seal of imperial Rome, and guarded by a hundred soldiers.

To His disciples Jesus said, "Ye shall drink indeed of my cup." Matthew 20:23. "The world hateth you." John 15:19. "A man's foes shall be they of his own household." Matthew 10:36.

Forecasting the future through the revelation to the apostle John, Jesus pointed out Satan's work of persecution through pagan, heathen Rome, as well as during the Dark Ages to follow. In the climax of the age-old conflict over Christ and the law of God, right down in the remnant of time, Satan will wage warfare against the true followers of Christ. (Revelation 12:10-17.)

To His faithful children of every age Jesus says, "In the world ye shall have tribulation: but be of good cheer; I have overcome the world." John 16:33.

It was Richard Baxter who said, "The way is strange to me, but not to Christ."

"Then trust in God through all thy days;
Fear not, for He doth hold thy hand;
Though dark thy way, still sing and praise,
Sometime, sometime, we'll understand."

Satan Climaxes His Work by Possession

Many questions have been raised concerning the matter of being "possessed of the devil." Christ presents the picture of an unclean spirit going out of a man, and later returning only to find the place empty. The spirit then proceeds to gather seven other unclean spirits more wicked than himself, and they all enter the man, making his last state worse than the first. (Matthew 12:43-45.)

Christ represents the human heart to be a field of battle, a zone of contest, to be occupied by the forces of good or the forces of evil. There can be no permanent neutral ground. Nor can there be any stopping this side of eventual complete possession by either Christ or Satan. It must be one or the other. This is the Bible view. This is the teaching of Christ.

Dr. J. H. Oldham, secretary of the Council of the Christian Faith and Common Life, wrote in the *Christian News Letter:*

"Satanic forces seem today to be in the saddle. Not only have the impulses of violence, cruelty, and lust broken loose in the world, but apart from the forebodings which these awaken, many people have a growing sense of a hostile element in the universe, a power of evil which wages malicious war against their spirits."

In concluding his statement he presents this conviction:

"Modern psychology confirms the Biblical view of man, not as a self-contained personality, master of his fate, but as a battleground of contending forces of good and evil, open on the one hand to possession by demoniac powers, and on the other hand to the invasion of redeeming grace."

This is not to say that man is foredoomed to evil or predestined to good. It is to declare that there are two ways, two principles, two powers. There is the upward way, and there is the downward way. There is the good principle, and there is the evil principle. There is the power of Christ, and there is the power of Satan.

Which way shall we take? Which principle shall reign in us? Who shall be our master, Christ or Satan? The choice is ours. A delicate scale of destiny has been entrusted to each one of us. God will not tip it. Christ will not force it. Angels may not touch it. Satan cannot move it. Only man, by casting in the weight of his own personal choice, may decide which way the scale beam moves, and what power shall be dominant in his life.

Given entrance to the life, Satan will in time take complete possession. "Then entered Satan into Judas surnamed Iscariot, being of the number of the twelve. And he went his way, and communed with the chief priests and captains, how he might betray him [Jesus] unto them. And they were glad." Luke 22:3-5.

A demon-possessed disciple bargained with the demon-possessed religious leaders, and betrayed the Saviour of the world into the hands of church prelates and civil power. The end was Calvary.

John adds the meaningful statement: "He [Judas] then . . . went immediately out, and it was night." John 13:30.

Yes, it was night for Judas. It was physical night. It was spiritual night, without a single star of hope. He whose life might have shone as one of the brightest stars in the firmament of the everlasting gospel went out in a void of black darkness. Satan led him to put a halter round his neck and hang himself from the limb of a tree. Under the weight of his body the rope broke, leaving his horribly mangled remains a feast for roving dogs—a mute symbol of the last end of serving sin, self, and Satan.

Three Things We Can Do to Overcome Satan

"They overcame him by the blood of the Lamb." Revelation 12:11.

Yes, Calvary is always the basic answer. Satan sought to make Calvary the final hour of defeat. Jesus made it the glorious, triumphant hour of victory.

"That through death he [Christ] might destroy him

that had the power of death, that is, the devil." Hebrews 2:14.

A great prairie fire, driven by a strong wind, swept relentlessly toward a farmer's homestead. The man quickly hitched his horses to the plow and made several furrows in the form of a large circle around his home. Then he set fire to the dry grass within the circle and burned it clean. The roaring, terrifying demons of the prairie, with giant tongues of leaping flames, charged down upon that home. But when it struck the furrows and the ground already burned over, it swirled round the circle and went on its devastating way. The farmer and his family, his house and barns, his machinery and stock, were saved. The fires of God's wrath against sin burned over Calvary, where you and I may gather around the cross of Jesus, safe from the fires of destruction.

Begin your march to heaven at the cross of Calvary. Keep close to the cross and to its Christ all the way you journey.

The second thing we can do is use the powerful "sword of the Spirit, which is the word of God." Ephesians 6:17.

After forty days of fasting and prayer Jesus was weak and weary. In this hour of His great weakness Satan came to Him with strong, almost overpowering temptation. He came once. Jesus said, "It is written." He came twice. Jesus said, "It is written." He came the third time, and Jesus said, "It is written." (Matthew 4:1-9.) Three thrusts of the two-edged sword of the Word of God, and Satan left for a season, lest he be divided asunder. (Hebrews 4:12.)

The third thing to keep in mind is to "resist the devil, and he will flee from you." James 4:7. "They overcame him . . . by the word of their testimony." Revelation 12:11.

We cannot lie flat on our backs or recline cushioned on flowery beds of ease for an idle ride to heaven.

We must speak up and bear our testimony for God, for Christ, and for truth. We must stand up and be counted for God, taking the shield of faith and the sword of the Spirit and going forth to "fight the good fight of faith," thus laying "hold on eternal life." 2 Timothy 6:12.

"The greatest want of the world is the want of men,—men who will not be bought or sold; men who in their inmost souls are true and honest; men who do not fear to call sin by its right name; men whose conscience is as true to duty as the needle to the pole; men who will stand for the right though the heavens fall."—MRS. E. G. WHITE, *Education,* p. 57.

CHAPTER 11

What Is God's Remedy for Sin?

GOD DID not originate sin, but He did originate a remedy for sin. "Sin is the transgression of the law" (1 John 3:4), but law is not the remedy for sin.

It is true, as the apostle Paul proclaims, "The law is holy, and the commandment holy, and just, and good." Romans 7:12. But the difficulty lies in the fact that man is not holy and just and good. The man cries out, "The Law is spiritual; we know that. But then I am a creature of the flesh, in the thraldom of sin." Romans 7:14, Moffatt.

It is true that God's law is eternal, and no man or men can change or abolish it. "All his commandments are sure. They stand fast for ever and ever, and are done in truth and uprightness." Psalms 111:7, 8. The problem is that the law is eternal, but we are temporary. "Surely the people is grass. The grass withereth, the flower fadeth: but the word of our God shall stand for ever." Isaiah 40:7, 8. "For what is your life? It is even a vapour, that appeareth for a little time, and then vanisheth away." James 4:14.

It is true as David sang, "The law of the Lord is perfect." Psalms 19:7. With this the great Moody agreed when he said, "Now men may cavil as much as they like about other parts of the Bible, but I have never met an honest man that found fault with the Ten Commandments."—DWIGHT L. MOODY, *Weighed and Wanting*, p. 11. The trouble is not that we can find one jot or tittle of fault with the Ten Commandments. The real trouble, and a very deep trouble, is that the Ten Commandments find so many and such grievous faults with us. "Sin is the transgression of the law," and the tragedy is that we have "all sinned." Romans 3:23.

What, then, is the remedy? It is always and ever the same. It was announced in Eden in these words: "I will put enmity between thee and the woman, and between thy seed and her seed; it shall bruise thy head, and thou shalt bruise his heel." Genesis 3:15. It was announced by Jesus in these words: "For God so loved the world, that he gave his only begotten Son, that whosoever believeth in him should not perish, but have everlasting life." John 3:16.

Years ago at Moody's meetings in Chicago a young man by the name of Moorhouse came over from England and spoke seven nights on John 3:16. Then he said:

"My friends, for a whole week I have been trying to tell you how much God loves you; but I cannot do it with this poor, stammering tongue. If I could borrow Jacob's ladder, climb up to heaven and ask Gabriel, who stands in the presence of God, to tell me how much God loves sinners, all he could say would be, 'God so loved the world, that He gave His only begotten Son that whosoever believeth in Him should not perish, but have everlasting life.' "

God created a good world and a good man. He gave the good man a good law, which was ordained to life. (Romans 7:10.)

The law was good, but the man became bad.

The law was eternal, but the man became temporary.

The law was perfect, but it revealed the imperfections of the man.

God remained always the same—a God of power, wisdom, beauty, law, and love.

God gave His Son.

The law was holy. Christ was holy. "Who did no sin." 1 Peter 2:22.

The law was eternal. Christ was eternal. "Whose goings forth have been from of old, from everlasting." Micah 5:2.

The law was perfect. Christ kept that perfect law. "I have kept my Father's commandments." John 15:10. Said Pilate, "Behold, . . . I find no fault in him." John 19:4.

This holy, perfect, eternal Christ, of whose character the law was a written transcript, and whose life was a living revelation of that same law—this Christ, God gave to save you. No other being in God's universe could meet the demands of the holy, unchangeable law of the eternal God, and make that obedience available to you. "Since the divine law is as sacred as God himself, only one equal with God could make atonement for its transgression."—*Patriarchs and Prophets,* p. 63.

He lived for you. (Matthew 20:28.) He died for you. (1 Peter 2:24.) He offers pardon to you. (1 John 1:9.) He offers grace and power to you. (Hebrews 4:16.) He offers heaven to you. (Matthew 19:27-29.)

Do you hesitate and say, "I do not understand how these things can be"?

God did not say, "Whosoever understandeth the science and philosophy of the atonement of My Son on Calvary shall have everlasting life." He said, "Whosoever believeth in him."

"Believe on the Lord Jesus Christ, and thou shalt be saved." Acts 16:31.

The dying thief looked, believed, and received assurance of Paradise. (Luke 23:42, 43.)

The living centurion, watching the dying Christ, said, "Truly this was the Son of God." Matthew 27:54.

The sinful, conscience-smitten publican cried, "God be merciful to me a sinner," and went down to his house forgiven. (Luke 18:13.)

Sinful David pleaded, "Cleanse me from my sin." "Create in me a clean heart," and God heard his prayer. (Psalms 51:2, 10.)

If you will believe, you shall receive. Do not trust to feeling. Take your sins to the cross. Exchange them for forgiveness. Ask God to give you a new heart, and write His holy law upon it, that you may love it and keep it. Believe that as you have prayed in the name of Jesus, God does this. Surrender your all to Him. Make no reservation. Give all. Receive all that God gives.

"These blessings we by faith receive,
By simple, childlike trust:
In Christ 'tis God's delight to give;
He promised, and He must."

SECTION THREE

MAN'S QUESTIONS ABOUT THE BIBLE

Review Pictures *Bernard Plockhorst, Artis*

Our Lord's companions were ignorant of the Scriptures, and Jesus therefore "expound unto them in all the scriptures the things concerning himself."

CHAPTER 12

What the Bible Is

THERE IS a story of a visitor who asked of a little boy, "How old are you?"

"Well," replied the boy, "according to my latest personal check my psychological age is twelve, my moral age is four, my anatomical age is seven, and my physiological age is six; but if you wish to know my chronological age, I am eight years old." Almost everyone today knows more large words than did his grandparents. Yet the Bible, which is the world's greatest book and the largest seller, is often read less and understood less than it was in the past.

In a check of nearly fourteen thousand New York City grammar school children, one out of every four had never heard of the Ten Commandments.

THE WORD *Bible*

Strange as it may seem, the word *Bible* is not found in the actual text of the Bible. It may be printed on the cover or on introductory or appended pages, but it does not appear in the writings of the Book itself.

What does the word *Bible* mean, and why are its writings called the Bible?

The word *Bible* comes from the Latin *biblia,* signifying books, which comes from the Greek *biblos,* book.

Thus the word *Bible* means "books." The Holy Bible therefore indicates the holy *books,* being indeed appropriate, since the Bible truly is composed of many books, thirty-nine in the Old Testament and twenty-seven in the New Testament, or sixty-six in all.

Bible's Name for Itself

What then is the Bible's own name for these writings?

To discover the more general title as found in the Bible, let us turn to four statements made by Jesus. The first is Luke 4:16-21:

"And he [Jesus] came to Nazareth, where he had been brought up: and, as his custom was, he went into the synagogue on the sabbath day, and stood up for to read. And there was delivered unto him the book of the prophet Esaias. And when he had opened the book, he found the place where it was written, The Spirit of the Lord is upon me, because he hath anointed me to preach the gospel to the poor; he hath sent me to heal the broken-hearted, to preach deliverance to the captives, and recovering of sight to the blind, to set at liberty them that are bruised, to preach the acceptable year of the Lord. And he closed the book, and he gave it again to the minister, and sat down. And the eyes of all them that were in the synagogue were fastened on him. And he began to say unto them, This day is this *scripture* fulfilled in your ears." Here we have the record of that dramatic scene in the synagogue at old Nazareth, on that memorable Sabbath day when Jesus announced His mission to the world, as predicted in the writings of Isaiah the prophet. Reading a portion, Jesus referred to it as "this scripture."

Again we read His words in Matthew 21:42: "Jesus saith unto them, Did ye never read in the *scriptures,* The stone which the builders rejected, the same is become the head of the corner."

Yet again we hear His words: "Ye do err, not knowing the *scriptures.*" Matthew 22:29. Once again He sums it up. It was after His resurrection, as He walked with two of His discouraged followers on the road from Jerusalem to Emmaus as night was drawing on. After their sad recital of the crucifixion He said to them: "O fools, and slow of heart to believe all that the prophets have spoken: ought not Christ to have suffered these things, and to enter into his glory? And beginning at Moses and all the prophets, he expounded unto them in all the *scriptures* the things concerning himself." Luke 24:25-27.

Thus the ancient writings of the Bible Jesus called the "scriptures." That word means "writings," so we often appropriately call the Bible the Sacred Scriptures, Holy Scriptures, or writings.

The Content of the Scriptures

What writings are included in the Scriptures? This is a most natural and important question. Since there was no New Testament in the time of Christ, His references to the Scriptures always denote the Old Testament.

There is no contradiction between the Old Testament and the New. They are a unit, standing or falling together. The Old is the foundation for the New. It has been written that there are more than 250 direct quotations from the Old Testament in the New Testament. Professor Milligan says that the book of Revelation is "absolutely steeped in the memories, incidents, thoughts and language of the church's past. . . . It is a perfect mosaic of passages from the Old Testament."

Someone else likens the Old Testament to a Damascus blade made of a cloth of woven wire, heated, forged, and tempered to take an edge that was irresistible. So the Old and New Testaments are in figure interwoven, then heated and welded in the fire of divine inspiration, until they come out as "the sword of the Spirit, which is the word of God." Ephesians 6:17.

What did Jesus say was included in the Scriptures, which in His time denoted only the Old Testament? The three main divisions of the Old Testament He gives us clearly in these words spoken after His resurrection from the dead:

"These are the words which I spake unto you, while I was yet with you, that all things must be fulfilled, which were written in the *law of Moses,* and in the *prophets,* and in the *psalms,* concerning me. Then opened he their understanding, that they might understand the *scriptures.*" Luke 24:44, 45.

Here is the threefold division of the Old Testament: the law of Moses, or the first five books of the Bible, Genesis, Exodus, Leviticus, Numbers, and Deuteronomy, called also the Pentateuch; the second division or the prophets, which took in all the rest of the Old Testament save that called the Psalms; the third portion included not only what we now call the Psalms, but Ruth, First and Second Chronicles, Ezra, Nehemiah, Esther, Job, Proverbs, Ecclesiastes, Song of Solomon, Lamentations, and Daniel.

It is true that the Roman Catholic Douay Bible has seven other books in the Old Testament not accepted by Protestants. They are Tobias, Judith, Wisdom, Ecclesiasticus, Baruch, and First and Second Maccabees. Other additions are six extra chapters to the book of Esther, and seventy more verses in the third chapter of Daniel.

In this connection it is important to note that Christ and the apostles never made any references to or quotations from these additional writings, which are known as the Apocrypha. Aside from these added books, however, the Catholic Douay Version of the Bible is an excellent translation.

The New Testament writings are also spoken of as

the Scriptures. Peter thus refers to the epistles of Paul:

"Our beloved brother Paul also according to the wisdom given unto him hath written unto you; as also in all his epistles, speaking in them of these things; in which are some things hard to be understood, which they that are unlearned and unstable wrest, as they do also the other scriptures, unto their own destruction." 2 Peter 3:15, 16.

So the apostle Peter refers to Paul's writings on the same basis as "the other scriptures."

Then Paul in 1 Timothy 5:18 quotes the record of Luke 10:7: "The labourer is worthy of his reward," and refers to the statement as "scripture."

Thus we reach the clear conclusion that the writings of both the Old and the New Testament constitute the Scriptures, the fundamental Bible name for the writings of the book we call the Bible.

"In more than fifty places in the New Testament an appeal is made to 'the Scripture' or 'the Scriptures' in such a way as to show that those words were as definite in their meaning then as they are now among evangelical Protestants."—G. FREDERICK WRIGHT, *The Divine Authority of the Bible,* p. 37.

Consider these two statements of Jesus: "The scriptures must be fulfilled." Mark 14:49. "The scripture cannot be broken." John 10:35.

Little wonder, then, that the apostle Paul insists on the unity and value and inspiration of *"all scripture"* (2 Timothy 3:16) and exclaims with the most sincere spirit of inquiry, "What saith the scripture?" (Romans 4:3.)

"How blest are we, with open face
To view Thy glory, Lord.
And all Thy image here to trace,
Reflected in Thy Word."

CHAPTER 13

What Men Say About the Bible

BEFORE PROCEEDING further with what the Bible says about itself, we would profit by considering something of what leading men have said concerning the Book of books.

UNITED STATES PRESIDENTS SPEAK

Woodrow Wilson: "A man has deprived himself of the best there is in the world who has deprived himself of intimate knowledge of the Bible."

Herbert Hoover: "The study of the Bible . . . is a postgraduate course in the richest library of human experience."

Calvin Coolidge: "There is no other book with which the Bible can be compared and no other reading that means so much to the human race."

Theodore Roosevelt: "Almost every man who has by his lifework added to the sum of human achievement of which the race is proud, of which our people are proud, almost every such man has based his lifework largely upon the teachings of the Bible."

Abraham Lincoln: "In regard to this great Book, I have only to say that it is the best Book that God has given to man."

Andrew Jackson: "That Book, sir, is the rock on which our Republic rests."

George Washington: "It is impossible to rightly govern the world without God and the Bible."

Other Voices in Chorus

Queen Victoria: "This is the secret of England's greatness, the Bible."

William E. Gladstone: "I have known ninety-five great men in my time, and of these, eighty-seven were all followers of the Bible. . . . Though assailed by camp, by battery, and by mine, the Holy Scriptures are nevertheless a house builded upon a rock, and that rock is impregnable."

Dr. James McGray:

"Despised and torn in pieces,
By infidels decried—
The thunderbolts of hatred,
The haughty cynics' pride—
All these have railed against it,
In this and other lands,
Yet dynasties have fallen,
And still the Bible stands!"

Immanuel Kant: "The existence of the Bible as a book for the people is the greatest benefit which the human race has ever experienced."

Thomas Huxley: "The Bible has been the Magna Charta of the poor and oppressed."

Daniel Webster: "If we abide by the principles taught in the Bible, our country will go on prospering and to prosper, but if we and our posterity neglect its instruction and authority, no man can tell how sudden a catastrophe may overwhelm us and bury our glory in profound obscurity."

General Douglas MacArthur: "Believe me, sir, never a night goes by, be I ever so tired, but I read the Word of God before I go to bed."

John Wanamaker: "I have of course made large purchases of property in my time, involving millions of dollars. But it was as a boy in the country, at the age of eleven years, that I made my greatest purchase. In the little mission Sunday school I bought a small red leather Bible for $2.75, which I paid for in small installments. Looking back over my life, I see that that little red Book was the foundation on which my life has been built and has made possible all that has counted in my life. I know now that it was the greatest investment and the most important and far-reaching purchase I ever made."

Dwight L. Moody: "I never saw a useful Christian who was not a student of the Bible. If a man neglects his Bible, he may pray and ask God to use him in His work, but God cannot make much use of him."

Canon Dyson Hague: "The depth of the Bible is infinite. Millions of readers and writers, age after age, have dug in this unfathomable mine and its depths are still unexhausted. . . . You cannot gild gold. You cannot brighten diamonds, and no artist can touch with final touch this finished Word of God. This proud-pinnacled century can add nothing to it. It stands as the sun in the sky. It has the glory of God."

Cordell Hull as Secretary of State of the United States: "Humanity desperately needs today a moral and a spiritual rebirth—a revitalization of religion. There is no sure way to this supreme goal save through adherence to the teachings of the Bible."

John Wesley: "I want to know one thing—the way to heaven: how to land safe on that happy shore. God Himself has condescended to teach the way. He hath written it down in a Book! Oh, give me that Book! At any price, give me that book of God!"

Henry Van Dyke: "No man is poor or desolate who has this treasure for his own."

John G. Whittier:

"We search the world for truth; we cull
The good, the pure, the beautiful,
From graven stone and written scroll,
From all old flower fields of the soul;
And, weary seekers of the best,
We come back laden from our quest,
To find that all the sages said
Is in the Book our mothers read."

 Frederic R. Gruger, Artist

God's Word is eternal. It outlives great kingdoms. World empires have crumbled t dust, but the living Word grows stronger and more potent than ever before.

CHAPTER 14

How the Bible Came to Us

WE HUMAN beings have a thirst to know where things come from. It is perfectly natural for us to inquire concerning the origin of this most famous Book in the world.

This is the book that H. L. Hastings said contains "history, genealogy, ethnology, law, ethics, prophecy, poetry, eloquence, medicine, sanitary science, political economy, and perfect rules for the conduct of personal and social life."

What is the primary source of the Scriptures? Men claim that the Bible is the world's greatest book. What does this Book have to say regarding its origin? Is it just the world's greatest book, or is it something more than human?

The Bible Testifies

The authority of the Bible prophets is greater than the words of any human being, even though he might rise from the dead a thousand years after he was buried. Said Jesus by way of a parable, "If they hear not Moses and the prophets, neither will they be persuaded, though one rose from the dead." Luke 16:31.

There are five important things to remember about the giving of the Scriptures.

The first and most significant is this positive declaration by that flaming, living torch of gospel truth, the apostle Paul: "All scripture is given by inspiration of God." 2 Timothy 3:16. This recognizes God as the fountainhead of "all scripture," the fundamental source of the whole Bible.

The second point is given by the great apostle Peter in these words: "Of which salvation the prophets have enquired and searched diligently, who prophesied of the grace that should come unto you: searching what, or what manner of time the Spirit of Christ which was in them did signify, when it testified beforehand the sufferings of Christ, and the glory that should follow." 1 Peter 1:10, 11. Thus we understand that *Christ* was intimately connected with the giving of the Scriptures, of which the prophecies are a portion.

The third agency in the giving of the Scriptures is set forth in connection with the fourth, as clearly stated by the same apostle Peter: "Prophecy came not in old time by the will of man: but holy men of God spake as they were moved by the Holy Ghost." 2 Peter 1:21. As God the Father, the Son, and the Holy Spirit cooperated in the creation of the world and the making of man, so here we find the three working together in giving to the world the Bible through men. Men "spake as they were moved by the Holy Ghost." David expressed the same truth when he said, "The Spirit of the Lord spake by me, and his word was in my tongue." 2 Samuel 23:2.

There is yet one more living agency involved in the giving of the Holy Scriptures. A beautiful picture of the process is presented in the first verse of the book of Revelation. "The Revelation of Jesus Christ which God gave to him, to shew unto his servants things which must shortly come to pass; and he sent and signified it by *his angel* unto his servant John." Revelation 1:1.

God gave the message to Christ, who sent it by His

angel to the prophet John; then John spoke or wrote the message for the people. The angel is the new agent brought to view in this scripture. This particular angel is called "his angel," generally considered to be Gabriel. (Daniel 8:16; 9:21; Luke 1:19, 26.)

From God, to Christ, to His angel, to the prophets who spoke or wrote as "they were moved by the Holy Ghost"—that was the method. Thus it was "God, who at sundry times and in divers manners spake in time past unto the fathers by the prophets." Hebrews 1:1. The Bible is the divine-human book, a book from Heaven given through men to men.

A Word About the Books and Writers

The Ten Commandments God Himself first spoke, then wrote upon two tables of stone, and "he added no more." Deuteronomy 5:22. This sacred law of Scripture stands apart and separate, spoken to men by God and written by Him.

Moses wrote the first five books of the Bible and is generally conceded to be the author of the book of Job. Joshua was also commissioned to write. (Joshua 24:26.)

Then came the long period of the kings, first David and Solomon, then the divided kingdom of Judah and Israel, with the books of Samuel, parts of Kings and Chronicles, David's Psalms, Solomon's Proverbs, Ecclesiastes, and Song of Solomon, also Isaiah, Jeremiah, Hosea, Joel, and Amos.

In close connection with the time of captivity in Babylon, there came the messages of Ezekiel, Daniel, Obadiah, Habakkuk, and Zephaniah. It is understood that the later portions of Kings and Chronicles were written then.

After the Jews were restored to their own land the books of Ezra, Nehemiah, Esther, Haggai, Zechariah, and Malachi were also added.

The Old Testament was completed some three or four hundred years before Christ. The New Testament was finished by about A.D. 100.

The whole Bible was thus brought into being over a period of more than fifteen hundred years, and portions were written by nearly forty different men. What a miracle is its origin, its preservation, its unity, its beauty, and its power!

WHAT MEN HAVE SAID

H. L. Hastings wrote, "Here are words written by kings, by emperors, by princes, by poets, by sages, by philosophers, by fishermen, by statesmen, by men learned in the wisdom of Egypt, educated in the schools of Babylon, trained up at the feet of the rabbis in Jerusalem. It was written by men in exile, in the desert, in shepherds' tents, in 'green pastures,' and beside 'still waters.' Among its authors we find the taxgatherer, the herdsman, the gatherer of sycamore fruit; we find poor men, rich men, statesmen, preachers, exiles, captains, legislators, judges; men of every grade and class. . . . It contains all kinds of writing; but what a jumble it would be if sixty-six books were written in this way by ordinary men. Suppose, for instance, that we get sixty-six medical books written by thirty or forty different doctors of various schools, . . . bind them all together, and then undertake to doctor a man according to that book! . . . Or suppose you get thirty-five ministers writing books on theology, and then see if you can find any leather strong enough to hold the books together."—*Will the Old Book Stand?* p. 21.

Voltaire said the Bible was an exploded book. His theory is what exploded, for he has been dead more than 150 years, and the Book is still here, read and loved by more people than ever.

Ingersoll, a man of rich talent, declared that the Bible

would not be read in ten years. It has been long years since he died, yet the Bible today outsells any one hundred other books put together.

Like a cube of granite, the Bible is right side up no matter how many times you overturn it, and it leaves its imprint everywhere it goes.

It has been translated into more languages and dialects than any other book. Completed nearly two thousand years ago the Bible or portions of it may be read today in more than one thousand tongues, and it is the most up-to-date book in the world.

Someone has written:

"The empire of Caesar is gone; the legions of Rome are mouldering in the dust; the avalanches Napoleon hurled upon Europe have melted away; the pride of the Pharaohs is fallen; the pyramids they raised to be their tombs are sinking every day in the desert sands; Tyre is a rock for fishermen's nets; Sidon has scarcely a rock left behind; but the Word of God survives. All things that threatened to extinguish it have aided it, and it proves every day how transient is the noblest monument that man can build, how enduring the least word God has spoken. Tradition has dug a grave for it; intolerance has lighted for it many a fagot; many a Judas has betrayed it with a kiss; many a Peter has denied it with an oath; many a Demas has forsaken it; but the Word of God still endures."

"Last eve I passed beside a blacksmith's door,
And heard the anvil ring the vesper chime;
Then looking in, I saw upon the floor
Old hammers, worn with beating years of time.

" 'How many anvils have you had,' said I,
'To wear and batter all these hammers so?'
'Just one,' said he, and then, with twinkling eye,
'The anvil wears the hammers out, you know.'

"And so, thought I, the anvil of God's Word,
For ages skeptic blows have beat upon;
Yet, though the noise of falling blows was heard,
The anvil is unharmed—the hammers gone."

—*Author Unknown.*

CHAPTER 15

Why Do Men Need the Bible?

THE BIBLE, which is generally known as the Scriptures, is also called "the book of the Lord" (Isaiah 34:16), "the gospel of God" (Romans 1:1), "the oracles of God" (Romans 3:2), "the good word of God" (Hebrews 6:5), and "the word of Christ" (Colossians 3:16).

This Book of divine origin Heaven has provided for man. Why? What is the purpose of the Book? Why do men need the Book?

Man's need of the Bible is just as universal as life and death. Sir Walter Scott, famous writer of Scotland, sickly as a child, robust as a man and successful beyond his fondest dreams, found himself upon his deathbed as a result of overwork in an effort to pay off debts from an unfortunate business collapse. In that twilight hour of his life he said to John Lockhart, his son-in-law and later biographer, "Read to me from the book."

Thinking of the vast writings of Sir Walter, John said, "Which book shall I read?"

Scott replied, "Need you ask? There is but one Book." So there at old Abbotsford, with his children gathered about him, and while the darkness of death deepened, he listened to the reading of God's Book, the Bible, and saw a great and comforting light as he fell asleep September 21, 1832.

The Bible is God's lamp of hope for all men. It is

God's antidote for despair. "For whatsoever things were written aforetime were written for our learning, that we through patience and comfort of the scriptures might have hope." Romans 15:4.

In these dark days of human history when black clouds of dire destruction hurry across our skies, the promises of the Bible have been given that "we might have a strong consolation, who have fled for refuge to lay hold upon the hope set before us: which hope we have as an anchor of the soul, both sure and stedfast." Hebrews 6:18, 19.

"It will firmly hold in the straits of Fear,
When the breakers tell that the reef is near;
Tho' the tempest rave and the wild winds blow,
Not an angry wave shall our bark o'erflow.

"When our eyes behold, in the dawning light,
Shining gates of pearl, our harbor bright,
We shall anchor fast to the heavenly shore,
With the storms all past forevermore."

—PRISCILLA J. OWENS.

OTHER SPECIFIC PURPOSES OF THE BIBLE

We now consider other specific purposes of the Bible, other reasons why men need the Scriptures. Perhaps the fullest summary in a few words is given by the apostle Paul in these two verses:

"All scripture is given by inspiration of God, and is profitable for doctrine, for reproof, for correction, for instruction in righteousness: that the man of God may be perfect, throughly furnished unto all good works." 2 Timothy 3:16, 17.

First in Paul's list is doctrine. The word *doctrine* means a teaching, a truth, a tenet of faith. In fact, the Revised Standard Version, Weymouth, and Moffatt read, "profitable," or "useful," "for teaching."

And according to the Scriptures, men need doctrines.

It is profitable for us to study doctrines. There may be at times a feeling within us which says, "I do not like doctrines. I want only the Spirit. Just give me spiritual things." Now, the truth is that doctrines are of the Spirit, for "all scripture is given by inspiration of God, and is profitable for doctrine." One of the greatest needs of the church and the world today is the setting forth in clarity and certainty of the great doctrines of true faith and morals. We need to believe something, and to know why we believe what we believe. Too many are vacillating, "carried about with every wind of doctrine." Ephesians 4:14. Many do not know what to believe, and are more sure of what they do not believe than of what they do believe.

It was the same in Jesus' day. He was just beginning His public ministry and was concluding His sermon on the mount. To the people He said, in essence, "If you will believe and do the things I say, you will be like a wise man who built his house upon a rock. If you do not believe and do the things I say, you will be like a foolish man who built his house upon the sand." That sounds the note of certainty. Matthew writes of this experience in chapter 7, verses 28 and 29: "It came to pass, when Jesus had ended these sayings, the people were astonished at his doctrine: for he taught them as one having authority and not as the scribes." Jesus believed something. He stood for something.

There has never been a great religious awakening without the preaching of great doctrines. One might as well try to build a substantial house without putting in a good foundation and without rugged framework, as to attempt the erection of strong Christian character without faith in great doctrines. A Christian without fundamental beliefs is like a body without bones. It has no rigidity to stand erect. It has no strength.

Truly the body needs more than bones, lest it be but a skeleton. Nevertheless, to be a successful body, it must have bones—good bones. Christian experience needs more than doctrines, but to be successful, it must have them. "All scripture . . . is profitable for doctrine."

Not only is all scripture profitable for doctrine, establishing us in an understanding of fundamental divine truths, but according to this same verse (2 Timothy 3:16), it is profitable for reproof.

None of us relishes reproof—not by nature. Yet God finds it necessary to reprove us. A man who does not think he is sick will not seek a physician. God cannot remedy our weaknesses if we do not have knowledge of them, and acknowledge them, though God does not delight in reproving man.

Christ was in conversation with a woman of questionable character. He talked to her about the water of life. He tried to help her without calling attention to her sin. Making little progress, He said to her, "Go, call thy husband, and come hither."

"I have no husband," she answered.

Jesus replied, "Thou hast well said . . . : for thou hast had five husbands; and he whom thou now hast is not thy husband." John 4:16-18. Christ placed His finger on her sin, and in this case was able to save the woman, howbeit she first sought to save face by arguing for her religion as against His, and her place of worship as against that of the Jews.

Secret sins of the heart, such as pride, envy, hatred, and covetousness, which may escape the view of man, are seen by God and are especially hateful in His eyes. The Scriptures are scheduled to reveal, as an X-ray, this inner trouble. In Hebrews 4:12 we read, "The word of God is quick, and powerful, and sharper than any two-edged sword, piercing even to the dividing asunder of soul and spirit, and of the joints and marrow, and is a discerner of the thoughts and intents of the heart." The Bible will reveal the crooked and misshapen bones of doctrine, and bring to view the selfish and evil thought. Thus does the Word of God become a reprover of sin, whether that sin be in a believer or unbeliever. It is no respecter of persons. Anyone who searches the Scriptures with honesty of heart will find that he will be reproved. Evil unreproved is dangerous.

Correction follows reproof. Mere reproof would be of little value if no change for the better could be effected. Here again the Word of God is the agent. "All scripture is given by inspiration of God, and is profitable for doctrine, for reproof, for correction." Moffatt says, "For amendment."

The Scriptures not only set up great beliefs, they not only reprove us individually for individual sins, but tend to correct the evil pointed out, to effect an amendment of life and to keep us on the right path.

Alexander McLeod tells somewhere of two young men who visited a great factory to discover the secret of a new machine that a clever man had invented, and to make secret drawings of it.

In their hotel room one of the young men opened a Bible to the twentieth chapter of Exodus and read the Ten Commandments. When he came to the eighth one he could go no farther, for its words seemed to flash like fire, and smote upon his conscience, "Thou shalt not steal." Those men went home without the secret of the machine, but with the secret of personal power. "Wherewithal shall a young man cleanse his way? by taking heed thereto according to thy word." Psalms 119:9.

Down in the ancient land of Egypt, youthful, lithe, and handsome Joseph was sold as a slave, only later to become the manager of the household of Potiphar, who was captain of the king's guard. When tempted to the scarlet sin at the invitation of Potiphar's wife, under the enticement of secrecy and the lure of favor and reward, Joseph said to her, "How then can I do this great wickedness, and sin against God?"

Day after day this sultry-voiced, dusky beauty of Egypt's land cast her eyes upon Joseph and engaged the stalwart youth of God in stealthy, whispered conversation. His answer was always No. He would neither betray his master on earth nor be untrue to his Master in heaven. He would not sell his better self to his lower self, even though it seemed that no one would ever know of his sin.

What did it cost him to say that word *no?* The price was prison, where they fettered his feet with chains and laid him in iron. (Psalms 105:18.)

What was the secret of his power? The principles of righteousness learned in his father's tent in Canaan were in his mind and heart. "Thy word have I hid in mine heart, that I might not sin against thee." Psalms 119:11. He lived as under the direct gaze of God, subject unto His word, and thus did he prevail in the hour of temptation. Standing on the very edge of a perilous precipice, he was steadied by the word and presence of God. One writer has said, "If God's Word were studied as it should be, men would have a breadth of mind, a nobility of character, and a stability of purpose that is rarely seen in these times."—MRS. E. G. WHITE, *Steps to Christ,* p. 95.

All that we have been saying is but to amplify the verses we have been studying: "All scripture is given by inspiration of God, and is profitable for doctrine, for reproof, for correction, for instruction in righteousness ["right doing," Weymouth] ["moral discipline," Moffatt]: that the man of God may be perfect ["complete," "proficient"], throughly furnished ["perfectly equipped," Weymouth] unto all good works." 2 Timothy 3:16, 17.

Greatest Purpose of the Bible

The greatest single purpose of the Bible we have left for the last, in order to make impressive the fact that it should be not only last but also first.

The Bible is likened to a lamp (Psalms 119:105), to food (Matthew 4:4), to a hammer and to fire (Jeremiah 23:29), to honey (Psalms 119:103), and to a sword (Ephesians 6:17). These and other interesting and important considerations we pass by for a brief look at the central figure of the Scriptures.

Concerning Himself the Son of man said, "Fear not; I am the first and the last." Revelation 1:17.

To the Jews at Jerusalem at the time of one of their religious feasts, when they were seeking to slay Him in the early days of His ministry, Jesus said, "Search the scriptures; for in them ye think ye have eternal life: and they are they which testify of me." John 5:39.

Of His actions after His crucifixion and resurrection we have this record: "Beginning at Moses and all the prophets, he expounded unto them in all the scriptures the things concerning himself." Luke 24:27.

In these words did Jesus make it unmistakably clear that from beginning to end the Scriptures brought revelations concerning Him.

"It was Christ who from the bush on Mount Horeb spoke to Moses saying, 'I AM THAT I AM. . . . Thus shalt thou say unto the children of Israel, I AM hath sent me unto you.' Exodus 3:14. This was the pledge of Israel's deliverance. So when He came 'in the likeness of men,' He declared Himself the I AM. The Child of Bethlehem, the meek and lowly Saviour, is God 'manifest in the flesh.' 1 Timothy 3:16. And to us He says, '"I AM the Good Shepherd." "I AM the living Bread." "I AM the Way, the Truth, and the Life." "ALL power is given unto ME in heaven and in earth." [John 10:11; 6:51;

14:6; Matthew 28:18.] "I AM the assurance of every promise." "I AM; be not afraid."' 'God with us' is the surety of our deliverance from sin, the assurance of our power to obey the law of heaven."—*The Desire of Ages*, pp. 24, 25.

CHRIST IN ALL THE BIBLE

In Genesis He is the Seed of the woman.
In Exodus, the Lamb of God foreshadowed.
In Leviticus, the High Priest typified.
In Numbers, the Star out of Jacob.
In Deuteronomy, the Prophet like unto Moses.
In Joshua, the Captain of the Lord's host.
In Judges, the Messenger of Jehovah.
In Ruth, our Kinsman and Redeemer.
In Samuel, the Lord and Seed of David.
In Kings and Chronicles, King over kings.
In Ezra and Nehemiah, Lord of heaven and earth.
In Esther, our Intercessor.
In Job, our risen Redeemer.
In Psalms, the Son of God.
In Proverbs, One brought up with God.
In Ecclesiastes He is above the sun.
In the Song of Solomon, altogether lovely.
In Isaiah He is the atoning and glorified Saviour.
In Jeremiah, the Lord our Righteousness.
In Lamentations, the Man of Sorrows.
In Ezekiel, Prince and Priest.
In Daniel, the Messiah cut off, and then Ruler of the world.
In Hosea He saves the backslider.
In Joel He utters His voice and shakes the earth.
In Amos He reproves and restores.
In Obadiah He is Lord of His kingdom.
In Jonah, the risen Prophet.
In Micah, the Ruler born in Bethlehem.
In Nahum, the Bearer of good tidings.
In Habakkuk, the Holy One with Calvary's scars.
In Zephaniah, a saving Lord in their midst.
In Haggai, the Desire of all nations.
In Zechariah, thy King, meek and lowly.
In Malachi, the Sun of Righteousness.

In Matthew, Emmanuel—God with us.
In Mark, the Stone which the builders rejected.
In Luke, the forgiving Debtor.
In John, Creator, Redeemer, and coming King.
In Acts, the ascended Lord.
In Romans, Justifier of the unjust.
In 1 Corinthians, the Hope of the resurrection.
In 2 Corinthians, Constraining Love.
In Galatians, Redeeming Grace.
In Ephesians, Head of the church.
In Philippians, Power of a resurrected life.
In Colossians, the First-born of every creature.
In 1 Thessalonians, the Voice that raises the dead.
In 2 Thessalonians He is feared of sinners, admired of saints.
In 1 Timothy He is the only Mediator between God and men.
In 2 Timothy, Giver of the crown.
In Titus, the Blessed Hope of the world.
In Philemon, the Author of peace.
In Hebrews, our great High Priest.
In James, the Lord whose coming draweth nigh.
In 1 Peter, the Lamb without blemish.
In 2 Peter, the Daystar to our hearts.
In epistles of John, the Word of life.
In Jude, Michael the Archangel.
In Revelation, King of kings and Lord of lords.

A father was left alone one evening with his small daughter. He wished to read, and the little girl wanted to play, and the combination did not work too well.

Finally the parent seized onto a solution, picked up a map of the world, took the scissors, and cut it into many pieces. "Now," he said to the child, "you can have a good time putting these pieces together, and when you are through you will have a map of the world." So saying, he turned to his reading, the little lady to her game, and all was quiet on the family front.

To the father's astonishment, it was only a short time until the daughter said, "Daddy, I'm all finished." And there lay on the floor a perfect map of the world. "How in the world did you put it together so quickly?" he asked in surprise.

"Oh, it was easy," said she, "because on the back of the map there was the picture of a big man, so I turned the map over, and when I got the man the world came out all right."

The Bible reveals the Man, and when men find the Man everything else will come out all right.

Have you found the Man of the Book? Have you made Him your Saviour, your Friend, your Pattern, your Power?

The Friend of yours is the Man of the Book. Faith in this Man is nourished by the Book. Stay close to the Man. Stay close to the Book. "This Book will keep you from sin, and sin will keep you from this Book." The secret of your perfection (2 Timothy 3:17) lies in your submission to, and association with, the perfect Man and the perfect Book.

"O Word of God Incarnate,
O Wisdom from on high,
O Truth unchanged, unchanging,
O Light of our dark sky,
We praise Thee for Thy radiance
That from the hallowed page,
A lantern to our footsteps,
Shines on from age to age.

. . . . .

"It is the golden casket,
Where gems of truth are stored;
It is the heaven-drawn picture
Of Christ, the living Word.

. . . . .

"O teach Thy wand'ring pilgrims
By this their path to trace,
Till, clouds and darkness ended,
They see Thee face to face."

—W. W. How.

CHAPTER 16

Is the History of the Bible True?

DID YOU know that when George Washington was President of the United States there was nothing definitely known, aside from the Bible, concerning the history of peoples of the world prior to the date 400 B.C., the date of the oldest reliable histories of Greece and Rome? In other words, at the time George Washington died there was not a single document known to be in existence which was written in the time of Old Testament history. Therefore the Old Testament had no witnesses to call to its aid when its statements of historical fact were challenged. Yet there was the Bible, claiming to give the history of the world back, not to four hundred years, but to four thousand years before Christ.

HISTORIANS QUESTIONED BIBLE HISTORY

Historians, with no evidence from other sources to support the Bible, raised questions as to the reliability of Biblical history. Scoffers pointed in scorn to stories of men and nations that they claimed never existed. Militant skeptics shot their arrows of unbelief, thinking that they could inflict a mortal wound on God's living Word. If the Bible record of Israel and the nations was true, why was there no other record of the same happenings? they asked. And they boldly assumed that because the Bible record stood alone it was most likely false.

Herbert Photos

Furthermore, they said that the art of writing was a comparatively modern art; therefore, the supposed records of Moses, for instance, could not be reliable, for the simple reason that people did not know how to write in Moses' day—fifteen hundred years before Christ, or some thirty-five hundred years ago. So they set later dates for these writings. They had particular objection to the book of Daniel, claiming that it was written long after the time of Babylon and Medo-Persia.

A Thing of Divine Providence

To those of us who believe the Bible, and its representation of God as one who definitely has something to do with the affairs of men, it seems a thing of divine providence that during the very time when the reliability of the Bible is questioned, great and notable discoveries have been and are being made which testify to the accuracy of the Bible record. The spade, pick, and shovel have unearthed the remains of ancient nations before known only in Bible history.

Mark B. Chapman says, "Great mounds that had lain untouched for millenniums have been dug up and thoroughly examined, and amid the debris of these buried and forgotten ruins have been found not only the remains of palaces, temples, monuments, and great buildings, but immense libraries, inscribed bricks, vases, tablets, and mural inscriptions, which have given us the history and chronology of those ancient and almost unknown people, with their manners and customs, their social surroundings and scientific knowledge, and their very thoughts and emotions."—*Mounds, Monuments, and Inscriptions,* pp. 9, 10. The history thus dug from the earth itself has borne mute but abundant testimony that the Bible record is reliable.

Another writer has said: "It must be accounted a wonderful providence of God that, at a time when so much is being said and done to discredit the Old Testament, so marvelous a series of discoveries, bearing directly on matters contained in its pages, should have been made."—JAMES ORR, *The Problem of the Old Testament* (Scribners), p. 396. This investigation of ancient ruins is known as archeology. The leading countries of the world have societies organized to carry on this work. In the light of discoveries made, Dr. Robert D. Wilson, professor of Semitic philology in Princeton Theological Seminary, said, "I have come to the conclusion that no man knows enough to assail the truthfulness of the Old Testament. Whenever there is sufficient documentary evidence to make an investigation, the statements of the Bible in the original texts have stood the test."

THREE CLASSES OF ANCIENT WRITINGS

According to Prof. W. W. Prescott, author of *The Spade and the Bible,* the ancient writings that have been unearthed fall into three general classes: the inscriptions, the papyri, and the ostraca.

The inscriptions include writings that have been found upon metal, stone, wood, or clay. One writer says, "'The bulk of the inscriptions are on stone, but to these must be added inscriptions cast or engraved in bronze or scratched on tablets of lead or gold, a few wax tablets, the scribblings (graffiti) found on walls, and the texts on coins and medals.'"—*The Spade and the Bible,* p. 19. There are hundreds of thousands of these inscriptions. The best known of these are the Moabite stone, the Rosetta stone, and the Behistun inscriptions, of which more will be said later.

Then there are the writings on papyrus, or the paper of those days. This paper was made of the pith of the papyrus plant, the method originated in Egypt. Milligan says: "The pith (*byblos*) of the stem was cut into long strips which were laid down vertically to form a lower or outer layer. Over this a second layer was then placed, the strips this time running horizontally. And then the two layers were fastened together and pressed to form a single web or sheet (*kollēma*), the process being assisted by a preparation of glue moistened, where possible, with the turbid water of the Nile, which was supposed to add strength to it. After being dried in the sun, the surface was carefully rubbed down with ivory or a smooth shell, and was then ready for writing."—GEORGE MILLIGAN, *Selections From the Greek Papyri,* Introduction, pp. xxi, xxii. (Copyright, 1910. Used by permission of The Macmillan Co.) A long sheet could be made by fastening many sheets together to produce the roll spoken of in the Bible.

The ink used, even in the days of the disciples, was "'made of soot, mixed with gum, and diluted with water. A color, which had a wonderful lasting power, was thus produced, as may be seen by examining any of the recently recovered texts.'"—PRESCOTT, *op. cit.,* p. 21.

"'The great bulk of the papyri,'" according to those who know, "'are of the non-literary character: as legal documents of the most various kinds, *e.g.,* leases, accounts, receipts, marriage contracts and wills, attestations, official edicts, petitions for justice, records of judicial proceedings, and a large number of documents relating to taxes, then letters and notes, exercise books, charms, horoscopes, diaries, etc., etc. . . . They enable us to revive a long period of ancient life.'"—*Ibid.,* p. 23.

The third class of writings, which has thrown light on the lives of ancient people and has been especially helpful in understanding New Testament Greek, is known as ostraca, or broken pieces of pottery found in the rubbish heaps of many cities. They were used by the poorer classes of the people in place of the papyrus, which was more expensive. The notes on these broken pieces of pottery are naturally briefer, but they give us an insight into the lives of the poorer classes.

Now, it is evident that with all these thousands and thousands of inscriptions, whether on wood, stone, metal, papyrus, pottery, clay brick, walls, or what not, we could gather no information unless we could decipher them to know their meaning. No living person knew how to read them.

So we turn to the fascinating story of how three stones yielded their secret to the perseverance of men, and unlocked the ancient languages to us, uncovering evidence in support of the history of the Bible. As long as we live there will always be room for doubt, but God provides ample evidence for us to believe. The Christ of your Bible is the Christ of a Book that has stood the storms of the ages. If you will accept Him and build on His Word, your Christian character building will withstand every wind, storm, and flood of doubt, destruction, grief, and temptation.

CHAPTER 17

When Stones Speak

JESUS CHRIST rode toward the city of Jerusalem, accompanied by a triumphal procession, which grew larger and larger as He neared the city. There went up a continual shout, "Hosanna to the son of David: Blessed is he that cometh in the name of the Lord." Matthew 21:9. Many Pharisees witnessing the scene sought to turn the current of popular feeling. They pressed through the crowd to Jesus, who was the object of the people's acclaim, and said to Him, "Master, rebuke thy disciples." Luke 19:39. Jesus replied, "I tell you that, if these should hold their peace, the stones would immediately cry out." Verse 40. In other words, when the time comes for God's plans to be carried out, they will be carried out, though perhaps not by the ones who should be expected to do it.

Our attention turns to the story about how three ancient stones gave up their secret, unlocking the old languages of Egypt and Babylonia, thus enabling men to decipher the writing found on metal, stone, wood, wax, paper, and pottery of millenniums ago, and bringing testimony to the truthfulness of Bible history.

You have all heard of Napoleon Bonaparte, that extraordinary light of military genius that flashed on the world, glowed brilliantly, and suddenly went out in darkness. Napoleon, impelled by dreams of conquest and glory, led a French expedition into Egypt in 1798. With him and

 Arlo Greer, Artist

One of the most significant discoveries of modern times is the finding, in 1799, of th famous Rosetta stone (inset) near the delta of the Nile by the soldiers of Napoleon

his four hundred transport ships were not only his brilliant generals and thirty-eight thousand men but more than one hundred distinguished scholars, scientists, artists, and engineers. In fact, the work of these one hundred men was to be of far greater value to the world than the battles of his army.

The Rosetta Stone

The following year, 1799, one of these men was doing some digging not far from the mouth of the river Nile, near the town of Rosetta, in Egypt. There he found a "strange looking granite stone. It was nearly four feet tall, about two and one-half feet wide, and nearly a foot thick. One face of the stone was smooth, and was divided into three parts, one above the other, and upon each part was an inscription. The inscription on the lowest portion was in Greek, and so could be read by the scholars, but the characters on the other two portions were strange and meaningless to them."—PRESCOTT, *The Spade and the Bible,* p. 25.

Nearly twenty years passed by before any adequate attempt was made to find the meaning of the two strange inscriptions. Finally a Frenchman by the name of Champollion set himself to the task. He proceeded on the theory that all three inscriptions actually said the same thing. The Greek inscription he could read, of course. But to prove that the other two should be read with the same meaning was not so easy, he found. For four years he labored before he could announce to the world that he had deciphered the mysterious writing on the stone.

One of the inscriptions proved to be the ancient picture writing of Egypt, the hieroglyphic, and the other a later form of picture writing known as the demotic. The discovery of this Frenchman made it possible for men to read the thousands of inscriptions found upon monuments, tombs, and tablets throughout Egypt. Thus was brought to light testimony to support the records of the Bible. This stone was the Rosetta stone, discovered in Egypt in 1799 and deciphered some twenty years later.

The Behistun Inscription

From Egypt and the Nile let us take a swift journey to the land of Persia. We go to the small town of Behistun, described as "a village at the foot of a precipitous peak some 1,700 feet high, in the Zangers range in Persia, on the right bank of the Samas-Ab, a tributary of the Kerkha."

Prescott says: "On the face of this high peak, about 500 feet from its base, Darius I, king of Persia, carved a great inscription in three kinds of ancient writing. . . . The lower part consists of eight columns about eleven feet high, three of the columns being in the Susian language and five in Persian. Above these columns is one column in the Babylonian language, and a large sculpture representing Darius putting his foot on the body of Gaumata, who attempted to usurp control of the country. This Behistun inscription was discovered in 1835 by Henry Rawlinson, a British army officer then located in that region."—*Ibid.,* p. 26. He spent parts of four years in making a copy. There was the inscription five hundred feet up the side of the great cliff. Just below the inscription was a ledge fourteen inches wide upon which a daring copyist might stand at the peril of his life while attempting to copy the inscription. The higher portions were reached by a ladder standing on this narrow ledge. A swing was let down from above for Mr. Rawlinson to copy the highest portion. Not only was he 500 feet up the side of the cliff, but below the base was a 350-foot chasm. After these four years of daring work it took eighteen years more of study to complete a translation of the strange characters that he had copied. He had followed the same principle that led to the deciphering of the Rosetta stone inscriptions. The greater part of the time Mr. Rawlinson studied on the inscription without the aid of books, for he was stationed where there were none.

The deciphering of this group of inscriptions unlocked to the world the cuneiform writing of old Babylonia, whose history was known only in Bible records.

THE MOABITE STONE

Now let us go fifteen miles east of the Dead Sea to a town named Dibon in the land of Moab. In 1868 a missionary discovered a stone four feet high, two feet wide, and fourteen inches thick, according to Prescott. He says that on one side of the stone was an inscription in Phoenician letters. The missionary dickered with the native Arabs for the stone, settling on a price of four hundred dollars. Meantime some French residents at Jerusalem heard of it, and offered four times the four hundred dollars for it. The superstitious natives, thinking that some magic must be in the stone, heated it, poured cold water on it, and broke it into several pieces and divided it among themselves. The scattered fragments were finally gathered together sufficiently to enable scholars to read it.

The stone had been erected by Mesha, king of Moab, to the god Chemosh, about 850 B.C., commemorating Moab's deliverance from Israel. Prescott says, "Israel is mentioned four times; Omri, the king of Israel, is named; Jehovah, the God of Israel, is recognized; and the domination of Omri over Moab is twice spoken of."—*Ibid.,* p. 29. Here is one of the many instances where the ancient writings confirm the historical trustworthiness of the Bible. The Bible gave us this record long, long ago, and the stones now cry out their testimony to the truthfulness of the Bible story, found in this instance in 2 Kings 3:4.

We may remember that this memorial stone is called the Moabite stone, found in the land of ancient Moab in 1868.

Oliver Wendell Holmes said, "I believe in the spade. It has fed the tribes of mankind. It has furnished them with water, coal, iron and gold. And now it is giving them truth—historic truth—the mines of which have never been opened till our time." The stones uncovered with the spade speak to us in favor of the old Book, God's Book, the Bible. Read it, believe it, practice it. This Book that presents the Creator presents also the Redeemer, the man of Calvary, who bore the cross and gave promises of the crown.

A modern friend of His wrote:

"I would not ask my Lord to take away
The cross He bids me carry when I pray,
For the heavy burden placed upon me there
Perhaps is but the answer to my prayer.

"Others may walk in brighter paths today
And find a lighter cross to bear away,
But the cross that Jesus chooses just for me
Is one that keeps me close to Calvary."

—MARJORIE LEWIS LLOYD.

CHAPTER 18

Other Evidence

THE BIBLE history of the Old Testament, long standing alone, now has abundant support from writings unearthed from the ruins of ancient times. Only a little can be cited here.

King Sargon and Nineveh

The prophet Isaiah, in Isaiah 21:1, mentions the name of Sargon, king of Assyria. No such name being known to secular history, the critics loudly asserted that no such king had lived and that the Bible, therefore, was unreliable. And then the French archeologist, Botta, excavating in the ruins of Nineveh, uncovered the very Assyrian palace built by King Sargon, covering twenty-five acres of gardens, lakes, and parks, surrounded by a high wall pierced by two gates on each side. Again the spade stood by the Word of God.

Belshazzar of Babylon

Every reader of the Bible is familiar with the story of the fall of Babylon, recorded in Daniel the fifth chapter. Daniel says that the king who was slain that night was Belshazzar. This would of necessity make Belshazzar Babylon's last king.

History gave us no such king, but listed Nabonidus as the last reigning king of Babylon. Thus the book of Daniel lay open to the charge of unreliability.

But the spade came to the rescue. Through the discovery of Sir Henry Rawlinson we now know that for many years Nabonidus lived in retirement at Tema, and "came not to Babil." We know, too, that his son, with the nobles and army, was in Babylon. One inscription reads: "And as to Belshazzar the exalted son, the offspring of my body, do thou place the adoration of the great deity in his heart; may he not give way to sin; may he be satisfied with life's abundance; and may reverence for the great divinity dwell in the heart of Belshazzar, my first-born favorite son."

So Daniel had it right, and the historians who said there was no Belshazzar had it wrong. When the Bible says one thing and men say another, it is safer to believe the Bible.

Take some detail like the reference in 1 Kings 4:26; 9:15-19; 10:28, 29. Here King Solomon is represented as gathering together so many horses that he had to stable them about in different cities. Along comes the excavator with his spade. At the spot of Megiddo, where Solomon had some of his horses, the very stables were found. There were stalls for large numbers of horses and quarters for their grooms as well as shelter for chariots. We may rely upon it that the Bible is true. The apostle Paul in Romans 3:4 said, "Let God be true, but every man a liar." When God speaks to us through His Word we may trust it to be true, even though some men have not yet found it out.

Why Belief Alone Is Not Sufficient

It is not enough merely to believe that the Bible is *true*. This can never suffice. "The devils also believe, and tremble," the Bible says. (James 2:19.)

Jesus said in Matthew 4:4, "Man shall not live by bread alone, but by every word that proceedeth out of the mouth of God." Thus we are to live by the Word of God. Jeremiah wrote, "Thy words were found, and I did eat them; and thy word was unto me the joy and rejoicing of mine heart." Jeremiah 15:16.

How can a man eat the words of God, you ask? How can the Word of God become food to us? Jesus said in John 4:34, "My meat is to do the will of him that sent me, and to finish his work." Thus it is. When a man studies the Word of God that he may know God's will, that by His grace he may do His will, and help to finish God's work on earth, that man will find God's Word to be food. This is in harmony with the statement of Jesus: "The words that I speak unto you, they are spirit, and they are life." John 6:63.

"Break Thou the bread of life,
Dear Lord, to me,
As Thou didst break the loaves
Beside the sea;

"Beyond the sacred page
I seek Thee, Lord;
My spirit pants for Thee,
O living Word!"

—MARY A. LATHBURY.

CHAPTER 19

Are the Prophecies of the Bible Reliable?

A CONVENTION of weather forecasters met in a certain city on a day selected as least likely for rain. It rained. With all the modern means of mapping air pressures, wind direction and velocity, and cold and warm air masses, yet today weather forecasters often miss the mark.

People have always had a keen interest in knowing about the future. Fortunetellers have plied their trade for ages. A person puzzled by having some female wizard tell him what his name is (most people know their names already), pays out good money for personal readings which purport to be reliable information on his future. Much of it is like the counsel that came from an ancient oracle to an army general. "A great army would be defeated" if he went into battle. The battle took place. An army was defeated. It was the general's own army. True, the enemy army might have been destroyed, but in either case the oracle would be correct. Much of man's prediction is double talk, like some radio commentators who say it may be this way and it may be that way. Then whatever way it turns out they proclaim their great prophetic ability.

Astrology is another prophetic line fed to Americans at the reported rate of two hundred million dollars' worth annually, soothing their worries with mumbo jumbo and horoscopes. People pay up to fifty dollars a session to learn how to get rich or stay rich. One stargazer is reported to have taken in fifty thousand dollars in one year from Wall Street people.

Top diplomats seek counsel on world affairs. More people just want to know, "Will I get married?" "Will I succeed?" "Where is Henry?" There is everything from business and vocational astrology to radix and sexual astrology.

What About Bible Predictions?

What can be said for the forecasting of Bible prophets?

First of all, what claim is made in Scripture for this type of thing? Does the Bible itself profess prophetic reliability? From Isaiah 42:8, 9 we read the following: "I am the Lord: that is my name: and my glory will I not give to another, neither my praise to graven images. Behold, the former things are come to pass, and *new* things do I declare: before they spring forth I tell you of them."

Then from the New Testament we note this invitation, challenge, and counsel: "Despise not prophesyings. Prove all things; hold fast that which is good." 1 Thessalonians 5:20, 21.

God asks no man to believe the prophecies of the Bible without testing them, proving them. Then if they stand up, hold fast to them.

The Exodus From Egypt

Let us first check a prediction made to Abraham more than one thousand years before the days of Isaiah. This would be one of the former things.

We read God's word to Abraham: "Know of a surety that thy seed shall be a stranger in a land that is not their's, and shall serve them; and they shall afflict them four hundred years. . . . But in the fourth generation they shall come hither again." Genesis 15:13-16.

Here was a prophecy of slavery and deliverance. Abraham died. His grandson, Jacob, with his household went down to Egypt in the days of his son Joseph's high office. From favor and freedom they fell into disfavor and slavery. Decades went by. The time of predicted deliverance was at hand. A proud Pharaoh, which knew not Joseph, declared, "I know not the Lord, neither will I let Israel go." Exodus 5:2.

Israel was up against a hard and adamant Pharaoh. The king of Egypt was up against a prophecy of God. Who would prevail? God said, "Let my people go." Pharaoh answered, "They stay." As well might man seek to bind in fetters the ebb and flow of the ocean tides or build a wall to stop the stars, as to challenge the power of the word of God. Said Jesus, "The scriptures must be fulfilled." Mark 14:49.

The fulfillment we read as follows: "It came to pass at the end of the four hundred and thirty years, even the selfsame day it came to pass, that all the hosts of the Lord went out from the land of Egypt." Exodus 12:41.

The Puzzle of Egypt's Decline

After the time of Isaiah, Ezekiel forecast the permanent decline of Egypt. This was one of the "new things" declared by God before it sprang forth. Of Egypt, Ezekiel wrote:

"It shall be the basest of the kingdoms; neither shall it exalt itself any more above the nations: for I will diminish them, that they shall no more rule over the nations." Ezekiel 29:15.

Egypt was not to disappear. It was to become a base nation. Egypt had been the "granary of the world," "the mother of science and letters and art. At the fire which burned upon her hearth, the nations had kindled the lamp of knowledge."

She has been pictured at that time as standing "alone among the nations, great, wise, and self-respecting; around her the choicest treasures of earth; her land filled with imperishable monuments of might and skill and genius; her people, in their order and enlightenment and civilization, a marvel of all time." When the Mohammedan hosts approached the city of Alexandria centuries later "the sight of its magnificence and wealth filled the children of the East with amazement."

Despite the grandeur and glory that seemed destined for unending ages, decay and disintegration have ravaged both people and objects. "The hopeless bondage of centuries has quenched every spark of ambition in the breasts of the descendants of the Pharaohs; and under the iron heel of oppression, genius and talent, and even intellect itself, seem to have been extinguished."

Thus God's declarations are fulfilled both specifically and generally.

"I am God, and there is none else; I am God, and there is none like me, declaring the end from the beginning, and from ancient times the things that are not yet done, saying, My counsel shall stand, and I will do all my pleasure." Isaiah 46:9, 10.

The Ebb Tide of Tyre

Tyre means "rock," and the city got its name from the double rock off the eastern Mediterranean coast, which was the supposed site of the first settlement. The historian Herodotus traces its traditional history back over two thousand years before the time of the prophecy concerning Tyre.

Tyre the beautiful had grown until she was known as "mistress of the sea." Rich with "the fine gold of Tarshish, the precious stones of Aram, . . . the beautiful ivories of Damascus, the fine linen of Egypt, . . . the

Combine Photos

The Jews for centuries have been mercilessly persecuted. More than four millic perished in World War II. Above: Jewish women huddled in a shed. Belov Hebrew men march to labor camp.

perfumes of Sheba, the slaves of Javan," she was the rival of Rome, and "the commercial center of the world."

At the very time when the tide of her power and glory was at its flood, around 600 B.C., the prophet Ezekiel lifted his voice in warning from God: "I will also scrape her dust from her." "And they shall lay thy stones and thy timber and thy dust in the midst of the water. . . . And I will make thee like the top of a rock: thou shalt be a place to spread nets upon; thou shalt be built no more: for I the Lord have spoken it, saith the Lord God." Ezekiel 26:4, 12-14.

Nebuchadnezzar of Babylon took the city after a thirteen-year siege, breaking down buildings and walls and slaying the people in savage fury.

Yet the ruins remained. Tyre had not had her timbers and stones thrown into the sea, nor her dust scraped to the top of the rock foundation.

Concerning the final fulfillment, Earle Albert Rowell says:

"Two and a half centuries passed, and still the ruins stood, a challenge to the accuracy of prophecy. Then through the East the fame of Alexander the Great sent a thrill of terror. He marched swiftly to attack new Tyre, 332 B.C. Reaching the shore, he saw the city he had come to take, with half a mile of water surging between them, for it was built upon an island. Alexander's plan of attack was especially formed and vigorously executed. He took the walls, towers, timbers, and ruined houses and palaces of the ancient Tyre, and with them built a solid causeway to the island city. So great was the demand for material that the very dust was scraped from the site and laid in the sea."—*Prophecy Speaks,* p. 20.

Though the judgments of God may linger, His Word is sure. After the flood tide of fame and riches and power and glory, Tyre the beautiful became but a lonely barren rock for the stretching of fishermen's nets, when her tide ebbed and prophecy was fulfilled.

"Who is like me? Let him come forward with his claim, let him state out his case before me. Who foretold the future long ago? Pray let us hear what is still to be? Fear nothing, dread not in the days to come; have not I foretold it and announced it long ago? You are my witnesses whether there is any god, any power at all besides me." Isaiah 44:7, 8, Moffatt.

The Miracle of the Jew

Frederick, the king of Prussia, asked a leading preacher of his country this question: "Tell me what is the greatest evidence that the Bible is inspired?" Without a moment's hesitation this prince of the pulpit replied, "The Jews, Your Majesty, the Jews!"

The gifts of God to the Jews, and thereby the gifts of the Jews to the world, are indeed very considerable.

Worshipers of our God, the Creator, depositaries of the Ten Commandments on tables of stone, observers of the weekly Sabbath of the fourth commandment as the sign of their allegiance to their Creator, believers in the coming of the Messiah as a great deliverer, the Jews were designed to be a blessing to all the world, and their Temple of worship a "house of prayer for all people." Isaiah 56:7.

One of the greatest Christian Jews who ever lived put it in these words: "What advantage then hath the Jew? . . . Much every way: chiefly, because that unto them were committed the oracles of God"; "who are Israelites; to whom pertaineth the adoption, and the glory, and the covenants, and the giving of the law, and the service of God, and the promises; whose are the fathers, and of whom as concerning the flesh Christ came, who is over all, God blessed for ever. Amen." Romans 3:1, 2; 9:4, 5.

Promises of Peace and World Leadership

The God of Israel made bold promises to His people, promises that would appeal to the heart's deepest desires for peace, quiet, and absence of fear, as well as for lawful ambition and the reward of intelligence, diligence, and integrity.

Through Moses, God said to them: "Ye shall keep my sabbaths, and reverence my sanctuary: I am the Lord." "If ye walk in my statutes, and keep my commandments, and do them; . . . I will give peace in the land, and ye shall lie down, and none shall make you afraid." Leviticus 19:30; 26:3-6.

Through the prophet Jeremiah there came to the Jews in a time of great spiritual declension, when their love of money had outrun their love of God, these thrilling words of daring promise: "It shall come to pass, if ye diligently hearken unto me, saith the Lord, to bring in no burden through the gates of this city on the sabbath day, but hallow the sabbath day, to do no work therein; then shall there enter into the gates of this city kings and princes sitting upon the throne of David, . . . and this city shall remain for ever." Jeremiah 17:24, 25.

But it was business first and religion second. So across the bright sky of Israel's hopeful future scurried the black clouds of trouble and tragedy.

Even the Jewish Prince of Peace must close His ministry of pity and love with words that rumbled a warning of coming destruction and desolation:

"O Jerusalem, Jerusalem, thou that killest the prophets, and stonest them which are sent unto thee, how often would I have gathered thy children together, even as a hen gathereth her chickens under her wings, and ye would not! Behold, your house is left unto you desolate." Matthew 23:37.

FOUR PROPHECIES CONCERNING THE JEWS FULFILLED

1. *To Be Scattered.*—"If thou wilt not observe to do all the words of this law," "the Lord shall scatter thee among all people, from one end of the earth even unto the other." Deuteronomy 28:58, 64.

"The whole remnant of thee will I scatter into all the winds." Ezekiel 5:10.

"My God will cast them away, because they did not hearken unto him: and they shall be wanderers among the nations." Hosea 9:17.

Tradesmen, bankers, musicians, publishers, scientists, doctors, writers, and entertainers—the Jews are found all over the world. Someone has said that they drink out of every river in the world from the Ganges to the Mississippi.

The estimated Jewish population was less than sixteen million in 1939. And five million may have perished in World War II, leaving but eleven million. Yet a traveler would think there were many times that number. Some five million reside in the United States. They seem to be everywhere, scattered among the nations.

2. *To Be Despised.*—"Thou shalt become an astonishment, a proverb, and a byword, among all nations whither the Lord shall lead thee." Deuteronomy 28:37. "I will . . . make them an astonishment, and an hissing." Jeremiah 25:9.

These prophecies have been fulfilled and continue to be fulfilled before our very eyes and in our very ears. Go any place where Jews in any number dwell, and you will find them a "byword" and a "hissing" among the people. This is true of them as of no other race.

When one first encounters this experience he is shocked at this almost universal spirit to despise the Jew. A leading American questioned a leading Jew, his friend, to learn his explanation of this seemingly abnormal feeling. Their friendship cooled. The situation is a delicate one, and in some ways mysterious. One must be on guard lest his own heart join with the multitude in this uncanny and practically universal attitude to hold in scorn and contempt this extraordinary race of men.

We can attempt no study of the varied intricacies of this baffling problem here. But we may know this: "The Jew received great light from God. He did not live it. He did not give it. He would accept no additional light. As a depositary of the truths of God he was rejected. For nearly two thousand years he has been a byword and a hissing on the lips and tongues of men in fulfillment of the Scripture prophecy. Jesus, the greatest Jew who ever lived, said to the Jews, 'The scripture cannot be broken.'"

3. *To Be Persecuted.*—"I . . . will draw out a sword after you." Leviticus 26:33. "And ye shall eat the flesh of your sons, and the flesh of your daughters shall ye eat" (verse 29), declared the God who loved them with "everlasting love" (Jeremiah 31:3).

Two million of them perished or went into a slavery worse than death when in A.D. 70 the Roman sword and slaughter broke through the siege of Jerusalem. And before that fateful day, in their starvation and desperation within the city, they ate the flesh of their own children.

Moses had once led them from Egyptian slavery, but God warned them: "The Eternal will take you back to Egypt . . . by a route which I said you would never tread again, and there you shall let yourselves be sold as slaves to your enemies." Deuteronomy 28:68, Moffatt. History tells of how they "were brought in droves, and sold as cheap as horses." (See H. H. MILMAN, *The History of the Jews,* vol. 2, p. 436.)

In Egypt many labored in the mines, men and women,

young and old, often in chains, driven under the lash until their wasted bodies crumpled under the sheer weight of their burden, and they perished with their last ounce of strength expended in slavish toil. These were the ancient counterpart of the modern slave-labor camps.

The rolling wheels of the centuries leave the ugly imprint of their sorrowful story embedded on the tragic trail of time.

Let the historian Milman tell it: "No fanatic monk set the populace in commotion, no public calamity took place, no atrocious or extravagant report was propagated, but it fell upon the heads of this unhappy caste. In Germany the Black Plague raged in all its fury, and wild superstition charged the Jews, as elsewhere, with causing and aggravating the misery and themselves enjoying a guilty comparative security amid the universal desolation....

"The same dark stories were industriously propagated, readily believed, and ferociously avenged, of fountains poisoned, children crucified. . . . Oppressed by the nobles, anathematized by the clergy, hated as rivals in trade by the burghers in the commercial cities, despised and abhorred by the populace, their existence is known by the chronicle . . . of their massacres."—*Ibid.,* vol. 3, pp. 222, 223.

In our day the tide of their terror increases. "It is known that in Poland under the Nazis eighty thousand were murdered in one night."—*America,* October 13, 1945, p. 32.

In World War II thousands were shot, hanged, or beheaded one by one. Hosts were enslaved, worked, starved, or beaten to death. They were put to death in gas chambers, burned in stacks, buried in huge mass graves. The Nazi call to exterminate the Jew brought destruction to the reported estimate of five million.

No modern picture can surpass in perfection of detail

the one painted by the prophetic hand of Moses, their great leader at the time of their first deliverance. Warning against disobedience, he predicted: "The Lord shall scatter thee. . . . And among these nations shalt thou find no ease, neither shall the sole of thy foot have rest: but the Lord shall give thee there a trembling heart, and failing of eyes, and sorrow of mind: and thy life shall hang in doubt before thee; and thou shalt fear day and night." Deuteronomy 28:64-66.

The terrific tension of their lives as a result of persecution is given in this striking and pitiful picture: "You shall be utterly crushed and broken continually, till you are driven mad by the sight of it all." Deuteronomy 28: 33, 34, Moffatt.

4. *To Be Indestructible.*—Although they were to be scattered, despised, and persecuted, they were not to die out as a people. Though God said, "I will break this people . . . as one breaketh a potter's vessel, that cannot be made whole again" (Jeremiah 19:11), yet they were not to disappear.

"Thus saith the Lord, which giveth the sun for a light by day, and the ordinances of the moon and of the stars for a light by night . . . : if those ordinances depart from before me, saith the Lord, then the seed of Israel also shall cease from being a nation before me for ever." Jeremiah 31:35, 36.

H. L. Hastings wrote: "Scattered through every land and in every clime; mingled among all people; adapting themselves to all circumstances, climates, conditions, and governments, and though oppressed and scorned and spurned, yet ever rising to honor when the pressure of persecution is removed; going from the prison house of Egypt to ride in the chariot of Pharaoh, and from among the children of the captivity to sit in the high places of Babylon and Persia; gaining influence, winning wealth, obtaining power, and defying competition; more prolific, orderly, temperate, healthy, and long-lived than any other race; more numerous, wealthy, and influential today, after eighteen hundred years of dispersion and oppression, than they were in the palmiest days of David and Solomon—the historian, the patriot, and philosopher cannot fail to observe in the existence of this scattered nation a phenomenon well worthy of the most careful consideration."—*Will the Old Book Stand?* p. 225.

Michael Beer, one of their own writers, says: "Braving all kinds of torments, the pangs of death, and still more terrible pangs of life, we have withstood the impetuous storm of time, sweeping indiscriminately in its course nations, religions, and countries, . . . like a column left standing amid the wreck of worlds and ruins of nature. The history of our people connects present times with the first ages of the world, by the testimony it bears to the existence of those early periods. It begins at the cradle of mankind; it is likely to be preserved to the very day of universal destruction."—*The Jewish Problem,* pp. 54, 55.

Summing It Up

The descendants of Abraham went into Egyptian slavery as God predicted to Abraham, and came out at the time forecast.

Egypt went into permanent decline to become one of the "basest," or least significant of nations, as foretold by Ezekiel the prophet.

Tyre, mistress of the sea as Babylon the Great was of the land, was to become but a barren rock, scraped clean of soil, a place for fishermen to dry their nets, and it is even so. Ezekiel the prophet was right.

The disobedient Jews were to be a scattered nation among the nations, taunted and despised, living under persecution and fear and tribulation, yet as indestructible as the indestructible Book that records with unerring accuracy the prophecies set forth concerning them.

Bible prophecy is God's challenge.

"Shew the things that are to come hereafter, that we may know that ye are gods." Isaiah 41:23.

"I am the Lord. . . . Behold, the former things are come to pass, and new things do I declare: before they spring forth I tell you of them." Isaiah 42:8, 9.

Prophecy is a distinctive badge of Bible inspiration and reliability. It is more sure than eyesight, and is God's great light to guide us till the rising of the Daystar. (2 Peter 1:16, 19.)

 Vernon Nye, Artist

There are many evidences, in addition to the Scripture record, that the world w
anciently destroyed by a Flood. Christ Himself referred to this disaster as a fa

CHAPTER 20

What About Noah and the Flood?

MANY PEOPLE ask about the Bible story of Noah and his great ship, the ark, some five hundred feet long and seventy-five feet wide, tossing on a shoreless ocean. Is the story of the Flood true or untrue, myth or reality, fact or fancy?

The settled views of some modern scientists and theologians would eliminate this story from the book of facts. They would make quick settlement of the whole question by saying, "The Flood story is a myth. It belongs to the pages of childish fables."

WHAT DOES THE BIBLE SAY?

What does Moses, author of the book of Genesis, say? In Genesis 7:4 God is represented as speaking: "I will cause it to rain upon the earth forty days and forty nights; and every living substance that I have made will I destroy from off the face of the earth." Verses 19 and 20 state, "And the waters prevailed exceedingly upon the earth; and all the high hills, that were under the whole heaven, were covered. Fifteen cubits upward did the waters prevail; and the mountains were covered." That is the story as given by the first Bible writer.

Now let us turn the pages to the writings of the apostle Peter, penned in New Testament times some fifteen hundred years later. In 2 Peter 3:3-6 he says: "There shall come in the last days scoffers, walking after their own lusts, and saying, Where is the promise of his coming? for since the fathers fell asleep, all things continue as they were from the beginning of the creation. For this they willingly are ignorant of [or forget], that by the word of God the heavens were of old, and the earth standing out of the water and in the water: whereby the world that then was, being overflowed with water, perished." Peter not only testifies to his belief in the Flood but prophesied that in the last days men would arise who would willingly forget the story of the Flood. Furthermore, he calls such persons "scoffers." It is impossible for us, in the light of these verses, to believe that Peter, in speaking of the Flood, was referring to some story he considered a fable.

What did the Son of God have to say regarding this question? To answer, let us read Matthew 24:35-39: "Heaven and earth shall pass away, but my words shall not pass away. . . . But as the days of Noe were, so shall also the coming of the Son of man be. For as in the days that were before the flood they were eating and drinking, marrying and giving in marriage, until the day that Noe entered into the ark, and knew not until the flood came, and took them all away; so shall also the coming of the Son of man be."

Without question Christ conceded the fact of the Flood, and said that as people in that day disbelieved and were lost, so at the time of His second coming men would refuse to believe, and thus be unprepared for His return.

The Popular Present-Day Theory

The popular scientific dogma of the present day is that no worldwide catastrophe or destruction, like the Flood, ever takes place. Nature, it is said, works uniformly, except for more or less small capricious outbreaks, as earthquakes, violent storms, and so forth. There never was any direct creation, nor was there any sudden destructive Flood as the Bible says, according to the decree of popular science. "All things continue as they were from the beginning of the creation"—so Peter prophesied that they would say. And that is what they are saying. They subject God to the laws of nature, which He has set in operation, and say that He can never change them. However, since the discovery of atomic explosion men are not quite so certain as they used to be that the future of man is safe in his own hands. Notwithstanding, they wish no hand of God to intervene in the laws of nature.

They are like two woodpeckers someone wrote about, which built their nest in a telegraph pole on the railroad right of way. At a certain time every day a train went by. The woodpeckers nested there season after season, and the train kept up a regular schedule. They reasoned to themselves, it is said, that that train had gone by their home each day at a given time, and therefore it always would. But one day the train did not come. The next day it did not come. In fact, it never did come any more. What had happened? Simply this: The management of the railroad had decided that the line would be discontinued. What had always been and what would always be, according to woodpecker thinking, discontinued.

The God of the universe may operate a long time on a given plan, but He is not limited to that plan. The Bible represents God as sending the Flood upon the world of the ungodly in a time of overwhelming wickedness. He either did or did not. Let us look now for evidence outside the Bible!

Evidence From Outside the Bible

Here is a quotation from Francois Lenormant, once professor of archeology at the National Library of France:

"The lengthy review of the subject in which we have just been engaged leaves us in a position to affirm that the account of the deluge is an universal tradition in all branches of the human family, with the sole exception of the black race. And a tradition everywhere so exact and so concordant cannot possibly be referred to as an imaginary myth. No religious or cosmogonic myth possesses this character of universality. It must necessarily be the reminiscence of an actual and terrible event, which made so powerful an impression upon the imaginations of the first parents of our species that their descendants could never forget it."—*The Beginnings of History,* pp. 486, 487.

Fishes and the Flood

In John M. MacFarlane's *Fishes the Source of Petroleum* we read: "It can be definitely said that, through all of the geologic formations in which fish remains occur, a large proportion of the remains consists of entire fishes or of sections in which every scale is still in position; every fin is extended as in life attitude; the bones of the head, though often crushed in and broken through subsequent diastrophic strains, still retain almost the normal positions; while near them may be coprolites of the same or some other types of fish in a practically entire state. All of this conclusively proves that when myriads of such fishes were simultaneously killed, their bodies were deposited or stranded within a few hours or a few days at most after death, so that the flesh, the liver, the alimentary canal and other soft parts were unquestionably enclosed and intact, when sediment sealed them up."—Page 400. Copyright, 1923. Used by permission of The Macmillan Co.

Not only do we find myriads of fish, killed and buried at the same time, and so quickly as to preserve them perfectly, but frequently the deep-sea specimens of life are found buried in this fashion, mixed with shore species and land plants. It is common knowledge that the deep floor of the ocean is so calm as never to have its ooze disturbed by the most violent surface storm. Only some violent upheaval as the Bible Flood, in which "the fountains of the great deep [were] broken up" (Genesis 7:11), would explain this mixture of the deep-sea specimens with those of shore and land, all covered and preserved by sudden destruction and burial.

Frozen Mammoths in Siberia

Let us go to faraway and cold Siberia, where the ground is frozen to a depth of a hundred feet or more—nature's refrigerator.

From this frozen depth men dig up the great Siberian mammoths, the tusks of which have been sold on the world market for a thousand years. Some of these beasts have been found with their flesh so well preserved as to be eaten by the explorers' dogs. In some instances the mammoths had undigested food in their stomachs and unchewed grass in their mouths.

It is indeed apparent that while hordes of these tropical animals were quietly feeding thousands of years ago, some mighty catastrophe overtook them, and buried them alive. And they have been preserved in cold storage to testify in these times to the truthfulness of the Bible story, and to deny the teaching of a slow, uniform procedure of nature at all times, as the modern dogma would require us to believe. The Manager of the universe sometimes does things differently, the modernist to the contrary notwithstanding.

Over an area of some ten thousand square miles the bodies of these mammoths are found. These tropical animals were thus caught in catastrophe and frozen. James D. Dana says the climate must have "become suddenly

Great mammoths, mastodons, dinosaurs, and other antediluvian animals perished su- denly in a worldwide watery catastrophe. Their remains are still being discovere

extreme as of a single winter's night."—Quoted in *The Phantom of Organic Evolution,* by George McCready Price, p. 51. God warned Noah of "things not seen as yet" (Hebrews 11:7), and he believed to his salvation. God's Word is true.

THE DINOSAURS

Take the mighty dinosaurs for another example—those giant animals, some about two hundred feet long, which roamed the earth long ago, and now are gone. R. S. Lull says, "One of the most inexplicable of events is the dramatic extinction of this mighty race."—*Ibid.,* p. 58. Had he believed in the Flood, the extinction would not be inexplicable. Henry Fairfield Osborn said that "the cutting off of this giant dinosaur dynasty was nearly if not quite simultaneous the world over."—*Ibid.,* p. 59.

We read from Oliver P. Hay: "Genera and families, even orders, were wiped out of existence, and these included some of the noblest animals that have graced the face of the earth, the elephants, the mastodons, tapirs, many species of bison, horses, saber-tooth cats, huge tigers, and gigantic wolves."—*The Pleistocene of North America and Its Vertebrated Animals,* p. 5.

The simple truth is that the most reasonable explanation of these things is the Flood of Noah's day.

Christ said, "As the days of Noe were, so shall also the coming of the Son of man be." Matthew 24:37. What Noah preached the people did not believe in his day, or believing, did not act upon the belief. Today the entire account is questioned as Peter said it would be. Jesus adds these significant words: "Heaven and earth shall pass away, but my words shall not pass away." Verse 35.

CHAPTER 21

How to Understand the Bible

SOMEONE HAS said that "light travels at remarkable speed until it meets the human mind."

"Thy word is a lamp unto my feet, and a light unto my path." Psalms 119:105. When this light strikes natural human minds it is ineffective, because "the god of this world hath blinded the minds of them." 2 Corinthians 4:4. How then can the darkened mind of man understand and receive the heavenly light of God's divine Book?

There are five simple steps, five rungs to the ladder, that assuredly lead to ever-increasing understanding of the Word of God.

1. Pray for Divine Guidance

Any responsible person can pray. He may not be able to read or write or even see, but he can utter a prayer, a soul cry, a heart longing for God's light. Prayer is a simple thing, and sincere prayer is likely to be simply stated. Here is one both simple and beautiful: "O send out thy light and thy truth: let them lead me." Psalms 43:3.

Here is the one reason why we should pray before studying the Bible. This Book was inspired by the Spirit of God, yet "the natural man receiveth not the things of the Spirit of God." 1 Corinthians 2:14. Therefore we need that Spirit to enlighten us. Paul says, "Now we have received . . . the Spirit of God; that we might know the things that are freely given to us of God." Verse 12. The thing to remember is that we receive the Holy Spirit through prayer. Said Jesus, "If ye then, being evil, know how to give good gifts unto your children: how much more shall your heavenly Father give the Holy Spirit to them that ask him." Luke 11:13.

God has warned us that if we walk in the light of our own fire and the sparks of our own kindling, we shall lie down in sorrow. (Isaiah 50:11.) But if our blind eyes are opened, we shall with the psalmist "behold wondrous things out of thy law." Psalms 119:18. "The God of our Lord Jesus Christ, the Father of glory, may give unto you the spirit of wisdom and revelation in the knowledge of him." Ephesians 1:17.

"Holy Spirit, light divine,
Shine upon this heart of mine,
Chase the shades of night away,
Turn my darkness into day."

—Andrew Reed.

2. Study the Scriptures

A curious-minded boy prowling about the house picked up a dust-covered Bible. Addressing his mother, he said, "Mamma, is this God's book?" "Why, yes, of course," was her quick response. "Well, then," said the boy, "I think we might as well send it back to Him. We never use it."

Some reject the Bible. More of us just neglect it, or consider that it is a little out of date in the pressing, surging life of today. Even during the dark days of World War II only one American out of ten read the Bible daily, and forty-four out of one hundred never opened it, according to a reported Gallup poll.

A writer in a popular magazine some years ago wrote: "The Bible is not actually lost, but it is almost un-

Charles Carey

There is no work of man, however masterly, that can do so much to bring life, h
and peace into human hearts as meditation upon the Holy Scriptures.

known. He is a rare person who spends much time with it. The majority of Christians are lukewarm to the Bible. . . . The world is so indifferent to it that even its enemies do not bother to criticize it. Only a few abuse it. It is just ignored. Even theological students lay it aside for other books. A recent graduate of a prominent theological seminary told me that it is not unusual to find no Bible in a student's room. . . . Men and women of education and culture are in large numbers ignorant of the Bible. . . . Ask the bookseller about people who buy Bibles. One of them told me recently that people who look intelligent and talk intelligently about other matters, come in and ask for a 'Methodist Bible,' a 'Baptist Bible,' a 'Lutheran Bible,' an 'Episcopal Bible.' . . . Many Bibles are bought for ornamental purposes. They are suitable for a home supposed to be religious. A Bible looks well on a library table, and most church people would be ashamed to confess that they did not own a copy. To some people the Bible is like a horseshoe; it brings good luck."

Many never permit any other article to be placed on top of a Bible, yet never lift a finger to open the Book that would get down to the very bottom of the greatest questions and problems of their own personal lives.

What counsel does the Book offer?

"Search the scriptures," said Jesus. John 5:39.

"Study to shew thyself approved unto God," said Paul. 2 Timothy 2:15.

"Take heed to thyself, and unto the doctrine." 1 Timothy 4:16.

"Man shall not live by bread alone," said Christ. Matthew 4:4.

"Thy words were found, and I did eat them." Jeremiah 15:16.

"Seek ye out of the book of the Lord, and read." Isaiah 34:16.

"Consider what I say; and the Lord give thee understanding." 2 Timothy 2:7.

Children should study the Bible. To Timothy the apostle Paul wrote, "From a child thou hast known the holy scriptures, which are able to make thee wise unto salvation through faith which is in Christ Jesus." 2 Timothy 3:15.

How may we wisely study the Scriptures under the direction of the Holy Spirit? Paul gives us a most valuable suggestion in 1 Corinthians 2:13: "Which things also we speak, not in the words which man's wisdom teacheth, but which the Holy Ghost teacheth; comparing spiritual things with spiritual."

In other words, we should compare scripture with scripture until we have what the Bible teaches on one topic. Then we may compare topic with topic. As Isaiah puts it, "Precept must be upon precept, precept upon precept; line upon line, line upon line; here a little, and there a little." Isaiah 28:10. Thus we avoid drawing a wrong conclusion from the study of one text or some limited portion of the Bible. It is the Bible and the whole Bible.

Ten minutes a week provides enough reading to make a superior Bible critic. An hour a day with the Word of God may make a humble saint.

"Sing them over again to me,
Wonderful words of life;
Let me more of their beauty see,
Wonderful words of life."

3. Be Willing to Learn

There is a story of a young man who came to the famous Greek scholar Socrates, asking, "What shall I do to become a learned man?" Whereupon Socrates led him into a pool of water, plunged his head under, and held it there. When the youth had struggled free and got his breath, Socrates said, "When your head was under the water, what did you most wish?"

"Air," gasped the young man.

"Very well," answered the sage; "when you want knowledge as much as you wanted air when your head was under water, you will find ways to get it."

Jesus Christ chose fishermen and taxgatherers instead of priests and religious leaders for one simple reason: they were willing to learn. He who closes his eyes to truth is neighbor to him who neglects to study.

A prominent church member took his minister to task after a sermon. "But was my point not according to the teaching of Christ?" asked the preacher.

"I'm not disputing that," responded the man; "it's a point Christ made that I don't believe." A closed mind is like a jug, corked and sealed—you cannot get anything into it.

Someone said: "If an angel brought a message containing all wisdom, few would be impressed. A great speech is one that tells us what we wish to hear and already know."

Here is counsel from a man who was willing to learn: "As newborn babes, desire the sincere milk of the word, that ye may grow thereby." 1 Peter 2:2.

Looking back on his preaching at Berea, Paul wrote: "These were more noble than those in Thessalonica, in that they received the word with all readiness of mind, and searched the scriptures daily, whether those things were so. Therefore many of them believed." Acts 17: 11, 12.

An open mind is a noble mind. A closed mind is another matter. "A man convinced against his will, is of the same opinion still."

The people of Berea were not "taken in" by every new

thing that came along, but they were open-minded. They studied diligently, and many believed what they had not known before.

"If any man seek for greatness, let him forget greatness and ask for truth, and he will find both," said the great Horace Mann.

If we do not make progress, we will go backward. Wrote the apostle Paul, "Though by this time you ought to be teachers, you need some one to teach you again the first principles of God's word." Hebrews 5:12, R.S.V. Then with earnest appeal he wrote, "Therefore let us leave the elementary doctrines of Christ and go on to maturity." Hebrews 6:1, R.S.V.

It seems most reasonable to suppose that in this critical hour of earth's history the Bible may have messages for us which are, as the apostle Peter put it, "present truth" (2 Peter 1:12), and as Jesus said, "meat in due season" (Matthew 24:45).

It may be that God will enlighten us through other men. "Go ye, therefore, and teach all nations," commanded Christ. If there are teachers commissioned of God, there will be those to listen.

He who already knows everything can learn nothing. When Paul was Saul the brilliant young Jewish prosecutor and persecutor, who thought he knew most of the answers, he was converted to Christ on the road to Damascus. Stopped in his mad war against the followers of Christ, and humbled in the dust, he said to Christ, "Lord, what wilt thou have me to do?" The answer was, "Arise, and go into the city, and it shall be told thee what thou must do." Acts 9:6. There in old Damascus he was instructed by a member of the very sect he had despised and persecuted. If we truly want to know God's way, we will accept His truth through the channel of His choosing.

Years ago a young officer of the English Navy discovered a small dangerous rock in the Mediterranean Sea, and reported it to the admiralty. All stations were immediately notified to mark the spot on all charts. An old captain was the first to sail that way, and he said, "There is no such rock. I've sailed this sea all my life. I know." So saying, he ordered the ship to be steered right over the spot under full sail. There followed a mighty crash, and the broken vessel with all hands went down. The captain knew too much, and refused to follow the chart of the seas.

"Seest thou a man wise in his own conceit? there is more hope of a fool than of him." Proverbs 26:12.

Conceit and pride of opinion keep the mind hidebound and creed bound, and play a man's life into the hands of that great enemy Prejudice.

Prejudice is pride gone on a spree. It is inordinate pride of opinion, race, place, politics, nation, and religion. Prejudice can get so concentrated that it even makes people proud of their prejudices.

Says a man, "Just so. I'm against these prejudiced people. There are a lot of them around here." It is a good thing for every man to remember that he who thinks himself to have no prejudices is living under as great a delusion as ever overshadowed a human soul. To break the bonds that bind the minds of men is more difficult than to loose the fetters that chain the feet of slaves.

Of all prejudices religious prejudice is probably more widespread, deeper dyed, and more devastating to the development of the human soul, than any other. There is but one adequate way to deal with it, and that is to call it *sin*. Let a man daily pray, "Lord, this one day save me, deliver me, from the sin of prejudice. Keep my soul filled with the love and the grace and the power of God, and my eyes open to light."

If we are to understand God's great Book, the Bible, we shall sincerely pray, "Teach me *thy* way, O Lord, and lead me in a plain path." Psalms 27:11.

When the Pilgrims were about to set sail for America, where they might be further removed from the chains of religious prejudice and tyranny, their pastor, John Robinson, spoke to them these noble words:

"For my part, I cannot sufficiently bewail the condition of the Reformed churches, who are come to a period of religion, and will go at present no farther than the instruments of their reformation. The Lutherans cannot be drawn to go beyond what Luther saw, . . . and the Calvinists, you see, stick fast where they were left by that great man of God, who yet saw not all things. This is a misery much to be lamented, for though they were burning and shining lights in their times, yet they penetrated not into the whole counsel of God, but were they now living, would be as willing to embrace further light as that which they first received."—DANIEL NEAL, *History of the Puritans* (1848), vol. 1, pp. 269, 270.

"Remember your church covenant, in which you have agreed to walk in all the ways of the Lord, *made or to be made known unto you.* Remember your promise and covenant with God and with one another to receive whatever light and truth shall be made known to you *from his written word.*"—W. CARLOS MARTYN, *The Pilgrim Fathers of New England* (1867), pp. 70, 71. (Italics mine.)

4. BE WILLING TO UNLEARN

To be wholeheartedly willing to unlearn, to give up an idea we have long held, is doubly difficult. It is like getting a horse to back a heavy load up a hill.

We have *many* lessons to learn, and *many, many* to unlearn. Our fathers believed the world was flat and that tomatoes were poisonous. It took them a long time to change their minds. Some never did.

More than three hundred years ago a seventeen-year-old boy sat in an Italian cathedral so intent on watching a lamp accidentally set swinging on its long chain that he forgot about prayers. This young Galileo began working on the idea of weights and gravitation, and delved deeper and deeper into the broad fields of physics, astronomy, and dynamics.

From the top of the famous leaning tower of Pisa he dropped a large and a small weight, and demonstrated that they fell at the same rate of speed. The philosophers saw it, but they refused to part with their prejudice. They chose to cling to the ideas of Aristotle, who told people two thousand years before that the heavier weight would fall faster.

Galileo taught that the earth was not the center of everything, and that the whole universe was in motion. Bruno had taught the same thing a few years previous to Galileo, and church leaders saw that he was burned at the stake.

Galileo invented a telescope that made objects seem thirty-three times nearer, and it helped him prove that the earth moves. But philosophers who could not give up an idea, especially when it was dangerous to do so, joined with church leaders of the Vatican and forbade him to teach this truth. For sixteen years he kept still. Then he began to write. The pope and philosophers got together, summoned the ailing old man to Rome, where the church cardinals examined him. After being held four months, in order to be released he agreed that the earth does not move. But it is said that as he departed he whispered under his breath, "She moves."

It takes more grit and grace of character to give up a popular idea long believed than to accept one that is brand-new. Yet what could be more foolish than slavishly to believe that what others think is necessarily right for us to believe? And what could be more wise than to exchange error for truth, even though others do not? If you be one of those who can consistently and persistently do this, you are one of the select, one of the "elect."

Here is Scriptural light and suggestion: "What is the chaff to the wheat? saith the Lord." Jeremiah 23:28. "To the law and to the testimony: if they speak not according to this word, it is because there is no light in them." Isaiah 8:20.

From these Old Testament appeals to choose wheat rather than chaff, and light instead of darkness, we turn to these significant statements of Jesus from the New Testament: "'You leave the commandment of God, and hold fast the tradition of men.' And he said to them, 'You have a fine way of rejecting the commandment of God, in order to keep your own tradition!'" Mark 7:8, 9, R.S.V. Jesus here employs a bit of irony, as if to say, "That is a fine way to do, isn't it? You believe in God. You make a high profession. But you reject the commandment of God that you may keep your own tradition!" Christ hoped to bring into their hearts some sense of shame, that they might turn away from error and accept the truth which would make them free. (John 8:32.)

5. Be Willing to Obey

The fifth and final rung of the ladder to Bible learning is *willingness to obey.* If we will pray for guidance, study diligently, be willing to learn, to unlearn, and to obey; then, and then only is God responsible for our guidance. Note carefully these words of Christ in John 7:17. They were spoken at the feast of Jerusalem amid much discussion among the crowds as to whether He was good or bad, of God or of the devil:

"If any man will do his will, he shall know of the doctrine, whether it be of God, or whether I speak of myself." The Revised Standard Version makes it very clear: " 'If any man's will is to do his [God's] will, he shall know whether the teaching is from God or whether I am speaking on my own authority.' "

How simple! How fair! Through His Son God says: "If you will choose to follow Me, I will show you the way. If your first purpose is to do My will, I will make clear to you whether a doctrine is true or false." Nothing in all this wide world can take the place of absolute honesty with God.

Jesus made this clear in the great parable where He is the sower, the Word of God is the seed, and the human heart is the soil. He described the unsatisfactory results of the Word of God on hard hearts that would not accept it; in shallow, changeable hearts which were merely emotional and dominated by feeling; and in worldly hearts overcome with care and riches and pleasures. Then He spoke of the successful Christian in these words:

"But that on the good ground are they, which in an honest and good heart, having heard the word, keep it, and bring forth fruit with patience." Luke 8:15.

Diogenes, of ancient Greece, is reported to have gone about day and night carrying a lantern and looking for an honest man. So the Holy Spirit of God searches the highways and habitations of men today looking for the honest in heart whose purpose is to know the will of God, that by His grace they may do it.

This fifth step of willingness to obey is the climax. It proves our sincerity in taking the four preceding steps. When Jesus called Matthew as he sat in the taxgatherer's booth, He said, "Follow me." What did Matthew do? "He arose, and followed him." Matthew 9:9.

That is what it takes—no more, no less. To us He

calls, "If any man will come after me, let him deny himself, and take up his cross, and follow me." Matthew 16:24.

Christ had His cross. We have ours. The apostle Paul gloried in the cross of Christ. (Galatians 6:14.) He also gloried in tribulation. (2 Corinthians 12:7-10.) Christ was obedient unto death. (Philippians 2:8.) Paul was faithful unto death. (2 Timothy 4:6-8.) "Be thou faithful unto death, and I will give thee a crown of life." Revelation 2:10.

The way of obedience is the way of learning. "I have more understanding than all my teachers: for thy testimonies are my meditation. I understand more than the ancients, because I keep thy precepts." Psalms 119:99, 100.

SECTION FOUR

GOD SPEAKS TO MAN ABOUT CHRIST

One Solitary Life

HERE IS A MAN who was born in an obscure village, the child of a peasant woman. He grew up in another village. He worked in a carpenter shop until He was thirty, and for three years He was an itinerant preacher. He never wrote a book. He never held an office. He never owned a house. He never had a family. He never went to college. He never put His feet inside a big city. He never traveled two hundred miles from the place where He was born. He never did one of the things that usually accompany greatness. He had no credential but Himself.

While still a young man, the tide of popular opinion turned against Him. His friends ran away. One of them denied Him. He was turned over to His enemies. He went through the mockery of a trial. He was nailed upon a cross between two thieves. His executioners gambled for the only piece of property He had on earth while He was dying and that was His coat. When He was dead He was taken down and laid in a borrowed grave through the pity of a friend.

Nineteen wide centuries have come and gone, and today He is the centerpiece of the human race and the leader of the column of progress.

I am far within the mark when I say that all the Armies that ever marched and all the Navies that were ever built, and that all the parliaments that ever sat and all the Kings that ever reigned, put together have not affected the life of man upon this earth as did that one Solitary Life.

—PHILLIPS BROOKS.

CHAPTER 22

Christ Forever

BRUCE BARTON wrote a book about Jesus Christ, calling it *The Man Nobody Knows.* Many claims have been made for and against Christ. Millions of words have been spoken about Him. An almost endless chain of books has been forged to link His day and His life with ours.

Napoleon Bonaparte pointed out that he and Julius Caesar had founded kingdoms upon force, which had been destroyed by force. In contrast, he said that Jesus founded a kingdom upon love, and millions of His followers would die for Him.

A Nazi youth of Nazi heyday said, "Hitler is so big, and Jesus Christ seems so little." Yet the name of Hitler has gone down in infamy, while the name of Jesus rises higher and higher, and remains as indestructible as time itself.

Consider here, if you will, what the Bible teaches concerning this outstanding character of world history. Ten great questions will be asked and answered. Ten great claims will be made concerning Him.

1. Is He the Son of God?

It was night. The city of Jerusalem was hushed in slumber. A famous ruler of the synagogue made his way with quiet steps through the silent streets to seek an in-

Review Pictures *H. Le Rolle, Ar*

The Son of God was born in humility. He died in humility. He rose from the gr in triumph. He is coming again in glory. The path to glory is through humil

terview with this Man Jesus in His place of secluded retirement.

That was a momentous meeting, a historic night. In no discourse, before or after, did Jesus set forth so simply, so beautifully, and so fundamentally the very heart of the gospel of salvation.

It was out there in the darkness of Olivet's garden that the handsomely robed Nicodemus got the answer to the very question that was troubling his mind. Was Jesus the Son of God or not? Nicodemus was sincere. He sought to know the truth. From the lips of Jesus there broke upon the stillness of night those immortal words that have brought more pure peace than all the volumes of the wisdom of man. "For God so loved the world, that he gave his only begotten Son, that whosoever believeth in him should not perish, but have everlasting life." John 3:16.

Christ was speaking of Himself. This Nicodemus understood. Jesus was the Son of God in a sense that Adam was not, though Adam is called the son of God. Jesus was the "only begotten Son" of God. God gave dominion to Adam. He gives great responsibility to the angels. But none occupies the place of the Son, as we read in Hebrews 1:5: "For unto which of the angels said he at any time, Thou art my Son, this day have I begotten thee?" So there stands that thrilling text, John 3:16, at once both the foundation and the highest pinnacle of redemptive truth. God gave His Son that we might have everlasting life.

In Matthew 16:13-17 we read the following: "When Jesus came into the coasts of Caesarea Philippi, he asked his disciples, saying, Whom do men say that I the Son of man am? And they said, Some say that thou art John the Baptist: some, Elias; and others, Jeremias, or one of the prophets. He saith unto them, But whom say ye that I am? And Simon Peter answered and said, Thou art the Christ, the Son of the living God. And Jesus answered and said unto him, Blessed art thou, Simon Barjona: for flesh and blood hath not revealed it unto thee, but my Father which is in heaven."

Here is language unmistakable in its meaning. Jesus claimed God as His Father in heaven, and made God responsible for having revealed to a fisherman on earth that He, Christ, was the Son of God.

We cannot rightfully hold that this teaching is a mere figment of the fanatical superstition and fanciful reasoning of ignorant fishermen. It is the open and freely avowed statement of Jesus Christ Himself. Jesus was, therefore, either a pious and deluded fanatic, thinking Himself to be what He was not, or a fraud and deceiver professing to be what He knew He was not, or He was what He claimed to be—the living Son of the living God, the Saviour of the sinful human race.

His testimony that He gave to His friends on numerous occasions His enemies later supported at His trial before Pilate:

"The Jews answered him, We have a law, and by our law he ought to die, because he made himself the Son of God." John 19:7.

Isaiah foretold, "Unto us a child is born, unto us a Son is given." Isaiah 9:6. Gabriel, that special messenger angel of heaven, spoke to the virgin Mary saying, "He shall be . . . called the Son of the Highest." Luke 1:32. Baptized of John the Baptist, He came forth from Jordan's water to hear the voice of God proclaiming, "This is my beloved Son, in whom I am well pleased." Matthew 3:17. When He died on Calvary with a great and awful cry, when the earth shook and the rocks were rent and the graves were opened, the Roman centurion exclaimed, "Truly this was the Son of God." Matthew 27:45.

2. Is Christ Called God?

It might be one thing to be called the Son of God and another thing to be called God. What is the word of both the Old and the New Testament on this vital question of whether Christ is God?

The Old Testament presents the Son of God as God: "For unto us . . . a Son is given: . . . and his name shall be called . . . The mighty God." Isaiah 9:6.

We consider also the words which Jesus spoke: "I and my Father are one." John 10:30. Then we turn to the book of Hebrews, where God is represented as speaking to His Son. "But unto the Son he saith, Thy throne, O God, is for ever and ever." Hebrews 1:8.

In the very first verse of the Gospel According to John are these striking words: "In the beginning was the Word, and the Word was *with* God, and the Word *was* God." Who was this Word who was with God in the beginning and who was God? The fourteenth verse gives us the New Testament answer: "The Word was made flesh, and dwelt among us, (and we beheld his glory, the glory as of the only begotten of the Father,) full of grace and truth."

In simple, straightforward language written for the commonest man to follow, the New Testament declares that Christ is God, and that the Word is God, and the Word is Christ, and that God the Father calls the Son God. How natural then the exhortation, "Let all the angels of God worship him." Hebrews 1:6.

> "All hail the power of Jesus' name!
> Let angels prostrate fall;
> Bring forth the royal diadem,
> And crown Him Lord of all!"

When we truly recognize the position to which God has lifted His Son, the Son will lift us to the place God has ordained for us.

3. Did Christ Exist Before Creation?

In order to get a clear view of the Bible teaching as to whether Christ existed before the creation of the world, we hear two witnesses—the Son of God Himself and an Old Testament prophet.

In the early days of Christ's earthly ministry He proclaimed, "I came down from heaven." John 6:38. On the last night of His earthly life before the crucifixion He prayed, "Now, O Father, glorify thou me with thine own self with the glory which I had with thee before the world was." John 17:5. Thus the Son of God laid claim to life and glorious existence with His Father before this world was ever made. This is known as the pre-existence of Christ.

From the Old Testament comes the voice of the prophet Micah, who not only forecast the birth of Christ in Bethlehem but turned the hands backward on the clock of eternity to a point beyond the reach of finite imagination. Of Christ he said, "Whose goings forth have been from of old, from everlasting." Micah 5:2.

"Before the heavens were spread abroad,
From everlasting was the Word;
With God He was, the Word was God!
And must divinely be adored.

"Ere sin was born, or Satan fell,
He led the host of morning stars;
His generation who can tell,
Or count the number of His years?"

—Isaac Watts.

4. Was Christ the Active Creator?

The very first verse in the Bible says, "In the beginning God created the heaven and the earth." Genesis 1:1. Then the twenty-sixth verse reads, "God said, Let us make man in our image." Who was the other divine person to whom God spoke? This is made plain in the following words: "God, who created all things by Jesus Christ." Ephesians 3:9. "All things were made by him" (the Word, or Christ). John 1:3. "One Lord Jesus Christ, by whom are all things." 1 Corinthians 8:6.

This eternal Christ fashioned suns and moons and systems with words that leaped from His lips in infinite power. At His command whirling worlds flew off into their appointed paths in space, and His hands molded the forms of beings into which He breathed the breath of life.

This is the Creator Christ, and to us He sends the saving news: "Therefore if any man be in Christ, he is a new creature: old things are passed away; behold all things are become new." 2 Corinthians 5:17. What a saving yeast would be working in society today if every professed follower of Christ were truly living the new life of His creative power. In the person of His Holy Spirit He is ready to respond to the invitation:

"Thou canst fill me, gracious Spirit,
Though I cannot tell thee how;
But I need thee, greatly need thee;
Come, O come and fill me now."

5. Was Christ Born of a Virgin?

Isaiah, often called the gospel prophet, foretold the Messiah's virgin birth in these words: "Therefore the Lord himself shall give you a sign; Behold, a *virgin* shall conceive, and bear a *son,* and shall call his name Immanuel." Isaiah 7:14.

In the very first chapter of the New Testament the angel of the Lord confirms this plan by saying to Joseph concerning the virgin Mary, "That which is conceived in her is of the Holy Ghost. . . . Now all this was done that it might be fulfilled which was spoken of the Lord by the prophet, saying, Behold, a virgin shall be with child, and shall bring forth a son, and they shall call his name Emmanuel, which being interpreted is, God with us." Matthew 1:20-23.

The story is told of an African Mohammedan Negro who was taken prisoner of war. His captors removed a small charm that he wore about his neck. He was grief-stricken and terrified. The charm was opened and found to contain a small piece of paper on which was written the word "God." This native trusted in the charm, and when it was returned to him by one of his captors, he bowed to the ground and kissed the man's feet—all this for a scrap of paper with the name of God upon it. In Christ, God Himself came to earth.

The mystery of the human birth of God in Christ is called the incarnation. "The Word [the Son] was made flesh." John 1:14. A new being was not brought into existence, but a change was made in the order of His being, the form of His being. "Who, being in the form of God, . . . made himself of no reputation, and took upon him the form of a servant, and was made in the likeness of men." Philippians 2:6, 7.

This is indeed a mystery. Human birth is a mystery. Digestion and assimilation of food are mysteries. Light and electricity are mysteries. The whole universe is a mystery. All life is mysterious. Sin is baffling and mysterious. There is mystery in the Bible and out of the Bible. Great minds have often pointed out that the mysteries outside the Bible may indeed outnumber those in the Bible. Therefore, let us believe God, though we know not the fullest explanation of the virgin birth. Those who accept the virgin birth believe the Bible. Those who do not must set aside the Book of God.

We do well to remember that when Joseph found his espoused and untouched virgin wife to be with child, it took more faith on his part to accept the idea that she was with child by the Holy Ghost than it does for us to believe it. Christ's gracious life, His powerful preaching, His mighty miracles, the spread of His gospel—these were all future. Yet Joseph believed and was blessed. With less test of faith, but with fuller understanding and more manifold evidence, we also may believe and be blessed.

"Though in the very form of God,
With heavenly glory crowned,
Thou didst partake of human flesh,
Beset with sorrows round.
Thou wouldst like sinful man be made,
In everything but sin,
That we as like Thee might become,
As we unlike have been."

V. F. Kienberger, in the *Homiletic and Pastoral Review,* tells of a reporter who approached persons at random and asked, "What was the most important happening in history?" Here are some of the replies:

"The settlement of Jamestown by the English."

"The defeat of the Saracens at Tours."

"The splitting of the atom."

"The defeat of the Japanese."

"The invention of the wheel."

The sixth answer came from a fourteen-year-old schoolboy: "The birth of Jesus Christ."

It was Micah, the prophet of old, who exclaimed, "But thou, Bethlehem Ephratah, though thou be little among the thousands of Judah, yet out of thee shall he come forth unto me that is to be ruler in Israel; whose goings forth have been from of old, from everlasting." Micah 5:2.

"O holy Child of Bethlehem,
Descend to us we pray;
Cast out our sin and enter in,—
Be born in us today."

6. Did He live a Sinless life?

Sin is defined to be the transgression of God's law. (1 John 3:4.) When Christ was here upon earth He said to His own disciples on the night of the sacred Passover feast, just preceding His crucifixion the next day, "I have kept my Father's commandments." John 15:10.

To the Jews, Jesus said, "Ye seek to kill me." "Which of you convinceth me of sin?" John 8:37, 46. Those who sought to destroy Him could point to no act of transgression against the divine law of God. And when they brought Him before Pilate and he had examined Him, this Roman governor was compelled by his conscience to say, "I find no fault in this man." Luke 23:4. Pilate's wife, being warned in a dream, sent urgent word to her husband: "Have thou nothing to do with that just man." Matthew 27:19. When vacillating Pilate had washed his hands before the people, he cried, "I am innocent of the blood of this just person." Verse 24.

We turn to the apostle Peter, who put it in brief, terse language, which is unmistakably clear: "Who did no sin, neither was guile found in his mouth." 1 Peter 2:22. And Paul climaxed the matter in these words: He "was in all points tempted like as we are, yet without sin." Hebrews 4:15.

What did Christ accomplish by living this sinless life? (1) He demonstrated that when the life of God dwells in the "likeness of sinful flesh," sin may be overcome in the flesh and obedience to God's law be experienced. (Romans 8:3, 4.) (2) He made His righteous life available to cover our sins. (Romans 3:25.) (3) He became more "able" to sympathize with and help man in his struggle against sin. (Hebrews 2:17, 18.) (4) He revealed God to man. (John 1:18.)

"Satan had pointed to Adam's sin as proof that God's

law was unjust, and could not be obeyed. In our humanity, Christ was to redeem Adam's failure. . . . For four thousand years the race had been decreasing in physical strength, in mental power, and in moral worth; and Christ took upon Him the infirmities of degenerate humanity. Only thus could He rescue man from the lowest depths of his degradation."—*The Desire of Ages,* p. 117.

"What the law could not do, in that it was weak through the flesh, God sending his own Son in the likeness of sinful flesh, and for sin, condemned sin in the flesh: that the righteousness of the law might be fulfilled in us, who walk not after the flesh, but after the Spirit." Romans 8:3, 4.

So the Son of God overcame in the flesh, condemning the theory that God's law cannot be kept, and He is ready to dwell in us by His Holy Spirit and fulfill His law in us. The flesh is not subject to the law of God, but the Spirit of God is. Thus we are to yield to the Spirit and receive power to obey. (Romans 8:6-9.)

Christ lived a life, "leaving us an example, that ye should follow his steps." 1 Peter 2:21. Ask the Hindu, "Is the life of your god, Krishna, a good example for you?" And if he is a good and intelligent Hindu, he will say, "No, Krishna was a god. We cannot follow his example and live as he did."

Emerson testified, "Jesus is the most perfect man of all men that have yet appeared." Renan declared, "All history is incomprehensible without Him. . . . Whatever may be the surprises of the future, Jesus will never be surpassed."—*Life of Jesus.* James Anthony Froude, historian and critic, wrote, "The most perfect being who has ever trod the soil of this planet was called the Man of Sorrows."

The Bible calls Him the Son of God and the Son of man, who "did no sin."

"Look upon Jesus, sinless is He;
Father, impute His life unto me.
My life of scarlet, my sin and woe,
Cover with His life, whiter than snow."
—F. E. BELDEN.

7. WHY DID CHRIST DIE?

A Chinese man, having heard the story of the cross, responded with this question: "What does one man's death have to do with another man's sins?" I think it safe to say that the complete answer to that question may never come. The human mind may never fully fathom the science, philosophy, and theology of the cross and its atonement. It is not necessary. But it is possible for the simplest man to touch with the fingers of his faith the hem of Calvary's crimson garment, and be made every whit whole. Christ is Christianity and Christianity is Christ. It is a personal experience. The cross of Christ is the center of that experience.

A great preacher wrote: "The cross was the gallows of His day—the electric chair of His age. It was the most cruel instrument of torture ever invented. Men were nailed upon it and hung there unsheltered from the biting cold or the scorching heat until they died of exhaustion or of heart-breaking suffering. We are told by historians that some lived for a week hanging upon the cross until the birds came and plucked out their eyes while they were still alive. The body of the Lord Jesus touched the cruel cross and immediately transformed it into the glory of the world."—CHARLES T. EVERSON, *Jesus,* p. 15.

This is not to say that we may be saved by hanging the cross on the wall of our house, or by wearing it as an ornament about the neck, or as the charm of a watch chain. But we may sincerely say, if we so choose, "God forbid that I should glory, save in the cross of our Lord

Jesus Christ, by whom the world is crucified unto me, and I unto the world." Galatians 6:14.

There are three things glorified by Calvary.

a. It glorifies the law of God. Not that the principles of the Ten Commandments needed to be glorified; rather, men needed to see their glory. This law was "ordained to life." (Romans 7:10.) Obedience brought happiness. Sin brought death. Had it been possible for God to abolish His law, the problem of sin could have been solved in this manner. But since the law was a very transcript of His character, He could not change its principles without changing His character. This He would not do and will not do.

When someone leaps to death from the window of a skyscraper, God does not change the law of gravitation to keep others from jumping to destruction. To do so would make the universe a chaos. If thousands perish in crashes from giddy speeds on the highways, God does not alter the laws of momentum governing moving bodies and masses.

Likewise, when God's created beings violate the moral law, God cannot change the law to suit their desires. That would mean the destruction of His government of which His law is the foundation. Said the psalmist, "Righteousness and judgement are the foundation of thy throne." Psalms 89:14, R.V.

The law could not save men because "all have sinned." Romans 3:23. Men could not save themselves. Angels were powerless to help. "Since the divine law is as sacred as God Himself, only one equal with God could make atonement for its transgression."

Thus we come to the eve of Calvary. There in an upper room in old Jerusalem, Jesus extended His hand, in which was held a cup of sweet wine, symbolizing His blood, and He said to His disciples, "This is my blood

Review Pictures *P. P. Rubens, Artist*

Christ was condemned for our sins, in which He had no share. He suffered the death which was ours, that we might receive the life which was His. His loss is our gain.

of the new testament, which is shed for many for the remission of sins." Matthew 26:28.

Isaiah the prophet had long before penned the words, "But he was wounded for our transgressions, he was bruised for our iniquities." And when Calvary was more than a quarter of a century past, the converted Peter wrote, "Who his own self bare our sins in his own body on the tree." 1 Peter 2:24.

From the cross of Christ there shines a light upon the law of God, gilding its holy precepts with a new glory, and making yet more plain to all the universe that "from everlasting to everlasting" are the unchanging commandments of the unchanging God and of His changeless Christ.

Calvary covers the throne of the universe with a new and radiant glory. The light of the cross beams upon the foundation stones of sacred precept, until, like spiritual diamonds, they glitter with added luster and unfading glory, as unfallen angels join men redeemed to renew their loyalty and allegiance to the eternal God and His eternal law.

Said Isaiah, "He will magnify the law." Isaiah 42:21. The cross of Calvary served this purpose to perfection. Jesus in His death sealed the doom of Satan's desire to abolish the law of God. He made forever plain to all the universe heaven's immovable position on these eternal words of God: "For ever, O Lord, thy word is settled in heaven." Psalms 119:89.

b. The cross glorifies the love of God. A British plane crippled by enemy fire dropped to the ocean and sank. Five of the crew managed to get into a rubber raft made for only four men. The raft began to sink. With calm heroism one young man stepped out of the raft and soon vanished beneath the waves. He gave his life that the four might live.

God is love. He always has been love. But up until the time when sin became a problem in His universe, His love had never been tested as to what it would do for a sinner. It is true that God and His Son knew what they would do, for we read, "Ye know that ye were . . . redeemed . . . with the precious blood of Christ, . . . who verily was foreordained before the foundation of the world, but was manifest in these last times for you." 1 Peter 1:18-20.

It is as though, far back in God's long eternity, the Father and the Son clasped hands in a mutual pledge of sacrifice, the Son saying, "If sin ever comes, I will go and redeem sinners"; and the Father saying, "I will give you to save the transgressor." This pledge was later fulfilled. Said Christ, "For God so loved the world, that he gave his only begotten Son." John 3:16. And again, "I lay down my life. . . . No man taketh it from me, but I lay it down of myself." John 10:18.

One leading writer has said, "God's love for the fallen race is a peculiar manifestation of love,—a love born of mercy; for human beings are all undeserving. Mercy implies imperfection of the object toward which it is shown. It is because of sin that mercy was brought into exercise."

This divine element of mercy was peculiar in the sense that it had never been observed before. It was not something new with God. Rather, there had not been any necessity or even opportunity for its manifestation. This purest gold of the love of God was there all the time, buried deep in the very heart of the mine, but it had not yet been brought to the surface.

Sin brought mercy to light. Satan rebelled against God, challenging the justice of the law, and questioning the love of God, which gave the law of God. God's answer was Calvary.

Somewhere God had caused a tree to grow. Its roots

'ent down into God's soil for nourishment. Its branches :ached up their leafy hands toward God's sky for air, ght, and moisture. One day men came, hewed down this 'ee, and of it made a cross. Upon it they nailed the Son f God.

Hanging there in His agony, He heard one crucified iief cry, "If thou be Christ, save thyself and us." Luke 3:39. Here was the voice of modernism, calling for some ther way of salvation—no atonement! no sacrifice! no ross!

The other thief, his heart smitten with a sense of uilt and repentance, pleaded earnestly, "Lord, remember ie when thou comest in thy kingdom." Verse 42. And esus answered, "Verily I say unto thee, To day"—here n this very hour of darkness and despair and death, I say :—"shalt thou be with me in paradise." Verse 43.

There upon the cross of Calvary the love of God was lorified and magnified to read, M-E-R-C-Y. There the ying voice of the Son of God was heard to say, "Father, orgive them; for they know not what they do." Verse 34.

"O Love that wilt not let me go,
I rest my weary soul in Thee;
I give Thee back the life I owe,
That in Thine ocean depths its flow
May richer, fuller be."

—George Matheson.

c. The cross glorifies the value of a human soul. It ias been said that when Napoleon was planning one of iis military campaigns, Metternich, Austrian minister at he French court, remarked, "This campaign will cost a nillion men." To this Napoleon replied, "What are a nillion men to me!"

In His practical life Jesus showed His great regard for :ven one individual. From the sinful woman at Jacob's well o the crooked little taxgatherer on the limb of a sycamore tree, Jesus loved the individual. There is no oth way to love the world. Dining with unchurched men, H bore the taunts of religious leaders who said, "This ma receiveth sinners, and eateth with them." Luke 15:2. T that He replied by relating that unforgettable parab which has perhaps brought more men to Christ than ar other—the prodigal son.

He sought to get men to see that God valued ther that He wanted to save them. Once He asked this que tion: "What is a man profited, if he shall gain the who world, and lose his own soul?" Matthew 16:26. Wh was Jesus trying to say? Simply this: "Any man of yo who will let God save you is worth more to Him than a the treasures of the world. And you yourselves will som day know the truth of this, whether you be saved or los If saved in heaven, you will say, 'The gilded treasures c earth are as but glittering sand in comparison to th glory and happiness of heaven.' If you are lost outside th city gates, you will say, 'Salvation and heaven would hav been worth more than all the world.'"

So Christ came down to give His life a ransom fc man, and He would have paid that price for one sou It was the *one* lost sheep, the *one* lost coin, the *one* los prodigal. The cross of Jesus glorifies the law of God, th love of God, and the value of a human soul saved in eter nity. Have you been down to Calvary?

"In the cross of Christ I glory,
Towering o'er the wrecks of time;
All the light of sacred story
Gathers round its head sublime."

—Sir John Bowring.

There is a striking story told of a certain Englishmar who in bygone days visited the old slave market in Cairc Egypt, and beheld a strong, intelligent young man on th ock for sale. Scarcely realizing it, he found himself bidng against the other buyers. Up and up went the price, ntil when the auctioneer cried, "Sold!" the Englishman d invested practically his whole life's savings in this range slave.

The slave eyed him with suspicion and hatred, saying himself, "Why should this man be free, and yet come re and barter my body for his own profit. If I get a ance, I'll drive a dagger through his heart."

The owner led him away, and said to him, "I bought u to set you free." When the slave heard this astoundg news he fell upon his knees and cried, "Oh, let me be ur slave forever!"

"All to Jesus I surrender,
All to Him I freely give;
I will ever love and trust Him,
In His presence daily live."

8. Did Christ Rise From the Dead?

There are six points to be borne in mind regarding e resurrection.

a. Christ said that He would rise from the dead. "From at time forth began Jesus to shew unto his disciples, ow that he must go unto Jerusalem, and suffer many ings of the elders and chief priests and scribes, and be illed, and be raised again the third day." Matthew 16:21.

b. The angel at the empty tomb testified to His esurrection. "He is not here: for he is risen, as he said. ome, see the place where the Lord lay." Matthew 28:6.

c. He was seen of more than five hundred persons t one time. "He was seen of Cephas, then of the twelve: fter that, he was seen of above five hundred brethren at nce." 1 Corinthians 15:5, 6.

d. After His resurrection Jesus affirmed it by personal estimony. "Behold my hands and my feet, that it is I myself: handle me, and see; for a spirit hath not flesh ar bones, as ye see me have." Luke 24:39.

e. Christ reaffirmed it through revelation. "I am he th liveth, and was dead; and, behold, I am alive for evermor Amen; and have the keys of hell and of death." Revel tion 1:18.

f. The resurrection belief was a driving force in th early church. When Judas, bent upon earthly glor watched Jesus wash the disciples' feet, including his ow he must have said to himself, "This is no king. Unle He shows His hand and takes over the reins of gover ment, I'm through." So this selfish office seeker sold h Lord for thirty pieces of silver in his determination force the issue. When He saw Jesus deliver Himself His enemies, Judas trembled with fear of both earthl and heavenly judgment. He went out and hanged himsel Had he believed that Christ would rise from the dead, l might not have betrayed his Lord or taken his own lif

As the disciples followed the rapid course of even from Gethsemane to Calvary, giant fingers of fe strangled the flow of saving faith in their souls. The Leader was dead upon a cross, lifted up between tw common criminals. They did not go and hang themselve as Judas did, however strong the suicidal urge may hav been. But they did watch their lamp of hope flicker an go out in utter darkness. For their faith it was night.

What restored their faith and hope? It was indeed th *resurrection.* The very first words of Peter's first epistl after the salutation, are these: "Blessed be the God an Father of our Lord Jesus Christ, which according to hi abundant mercy hath begotten us again unto a lively hop by the resurrection of Jesus Christ from the dead." 1 Pete 1:3.

What is Peter saying? This: "When Jesus died m hope died. When Jesus rose again my hope was bor

;ain." The cross of Calvary is significant because it bore e body of a sinless Christ, who was to break the bonds death and come forth a victor in the resurrection. "I n he that liveth, and was dead."

What sent the church forth "conquering and to con- ıer"? It was the belief that this sinless Son of God, born a virgin, and crucified upon Calvary as an atonement, ıd risen from the dead.

What message bore Peter, the mighty preacher of entecost? "Him . . . ye have taken, and . . . crucified . . . hom God hath *raised up*." Acts 2:23, 24. As he pressed e point by referring to a prophecy of David, and spoke ith great assurance, thousands of smitten consciences sulted, and men cried, "What shall we do?" Peter re- ›onded, "Repent, and be baptized." Writing of baptism ter, he said, "The like figure whereunto baptism doth so now save us . . . by the resurrection of Jesus Christ." Peter 3:21. Every Bible baptism is a symbol of faith in e death and resurrection of Christ. Pentecost was aflame ith this hope, as "with great power gave the apostles itness of the resurrection of the Lord Jesus." Acts 4:33.

What was the burden of Paul's preaching? In the nagogue and market place of ancient Athens, seat of isdom and learning, he "preached unto them Jesus and e resurrection." Acts 17:18. On Mars' Hill he repeated e assurance that God "hath raised him from the dead." erse 31.

He was arrested in Jerusalem. Pleading his own case, e said, "Of the hope and the resurrection of the dead I n called in question." Acts 23:6. Carried to Caesarea and rought to trial before Felix, the Roman governor, he enied that he had done any evil, "except it be for this ne voice, that I cried standing among them, Touching e resurrection of the dead I am called in question by ou this day." Acts 24:21.

Fug[cut off]

The resurrection of Christ was a demonstration of divine power over the [cut off]
and an assurance that "the dead in Christ shall rise" in the final resurrec[cut off]

To the Romans he wrote, "Paul, . . . separated unto e gospel of God, . . . concerning his Son Jesus Christ . . . , and declared to be the Son of God with power, cording to the spirit of holiness, by the resurrection om the dead." Romans 1:1-4.

To the Christians in the corrupt city of Corinth he eclared, "And if Christ be not risen, then is our preachg vain, and your faith is also vain. . . . Ye are yet in ur sins." 1 Corinthians 15:14-17.

And finally, in his own personal experience, the resrrection was his hope of daily power, and of the future surrection from the dead. "That I may know him, and e power of his resurrection, and the fellowship of his fferings, being made conformable unto his death; if by y means I might attain unto the resurrection of the ead." Philippians 3:10, 11.

We are told that at the battle of Inkerman, famous nflict of the Crimean War, a wounded soldier crawled to his tent. They found him there, face down, his hand lued by his own blood to the pages of an open Bible. Vhen his hand was lifted these printed letters were seen aced upon it, "I am the resurrection, and the life: he at believeth in me, though he were dead, yet shall he ve." John 11:25.

The early Christian believers went forth in spiritual onquest. Before them were the hatred of the Jews and e scorn of the Romans. They faced the mouths of lions nd the fires of the stake. Their bodies, soaked in oil, were ade into living, burning torches to light the playgrounds f Rome.

They perished in prison and dungeon. They felt e sharp cutting edge of the sword, the stab of the agger, and the blow of the headsman's ax. Thousands ved in the dark, dank catacombs in the bowels of the arth beneath the city of Rome. What sustained them through those earthly terrors? Faith in the crucified and risen Christ.

"Up from the grave He arose,
With a mighty triumph o'er His foes;
He arose a Victor from the dark domain,
And He lives forever with His saints to reign.
He arose! He arose!
Hallelujah! Christ arose!"

—ROBERT LOWRY.

We resist the temptation to discuss at length the technical problem of the empty tomb. We might consider the trumped-up charge of the Roman guards who had been bribed by the church leaders to say that the disciples "stole him away while we slept." Matthew 28:11-13. But had not these very soldiers been warned by these very church leaders to be on guard against just such a possibility? (Matthew 27:63-66.) And if the guards were asleep, how could they know what happened? And what would the disciples have done with the dead body? And how could it have inspired them to die for their faith in a *risen* Lord? Edwin Markham wrote a poem which agrees with the Bible account:

"I was a Roman soldier in my prime;
Now age is on me and the yoke of time.
I saw your Risen Christ, for I am he
Who reached the hyssop to Him on the tree;
And I am one of two who watched beside
The Sepulcher of Him we crucified.

. . . . .

"Years have I wandered, carrying my shame;
Now let the tooth of time eat out my name.
For we, who all the wonder might have told,
Kept silence, for our mouths were stopt with gold."

—Reprinted by permission.

We could talk of the theory that Christ did not really die, but that He only fainted on the cross. Whence then came the water and blood from His spear-pierced side? And are we to believe that this mangled man revived, and on the second night Himself rolled away the great stone from the sealed rock tomb? What nonsense in the name of murder mystery! It could never be charged to a Sherlock Holmes.

Could it be that the disciples saw only a ghost? Were they anxious to see one? I tell you, nay! Their faith was so shattered that they were skeptical of every report. Friends said they had seen Him, but they said, "Idle tales." Luke 24:11. Two reliable followers rushed in from Emmaus, where they had seen Him, but the account says, "Neither believed they them." Mark 16:13.

Then while the disciples were behind closed doors Jesus appeared. Then they *did* think they had seen a ghost and were terrified. (Luke 24:37.) They did not reckon this as a resurrection, and they wanted nothing to do with ghosts.

Then it was that Jesus had them feel of His flesh and bones, and ate food before them, that they might know that it was really their risen Lord. The record says, "Then were the disciples glad, when they saw the Lord." John 20:20. Not some seducing spirit impersonating the Lord. Not a hallucination spun by the heated imagination of unscientific men. But the actual, literal, resurrected, glorious body of Jesus Christ.

The Bible brings us the past record of at least eight appearances of Christ to men after His resurrection, including one company of five hundred. Today brings us the power of a resurrected life. "For if, when we were enemies, we were reconciled to God by the death of his Son, much more, being reconciled, we shall be saved by his life." Romans 5:10. Tomorrow holds the hope of opened graves and immortality. (1 Corinthians 15:51-57.)

Let no lips seal off the praise of the heart that has found fellowship with Christ the crucified and risen Lord.

"He lives, He lives, Christ Jesus lives today!
He walks with me and talks with me
Along life's narrow way.

"He lives, He lives, salvation to impart!
You ask me how I know He lives?
He lives within my heart."

—A. H. ACKLEY.

9. WHAT IS CHRIST DOING NOW?

Luke gives us the record of what happened forty days after the resurrection: "He led them out as far as to Bethany, and he lifted up his hands, and blessed them. And it came to pass, while he blessed them, he was parted from them, and carried up into heaven." Luke 24: 50, 51.

The record of Acts 1:9-12 gives this account of the ascension from the Mount of Olives: "When he had spoken these things, while they beheld, he was taken up; and a cloud received him out of their sight. And while they looked stedfastly toward heaven as he went up, behold, two men stood by them in white apparel; . . . then returned they unto Jerusalem from the mount called Olivet."

It was no doubt a cloud of angels which enveloped the Son of man in glory as He ascended to heaven, there to be received in adoration and acclaim as forecast in the prophetic poetry of the twenty-fourth psalm, verses 9, 10:

"Lift up your heads, O ye gates;
Even lift them up, ye everlasting doors;

And the King of glory shall come in.
Who is this King of glory?
The Lord of hosts, he is the King of glory."

What is Christ doing now? What was His work in heaven to be? Speaking of this, Paul says, "Now of the things which we have spoken this is the sum: We have such a high priest, who is set down on the right hand of the throne of the Majesty in the heavens." Hebrews 8:1. Using another word, the apostle states the same truth in 1 Timothy 2:5: "There is one God, and one mediator between God and men, the man Christ Jesus." So there is a high priest in heaven, who is the mediator between God and men.

What does this all mean to us? It means that there has been a separation between God and us. Our sins have brought about an estrangement. There is a matter of difference, a wall of partition. There must be a getting together.

If such were not the case, there would be no need for reconciliation. If I should say to two strangers, "Let me act as an arbitrator between you," they would respond, "We don't even know each other. We have never had any differences." If I should approach two good, lifelong friends and say to them, "Let me serve as a mediator between the two of you," they would exclaim, "We are friends. We have no differences."

But consider a case where there has come in a difference, a cleavage, a separation. A young couple go through a glowing courtship, a beautiful wedding, a happy honeymoon, and years of life's closest union. Then one of them breaks the holy bonds that held them together. There is separation, bitterness, and a trail of tragedy with many broken hearts. Peace and harmony give place to strife and confusion. What is needed? A mediator, a peacemaker.

One of the last things the great John Bunyan ever

did in this world was to make a trip in a cold rain to make an effort to bring peace between a father and a son. Having succeeded, he reached home soaked to the skin, contracted pneumonia, and died.

Christ Jesus is the peacemaker of the universe. He died that men might be reconciled to God. Not that God was a tyrant, and only Jesus was benevolent, but rather they were both together in this plan. We read, "To wit, that God was in Christ, reconciling the world unto himself." 2 Corinthians 5:19.

Peace was made through the blood of Christ. "God purposed through Him to reconcile the universe to Himself, making peace through His blood, which was shed upon the Cross." Colossians 1:20, Weymouth. Only eternity will reveal the mighty host of sinners who have found peace and reconciliation at the foot of Calvary.

Christ died to make peace, and He lives to make peace. He is our mediator now. He is our high priest of reconciliation today. "Wherefore he is able also to save them to the uttermost that come unto God by him, seeing he ever liveth to make intercession for them." Hebrews 7:25.

Today we often see thousands of men trust their hopes for mediation to the hands of some representative from their own ranks. Labor pins its faith to some man who has been through the grind and over the road—through the grind they endure, over the road they travel. This bond of sympathy and understanding is hard to break.

Jesus was "made like unto his brethren, that he might be a merciful and faithful high priest . . . , to make reconciliation for the sins of the people." Hebrews 2:17. "For we have not an high priest which cannot be touched with the feeling of our infirmities; but was in all points tempted like as we are, yet without sin." Hebrews 4:15.

Our mediator is the man Christ Jesus. (1 Timothy

2:5.) On the one hand He is the Son of man, and on the other hand He is the Son of God. Thus does He become the perfect peacemaker, mediator, and high priest between God and man.

When Lincoln was in the White House he had one boy they called Tad, a lively fellow who never regarded anyone as a stranger. One day among the many who waited in the reception room to see the President personally there sat a sad and troubled soldier. Tad made friends with him. When he heard the soldier's story and saw how anxious he was to see Mr. Lincoln, and how fearful he was that there would be no time, he said, "Don't you worry. I'll see that you get in." The lad disappeared, and the hours wore on. Finally the President's secretary stepped out and announced, "Mr. Lincoln is very sorry, but he can see no one else today." The soldier's heart sank as he turned to leave. Then in a sudden desperation he faced the secretary and said, "Tad told me he would see that I got an audience with the President today." The secretary eyed the soldier to read upon his face a simple sincerity, and replied, "If Tad said you could see Mr. Lincoln today, you shall see him. He never turns Tad down."

This is not an exact picture of spiritual truth, but it serves to point sharply this practical approach to God. Declared Jesus, "No man cometh unto the Father, but by me." John 14:6. And again, "Him that cometh to me I will in no wise cast out." John 6:37.

Have you made contact with this Mediator, this Friend of sinners, this Son of man who has been over the road you travel and understands your problems? This is the God-man. One of His hands clasps the hand of His Father in heaven. The other nail-scarred hand reaches down to earth and is "mighty to save." Clasp that hand today! Meet your Mediator!

"Arise, my soul, arise, shake off thy guilty fears;
The bleeding Sacrifice in my behalf appears;
Before the throne my Surety stands,
My name is written on His hands."

—CHARLES WESLEY.

10. WILL CHRIST COME BACK AGAIN?

We come now to the climax of this lesson on "Christ Forever." We have seen that He is the Son of God one with God, and is called God; that He existed with God before creation, and cooperated with God in creation; that He was born of a virgin, lived a sinless life died an atoning death, rose from the dead, and ascended to heaven to become our high priest and mediator.

Since the remaining chapters of this section all deal with the second coming of Christ, we here but briefly present it as the climax in this ten-point study of Christ

Bethlehem symbolizes to us the incarnation, when the Son of man was born of a virgin. Calvary is the place where the Son of God, as the Lamb of God, died for our sins. Mount Olivet is the place from which He ascended to heaven to become our mediator, and fitly symbolizes our hope of His glorious return. It was here that the angels said, "This same Jesus, which is taken up from you into heaven, shall so come in like manner as ye have seen him go into heaven." Acts 1:11.

This declaration by the angels on Olivet brought vivid memories of a few weeks before when "as he sat upon the mount of Olives, the disciples came unto him privately, saying, Tell us, when shall these things be? and what shall be the sign of thy coming?" Matthew 24:3. They remembered also the words He spoke to them just before He entered into the deep shadows of Gethsemane and Calvary: "Let not your heart be troubled: ye believe in God, believe also in me. In my Father's house are many mansions: if it were not so, I would have told you. I go to prepare a place for you. And if I go and prepare a place for you, I will come again, and receive you unto myself; that where I am, there ye may be also." John 14:1-3.

This is the Christ who like a mighty bridge spans the two eternities. He reaches back into the eternity of the past. His life and love arch the dark abyss of the present like an eternal rainbow. He reaches forth to that never-ending future to be ushered in when He comes back again.

If we truly know Him now, He will know us then—not mere profession, not the mere recital of prayer, or the participation in ritual, not the trust in sudden feeling and passing emotion, but the day-to-day faith in, surrender to, and fellowship with, this divine Son of man.

Someone tells of an actor and a minister who attended a social gathering. The actor had greatly pleased those present with his portrayal of characters from Shakespeare. It was suggested that both the minister and the actor take turns in reciting the twenty-third psalm. The actor gave his rendition first, and there followed great applause. The man of God was fearful. He scarcely looked up as he slowly spoke the familiar words of that wonderful shepherd psalm. When he finished there was no applause. He felt a sinking in his heart and wished he had never come. Then he looked up and saw the guests silently weeping. The skillful actor turned to him and said, "You see, I knew the *psalm,* but you knew the *Shepherd.*"

Today that Shepherd guards His faithful sheep. He seeks His straying sheep. He calls to those who have never yet been in His fold. "He goeth before them, and the sheep follow him: for they know his voice." "I . . . know my sheep, and am known of mine." John 10:4, 14. To those who know and follow Him all the way He will someday say, "Come, ye blessed of my Father, inherit the kingdom prepared for you from the foundation of the world." Matthew 25:34. Concerning those who do not know Him, though they may make great profession, He says, "Then will I profess unto them, I never knew you: depart from me, ye that work iniquity." Matthew 7:23.

The choice is mine. The decision no other may make for me. "What shall I do then with Jesus, which is called Christ?"

"O Jesus, my Redeemer,
Thou art my joy and song,
My Saviour and my solace
When griefs around me throng.

. . . . .

"O Jesus, my Redeemer,
My song shall be of Thee;
No other friend so constant,
No friend so dear to me."

CHAPTER 23

The Coming Man of Destiny

OPEN YOUR Bible to the book of Genesis, and there in the third chapter and the fifteenth verse you will read a prophecy of God. It tells about the seed of the woman, the coming Christ, who was one day to bruise the head of Satan the serpent.

Beginning at that point in Genesis, you may trace, like the scarlet thread in every inch of English navy rope, the golden line of promises and predictions of Christ's first coming—His birth, His birthplace and the little town in which He grew up, His message and its rejection by church leaders, His call to lowly men, His ministry of blessing to all classes, His betrayal, His humility and suffering and trial, His crucifixion and burial and resurrection, and His magnificent reception in heaven.

The prophetic voice is like a melody, mingling the strains of promise, tragedy, and hope: "There shall come a Star out of Jacob, and a Sceptre shall rise out of Israel." Numbers 24:17. "Until Shiloh come." Genesis 49:10. "A man of sorrows." Isaiah 53:3. "The Prince of Peace." Isaiah 9:6. But the refrain is ever the same: "He is coming! He is coming!" This was His first coming, His first advent.

WHAT OF HIS SECOND COMING?

Did the Old Testament prophets see beyond the first coming and the cross to the second coming and the

Franklin Booth, Artist

The central theme of the Holy Scriptures is Christ. It is on Him that all the proph have focused as the Saviour of mankind, "the same yesterday, to day, and for eve

crown? Here is a sweeping answer from the New Testament: "He shall send Jesus Christ, which before was preached unto you: whom the heaven must receive until the times of restitution of all things, which God hath spoken by the mouth of all his holy prophets since the world began." Acts 3:20, 21. Here we are assured that *all* the prophets of old understood that there was to be a glorious coming of the Messiah and a restoration of righteousness, and of God's original plans for man.

"The second coming of Christ is mentioned 1,518 times in the Bible, and over 300 times in the New Testament. This goes to prove God's emphasis on this important doctrine."—*The Free Methodist.*

If this statement be correct, there are some one thousand two hundred references in the Old Testament to the glorious day of the second coming of Christ and the restitution of all things. Dwight L. Moody estimated that the second coming of Christ is referred to two thousand five hundred times in the Bible. On this basis there would probably be some two thousand allusions in the Old Testament to this climax of the ages. This is not to say that God's people in those times had the fullest understanding of the distinct difference between the first and second comings of Christ, nor the place of what may be called the third coming of Christ. God continued to give increasing light as time went by.

Jude, next to the last book of the New Testament, names one of the first Old Testament prophets who preached the Second Advent of Christ: "Enoch also, the seventh from Adam, prophesied of these, saying, Behold, the Lord cometh with ten thousands of his saints, to execute judgment upon all, and to convince all that are ungodly among them of all their ungodly deeds which they have ungodly committed, and of all their hard speeches which ungodly sinners have spoken against him." Jude

14, 15. Here is a man but the seventh generation from Adam who long before the Flood painted a word picture of Christ's coming which fairly matches the finished pen of John the revelator.

Consider the patriarch Abraham also. Said Christ "Your father Abraham rejoiced to see my day: and he saw it and was glad." John 8:56. Christ's day includes His second coming and reign of glory. Is there any doubt that Abraham understood? Hear the testimony of Paul: "He [Abraham] looked for a city which hath foundations, whose builder and maker is God." Hebrews 11:10. This dweller in tents, wandering in strange lands, died in faith, as did his faithful descendants, who "not having received the promises, but having seen them afar off, and were persuaded of them, . . . embraced them." Verse 13. What a picture of saving faith! With eyes of faith they saw the fulfillment of promises while they were yet afar off, and with the arms of faith they embraced the hope of God's future day of glory.

Then there was Job. A man of means, character, honor, and influence, he found himself suddenly thrust into financial ruin, social unpopularity, sickness nigh unto death, and the deepest distress of soul. In this dark hour, when it might aptly be said that he had both feet in the grave, his faith exclaimed, "I know that my redeemer liveth, and that he shall stand at the latter day upon the earth: and though after my skin worms destroy this body, yet in my flesh shall I see God." Job 19:25, 26. What a striking presentation of the second coming of Christ and the resurrection of the dead!

The psalmist David writes as in vision, "Our God shall come, and shall not keep silence: a fire shall devour before him, and it shall be very tempestuous round about him. He shall call to the heavens from above, and to the earth, that he may judge his people. Gather my saints together unto me; those that have made a covenant with me by sacrifice." Psalms 50:3-5.

Zechariah describes His final coming, "His feet shall stand in that day upon the mount of Olives, which is before Jerusalem on the east, and the mount of Olives shall cleave in the midst thereof toward the east and toward the west, and there shall be a very great valley; and half of the mountain shall remove toward the north, and half of it toward the south." Zechariah 14:4.

The message of the Old Testament rings forth, "He is coming!" Coming in humility and suffering, then coming in power and glory. But always, without a wavering note. He is coming!

THE NEW TESTAMENT MESSAGE

The first great added note of the New Testament is, He has come! "Unto you is born this day in the city of David a Saviour, which is Christ the Lord." Luke 2:11. He has come as a babe born of a virgin, as a man clothed in the garb of a carpenter, as the Messiah baptized of John in Jordan, anointed with the Holy Ghost, and certified of God. He has come as the overcomer, tempted in all points as we are, yet without sin. He has come as the master teacher, the divine healer, the great comforter. He has died on Calvary for the sins of men. He has risen from the tomb with the keys of hell and death snatched from the sealed and stony sepulcher, and ascended into heaven as the Son of man to be our merciful mediator. All this *He has done.* Yes, He *has* come. That was the *first advent.*

The second triumphant strain of the New Testament is, "He is coming *again!*" From the milder tones proceeding from some of the parables of Jesus the music rises to a magnificent crescendo and grand finale in the book of Revelation. The curtain rings down on a sin-cursed world and rolls up to reveal the indescribable glories of eternity. "Surely I come quickly. Amen. Even so, come, Lord Jesus." Revelation 22:20.

In rapid review we bring to mind the actual New Testament words.

First, let us give an ear to the sayings of Jesus. Under questioning by His disciples He said, "Then shall all the tribes of the earth mourn, and they shall see the Son of man coming in the clouds of heaven with power and great glory." Matthew 24:30.

On trial before the high priest a few hours before Calvary, Jesus was put under oath to answer the question as to whether He was the Son of God. Standing there before the throne of the arrogant Caiaphas, bound as a criminal and flanked by guards, "Jesus saith unto him, . . . Hereafter shall ye see the Son of man sitting on the right hand of power, and coming in the clouds of heaven." Matthew 26:64. These words served to affirm in open testimony before a religious court what He had privately said to His disciples a few hours before: "I go to prepare a place for you. And if I go and prepare a place for you, I will come again." John 14:2, 3.

Since Christ is the central and authoritative figure of Christianity, therefore upon the reliability or unreliability of His recorded promise to come again, Christianity stands or falls.

Then there came the testimony of angels after His ascension: "This same Jesus . . . shall so come in like manner as ye have seen him go into heaven." Acts 1:11.

The apostle Paul, ready for execution by Nero's decree, exclaimed, "Henceforth there is laid up for me a crown of righteousness, which the Lord, the righteous judge, shall give me at that day: and not to me only, but unto all them also that love his appearing." 2 Timothy 4:8.

It is said that in the era of that early pagan persecution Christian believers passing each other at night on the streets of Rome exchanged the greeting, *"Maranatha,"* meaning "The Lord is coming." They did not understand how far in the future that coming was really to be, but they did experience the heavenly thrill of its hope in their hearts.

The careful, conservative apostle James, presenting a picture of certain conditions to come in the last days, said, "Be ye also patient; stablish your hearts: for the coming of the Lord draweth nigh." James 5:8.

The positive and more dramatic Peter gave point to his faith by saying, "The day of the Lord will come. . . . What holy and pious men ought you to be in your behaviour, you who expect and hasten the advent of the Day of God." 2 Peter 3:10-12, Moffatt.

John, the beloved saint and prisoner of Patmos, out of tribulation brought the Revelation of Jesus Christ concerning that final day when the destiny of all men shall have been settled. The good are good. The bad are bad. The saved are saved. The lost are lost. Then is heard rolling through the universe the words of the returning King: "Behold, I come quickly; and my reward is with me, to give every man according as his work shall be." Revelation 22:12. This is the Second Advent.

March 11, 1942, was a dark day for the freedom-loving peoples of the world. General Douglas MacArthur was ordered by his superior command to leave the Philippines. The overwhelming forces of the enemy were sweeping in. In that black and bitter night this man of faith and deeds reached within his soul and brought forth something that he struck against the rough, hard wall of unfriendly fate.

There sprang forth a light that illuminated and electrified the world, when he said, "I shall return." Two and a half years later, on October 20, 1944, he broadcast to the people of the Philippines, "I have returned."

In the dark shadows of the cross Jesus said simply, "I will come again." Someday, amid the contrasting scenes of celestial glory and earthly chaos, He will proclaim, "I have returned."

What Christians Have Said

A deep and abiding faith in the second coming of Christ has a tremendous purifying and uplifting power. The devil knows that. Two methods he uses to destroy the influence of this great doctrine. Sometimes he tries to minimize the importance of it by liberal thinking. Thus the "blessed hope" is practically destroyed. Second, he uses fanaticism to bring it into disrepute. But the towering leaders of the church have clung to this hope with tenacious faith.

Martin Luther wrote, "I ardently hope that, amidst these internal dissensions on earth, Jesus Christ will hasten the day of His coming." He thought that it would be about three hundred years in the future from his day. We live in the time when he thought it would be near.

The intrepid John Knox wrote, "We know that He shall return, and that with expedition."

The fervent John Wesley, commenting on the closing verses of Revelation, said, "The Spirit of adoption in the heart of every believer says, . . . 'Come and accomplish all the words of this prophecy.' "

John Milton sublimely wrote, "Come forth out of Thy royal chambers, O Prince of all the kings of the earth; . . . take up that unlimited scepter. . . . For now the voice of Thy bride calls Thee, and all creatures sigh to be renewed."

Moody said, "The church has very little to say about it. Now I can see a reason for this; the devil does not want us to see this truth, for nothing would wake up the church so much."

During World War II the island of Malta in the Mediterranean Sea was subjected to one of the most drawn-out, terrifying, and nerve-racking bombings on record. Lieutenant General Sir William Dobbie, former governor of Malta, made a speech in London in which he is reported to have said that during those days of terrific blasting he "had been unfailingly conscious of the Lord's impending return."

Three Things That Will Happen When He Comes

In this preliminary discussion we touch briefly on but three things that are connected with His second coming.

First, the righteous dead will be resurrected. "The Lord himself shall descend from heaven with a shout, with the voice of the archangel, and with the trump of God: and the dead in Christ shall rise first." 1 Thessalonians 4:16.

Second, the righteous living will be taken up. "Then we which are alive and remain shall be caught up together with them in the clouds, to meet the Lord in the air: and so shall we ever be with the Lord." Verse 17.

Third, the bodies of all the righteous will be changed. This is made plain beyond controversy in these words: "Our conversation is in heaven; from whence also we look for the Saviour, the Lord Jesus Christ: who shall change our vile body, that it might be fashioned like unto his glorious body, according to the working whereby he is able even to subdue all things unto himself." Philippians 3:20, 21.

Thus our bodies will be changed to resemble Jesus' glorious body, His resurrected body, which was very real. He Himself said, "A spirit hath not flesh and bones, as ye see me have." Luke 24:39. And again we read in 1 John

3:2, "When he shall appear, we shall be like him." Those who are alive and ready for His coming will be changed "in a moment, in the twinkling of an eye, . . . and this mortal shall put on immortality." 1 Corinthians 15:52-54. The righteous dead will also be changed. "So also is the resurrection of the dead. It is sown in corruption; it is raised in incorruption." Verse 42. Our loved ones whose bodies were twisted and racked with pain, mutilated or wasted by disease, disfigured by accident and tragedy, will come forth from the tomb with the bloom of eternal health.

The living followers of Christ, whether tormented by various physical ills or blessed with normal health, will feel a surging charge of new life in every fiber of their being. United with their loved ones from whom they have been separated by death or distance, and seeing their Redeemer face to face, the saved of all ages shall meet to part no more when Christ comes back to earth again.

The Book and the Man

The Bible is the Word of God written by man. Christ is the Son of God born of woman. The Bible is thus divine and human. Jesus is also divine and human—the Son of God and the Son of man. The central figure of this divine and human Book is the divine and human Christ. His first coming was forecast by prophets and heralded by that prophet of prophets, John the Baptist. His second coming was prophesied by Christ Himself, and "by the mouth of all his holy prophets since the world began." Acts 3:21.

The first coming of Christ is like the planting, seed-sowing time. The second coming is like the harvest. The first coming brought the cross. The second coming brings the crown. It is the glad harvesttime, the happy wedding day, the magnificent coronation hour, an event of splendor the like of which the universe has never witnessed. Little wonder that Paul wrote, "Looking for that blessed hope, and the glorious appearing of the great God and our Saviour Jesus Christ." Titus 2:13.

"He will gather the wheat in His garner,
But the chaff will He scatter away;
Then how shall we stand in the judgment
Of the great resurrection day?"

—HARRIET B. M'KEEVER.

The answer to that heart-searching question is ever the same. We may wear the crown of everlasting life then, if we surrender in simple faith to the Christ of the cross now. This surrender includes the taking up of our cross and following Him daily in loving service and in advancing light.

To the rich young man Jesus said, "Go sell and give, and thou shalt have treasure in heaven: and come and follow Me." But the young man was sad at the saying. His answer was No. A religious leader said to Jesus, "I will follow you anywhere." Jesus answered, "Foxes have holes, and the birds of the air have nests; but the Son of man hath not where to lay his head." When the man heard that he changed his mind. Another disciple said, "I will follow thee, but I must stay with my father until he dies. After that I will go." Said Jesus, "Let the dead bury their dead." He knew that the man was only making an excuse for not taking up his cross.

When Christ called Peter and Andrew from their fishing, "they straightway left their nets, and followed him." Matthew 4:20. When He called James and John from their fishing smack, "They immediately left the ship and their father, and followed him." Verse 22. Seeing Matthew sitting at the tax-collection booth, He said to him, "Follow me. And he arose, and followed him." Matthew 9:9.

When Peter "said unto him, Behold, we have forsaken all, and followed thee; what shall we have therefore?" Jesus replied that they would have everlasting life, and sit on twelve thrones judging the twelve tribes of Israel. (Matthew 19:27-29.) "If we suffer, we shall also reign with him: if we deny him, he also will deny us." 2 Timothy 2:12.

CHAPTER 24

Christ's Ten Signs of His Second Coming

"THIS IS the thing that puzzles me," said one man: "Christ foretold His Second Advent and counseled His followers to be ready. His disciples preached of His return. Today thousands of voices unite in giving the message. Yet nearly two thousand years have passed, and He is not here. Might not two thousand more years go by and He not come? Even ten thousand years? What can we actually know about the matter, if anything?"

This is a fair question. For an answer we turn to the testimony of Christ, who declared, "I will come again." John 14:3. What did He say regarding the signs of His return?

A few days before Calvary, Jesus made a dire pronouncement. To the Jews He said, "Behold, your house is left unto you desolate." Matthew 23:38. Immediately following are these significant words: "And Jesus went out, and departed from the temple: and his disciples came to him for to shew him the buildings of the temple. And Jesus said unto them, See ye not all these things? verily I say unto you, There shall not be left here one stone upon another, that shall not be thrown down. And as he sat upon the mount of Olives, the disciples came unto him privately, saying, Tell us, when shall these things be? and what shall be the sign of thy coming, and of the end of the world?" Matthew 24:1-3.

Let us bear in mind the picture. Jesus here forecast the utter desolation of Jerusalem, deserted by God and destroyed by man. The stunned disciples could not conceive of such a thing except in connection with Christ's glorious kingdom and the end of the world.

Jesus therefore proceeded to give to His disciples ten great signs. Some of these signs relate to the destruction of Jerusalem, which took place forty years later in A.D. 70. Some of the signs referred to His second coming. Some are applicable to both—most of them, in fact. We shall here consider ten specific signs that were to be seen in the period of the last days, just before the second coming of our blessed Lord. Not one or two signs, but ten of them—signs given, not by Peter and Paul, or James and John, but by Jesus the Son of God Himself.

1. False Christs and False Prophets

Immediately after the question of His disciples, "What shall be the sign of thy coming?" we read this statement: "And Jesus answered and said unto them, Take heed that no man deceive you. For many shall come in my name, saying I am Christ; and shall deceive many." Matthew 24:4, 5.

Some years ago there was a man in southern California who claimed to be the Messiah. As many as twenty thousand people were said to gather at his night sessions on low foothills, and many remained unto the break of day. Miraculous healings of the crippled, ill, deaf, dumb, and blind were reported. This type of deception Jesus foretold. Said He again, "There shall arise false Christs and false prophets, and shall shew great signs and wonders; insomuch that, if it were possible, they shall deceive the very elect." Verse 24. There will undoubtedly be the most spectacular manifestations in this direction, and not always by some apparently fanatical person.

Literally millions are today being blown about by every wind of doctrine, because they innocently trust in miracles and wonder working as a sign of truth. Christ made it clear that this cannot safely be done. Said He, "Behold, I have told you before." Verse 25. In Revelation, Christ predicts that a power "maketh fire come down from heaven on the earth in the sight of men, and deceiveth them that dwell on the earth by the means of those miracles which he had power to do." Revelation 13: 13, 14.

You may be invited to go to the desert to see a Messiah. "Go not forth," said Christ. (Matthew 24:26.) Someone may say to you, "Christ appeared to a group of people in a darkened, secret chamber, and His form glowed with celestial light." Said Christ, "Believe it not." (Verse 26.)

It is vital to remember that deception concerning the truth and nature of His coming will be widespread among the very people interested in that event. Let not your faith in the second coming of Christ and your desire for sanctification lead you to allow miracle working to determine what you believe or do. "Sanctify them through thy truth: thy word is truth." John 17:17. Does God never work a miracle? Yes. But we here emphasize and reemphasize that miracles, or apparent miracles, are not to determine our faith and actions. Widespread interest in "great signs and wonders," performed through men, resulting in millions being deceived thereby—this is the first sign which Jesus gave of His second coming. You may witness it on every hand as more and more persons become interested in Christ's return.

2. World Wars

"How could war be a dependable sign of the coming of Christ?" asks one. Have there not been "wars and rumours of wars" for all recorded time? The answer to the last question must be Yes. It has been said that war has been on the average thirteen times as prevalent as peace. Men have figured out the number of warless years, and they have been comparatively few. Therefore, mere war and talk about war cannot, alone, be a sign of Christ's return.

We turn to His own words: "Ye shall hear of wars and rumours of wars: see that ye be not troubled: for all these things must come to pass, but the end is not yet." Matthew 24:6. Jesus Himself was saying, "Wars and rumors of wars will mark the period preceding My return, but these are but a prelude to something vastly greater." Then He proceeds, "For nation shall rise against nation, and kingdom against kingdom." Verse 7.

How clear is the picture! Wars and rumors of wars had always been part of a sinful world. But the real and new war sign was to be *world war!* War on an international scale, global war, war so completely dwarfing everything preceding it that it would stand apart from all recorded warfare. It would constitute a sign of His coming.

On June 28, 1914, Archduke Francis Ferdinand, nephew of the emperor of Austria and heir to the throne, was, with his wife, assassinated in the streets of Sarajevo, capital of Bosnia. The fuse to World War I was lighted that day. The slaying was performed by men who were members of the Serbian race. So, one month later, Austria declared war on Serbia, and World War I began.

It has been estimated that before the terrible catastrophe was over, seven eighths of the world was at war. Nearly sixty million men were under arms. Over ten million soldiers were killed, as many civilians were dead, and millions of war widows, orphans, and refugees were left as an aftermath. The financial cost has been reckoned at from two hundred to four hundred billion dollars, depending on what items were included. The whole thing was so different, so gigantic, so staggering, that great men could only throw up their hands and say, "The curtain has been rung down upon a world never to be seen again, and has gone up on a new age."

A brief twenty years slipped by. Just long enough for a completely new crop of soldiers to come upon the stage of action, men who remembered nothing of war. Then with blitzkrieg suddenness came the sickening shock of World War II. The Bank of International Settlements of Basel, Switzerland, gives the cost of this conflict as $1,352,000,000,000. This is about four times the cost of World War I, as given by the same source. In fact, it has been said that it cost 75 cents to kill one soldier in Caesar's time, and $50,000 to kill one soldier in World War II. Taking the general estimate of twenty million men killed in World War II, and the total cost as above presented, you may easily figure the cost at $67,600 per man killed. It was at this fabulous cost in money, and the yet greater cost in suffering and loss, that the world sacrificed twenty million of its young men in that wild orgy of blood, fire, and explosives. The earth and sea and sky never before witnessed such widespread and violent destruction by war. "It shall be a sign," Christ declared.

In 1938, just before World War II, the *World Almanac and Book of Facts,* on page 710, gave this statement, "After an analysis of 902 wars and 1,615 internal disturbances in 2,500 years, Professor Pitirim A. Sorokin, chairman of the Department of Sociology at Harvard, reports that the war index for the twentieth century reached 'a total eight times greater than all the preceding centuries.'" And we remember that this did not include World War II and those following it.

The year 1945 marked not only the end of World War II but the discovery, manufacture, and use of the atom bomb. It was first dropped for destructive purposes on the

Japanese city of Hiroshima on August 6, 1945. According to one writer, "in a city of two hundred and forty-five thousand, nearly a hundred thousand people had been killed or doomed at one blow; a hundred thousand more were hurt."—JOHN HERSEY, "Hiroshima," *The New Yorker,* Aug. 31, 1946, p. 22. On the second anniversary of that terrible day a message from General Douglas MacArthur was read to the remnant of Hiroshima. "He warned 'all men of all races that the harnessing of nature's forces in furtherance of war's destructiveness will progress until the means are at hand to exterminate the human race.'"—*Time,* Aug. 18, 1947. Courtesy of *Time,* copyright Time, Inc., 1947.

According to the Smythe report, 1945 was the year when civilization "acquired the means to commit suicide at will." In other words, not only was World War II a world war, but it unleashed forces that could bring world destruction. This awful possibility has caused a universal cry among the great leaders of the world, "We must have one world or no world!"

We thus clearly see that Jesus foresaw the last-day development of world wars. He stated in the simplest language that these conflicts would be a sign of His second coming. Where dwells a man today who has not read about, heard of, or seen this sign?

3. Widespread Famine

Said Christ, "There shall be famines." Matthew 24:7. Again, this sign would have to involve famines on an unusual scale to constitute a clear indication of Christ's return.

After World War I, China's great famine numbered in its grip fifteen million starving and three million dead. Russia's famine, according to the noted explorer Nansen, was the "most appalling in the recorded history of man."

The unspeakable tragedies of that disaster will probably never be fully told till the judgment day. Until then we have but the spotted reports of noted correspondents.

China's famine of 1936 in the Szechwan Province was the result of years of feeding armies and robbing harvests. Dispatches reported that "15,000,000 peasants—a number equal to the entire population of New York State, Connecticut, and Vermont—have crawled into their mud-huts to perish of hunger. Others, driven by despair, are selling their wives for thirty cents' worth of rice, their young daughters for a dollar."—*The Literary Digest,* May 9, 1936, p. 16.

In connection with and following World War II widespread famine conditions prevailed. Reliable authorities estimated that the grizzly specter of starvation haunted 140,000,000 in Europe, and 500,000,000 in the world. In 1943 Hallett Abend estimated that of the 604,000,000 in Germany and German-occupied countries, 10 per cent were "already doomed to die of starvation or of diseases resulting from malnutrition."—"Millions Must Starve," *The Saturday Evening Post,* Oct. 23, 1943, p. 22. On October 31, 1943, in an editorial the New York *Times* reported that in the province of Bengal, India, people were dying of starvation, cholera, and dysentery at the rate of almost 100,000 a week.

The world food problem has not been solved. In *Time,* May 31, 1948, are these ominous words: "'It is not the atomic bomb, but the food crisis that may destroy us.' . . . In the race between population and food supply . . . population is winning. . . . Harvests that would have seemed bountiful ten years ago are inadequate now." (Courtesy of *Time,* copyright Time, Inc., 1948.) These are statements of Sir John Boyd Orr, who was at the time director general of the United Nations Food and Agricultural Organization.

The simple facts seem to be that there are about four billion acres of tillable land in the world. For one man to feed and care for himself properly, it requires on an average two and a half acres. But with 2,250,000,000 people there is actually less than two acres per person. Two thirds of the world is always undernourished, says Mr. Orr.

But this is not all. The land is getting poorer and poorer. Then population is becoming greater and greater, despite war, famine, disease, accident, suicide, murder, and old age. It is increasing at the rate of twenty million every year. In less than one hundred years it is estimated that the population will be doubled. Can the food supply be doubled? Already in many places men are pumping out more water from the earth than nature is putting back in. There is soil-building and erosion control, but this provides no foreseeable answer. One writer speaks of "universal hunger." Jesus Christ predicted worldwide war and world food shortage as signs of His coming.

4. Pestilences

"There shall be famines, and pestilences." Matthew 24:7.

In 1918, the year that marked the end of World War I, the influenza epidemic struck, taking a toll of an estimated eighteen million lives. In addition to disease epidemics, we face two other grim possibilities of pestilence. One is deliberate man-made famine. This may be caused by certain governments' denying seed to certain farmers in order to force them into line with government policies. Or it may be brought about by the spread of plant-destroying germs, insects, and chemicals. Where there is hunger pestilence follows. The other horrifying outlook is possible directly produced pestilence and disease.

"The most terrible of all poisons known to man, the

toxin of the botulinus bacillus, now can be produced in quantity by the U.S. Chemical Warfare Service. The substance has long been known to scientists, but this is the first time it has been sufficiently purified to become a dread weapon of war. Botulinus toxin is a thousand times more deadly than mustard gas; so that an ounce could kill, swiftly and quietly, every single person in the United States and Canada. . . .

"Spread through the air in tiny and invisible droplets by planes or by the poisoning of the water supply of an entire city, the toxin can be used to decimate entire populations. . . .

"Biological warfare . . . might conceivably include attacking enemy troops or peoples with virus diseases, as for example, influenza, infantile paralysis, smallpox, and sleeping sickness; with such bacteria as cholera, anthrax, dysentery, leprosy and typhoid; with rickettsia-like typhus, Rocky Mountain spotted fever; or with body-infiltrating fungi and tissue-eating yeasts."—JACK SCHUYLER in *America,* Feb. 21, 1948.

To His disciples Christ put it in one word, *"pestilences."* That the world, despite medical science, is yet to pass through unbelievably horrifying experiences with pestilence seems a definite certainty. "Signs of My return," said Jesus.

5. EARTHQUAKES

"There shall be famines, and pestilences, and earthquakes, in divers places." Matthew 24:7.

Near the end of 1946 an earthquake devastated a part of Japan. It is reported that Dr. Hagiwara, leading seismologist, estimated the force of this earthquake as equal to one hundred thousand atom bombs.

In 1945, B-29 bombers swarmed over the city of Fukui, Japan, and its thousands of shanty buildings were destroyed by blast and fire. Three years later the city was

60 per cent rebuilt of substantial structures for permanency. Then it came—the earthquake in 1948.

Carl Mydans, *Time* correspondent, wrote: "There wasn't any warning—the floor just pushed up under us, and great chunks of wall and ceiling began to crash about us. . . . We flung ourselves on the compound lawn, but the earth shook so violently that some of us were jerked upright and bounced about like popcorn. . . . Ripping, crackling and crushing sounds. . . . Yellow dust rose over the city, and suddenly a strong, crazy wind blew up, first from one direction, then another. After a moment's silence came the small voices of human beings—shouts and cries which rose into a din throughout the city. . . . A thin grey wisp of smoke crawled up behind the sagging department store. It grew larger. The fire had begun. . . . The people of Fukui say that tonight's quake was worse than the B-29's."—*Time,* July 12, 1948, Courtesy of *Time,* copyright Time, Inc., 1948.

After World War I China was rocked by a quake in 1920 that took a toll of 200,000 lives. Three years later in 1923 came the terrible quake in Japan. In that awful catastrophe 150,000 human beings perished. In ten years the world saw its greatest war to that time, its two greatest famines, and two of its most devastating earthquakes.

Up to date we know of no plans for man-made earthquakes to destroy nations, but we are sure that if such a thing could be worked out, this too would be added to the list of possibilities. We do know that earthquakes have increased, as shown by the following report from the British Association for the Advancement of Science:

First Century A.D.	15	Destructive	Earthquakes
Sixteenth Century A.D.	253	"	"
Eighteenth Century A.D. ..	640	"	"
Nineteenth Century A.D. ..	2,119	"	"

Said the Saviour, "There shall be . . . earthquakes in divers places"; that is, in many places. He predicted an increase in earthquakes as a sign of His coming.

6. Persecution of God's People

World wars, famines, pestilences, and earthquakes in divers places—"All these things are the beginning of sorrows," said Christ. (Verse 8.) Reading on, we find these words: "Then shall they deliver you up to be afflicted, and shall kill you: and ye shall be hated of all nations for my name's sake." Verse 9.

Not only here but in other scriptures is it made plain that freedom will be denied to the people of God in the closing days of the world's history. Christians should not court persecution. One may be persecuted and not be a true Christian. Persecution, standing alone, is not a sign that the persecuted is a child of God. But Jesus did predict affliction for His people in the day just before His return. Much could here be said on this matter, but it will be touched upon in later chapters.

7. Abounding Wickedness, Declining Love

"Then shall many be offended, and shall betray one another. . . . And because iniquity shall abound, the love of many shall wax cold." Verses 10-12. The Revised Standard Version reads, "Because wickedness is multiplied, most men's love will grow cold." Verse 12.

The Son of God thus bears witness that abounding, multiplied wickedness would so overflow the world that most men would be swept along with it. Social pressure is a tremendous thing. Children incline to do what other children do. Young people lean to the thinking and acting of other youth. Everyone does thus and so because everyone else does thus and so. Jesus pleaded for His followers,

"I pray not that thou shouldest take them out of the world, but that thou shouldest keep them from the evil." John 17:15.

He knew what would come in the last days. While still answering His disciples' question about signs of His coming, He said, "As the days of Noe were, so shall also the coming of the Son of man be. For as in the days that were before the flood they were eating and drinking, marrying and giving in marriage, until the day that Noe entered into the ark." Matthew 24:37, 38. Concerning those dark days before the Flood, we read, "God saw that the wickedness of man was great in the earth, and that every imagination of the thoughts of his heart was only evil continually." Genesis 6:5.

There are three ugly tragedies in these portrayals of the Book of God, and one gleaming hope.

The first tragedy is that wickedness is multiplied and iniquity abounds. So much so that the wisest statesmen of our time are concerned for the very existence of civilization.

The second and sadder tragedy is that most professed followers of Christ are experiencing a waning and dying love for Him. Swept along by the current of evil, they become less and less like Christ and more and more like the world. They seek the same pleasures, bet on the same horses, gamble with the same cards, call for the same liquor, buy the same cigarettes, watch or listen to the same prize fights, attend the same movies, read the same comics, follow the same murder mysteries, fawn over the same actors and actresses, pick up the same profanity, dance to the same music, and divorce in the same courts. Prayer gives place to pining for the world, and the Bible gives place to the daily newspaper and fiction.

The third tragedy is that Christians who first betray themselves and their Christ will one day betray His followers. "Then shall many be offended, and shall betray one another, and shall hate one another." Matthew 24:10.

What is the gleam of hope painted into this modern scene more than one thousand nine hundred years ago? "He that shall endure unto the end, the same shall be saved." Verse 13. There are those who in this time of mounting evil will endure unto the end. With a faith founded upon Christ and fed by the Word of God, they "hold fast the beginning of our confidence stedfast unto the end," refusing to cast it away, for it "hath great recompence of reward." Hebrews 3:14; 10:35. "What is a man profited, if he shall gain the whole world, and lose his own soul?" is the urgent question of the Christ who gave us the signs of His coming.

"Drifting away from the Saviour,
Casting reproach on the Lord;
Drifting away from His temple,
Heeding no longer His word."

A few years ago an accomplished man of letters committed suicide. He left a note telling why. He was not ill. He had not failed. He was not a disgrace. He had friends, home, and fortune. But he said, "My spiritual home has destroyed itself. After one's sixtieth year unusual powers are needed to make a wholly new beginning. Those that I possess have been exhausted by years of wandering."

"Drifting away from the Saviour,
Lonely and helpless thou art;
Drifting away from His people,
Ever so dear to His heart.

. . . .

"Drifting away from the Saviour,
Still He is mindful of thee.
Come unto Him and believing,
Pardoned through grace thou shalt be."

—FANNY J. CROSBY.

8. Sun, Moon, and Stars

As Christ continued giving the signs of His coming He said in Luke 21:25, "There shall be signs in the sun, and in the moon, and in the stars."

In Matthew 24:29 the timing of such signs is more definitely given: "Immediately after the tribulation of those days shall the sun be darkened, and the moon shall not give her light."

When was the great tribulation here spoken of? There was one great period of tribulation in connection with the siege and fall of Jerusalem in A.D. 70. Then there followed the satanic persecution of the early Christians by pagan Rome. But neither of these could be the one here referred to, for the simple reason that they took place not less than fifteen hundred years ago. They could not be signs of the second coming of Christ.

The other great tribulation came especially under the later centuries of what is sometimes called the Dark Ages, as far as the church is concerned. For 1260 years, or from A.D. 538 to A.D. 1798, the professed Christian church rode high in the affairs of the world.

In connection with the rise of the Protestant Reformation, and in order to halt its progress, the great ecclesiastical system of that day set up the Inquisition. This was a church court to try those charged with heresy. It was not until 1542 that this court became more or less the supreme tribunal for the whole church. This was just four years before the death of Martin Luther. Persecution, which in preceding centuries had been more or less spotted, now spread all over Europe. Millions perished because they dared to believe contrary to the doctrines of the church in power.

Jesus said, "Except those days should be shortened, there should no flesh be saved: but for the elect's sake those days shall be shortened." Verse 22. God had set the time for this persecuting power as 1260 years (which ended in 1798, as we shall see), and Jesus' prophecy indicated that persecution would be cut off in the latter time of this period. Note His prophecy in Mark 13:24: "But in those days after that tribulation, the sun shall be darkened." Thus persecution was to cease before the year A.D. 1798. Between the time of the ending of the persecution and the date 1798, the sun was to be darkened, and the moon was to withhold its light.

When did the persecution cease? One is fully safe in saying not later than A.D. 1776. The Protestant Reformation could not be stopped. The persecution by the Jesuits had been suppressed. Freedom was avowed in the United States. The day of liberty was dawning for the world.

Was there a darkening of the sun in this short period? The answer is Yes, on May 19, 1780, or eighteen years before the ending of the 1260-year period in 1798, and shortly after persecution had practically ceased. What records do we have of this event? They are numerous, and space will permit but a brief picture.

From an eyewitness in Massachusetts comes this description: "In the morning the sun rose clear, but was soon overcast. The clouds became lowery, and from them, black and ominous, as soon as they appeared, lightning flashed, thunder rolled, and a little rain fell. Toward nine o'clock, the clouds became thinner, and assumed a brassy or coppery appearance, and earth, rocks, trees, buildings, water, and persons were changed by this strange, unearthly light. A few minutes later, a heavy black cloud spread over the entire sky, except a narrow rim at the horizon, and it was as dark as it usually is at nine o'clock on a summer evening.

"Fear, anxiety, and awe gradually filled the minds of the people. Women stood at the door, looking out upon the dark landscape; men returned from their labor in the fields; the carpenter left his tools, the blacksmith his forge, the tradesman his counter. Schools were dismissed, and tremblingly the children fled homeward. Travelers put up at the nearest farmhouse. 'What is coming?' queried every lip and heart. It seemed as if a hurricane was about to dash across the land, or as if it was the day of the consummation of all things.

"Candles were used; and hearth-fires shone as brightly as on a moonless evening in autumn. . . . Fowls retired to their roosts and went to sleep, cattle gathered at the pasture-bars and lowed, frogs peeped, birds sang their evening songs, and bats flew about. But the human knew that night had not come."—*The Essex Antiquarian,* vol. 3, no. 4 (April, 1899), pp. 53, 54.

What of the night following this unusual day? I quote, "Nor was the darkness of the night less uncommon and terrifying than that of the day; notwithstanding there was almost a full moon, no object was discernible but by the help of some artificial light, which, when seen from the neighboring houses and other places at a distance, appeared through a kind of Egyptian darkness which seemed almost impervious to the rays." —Thomas' *Massachusetts Spy,* vol. 10, no. 472 (May 25, 1780).

Another eyewitness wrote, "'I could not help conceiving at the time, that if every luminous body in the universe had been shrouded in impenetrable shades, or struck out of existence, the darkness could not have been more complete. A sheet of white paper held within a few inches of the eyes was equally invisible with the blackest velvet.'"—Letter of Dr. Samuel Tenney, dated Exeter, New Hampshire, December, 1785; cited in *Collections of Massachusetts Historical Society,* vol. 1, 1792.

This is another picture: "'The darkness somewhat increased all day, and before time of sunset, was so intense that no object whatever could be distinguished. Anxiously and tremblingly, people waited for the full moon to rise at nine o'clock, and even little children with strained eyes, sat silently watching for its beautiful beams to appear. But they were disappointed, the darkness being unaffected by the moon.' "—REV. W. R. COCHRANE, *History of the Town of Antrim, New Hampshire,* pp. 58, 59.

Thus the sun was darkened and the moon did not give her light. And history records the day as "The Dark Day." Noah Webster's dictionary, edition 1869, gives this: "The Dark Day, May 19, 1780—so called on account of a remarkable darkness on that day extending over all New England. . . . The true cause of this remarkable phenomenon is not known."

Another writer says, significantly, "The causes of these phenomena are unknown. They certainly were not the result of eclipses."—*The Guide to Knowledge, or Repertory of Facts,* edited by Robert Sears, p. 428.

Was this darkness natural or supernatural? I do not here attempt to decide that matter. The sign came at the right time, and whether natural or supernatural, or a combination of both, it seems the definite fulfillment of the Saviour's prophecy.

I submit this thought from Dr. Samuel Stearns: "The primary cause must be imputed to Him that walketh through the circuit of heaven, who stretcheth out the heaven like a curtain, who maketh the clouds His chariot, who walketh upon the wings of the wind. It was He, at whose voice the stormy winds are obedient, that commanded these exhalations to be collected and condensed together, that with them He might darken both the day and the night; which darkness was, perhaps, not only a token of His indignation against the crying iniquities and abominations of the people, but an omen of some future destruction."—Letter in *Independent Chronicle,* Boston, June 22, 1780.

The next sign was the falling of the stars, or the great meteoric shower of November 13, 1833. "And the stars shall fall from heaven," said Christ. Matthew 24:29. This naturally does not refer to the falling of the great suns of the sky, or of the planets, but of the meteors which strike our atmosphere and burn as they fall. Falling stars, or shooting stars, we call them. This grand display was seen over all the United States, a part of Mexico, and the West Indies.

A writer on astronomy gives this description: "On the night of November 12-13, 1833, a tempest of falling stars broke over the earth. North America bore the brunt of its pelting. From the Gulf of Mexico to Halifax, until daylight with some difficulty put an end to the display, the sky was scored in every direction with shining tracks and illuminated with majestic fireballs."—AGNES M. CLERKE, *History of Astronomy in the Nineteenth Century,* p. 328.

A Yale professor gives us this picture: "The morning of November 13th, 1833, was rendered memorable by an exhibition of the phenomenon called shooting stars, which was probably more extensive and magnificent than any similar one hitherto recorded. . . . Probably no celestial phenomenon has ever occurred in this country, since its first settlement, which was viewed with so much admiration and delight by one class of spectators, or with so much astonishment and fear by another class. For some time after the occurrence the 'meteoric phenomenon' was the principal topic of conversation in every circle."—DENISON OLMSTED in *The American Journal of Science and Arts* vol. 25 (1834), pp. 363, 364.

An observer in Missouri wrote: "Though there was no moon, when we first beheld them, their brilliancy was so great that we could, at times, read common-sized print without much difficulty, and the light which they afforded was much whiter than that of the moon, in the clearest and coldest night, when the ground is covered with snow. . . . There was a grand, peculiar, and indescribable gloom on all around, an awe-inspiring sublimity on all above: while

> 'the sanguine flood
> Rolled broad slaughter o'er the plains of heaven,
> And Nature's self did seem to totter on the brink of time!'

". . . There was scarcely a space in the firmament which was not filled at every instant with these falling stars, nor on it, could you in general perceive any particular difference in appearance; still at times they would shower down in groups—calling to mind the 'fig tree casting her untimely figs when shaken by a mighty wind.'" —Letter from Bowling Green, Missouri, to Professor Silliman, in *The American Journal of Science and Arts,* vol. 25 (1834), p. 382.

The writer just quoted, in referring to the fig tree, was thinking of this prophecy in Revelation 6:13: "The stars of heaven fell unto the earth, even as a fig tree casteth her untimely figs, when she is shaken of a mighty wind."

One eyewitness, with this in mind, says:

"The stars fell 'even as a fig tree casteth her untimely figs, when she is shaken of a mighty wind.' Here is the exactness of the prophet. The falling stars did not come as if from *several* trees shaken, but from *one.* Those which appeared in the east fell toward the east; those which appeared in the north fell toward the north; those which appeared in the west fell toward the west; and those which appeared in the south (for I went out of my residence into the park) fell toward the south; and they fell, not as the ripe fruit falls; far from it; but they *flew,* they were *cast,* like the unripe fig, which at first refuses to leave the branch; and when it does break its hold, flies swiftly, straight off descending; and in the multitude falling, some cross the track of others, as they are thrown with more or less force.

"Such was the appearance of the above phenomenon to the inmates of my house. I walked into the park with two gentlemen of Pearl Street, feeling and confessing that this scene had never been figured to our minds by any book or mortal, save only by the prophet."—A correspondent in the *New York Journal of Commerce,* vol. 8, no. 534 (Nov. 16, 1833).

Was this a supernatural event? Again I say, "It does not matter." What does matter is that Jesus Christ selected a period of the earth's history, and precisely forecast a falling of the stars which would stand out so distinctly as to be a matter of general record and a sign of His return. The fact that more than a century has gone by since the falling of the stars merely adds to the significance of the times in which we live.

9. A World of Fear

"There shall be . . . upon the earth distress of nations, with perplexity; . . . men's hearts failing them for fear, and for looking after those things which are coming on the earth: for the powers of heaven shall be shaken." Luke 21:25, 26.

Fear! This is the word that has been written large within the heart of modern man. The most intelligent, the most highly informed, and those entrusted with the greatest responsibility of world leadership know that it is time to fear. Even when some say there is nothing to fear but fear, large sums are spent and great efforts are put forth for fear that men will not have enough fear. Leaders fear what is coming, and are afraid the people do not understand how terribly dangerous the situation is.

&H Pub. Assn. Arlo Greer, Artist

has not left man to grope his way to heaven in the dark. The traveler with road map—the Bible—may easily follow the signs on the highway to heaven.

 Lester Qua

We have entered the Atomic Age. It is an age for foreboding and fear. Our ho and great cities, which we thought to be safe from attack, are now vulnera

Dorothy Thompson, commentator, says: "The scientists are alarmed. They rush about warning that it is quite possible that the world may come to an end. People believe them, but it is almost as though they did not care much if the world came to an end. I never remember anything like this before in America."

Dr. Harold C. Urey, atomic bomb scientist, said in a Town Meeting of the Air broadcast, "I am the apostle of doom. I am still a frightened man, and I wish you to be frightened."

Robert Hutchins, noted educator of the University of Chicago, in a widely quoted radio address, declared: "It is very late. Perhaps nothing can save us. But the handwriting on the wall is plain enough. It says to the people of the earth, 'unite or die.' " He gave his opinion that some solution would need to be found within five years if the world was to be saved from disaster at some time not too far distant. "There is very little time remaining," he said.

President Truman was quoted in the New York *Times* as saying that if we had another war, "nothing would be left but a world reduced to rubble. Gone would be our hope for the greatest age in the history of mankind."

The late Field Marshal Jan Smuts of South Africa asserted, "To-day there is no time to think things out. If we are not prepared we cannot recover ourselves or retrieve ourselves. To-morrow the situation may be irretrievably lost."—Cited in *Cape Times,* March 2, 1948, p. 1.

Dr. Cyrus Forster Garbett, archbishop of York, wrote, "The Biblical declaration that the end of the world will come suddenly is driven home to us with fresh meaning. . . . The writing on the wall of threatened doom and destruction can now be read clearly by all thoughtful men."—Diocesan letter, November, 1945.

So men are afraid—afraid of war with atomic bombs and disease-spreading bombs, and of possible utter devasta-

T. K. Martin, Art

He who inspired the prophets to write the Holy Scriptures has attended its rapid sp around the world. The gospel is now read in more than 1,000 languages and dia

tion and destruction; afraid of peace with its perils of debt, its class struggles, its flouting of the laws of God and man, and its increasing sense of insecurity. Never has government tried to do so much for people. Never were people more dissatisfied and so disposed to seek protection from the cradle to the grave. More and more people are climbing into the "lap of government" for security.

Men talk about "the end of life on this star," "time running out," "the end of the world," and "doom and destruction."

What does this all mean? Two things. One, that the prophecy of Jesus Christ is being fulfilled before our very eyes, and His coming is drawing nigh, though the day and hour no man knows. The other is that men's hearts are full of the fear of man and things because they have lost the fear of God.

Carl Hambro, president of the much-talked-of League of Nations, is quoted from back in 1939 as saying, "Here at Geneva we have every fear but the fear of God." So it is. The fear that men need they do not have, and the fears they have, come as a result of not having the one fear that they need. If men loved God and feared to sin against His holy will, what a change would be seen in the picture of the world! "The fear of the Lord is the beginning of wisdom." Psalms 111:10.

10. The Worldwide Gospel

"This gospel of the kingdom shall be preached in all the world for a witness unto all nations; and then shall the end come." Matthew 24:14.

This is the climax of the signs that Jesus gave. Three points are made clear: (1) The gospel was to be preached to all the world in the period covered by the other signs. (2) This would serve as a witness to the nations. There is here no suggestion of world conversion to Christ; in fact, the array of signs already studied indicates the opposite of this idea. (3) When the worldwide witness has been given "then shall the end come."

What are the facts concerning the giving of the simple gospel as it was brought out anew through the Protestant Reformation? There are five things to bear in mind.

First, from the days of Luther when the Reformation really began to move, more than 250 years passed before the churches became really interested in missions; that is, in giving the gospel to *all* the world. This does not indicate that nothing was being accomplished, because even under bitter persecution the Reformation had spread and rooted down. But as for the heathen, that was another thing. It is said that a young man in England rose in a meeting of the clergy. He unburdened his heart about giving the gospel to the heathen. The chairman of the meeting interrupted him and said, "Young man, sit down; when God is pleased to convert the heathen world, He will do it without your help or mine."

The second thing to remember is that a great and mighty change came as the world moved toward the year 1800. "It was then that for the first time since the apostolic period, occurred an outburst of general missionary zeal and activity. Beginning in Great Britain, it soon spread to the Continent and across the Atlantic. It was no mere push of fervor, but a mighty tide set in, which from that day to this has been steadily rising and spreading. . . . It was the plain people, the masses, that now began to pray and give and go, not tarrying in the least for king or prelate to hoist the signal."— DELAVAN L. LEONARD, *A Hundred Years of Missions,* pp. 69, 70.

The providential hour had struck for the gospel to go to *all* the world. The 1260 years of the church's night was to end in 1798. The period of persecution had been cut short. The sun was darkened May 19, 1780. Just twelve years later, in 1792, there was organized the Baptist Missionary Society, which sent William Carey to India the following year.

The date 1792 and the name of William Carey mark the morning of the rising sun of modern missions. Leonard says, "We may speak of the 'Carey Epoch' with every whit as much propriety as of the Luther Reformation. We may as fitly term him the apostle of modern missions as Paul the apostle to the Gentiles."—*Ibid.,* p. 71.

In that same year three Moravian missionaries went to Africa to kindle again the light that flickered at the death of George Schmidt.

In 1795 the London Missionary Society was founded.

In 1797 it sent out five workers, including medical, to Africa.

In 1806 young Samuel Mills entered Williams College at the age of twenty-three, and at the now-famous meeting under a haystack during a thunderstorm sparked the fire of foreign missions in America.

In 1807 the consecrated Robert Morrison, refused passage by the British East India Company, sailed to China from America. The shipping agent cynically remarked, "And so, Mr. Morrison, you really expect that you will make an impression on the idolatry of the great Chinese Empire?" "No, sir," replied Morrison; "I expect GOD will."

In 1808 in a room of old East College, Samuel Mills and his fellows organized what has been called the first foreign missionary society in America. To a friend he said, " 'Though you and I are very little beings, we must not rest satisfied until we have made our influence extend to the remotest corner of this ruined world.' "—CLIFFORD G. HOWELL, *The Advance Guard of Missions,* p. 139.

In 1810 these young men set their plans before the General Association of Independent Ministers of Massachusetts. "Shall we go to a heathen land under the patronage of a mission society of America, or seek connection with a European society?" That was the question. The answer was the birth of the American Board of Commissioners for Foreign Missions, the first such organization west of the Atlantic.

In 1812 Judson, Newell, Hall, and Rice sailed from America to India, following the trail blazed by Carey.

In 1813, at Blantyre, Scotland, there was born a baby boy destined under God to break open furrows in Africa from end to end and side to side. They named him David Livingstone.

In 1816 the American Bible Society was founded.

In 1817 Robert Moffat, just turned twenty-one, landed at Cape Town, South Africa. This is the man who cried out, "O that I had a thousand lives, and a thousand bodies! All of them should be devoted to no other employment but to preach Christ to these degraded, despised, yet beloved mortals!" This is the soul winner who sought the black man Africaner, terror of the land, upon whose head the British Government had set a price of one thousand pounds. Moffat brought him to Christ.

Thus did the mighty tide of missions set in at the very time indicated in Bible prophecy.

A third observation is this. No sooner had this mission movement gained momentum, until hundreds of ministers over the world began to preach with special emphasis the message of Christ's second coming. And why not, since the worldwide preaching of the gospel was to be one of the signs of Christ's return! Dr. Joseph Wolff, alone, preached this truth with power in more than eighty countries.

A fourth significant fact is that at the very time this era of missions got under way modern inventions began to be born. In fact, just six years before Carey sailed to India, two men in Scotland built a steam engine pleasure boat, and John Fitch, of Philadelphia, navigated the Delaware with his steamboat. In 1793, the year Carey sailed, that famous American of Irish blood, Robert Fulton, was tinkering with the notion of applying steam to navigation. In 1807 he stepped into his renowned vessel, the *Clermont,* and drove it nearly 150 miles up the Hudson River to Albany, New York, in 32 hours. Modern power transportation was here in the year that Morrison sailed for China. The God who gave us the gospel of His Son and of His Son's return was preparing the way for a rapid giving of the full gospel to the whole world.

And finally, at the very hour when the era of modern missions was being born, the earth was bringing forth a new nation, destined to be the mightiest ever to appear on the earth. In 1793, when William Carey sailed to India, George Washington was serving his first term as the first President of the United States of America. Here was a rising republic dedicated to the proposition that all men are created equal. From this cradle of freedom consecrated men of religious fervor would travel to lands afar, supported by the prayers and the means of a gracious Providence. Could it be that this nation had some foreordained purpose specified in the prophecies of God?

Christ's Personal Counsel

In closing this survey of Christ's ten signs of His coming, we turn to His own words for personal counsel.

First, His explanation as to the meaning of the signs, "'From the fig tree learn its lesson: as soon as its branch becomes tender and puts forth its leaves, you know that summer is near. So also, when you see all these things, you know that he is near, at the very gates. Truly, I say to you, this generation will not pass away, till all these things take place.'" Matthew 24:32-34, R.S.V. The generation living in the time of those signs connected with the destruction of Jerusalem lived to see the destruction come.

The generation that today may see and recognize the signs (all these things) of Christ's second coming—this generation will not pass until "all these things be fulfilled." When this gospel is "preached in all the world for a witness unto all nations; . . . then shall the end come." Verse 14.

Here is caution and admonition: "Of that day and hour knoweth no man, no, not the angels of heaven, but my Father only." Verse 36. "Watch therefore: for ye know not what hour your Lord doth come." Verse 42.

The Saviour's counsel of comfort and joy is given in these words: "When these things begin to come to pass, then look up, and lift up your heads; for your redemption draweth nigh." Luke 21:28. True believers in the second coming of Christ may agree with the leaders of our day that the world outlook is dark, but they know also that the uplook is bright. "Look up, and lift up your heads," is the Saviour's admonition.

What Difference Does It Make?

What difference does it make whether one concerns himself with this belief? Here is one thought: "We know that, when he shall appear, we shall be like him; for we shall see him as he is. And every man that hath this hope in him purifieth himself, even as he is pure." 1 John 3:2, 3.

Another is given by the apostle Paul in almost his final words to the church before his execution: "Henceforth there is laid up for me a crown of righteousness, which the Lord, the righteous judge, shall give me at that day: and not to me only, but unto all them also that love his appearing." 2 Timothy 4:8.

An understanding love of His second coming will tend to purify the life. Sincere faith in the glorious prospect brings a power to prepare for it. Belief in the soon return of Christ intensifies the desire for quick and thorough preparation. As the moment draws near for the departing of a train, the passengers make doubly sure that everything is ready.

> "Lift up the trumpet, and loud let it ring:
> Jesus is coming again!
> Cheer up, ye pilgrims, be joyful and sing;
> Jesus is coming again!"
>
> —JESSIE E. STROUT.

CHAPTER 25

Christ and the Modern Floodlights

IMAGINE THE present population of the world, more than two billion, seated in a vast outdoor amphitheater. It is in the time just preceding the year 1800. The United States of America has been born as a nation with clear marks of destiny upon it. George Washington is its first President.

It is night. The moon sheds its light upon the two billion human beings seated in the gigantic bowl. Great candles compete with moonbeams to light the central area.

Suddenly a small battery of floodlights is switched on. The moon turns slightly pale. The candles become a little more yellow. A second battery of lights comes on. Then a third. The moon looks sickly. The candlelight is becoming lost in the glow of something men have not seen before. When the floodlights of batteries four and five come on, the light becomes that of open day. Candles are as nothing, and the moon has turned to a small disk of white cloud. While we watch in admiration, the light increases as though the brightest sun moved toward the noonday hour.

The Modern Floodlights of Knowledge

Yes, that is the answer. Those floodlights are modern knowledge, science, and invention. They have changed the world from moonlight and candlelight to the blazing rays of the shining sun.

The marvels of the past century are such as to defy adequate description. It takes libraries to contain the books that make feeble attempts to tell the startling story. It is as though from out the sleeve of darkness some magic hand was thrust, whose fingers turned the switch of genius in a million brains to give us light to flood the world. If George Washington should rise from the dead today, he would be as startled and bewildered as would the patriarch Abraham, who died four thousand years ago.

Switching Off the Lights

Let us start backward, and turn off one at a time the five batteries of floodlights.

First let us go to about 1900, when Theodore Roosevelt was soon to become President of the United States after the assassination of William McKinley. Step up to the switch yourself. Turn off battery No. 5.

Now look around. Your radio is gone. The dial telephone has disappeared. There is no modern automobile highway in the nation, and few persons have ever seen the first automobile models. No motorcycle speeds along anywhere. The airplane is still a dream. Aluminumware is gone from your kitchen, the color and talkies are not used in motion pictures, and nearly all types of electrical appliances have suddenly vanished. We are in a different world—quiet, slow, and dreamy. That is only back to 1900.

We move back twenty more years to 1880, the days of the United States under President James Garfield. Switch off floodlight battery No. 4.

What do we see? Not a boy or girl on a bicycle anywhere, and not a disk plow in any farmer's field. No submarine plumbs the ocean depths. No motion-picture machine throws moving life upon a screen. Carbide lights go out. The recording adding machine leaves every office in the land. The linotype vanishes from the print shop, trolley streetcars from the tracks, and the knot-tying harvester from the fields of grain. The great Marconi is still fifteen years from wireless telegraphy. And, mind you, that's just 1880, yet it seems as though we have traveled a thousand years of time.

Back another twenty years to 1860, the later days of Abraham Lincoln. Switch off battery No. 3. Then what?

The arc light goes out. All dynamos stop. Dynamite is dead. The incandescent light disappears. There are no telephones, differential mowing machines, typewriters, celluloid, air brakes, machine guns, or steel battleships. The light of modern knowledge, science, and invention is growing dim. We seem transferred to another world.

Now back to switch No. 2. It's thirty more years to President Andrew (Old Hickory) Jackson, 1830. Turn that switch, but be prepared.

There are only 122 miles of railroad in the United States. The cars are horse drawn. The speed is eight miles an hour. You cannot buy a vulcanized rubber band, shoot a revolver, send a telegram, sew garments on a machine, fasten your clothes with a safety pin, or strike a phosphorus friction match. Yes, the lights of modern genius are just about out. There is one more switch.

We are back to 1800, or thereabouts, where we began the story of this chapter. If you have the courage, reach up and turn off switch No. 1, the last of the modern floodlights of invention. Meet George Washington.

Do you need a tack? There isn't a machine to make one. Want to buy nails? No machine to make them. Take a trip on a train? No trains, no tracks, no steam engines. Trip on a boat? No screw propellers, no steamboats. Like modern clothes from modern cloth? No wool-carding machines, weaving or thread machinery. Pain around your appendix? Bad news—no anesthetics. What more shall we say? To tell the truth, there is not much more to take away. You have only to throw away your false teeth, blow out the kerosene light, and you are back to moonlight and candles.

WHAT DO THESE THINGS MEAN?

Our modern world stands sharply apart from all history. Knowledge had burst forth like a veritable flood of light. Why?

For one thing, God predicted that these very circumstances would prevail. Here is the prophecy: "But thou, O Daniel, shut up the words, and seal the book, even to the time of the end: many shall run to and fro, and knowledge shall be increased." Daniel 12:4. Consider three thoughts in this verse.

1. The increase of knowledge was to be a sign that the world had reached a period in its history called "the time of the end." This flooding of the world with knowledge was to be a sign that the climax of the ages was at hand.

2. The second thing is that the prophetic book of Daniel was to be unsealed in this same period; that is, prophecies of that book not adequately understood before, or having particular application to our day, were to be presented to the world. That is exactly what has been taking place. Yes, confusion and error may be taught, but God has declared the unsealing of the book. The truth is there and full of meaning for all the world today. Spiritual knowledge was to be increased.

3. The third point is that many were to run "to and fro." Not only were men to search to and fro in the Scriptures, but to run to and fro in the earth.

That is modern transportation. Every person in the United States could ride in automobiles at the same time. Will Rogers said that if America goes to the poorhouse, she will go in automobiles. The sky is heavy with the drone and swoosh of planes. Trains are loaded with people. Bicycles, motorcycles, elevators, escalators, ships, boats, submarines, streetcars, busses, and subways unite with planes and trains to carry more people faster and farther than men ever dreamed of before.

A grandmother of Pittsburgh, Pennsylvania, is traveling to San Francisco to visit her daughter and grandchildren. Another grandmother of Los Angeles is on her way to Baltimore to see her son and grandchildren. These two grandmothers represent the modern, restless, moving, speeding world. "Many shall run to and fro."

Ever-increasing Speed

Man drives an automobile at the hair-raising speed of over four hundred miles an hour. It seems well-nigh impossible. Planes travel faster than the speed of sound, which is about 750 miles an hour. Above that is supersonic speed. There is no use to talk about a mere one thousand miles an hour, for no one can accurately foresee the limit of speed.

Already planes, if sufficiently fueled, could circle the world in one day at the latitude of Winnipeg, Canada. At the National Airport in Washington, D.C., an acute problem of congestion was created at the auto parking circle. People left their cars parked for three or four days while they hopped to Europe and back. Parking meters had to be installed. As children we sang about how "the cow jumped over the moon." Of course, even then we did not believe it. But today he is a hardy soul who will say what can't be done.

God's Purpose

The Bible prophet foresaw our day of marvels. What is Heaven's purpose in this stupendous display of the very fireworks of knowledge? The purpose is twofold.

The one is to open the way for the removal of every barrier between man and man. Through science all men have become neighbors.

The war of 1812-14 might never have been fought had our Congress known of peaceful moves made in the British Parliament only two days before war was declared. At the close of that war the Battle of New Orleans was fought two weeks after the treaty of peace had been signed. The conflicting forces did not know the war was over.

God is giving man one last chance for human understanding, for peace and unity. What man does with this golden opportunity is, of course, quite dependent upon his decisions.

The second and likewise urgent purpose of God is very clear. "He [God] will finish the work, and cut it short in righteousness: because a short work will the Lord make upon the earth." Romans 9:28.

Christ put it in these words: "This gospel of the kingdom shall be preached in all the world for a witness unto all nations; and then shall the end come." Matthew 24:12.

When did the church arouse to the task of going to the world with the gospel? Just when the world was turning from candlelight to the floodlights of modern knowledge and invention—about 1800.

Today missionaries can reach distant points in a very few hours or days. Transportation of every kind is becoming more efficient and universal.

Communication is made by telephone, telegraph, cable, wireless, and radio. The wonders of television are now upon us.

The spread of education makes the press more powerful as the gospel goes forth in more than one thousand tongues. Books, magazines, and pamphlets are scattered as the leaves of autumn.

Modern knowledge and invention were to spring forth in the "time of the end." The prophecies of Daniel were to be opened up to man. The gospel was to be preached in all the world for a *witness* unto all nations. "Then shall the end come," said Jesus. We live in the "time of the end."

Can Knowledge Save Us?

The possession of mere knowledge and the enjoyment of its benefits tend to pride. We bathe in a porcelain tub in a tiled bathroom and feel superior to our forebears, who scrubbed in a wooden tub in the kitchen. But it takes more than good plumbing to save the world. We flick on the modern lights and turn our night into day. Our fathers blew out the kerosene light and went to bed. They blazed trails. We burn up roads. We are smart. They may have been wiser.

Someone said that modern life is a race between education and catastrophe, and it looks as if catastrophe is the black horse. It might more wisely be said that life is the steady teamwork of education and character. If education, science, and information keep on running ahead of character, the vehicle we call civilization will be pulled off into the ditch of destruction.

What Men Are Saying

One of our most popular modern philosophers said something like this in a public address:

"I am called an intellectual. My father was a working man. He rose at five in the morning, went downstairs, built a fire, cooked and ate his breakfast, prepared his lunch, and went to his work. When I consider the sheer character that led him, without complaint, to meet the stern realities of life week in and week out, year in and year out, I always stand in his presence and feel that I am a pigmy."—C. E. M. JOAD, *Philosophy of Our Times*, p. 9.

The atom bomb has pricked our senses, and made our most sober leaders understand that science has given us a handy tool for self-destruction.

"Something is, it is obvious, grievously wrong with our civilization. Science has won for us powers fit for the gods, yet we bring to their use the mentality of school boys or savages."—*Ibid.*

It might be said that modern man has considerable mentality. What he needs is character and spirituality. "Mechanically, we are moving at the speed of a jet plane. Socially, we are driving an oxcart," Eric Johnston is reported as saying. Why not face it? It is the spirit of man that needs fixing.

THE ONLY REMEDY

The remedy is regeneration of men and women. Many think it is federation of religions. It is not so much federation but *operation* of religion—true religion—that is needed.

The Jews were pretty well federated. Of course there were Pharisees and Sadducees. But they held together when it came to sidestepping Samaritans and putting pressure on politicians. They were federated enough to destroy the Prince of Peace, the Man who said, "Ye must be born again."

We read of the necessity of German's experiencing a sense of guilt and confessing the same. The simple truth is that the whole wicked sinning world needs a trip with Nicodemus down to Calvary. The Pharisee sinners need to go. The publican sinners need to go. There is no other place to go. There is where a man may see his sins in the light of what they cost, in the light of divine law and justice, and in the light of love. Comparing ourselves

Russ Harlan, Ar

Our Lord truly said, "I, if I be lifted up from the earth, will draw all men unto m
"Come unto me, all ye that labour and are heavy laden, and I will give you re

among ourselves, we "are not wise." (2 Corinthians 10: 12.)

Down there at Calvary repentance will steal in upon a man. It is the old story of the man who wandered all over the world seeking true repentance. But to no avail. At last he came to Calvary. There he found what he had been longing for. From the cross there came a voice saying, "You will always find Me here, and the way of this cross leads home."

Have you been down to Calvary and found out why Christ was bleeding there?

> "O, never till my latest breath
> Can I forget that look;
> It seemed to charge me with His death,
> Though not a word He spoke."
>
> —ISAAC WATTS.

"Let not the wise man glory in his wisdom." Jeremiah 9:23. Let not the scientist glory in his science, the philosopher in his philosophy, or the inventor in his genius. These cannot save us.

Let the world go down to Calvary, find there repentance and regeneration. When will the world go? Only when we go as individuals. Salvation is not by masses but by individuals.

> "Down at the cross where my Saviour died,
> Down where for cleansing from sin I cried,
> There to my heart was the blood applied.
> Glory to His name."
>
> —E. A. HOFFMAN.

CHAPTER 26

Christ and World Peace

"LET THE leaders contrive to put an end to our present troubles. The treaties of peace are insufficient for their purpose; they may retard, but cannot prevent our misfortunes. We stand in need of some durable plan, which will forever put an end to our hostilities, and unite us by the lasting ties of mutual affection and fidelity."

Thus wrote Isocrates in his *Panegyricus* three hundred and eighty years before the birth of Christ. A durable peace plan! That has been the hope ever springing from the innermost fountain of man's faith and fears.

Bible Prophecies About Peace

Man's desire for peace is as universal as his instinct to worship. The Bible responds to this God-implanted desire of mankind by holding forth the hope of universal peace.

"He maketh wars to cease unto the end of the earth; he breaketh the bow, and cutteth the spear in sunder; he burneth the chariot in the fire." Psalms 46:9.

Isaiah prophesied of a coming Man of Peace, "Unto us a child is born, unto us a son is given: and the government shall be upon his shoulder: and his name shall be called Wonderful, Counsellor, The mighty God, The everlasting Father, The Prince of Peace." Isaiah 9:6.

When this Prince of Peace was born in Bethlehem an angel announced the joyful news to shepherds who kept watch over their flocks that night. "Suddenly there was with the angel a multitude of the heavenly host praising God, and saying, Glory to God in the highest, and on earth peace, good will toward men." Luke 2:13, 14.

When we turn to the closing portion of the Bible's last book we read these hopeful words: "God shall wipe away all tears from their eyes; and there shall be no more death, neither sorrow, nor crying, neither shall there be any more pain: for the former things are passed away." Revelation 21:4.

Since these words are spoken concerning this earth, we face the undeniable and most glorious hope of a warless world someday. God has promised it, and He cannot lie. (Hebrews 6:18.)

Bible Prophecies of War

As we turn to this phase of the question our minds go immediately to Christ's prophecy given in answer to His disciples' question: "What shall be the sign of thy coming, and of the end of the world?" Matthew 24:3.

Said He, "Ye shall hear of wars and rumours. . . . For nation shall rise against nation, and kingdom against kingdom." "And upon the earth distress of nations, with perplexity; . . . men's hearts failing them for fear. . . . And then they shall see the Son of man coming in a cloud with power and great glory." Matthew 24:6, 7; Luke 21:25-27.

Here, under direct questioning, Jesus made it unmistakably plain that war and trouble would continue until His return.

These two references from the book of Revelation are in complete agreement with the record of Matthew and Luke:

"The nations were angry, and thy wrath is come, and the time of the dead, that they should be judged, and that thou shouldest give reward unto thy servants the prophets, and to the saints, and them that fear thy name, small and great." Revelation 11:18.

"They are the spirits of devils, working miracles, which go forth unto the kings of the earth and of the whole world, to gather them to the battle of that great day of God Almighty." Revelation 16:14.

The nations were to be angry in the hour of the judgment, which is in direct connection with the appearing of Christ. (2 Timothy 4:1.) Spirits of devils would incite the leaders of nations to gather for conflict. It is indeed interesting to note that the central point of this last great issue of war is Armageddon in Palestine. (Revelation 16:16.) The land of peace and promise becomes the center of war and conflict involving the whole world.

From the Old Testament comes the prophetic trumpet call of war: "Proclaim ye this among the Gentiles; Prepare war, wake up the mighty men, . . . beat your plowshares into swords, and your pruninghooks into spears: let the weak say, I am strong. . . . Let the heathen be wakened." Joel 3:9-12.

When was this universal awakening of the heathen and worldwide preparation for war to take place? Verse 13 says, "Put ye in the sickle, for the harvest is ripe." Jesus declared the "harvest" to be the "end of the world." (Matthew 13:39.) Joel continues his picture thus: "Multitudes, multitudes in the valley of decision: for the day of the Lord is near in the valley of decision." Joel 3:14.

Bible prophecy paints a picture of worldwide, feverish, satanic war and preparation for war, eventually centering in Palestine. The time is immediately preceding the coming of Christ. Small nations prepare for war. All the heathen awaken and prepare for war.

What have we seen in the past century? Charles D. Hazen, of Columbia University, wrote: "Europe became in the last quarter of the nineteenth century what she had never been before, literally an armed continent. The rivalry of the nations to have the most perfect instruments of destruction . . . became one of the most conspicuous features of the modern world."—*Modern European History* (Holt), p. 590.

In olden times a soldier or knight fought in metal armor. The more armor he put on, the more his adversary put on, until at last it took a good share of his energy just to carry the war plating.

Today we see wars fought all over the world, in the heavens above, in the earth beneath, and in the waters under the earth. We have seen nations gear their brain and scientific power and their industrial might to the one purpose of war production.

Cost money? In 1933 the U.S. national debt was twenty-one billion dollars. We began borrowing four or five billions a year to prime the pump that had run dry from aftereffects of the first world war. When World War II came it took us just five years to pile up a colossal debt of $262,000,000,000.

Today we think nothing of fifty billions in annual taxes. We modern knights are just about to wear ourselves out with our war armor, plus all that goes with being governed.

Besides, it is estimated that from 1941 to 1945 we used up one fourth of our known oil, zinc, and lead reserves, one fifth of commercial copper reserves, and 7 per cent of our commercial iron reserves; and when we think of pensions and the future war program the mind staggers. When we consider World War III, we automatically write, *"Bankruptcy."*

How wonderful if we could all stop fearing and fighting, and start controlling ourselves more so we could be governed less! Then the tax collector would have time to work at something productive. But the world seems swept on to new terrors of more war and greater preparation therefor. War thrives on science and industrial capacity, and these in turn learn new things from war. Thus the vicious circle: Brilliant science and great industrial capacity make greater wars possible. Greater wars teach science and industry new tricks to serve in yet greater wars.

Bible prophecy predicts world wars and universal war preparation. The historian writes the story in endless volumes. Magazines are filled with the reports. Radio, pulpit, and platform resound with the message.

Bible Prophecy on Peace Plans of Men

Having noted the Bible predictions concerning a coming day of universal peace, and its prophecies of war right up to the second coming of Christ, we face the question: "What of the worldwide peace plans of men?" Does the Bible have any word concerning these noble peace movements?

Let us hear the prophetic testimony of the great prophet Isaiah: "It shall come to pass in the last days, that the mountain of the Lord's house shall be established in the top of the mountains, and shall be exalted above the hills; and all nations shall flow unto it." Isaiah 2:2.

Here is a clear picture of the exaltation of the professed church in the last days. World church movement! World church federation! And the nations will join in this plan. What is the twofold purpose of this mighty movement?

The next verse gives us the first purpose. "Many people shall go and say, Come ye, and let us go up to the mountain of the Lord, to the house of the God of Jacob; and he will teach us of his ways, and we will walk in his paths: for out of Zion shall go forth the law, and the word of the Lord from Jerusalem." Verse 3.

"Many people" will join this chorus and say, "We must get back to God and religion." This is what the people say.

The second thing the people say is recorded in the next verse: "And he shall judge among the nations, and shall rebuke many people: and they shall beat their swords into plowshares, and their spears into pruning-hooks: nation shall not lift up sword against nation, neither shall they learn war any more." Verse 4.

Clear as the noonday sun, the Bible prophecy foretells this sweeping internation and interchurch movement toward religion and peace. The people, "many people," were to join in this world call in the last days.

In other words, Christ and the prophets predict war for the last days; but the church and the nations predict peace, however much it may seem to them like whistling in the dark to quiet their fears. They cry for peace, and say, "Let us beat our swords into plowshares." God says, "While you say that you will beat your swords into plowshares, you will actually beat your plowshares into swords."

America's silver-tongued peace orator, William Jennings Bryan, like "many people," thought God had predicted peace in our time. So he had a sword made into small plowshares, to serve as desk paperweights. On each was inscribed the text: "And they shall beat their swords into plowshares." Then he sent these paperweights to world leaders to strengthen their faith in peace. But Mr. Bryan was mistaken. He failed to see that God had not predicted peace, but had only predicted that men would organize a great peace movement.

What would the result be? The answer is given by the apostle Paul, speaking of this very time:

"When they shall say, Peace and safety; then sudden destruction cometh upon them." 1 Thessalonians 5:3.

This refers primarily to the destruction in connection with Christ's coming. However, it is interesting to look at the record of world peace conferences and what followed them.

A Look at the Record

Professor Hazen opens his chapter on "The Peace Movement" with these words: "The contemporary world, to a degree altogether unprecedented in history, has been dominated by the thought of war, by extraordinary preparations for war, and by zealous and concerted efforts to prevent war."—*Ibid.*

This is exactly the way God puts it, war and preparation for war side by side with, or alternating with, peace movements. The Scriptures add the prediction that disappointment and destruction follow on the heels of the peace-and-safety cry.

Let us examine the record.

The first world peace conference was held at The Hague in Holland in 1899, with twenty-six nations represented, including the United States, Mexico, Japan, China, Persia, and Siam. This first Hague International Peace Conference was called by Czar Nicholas II of Russia. His war machine was out of date or worn out, and he hoped to avoid the necessity of getting a new one.

The conference convened for more than two months, and in less than three months after it closed, England was engaged in the Boer War of South Africa, which lasted over three years. In less than two years after the close of the Boer War, the bloody Russo-Japanese War started on the night of February 8-9, 1904. There were battles with 500,000 men. Mukden cost 120,000 killed and wounded in four days. Two Russian fleets were defeated and one was annihilated. President Theodore Roosevelt got the warring leaders to a peace table in Portsmouth, New Hampshire. They signed for peace September 5, 1905. So we see how sudden, destructive war followed the world peace conference.

What would you expect next? Yes, another world peace conference within twenty months.

The second International Hague Peace Conference was called by the same Czar Nicholas II of Russia. It is interesting to notice these peace calls of Russia. This time forty-four of the world's fifty-seven sovereign states convened on June 15, 1907, and remained in session just over four months, to October 18, 1907.

Watch the chain of war forged link by link the following seven years, as military and naval appropriations increased and the preparation for war intensified.

Let us follow it year by year.

In 1908, first year after the peace conference, occurred the Turkish bloodless revolution. Young Turks overthrew the vile regime of Abdul Hamid. Austria took over Bosnia and Herzegovnia. Bulgaria and Crete broke away from Turkey. All this was in violation of the Treaty of Berlin. The Balkan States were becoming the storm center of the world. This is what the first year after the second world peace conference gave to the world. Destructive forces went into "sudden" action.

In 1909 there was a counterrevolution in Turkey, and the seeds of the Balkan wars were germinating. Edwin Ginn set aside a million dollars to be used after his death to endow a World Peace Foundation.

In 1910 the Carnegie Endowment for International Peace was set up with ten million dollars, and backed the reorganization of the American Peace Society.

Next, in 1911-12, Turkey and Italy went to war. Italy won. This encouraged the Balkan peoples to rebel against Turkish rule, and the tinderbox of Europe was lighted. So in 1912, the very day the peace was signed between Turkey and Italy (October 18, 1912), four Balkan States made war on Turkey and practically drove her from Europe. That was the first Balkan war.

In June, 1913, less than a month after the end of the first Balkan war against Turkey, the Balkan States fell to warring among themselves in the second Balkan war.

Next year, 1914, the fuse of World War I was lighted down in the Balkan territory of Bosnia. Thus from 1907, date of the second world peace conference, to 1914, every year was marked by significant conflict, except 1910, which was a year of two peace gestures by Mr. Ginn and Mr. Carnegie. We draw attention to these facts that it may be plain how great peace conferences held to end war are followed by the very things they were designed to avoid.

The first world war was fought to end all war. It was to make the world safe for democracy. It lasted over four years, ending by an armistice on November 11, 1918. The world had been bled to the point of exhaustion. Its moral sense was either shocked or shattered. It has been said that 134 treaties of peace made before 1914 were broken during those four wild years. One powerful nation of sixty-five million attacked another of only seven million, whose neutrality she had sworn to regard. Treaties were but worthless scraps of paper.

What would be expected next? Another great peace conference? Yes, several of them. Let us take a brief glance at these efforts of frightened men to save civilization from destruction.

On January 8, 1918, Woodrow Wilson, President of the United States, suggested a League of Nations to preserve peace. This was ten months before the end of the war.

Next year, in 1919, the actual formation of the league plans took place at the Versailles Peace Conference in France.

The next year, January 20, 1920, at 4:14 P.M., a solemn agreement between sovereign nations to limit their complete freedom for the good of all was entered into.

On November 15 of that year the first meeting of the League of Nations convened at Geneva with forty-one nations represented.

Next year, November 11, 1921, the Washington Conference convened. Here the United States, Great Britain, France, Japan, China, Italy, Belgium, The Netherlands, and Portugal agreed to certain limitation of naval armament. Other agreements were also made.

The next year, 1922, the World Court formally opened on February 15.

On October 16, 1925, at Locarno, Switzerland, the Locarno treaties were signed, and six weeks later were ratified at London. Mr. Briand, the French minister, is reported to have said, "It is the most important step in the history of the modern world."

The Associated Press reported Austin Chamberlain of England as saying, "The treaties . . . banished war." And Dr. Edouard Benes, the Czechoslovakian minister, was reported to have said, "The Locarno Pact has solved the international problems of Europe."

In 1928 the grand climax came. The Kellogg-Briand Anti-War Treaty, so called because it was sponsored by F. B. Kellogg, U.S. Secretary of State, and A. Briand, minister of France, was signed at the time when the arbitration treaty between France and the United States was due to expire, February 27, 1928. It is sometimes called the Pact of Paris, because the first signing by representatives of fifteen nations took place in Paris, August 27, 1928. Later the document received the signatures of fifty-eight nations.

What did these fifty-eight nations promise to do?

"ARTICLE I.—The High Contracting Parties solemnly declare in the names of their respective peoples that they condemn recourse to war for the solution of international controversies, and renounce it as an instrument of national policy in their relations with one another.

"ARTICLE II.—The High Contracting Parties agree that the settlement or solution of all disputes or conflicts of whatever nature they may be, which may arise among them, shall never be sought except by pacific means."

News wires and radios and the hearts of men around the world vibrated in unison at such a significant event.

Mr. Kellogg said, "This truly marks the end of war."

Charles Clayton Morrison, editor of *The Christian Century,* wrote: "I handled the finished pact. . . . I looked at the signatures and seals, and I cannot do otherwise than command my pen to write these words: *'To-day international war was banished from civilization.'*"

President Hoover reportedly said, "We are at the beginning of a golden age."

How little did these honest and honorable men realize that the "golden age" would be spitting lead and steel and fire, and exploding in a vast and unheard-of destruction within a dozen years.

In February, 1932, less than four years after the signing of the Kellogg-Briand Pact, the World Disarmament Conference was scheduled to meet at Geneva. This conference was suggested to be but the first of others to follow. It opened February 2, 1932, with delegates from fifty-nine nations. The long months of this conference and its special commission ended in almost total failure. On October 2, of this very year of 1932, Japan withdrew from the League of Nations.

Next year on January 30, 1933, President Von Hindenburg called Adolf Hitler to the chancellorship of Germany. From that day on the disarmament conference was practically doomed. On October 14 Germany suddenly withdrew from the conference and from the League of Nations.

Next year, in 1934, Japan gave notice that she planned to end the agreement to limit her navy ship building. Hitler styled himself *Der Führer.*

In 1935 Hitler declared universal military conscription.

In 1936 he took over full sovereignty of the Saar Basin, and marched troops into the demilitarized Rhine zone in violation of the Locarno Pact.

In 1937 Japan was engaged in full-scale war with China.

In 1938 German labor went to a fourteen-hour maximum day in feverish war preparation. Backed by the world's strongest army, Hitler annexed Austria in March and took over the Sudetenland portion of Czechoslovakia in October. Also Hitler concluded a nonaggression agreement with Russia. This left him free to fight on only one front in case of war.

In 1939, without any declaration of war, Germany invaded Poland. The world saw its first demonstration of blitzkrieg warfare. Neville Chamberlain broadcast to the world Britain's declaration of war on Germany.

Poland was defeated in less than thirty days. Russian troops also entered Poland. The year 1940 witnessed Germany's invasion of Norway, the subjugation of practically all Europe, the occupation of the Balkans, and the air raids on England. In this violent air war as many as 185 German planes were brought down in one day.

December 7, 1941, Japan attacked Pearl Harbor. The next day the United States Congress, in joint resolution, declared war on Japan. On December 11 Germany and Italy declared war on the United States, and the United States replied in kind the same day. The fires of the European war had leaped the Atlantic to America on the east, and the flames of the Asiatic conflict had arched the Pacific to Pearl Harbor and touched off the blazing war on the west. World War II in all its horror and destruction was here.

In 1945, six years from the month of Hitler's march into Poland, the war ended. Germany signed terms of unconditional surrender May 8, 1945. Japan fought on. The climax of horror came with the dropping of an atomic bomb, of greater power than twenty thousand tons of TNT, on Hiroshima, Japan, August 6. Reports say one hundred thousand were killed or doomed and another one hundred thousand hurt. Three days later a second bomb was loosed on Nagasaki. Five days later, on August 14, 1945, Japan surrendered with formal signing on September 2. The ghastly business of World War II was over. The crushing problems of peace were at hand.

According to Bible prophecy, what would we expect next? A world organization for peace? Yes. This time we have the United Nations.

On April 18, 1946, the League of Nations met for the last time, to transfer both its records and its functions to the United Nations. On every hand was heard the cry: "One world or no world!"

What Do These Things Mean?

What do these world wars and world organizations for peace mean? On man's part war shows up the human heart as desperately wicked. The organizations for peace reveal men's desires for peace and the gnawing fear of utter destruction as the only alternative.

On God's part and by Bible declaration world wars and world peace movements mean that the coming of the Prince of Peace draws nigh.

Before World War I men had been lulled into a sense of security. A prominent university professor declared, "Today we have no fear of war, famine, pestilence, or failing resources." A leading minister said, "Laws are becoming more just, rulers more humane, music is becoming sweeter and books wiser, homes are happier, and the individual heart is becoming at once more just and more gentle."

When World War I broke in 1914 the news came to

a group of Y.M.C.A. conference workers as they were seated at the dinner table. One minister is reported to have exclaimed, "And to think only last Sunday I told my congregation that there would never be another great war!"

But the war came. It was to end all war. It was the same with World War II. Even as late as September 30, 1938, England's prime minister, Neville Chamberlain, returned from Munich, Germany, with the British-German peace pact, containing agreements with Hitler which promised "peace for our time." In six months the hope was shattered. In less than a year Chamberlain himself broadcast to the world England's declaration of war. Fourteen months later he was dead.

Surely the modern prophets of peace have fulfilled the saying of Jeremiah, the seer of old, when he said, "They have healed also the hurt of the daughter of my people slightly, saying, Peace, peace; when there is no peace." Jeremiah 6:14.

Nothing in all this world is more important for you and me than to know that we have made our peace with God through the cross of the Prince of Peace. "And, having made peace through the blood of his cross." Colossians 1:20.

Jesus Christ, the Prince of glory, gave His life to deliver us from the clutches of evil, the chains of the prison house of sin and death. He is the golden chain let down from heaven to earth, the connecting link between man and God. Let us fix our eyes on Him, "looking for that blessed hope, and the glorious appearing of the great God and our Saviour Jesus Christ." Titus 2:13.

SECTION FIVE

GOD SPEAKS THROUGH THE PROPHECY OF DANIEL

 Harry Anderson, Artist

The unmistakable signs of prophecy point to the fast-approaching end. We live this climactic hour. Soon the heavens will reveal the great Redeemer of manki

CHAPTER 27

When God Unites the Nations

Based on Daniel 2

IT WAS some six centuries before Christ, over 2,500 years ago. A noted monarch retired to his regal couch for a night's rest from the busy cares of world dominion. Would the mighty empire that he had built stand the test of time, or would it break and crumble into pieces as Egypt and Assyria had broken and crumbled? Such were the thoughts of his mind as he fell asleep.

A Monarch Dreams

Then he dreamed. So startling and significant did his night vision seem that "his spirit was troubled, and his sleep brake from him." Daniel 2:1. Strangely, he could not recall the details of the dream.

Deeply disturbed, he called together the leading wise men of his court. "Bring back my dream and give to me its meaning, and you shall live in honor. Fail, and you shall die; you shall be cut in pieces." Such was the import of his words to men who professed ability to recall and interpret dreams.

Caught unprepared by this stern test of their false pretensions, the wise men cried, "There is not a man upon the earth that can shew the king's matter. . . . And it is a rare thing that the king requireth, and there is none other that can shew it before the king, except the gods, whose dwelling is not with flesh." Daniel 2:10, 11.

Sensing the shame of their science falsely so called, this Nebuchadnezzar, king of Babylon, decreed death for these deceptive mediums of mystery and knowledge.

The Hand of God Intervenes

Among the learned men of Babylon were some newly come—Daniel and three other young Jews. Some few years before the dream episode Nebuchadnezzar had in war taken the city of Jerusalem, subjected the land, and carried away choice Jewish captives to Babylon. Among them were Daniel and his fellows. At this time they had finished the king's court school, and were henceforth to be reckoned among the wise men.

Daniel sought and received consent to speak with the king, who granted him time to see what he and his companions could do about the mysterious dream.

That night the young men prayed. "Then was the secret revealed unto Daniel in a night vision." Verse 19.

Through proper arrangement Daniel was brought again into the presence of the earthly ruler of the world. Before Daniel could say a word the anxious king asked, "Art thou able to make known unto me the dream which I have seen, and the interpretation thereof?" Verse 26. The next two verses state, "Daniel answered in the presence of the king, and said, The secret which the king hath demanded cannot the wise men, the astrologers, the magicians, the soothsayers, shew unto the king; but there is a God in heaven that revealeth secrets."

Down the long, long corridor of time come ringing and echoing these words of faith, "There is a God in heaven." To the king upon his throne, to the beggar in the street, and to each and every one of us this God would reveal Himself.

Before telling the king the content of his dream Daniel pointed out two things. First he said, "As for me, this secret is not revealed to me for any wisdom that I have more than any living." Verse 30. He took no credit to himself. Yet he added, "But *for their sakes* that shall make known the interpretation to the king." Thus did Daniel courteously remind the king that, though his decree had sentenced Jewish captives to death along with other men, God's hand was intervening. God gave the king a dream. He gave His servants the interpretation. They gave it to the king. Their lives were saved. God's eye is on His people. "For their sakes" He stepped in.

"Truth forever on the scaffold,
  Wrong forever on the throne—
Yet that scaffold sways the future,
  And, behind the dim unknown,
Standeth God within the shadows,
  Keeping watch above his own."

God Sets Up and Removes Kings

In his prayer Daniel said, "Blessed be the name of God. . . . He changeth the times and the seasons: he removeth kings, and setteth up kings." Verses 20, 21.

"The power exercised by every ruler on earth is Heaven-imparted; and upon his use of the powers thus bestowed, his success depends. To each the word of the divine Watcher is, 'I girded thee, though thou hast not known Me.' Isaiah 45:5. . . . And 'Break off thy sins by righteousness, and thine iniquities by showing mercy to the poor; if it may be a lengthening of thy tranquillity.' Daniel 4:27."—*Prophets and Kings,* p. 502.

Said the Holy Watcher from heaven to Nebuchadnezzar: "That the living may know that the most High ruleth in the kingdom of men, and giveth it to whomsoever he will, and setteth up over it the basest of men." Daniel 4:17.

"In the annals of human history, the growth of nations, the rise and fall of empires, appear as if dependent on the will and prowess of man. . . . But in the word of God the curtain is drawn aside, and we behold, above, behind, and through all the play and counterplay of human interest and power and passions, the agencies of the All-merciful One, silently, patiently working out the counsels of His own will."—*Ibid.*, pp. 499, 500.

Daniel made it clear that Nebuchadnezzar's dream had to do with the future—the very future with which the king's thoughts had been playing when he lay down to rest on his golden bed and dreamed.

Said Daniel, "There is a God in heaven that revealeth secrets, and maketh known to the king Nebuchadnezzar what shall be in the latter days. . . . As for thee, O king, thy thoughts came into thy mind upon thy bed, what should come to pass hereafter: and he that revealeth secrets maketh known to thee what shall come to pass . . . that thou mightest know the thoughts of thy heart." Daniel 2:28-30.

God Rolls Back the Curtain of the Future (Amos 3:7)

Daniel now turns to the king's dream. "Thou, O king, sawest, and behold a great image. This great image, whose brightness was excellent, stood before thee; and the form thereof was terrible. This image's head was of fine gold, his breast and his arms of silver, his belly and his thighs of brass, his legs of iron, his feet part of iron and part of clay. Thou sawest till that a stone was cut out without hands, which smote the image upon his feet that were of iron and clay, and brake them to pieces. Then was the iron, the clay, the brass, the silver, and the gold, broken to pieces together, and became like the chaff of the summer threshingfloors; and the wind carried them away, and no place was found for them: and the stone that smote the image became a great mountain, and filled the whole earth." Verses 31-35.

The king listened. To himself he said, "That indeed is the very subject of my dream." He leaned forward with breathless interest, that he might now discover the meaning of the dream.

These were the first words he heard, "This is the dream; and we will tell the interpretation thereof before the king. Thou, O king, art a king of kings: for the God of heaven hath given thee a kingdom, power, and strength, and glory. . . . Thou art this head of gold." Verses 36-38.

How delightful must these words have been to the troubled king! Like pleasant music they fell upon his ears and tended to set at ease the tension of his restless heart. Was he not the God-recognized ruler of Babylon, the monarchy of the world? Had not the prophet of God just so said? What now of the future?

Babylon to Pass Away

These and a multitude of thoughts swarmed within his mind as Daniel calmly and courteously spoke without interruption. Said he, "And after thee shall arise another kingdom inferior to thee." Verse 39.

What? Was his mighty golden empire to fall to an inferior power, as silver is inferior to gold? Upon the walls of his house there had been inscribed: "For the astonishment of men I have built this house. These portals for the astonishment of multitudes of people with beauty I adorned." "Thus I completely made strong the defenses of Babylon." "May it last forever." Large numbers of bricks dug from Babylonian ruins bear the name and title of Nebuchadnezzar.

Babylon was the first of what history knows as the

four great monarchies. Her glorious capital city was laid out in a perfect square. It is supposed by some to have been fifteen miles on each side, sixty miles around her walls, which are said to have been over three hundred feet high and wide enough on top for five chariots to race abreast.

"Gleaming in the sun, its lofty palaces and temple towers stabbed the sky above the towering walls and thrilled the approaching traveler while he was yet miles away."

Through the city flowed the river Euphrates, flanked by great inner walls and giant gates. The streets of the city were broad and straight, crossing each other at right angles. The city was laid out in luxuriant pleasure grounds and dotted with magnificent dwellings, royal palaces, and glorious temples. Here were the famous Hanging Gardens, one of the seven wonders of the world.

But Babylon, the "head of gold," was to pass away. Yes, "Babylon, the glory of kingdoms, the beauty of the Chaldees' excellency, shall be as when God overthrew Sodom and Gomorrah." Isaiah 13:19. She was to remain but heaps of ruins, covered with the drifting sands of the centuries, a home only for owls, doleful creatures, and beasts of the wild; a place of uninhabited desolation, where even the roving Arab would disdain to pitch his tent or the shepherd to make fold there. Babylon's time "is near to come, and her days shall not be prolonged." Verse 22. (See also Jeremiah 51:6, 7.)

So "Darius the Median took the kingdom." Daniel 5:31. Cyrus the Persian led the successful attack in taking Babylon 538 years before Christ, about sixty-five years after Daniel's prophecy. Medo-Persia, the breast and arms of silver, ruled. God had said to Nebuchadnezzar, "After thee shall arise another kingdom." Medo-Persia was that kingdom. (Isaiah 13:17.)

Medo-Persia and Grecia to Rise and Fall

This silver kingdom of Medo-Persia was in supremacy for some two hundred years. But it was also to give way to yet "another third kingdom of brass, which shall bear rule over all the earth." Daniel 2:39. This third universal kingdom was that of Greece. How well do we all remember the maps of these nations as we studied them in high school. A full reading of the eighth chapter of Daniel will reveal that Grecia was to follow Medo-Persia. Alexander the Great reached the deciding point over the Medo-Persians at the famous Battle of Arbela, 331 B.C., or 207 years after Babylon's fall.

In five short years Alexander, through swift movement and audacious attack day or night, swept to victory at the age of twenty-five years. Seven years later he was dead. At the age of thirty-two, like a meteor in the night, his light suddenly went out. So swiftly does earthly glory fade! The decisive Battle of Pydna, 168 B.C., is often given as a definite point in Grecia's decline. The brass kingdom was through.

Rome to Rule

Daniel continues his brief and graphic picture of the future, while Nebuchadnezzar listens in amazement at this thumbnail sketch of world history.

"And the fourth kingdom shall be strong as iron: for as much as iron breaketh in pieces and subdueth all things: and as iron that breaketh all these, shall it break in pieces and bruise." Verse 40.

Iron Rome was to rule. "The iron monarchy of Rome" came to break in pieces, bruise, and subdue for nearly six hundred years. Jesus was born in this era and was crucified under Rome's authority.

Hippolytus, who lived from about A.D. 170 to A.D. 236, wrote, "Rejoice, blessed Daniel! thou hast not been in error. . . . Already the iron rules." He spoke of Rome. *The Catholic Encyclopedia* says, "Hippolytus was the most important theologian and the most prolific religious writer of the Roman Church in the pre-Constantinian era."

Gibbon says, "The images of gold, or silver, or brass, that might serve to represent the nations and their kings, were successively broken by the iron monarchy of Rome."

Rome Was to Be Divided

With simple boldness Daniel presented to the king the rise and fall and division of great empires yet unborn, as though he were giving a demonstration of addition, subtraction, multiplication, and division on a blackboard. The king listened in astonishment.

"And whereas thou sawest the feet and toes, part of potters' clay, and part of iron, the kingdom shall be divided; but there shall be in it of the strength of the iron, forasmuch as thou sawest the iron mixed with miry clay. And as the toes of the feet were part of iron, and part of clay, so the kingdom shall be partly strong, and partly broken." Daniel 2:41, 42.

Rome was to be divided. Here is something new. Another world kingdom was not to follow. Division was to come. Rome's mighty empire began to decay. Luxury, poverty, vice, and weakness, like white ants, burrowed from within. The Germanic tribes invaded from without, and the Roman kingdom was divided.

Ridpath says, "At last the seals were loosed, and the barbaric tornado was poured out of the North. Through the Alpine passes came the rushing cohort of warriors, each with the rage of Scythia in his stomach and the icicles of the Baltic in his beard. The great hulk of Rome tottered, fell, and lay dead on the earth, like the stump of Dagon."—*History of the World,* vol. 3, pp. 28, 29.

The ten main divisions, corresponding to the ten toes, are given as the Alamanni (Germans), the Franks (French), the Burgundians (Swiss), the Suevi (Portuguese), the Saxons (English), the Visigoths (Spanish), the Lombards (Italians), the Heruli, the Vandals, and the Ostrogoths. These tribes made victorious invasion as early as A.D. 351. History gives A.D. 476 as the date of Rome's fall, when Emperor Augustulus (Little Augustus) was deposed.

The modern nations of Europe developed from these barbarian tribes of the old Roman Empire. Some were to be strong and some weak. Thus it has been and is.

Can the Nations Be United by Man?

Daniel now presents to Nebuchadnezzar the long and tragic efforts of men to unite Europe and bring order to the world. Continuing the figure of the feet and toes of clay and iron, he says, "And whereas thou sawest iron mixed with miry clay, they shall mingle themselves with the seed of men: but they shall not cleave one to another, even as iron is not mixed with clay." Daniel 2:43.

Thus does the Bible declare with the utmost simplicity and clarity that the nations of our time cannot be permanently united by human effort.

Six notable characters have stepped upon the stage of history and sought to demonstrate that the kingdoms of Europe could be successfully ruled by one throne or under one federation. In 1939 the sixth set out to try it.

The first and one of the most notable was Charles the Great, or Charlemagne. He began to rule at the age of twenty-nine. Fourteen years before his death, while Charlemagne was kneeling in worship at Rome on Christmas Day, A.D. 800, the pope placed upon his head the crown of the Holy Roman Empire.

Two strong factors were in his favor: First, the church

desired the unity of Europe and it approved of him as emperor. Second, an enemy religious group, the Mohammedans, were ever menacing Europe from beyond the Pyrenees in Spain. Charlemagne's illustrious grandfather, Charles Martel, had defeated them at the Battle of Tours sixty-eight years before.

But Charlemagne died, weary from nearly half a century of fighting all over Europe. He could not make the clay and iron fuse together.

Charles V, emperor of the Holy Roman Empire, and Louis XIV, the vain Frenchman, we shall pass by as two more who failed to unite the nations of Europe.

Then comes that master man of destiny—an Italian by blood, a Corsican by birth, a Frenchman by nationality—Napoleon Bonaparte!

Born in 1769, he grew to a stature of only five feet and two inches. Thin-faced, sallow-complexioned, and round-shouldered, he yet developed one of the most remarkably rapid, clear-thinking, and tireless brains ever to function in a human cranium. His personality was utterly overmastering, his mind gazing out through eyes which crushed the strongest.

At the age of twenty-six, in 1796, two days before his marriage to Josephine, he was appointed head of one third of the armies of France. Two days after his marriage he departed for the war front. Passionate love messages went back to Josephine from every station as he set forth to "tear the heart out of glory." And he did.

Three years later, 1799, he overturned the government of France and seized control. Then he set out to unite Europe—to give it "one ruler, one code, one court of appeal, one coinage." This is a story of sixteen years of unparalleled military action by a man who loved power "as a musician loves his violin," and whose capacity for work seemed to know no limit.

For purposes of political unity he divorced Josephine to marry Marie Louise, of Austria.

He established the Napoleonic order in Europe, placing his kin in leadership and arranging marriages to cement the states together, a method the Bible said would be used. "They shall mingle themselves with the seed of men." Daniel 2:43.

But after his disastrous Russian campaign in 1812, his European federation soon fell like a house of flimsy cards. At Waterloo, June 18, 1815, just as the sun went down, the sun of his career set. He was through. "God Almighty has been too much for me," he said.

The Kaiser of Germany found the same thing to be true in World War I.

Adolf Hitler almost wrecked the world in his effort to unite Europe and set up a German rule to last for 1,000 years.

After World War I the League of Nations sought some sort of "cleaving together" of the nations, but with dismal failure.

After World War II came the United Nations and new talk of a United States of Europe. The ugly specter of communism arose to challenge the best efforts of great men to unite anything.

No present ruler, no set of rulers, no league of nations of any kind, no federation of religions, can ever unite Europe and the world permanently. "They shall not cleave one to another."

When God Unites the Nations

At this point in the narrative King Nebuchadnezzar must have been puzzled indeed. Daniel's dark forecast rang the death knell of Babylon, Medo-Persia, Greece, and Rome. Then it predicted the new situation—a division of Rome's kingdom and the utter inability of men to form any successful union of the nations. Glowing dreams would end in shattered hopes. Would the future of modern man be one of never-ending disunity?

Daniel gave the answer to the king's thoughts: "And in the days of these kings [the kingdoms of divided Europe] shall the God of heaven set up a kingdom, which shall never be destroyed: and the kingdom shall not be left to other people, but it shall break in pieces and consume all these kingdoms, and it shall stand for ever. Forasmuch as thou sawest that the stone was cut out of the mountain without hands, and that it brake in pieces the iron, the brass, the clay, the silver, and the gold; the great God hath made known to the king what shall come to pass hereafter: and the dream is certain, and the interpretation thereof sure." Daniel 2:44, 45.

Six Significant Statements

In this basic prophecy of the Bible six vital truths stand out.

1. There is a God in heaven.
2. He has servants on earth.
3. His hand is in earthly affairs.
4. He predicted the history of the world from Babylon, through Medo-Persia and Grecia to Rome and her breakup into ten main divisions.
5. He forecast man's failure, in every case, to truly unite the nations of the world again. The kingdom of God will not come through the gateway of politics or of religion and politics.
6. God's kingdom is to be set up after the final breakdown of man's plans.

"The dream is certain, and the interpretation thereof sure." Today we live in the feet and toes of human history. Christ will come and take the initial steps for a reign of peace on earth.

Martin Luther's Teaching

"The first kingdom is the Assyrian or Babylonian kingdom; the second, the Medo-Persian; the third, the great kingdom of Alexander and the Greeks; and the fourth, the Roman Empire. In this the whole world agrees, and history supports it fully in detail.

"But the prophet has the most to say about the Roman empire, . . . the legs, the feet, and the toes. The Roman empire will be divided. Spain, France, England, and others emerged from it, some of them weak, others strong, and although it will be divided there will still be some strength, as symbolized by the iron in it. . . . This empire shall last until the end; no one will destroy it but Jesus Himself, when His kingdom comes."—Translated from Luther, *Schriften,* vol. 6, cols. 898-900.

Two Great Questions

The first important question for me is, How can I find entrance into that kingdom of God?

The apostle Paul wrote, "Know ye not that the unrighteous shall not inherit the kingdom of God?" 1 Corinthians 6:9. And we are all unrighteous, "for all have sinned, and come short of the glory of God." "There is none righteous, no, not one." Romans 3:23, 10.

To Nicodemus, morally reputable, and accepted ruler of the synagogue, Jesus said, "Verily, verily, I say unto thee, Except a man be born again, he cannot see the kingdom of God." John 3:3.

It is therefore by way of the new birth, spiritual regeneration, that I must enter into the kingdom of God.

The kingdom of God must come into me before I shall be prepared to go into it. For God has two kingdoms: the spiritual kingdom of grace and the literal kingdom of glory. The kingdom of grace is within me. (Luke 17:20, 21.) It brings righteousness and peace and joy.

(Romans 14:17.) It is present. (Colossians 1:13.) The kingdom of glory is future. Christ will "sit upon the throne of his glory" (Matthew 25:31) and reign forever. Then the kingdoms of the world will become the kingdoms of our Lord and of his Christ. (Revelation 11:15.)

The second and most pressing personal question is, "What shall I do to be born into this kingdom?"

The answer is, "I must go up to Calvary, and see there the love of God in giving His Son to die for my sins, for my transgressions of a holy law that could not be changed." If my heart does not resist this love, it will be broken in sincere repentance, and love to God and His law will be born. There is no other place to go—nowhere but Calvary.

The Gateway of the Kingdom

The gateway to the kingdom of God is the cross of Christ. Nicodemus found it when he watched Christ die for his sins. So may I find the entrance also.

The gateway of the cross swings both ways. It opens a way into my heart, and the kingdom of His grace comes in. It one day will swing the other way, and I shall enter into that eternal kingdom of glory and bliss forevermore.

"A land upon whose blissful shore
There rests no shadow, falls no stain;
There those who meet shall part no more,
And those long parted meet again."

"Perhaps you are saying within your heart, 'I admit that I am not what might be called a real Christian, but I believe I have as good a chance for heaven as some people I know who profess to belong to Christ.'

"Let me give you an illustration that I hope will make this matter of the need of accepting Christ still clearer. In Rome, Italy, some years ago, there entered the office of the American embassy a man who appeared to be in great distress. When he finally secured an audience with the ambassador, he stated his case, a very serious one, and then implored the ambassador for help.

"The ambassador immediately asked the man, 'Are you a citizen of the United States?' The man replied, 'I lived in the United States for twenty-five years. I have reared my family there. I have always paid my taxes, and contributed to all worthy enterprises.' 'But,' interrupted the ambassador, 'are you a citizen of the United States?'

"He answered slowly, 'No, I have never taken out citizenship papers, but I believe I have done my duty toward the Government just as fully as those who have taken out their citizenship papers.'

"The ambassador replied, 'I am sorry for you, but I cannot help you because you are not a citizen of my country.'

"Some years later a man entered the same embassy, and talked to the same ambassador. The man was trembling with fear and emotion, for his case was desperate. He spoke in broken English, but he stated his case to the ambassador with sufficient clearness to make him understand his situation.

"The ambassador directed the same question to this man that he had asked the other man some years before: 'Are you a citizen of the United States?'

"In a faltering manner he explained to the ambassador that some years before he had taken out his first papers, and just before he sailed for Italy, he had received his last papers, and so he was a full-fledged citizen of the United States.

"The ambassador exclaimed, 'You are a citizen of my country. I extend to you the full power of the United States for your protection.' . . .

"No foreigner can become a citizen of a country without making a positive, definite decision to take out his citizenship papers. Everyone is a foreigner by nature with respect to the kingdom of heaven. But we may become 'fellow citizens with the saints,' as Paul expresses it in Ephesians 2:19.

"So may I ask you the question, 'Have you taken out your citizenship papers which entitle you to a place in the kingdom of heaven?'

"It is not a question of how near you think you come to doing as well as your neighbors who are Christians, but have you taken out your citizenship papers? Is Christ the King of your heart now?

"You say, 'I do not know how to take out citizenship papers for heaven?' If you are willing to acknowledge Christ as your personal Saviour, to follow Him all the way, He will accept you as a citizen of His Kingdom, and you will become right now a citizen of the kingdom of grace.

"You cannot do His will without His help; so it is useless to talk about being saved at last unless He has entered your heart and taken up His abode there. Our part of the transaction is to be willing to do God's will. Christ's part is to furnish the power to do the thing you will to do."—CHARLES T. EVERSON, *Jesus,* pp. 27-30.

The palsied, bedridden man of Luke 5:18 was told by Christ to rise up and walk. How could he walk? Had he not tried many times? Yet at Christ's command he willed to walk, and he walked. Christ gave him the power.

Let not one person make delay, but decide in Christ's favor at His cross; then take up your cross and follow Him.

"I will follow Thee, my Saviour,
Wheresoe'er my lot may be.
Where Thou goest I will follow;
Yes, my Lord, I'll follow Thee."
—JAMES LAWSON.

CHAPTER 28

The Church That Ruled the World

BASED ON DANIEL 7

GOD KNOWS the future, "declaring the end from the beginning." Isaiah 46:10. And "he revealeth his secret unto his servants the prophets." Amos 3:7.

A few days before His death Jesus urged the importance of reading and understanding the prophecy of Daniel. Said He, "When ye therefore shall see the abomination of desolation, spoken of by Daniel the prophet, stand in the holy place, (whoso readeth, let him understand:) then let them which be in Judaea flee into the mountains." Matthew 24:15, 16. We need no further support for belief in the prophecy of Daniel.

Daniel was but a youth when God gave him the vision of the future as symbolized by the great image of Nebuchadnezzar's dream in Daniel 2. In the seventh chapter Daniel was given another most important vision. He was now an old man, certainly past eighty years of age. Babylon had also grown gray and weak, and was soon to be conquered by the Medo-Persians.

THE FOUR WINDS ON THE GREAT SEA

"Daniel spake and said, I saw in my vision by night, and, behold, the four winds of the heaven strove upon the great sea." Daniel 7:2.

In symbolic Bible language the four winds signify strife. Here is an example: "Upon Elam will I bring the four winds. . . . For I will cause Elam to be dismayed before their enemies." Jeremiah 49:36, 37.

The sea, or waters, indicate multitudes of people, for we read, "The waters which thou sawest . . . are peoples, and multitudes, and nations, and tongues." Revelation 17:15.

The scene of turmoil is one familiar on the walls of history—the picture of war and conflict, of battle and blood, of strife and confusion, with one nation coming up and another going down. How wonderful it will be when the bugle of war will be blown no more, and our ears will hear only the sweet sounds of peace and harmony. It will be like coming out of a madhouse into a haven of sanity. That day will be ushered in when the Saviour comes to earth again.

"That morn everlasting, that day free from tears
Is swiftly approaching as on roll the years;
The wheat, rudely scattered by sin's cruel blast,
Then hasten to gather, e'er autumn be past."

—F. E. BELDEN.

THE FOUR BEAST KINGDOMS

Daniel was watching the great sea being lashed into fury by cyclonic winds, "and four great beasts came up from the sea, diverse one from another." Daniel 7:3. The general meaning is made clear in verse 17: "These great beasts which are four, are four kings, which shall arise out of the earth." That these four kings stand for kingdoms rather than individual kings is clearly set forth in verse 23: "The fourth beast shall be the fourth kingdom upon earth."

It is therefore plain that the history of the world from Babylon to the setting up of God's kingdom is again presented in Daniel 7 as in Daniel 2. There were to be but four world, or universal, political kingdoms. In both chapters they succeed each other, and God's kingdom comes as the glorious climax. The same ground is re-covered in chapter 7 to add certain details, and to present two new and important features.

The Lion With Eagle's Wings

The four beasts came up in order. "The first was like a lion, and had eagle's wings: I beheld till the wings thereof were plucked, and it was lifted up from the earth, and made stand upon the feet as a man, and a man's heart was given to it." Verse 4.

The lion with eagle's wings represented Babylon, corresponding to the head of gold in Daniel 2.

It is common knowledge that the winged lion was one of Babylon's outstanding symbols. Modern excavations of Babylon reveal it set up flanking the entrances to public buildings and otherwise in prominence. (See Jeremiah 4:7.)

The lion is recognized as the king of beasts and the eagle as the king of birds. So Babylon was the glory of kingdoms. (Isaiah 13:19.) It was the head of gold, most precious metal in the image of Daniel 2.

In Habakkuk 1:8 the Chaldeans, or Babylonians, are represented thus: "They shall fly as the eagle that hasteth to eat." This indicates the swiftness of her conquests.

However, the wings were to be plucked, and it was to stand on its feet as a man and be given a man's heart. How true is the picture to the later painting on history's canvas! (Read Jeremiah 51:30.) Babylon went down on a night of women and wine, feasting and reveling. (Daniel 5.)

The One-sided Bear

"And behold another beast, a second, like to a bear, and it raised up itself on one side, and it had three ribs in the mouth of it between the teeth of it: and they said thus unto it, Arise, devour much flesh." Daniel 7:5.

The bear symbolized Medo-Persia. It raised itself on one side. It was a dual monarchy of Medes and Persians. One power was stronger than the other. (See Daniel 8:3, 20.) It was a cruel and bloodthirsty power. The three ribs could well represent the triple alliance of Babylon, Libya, and Egypt, against which the bear fought. This is the silver kingdom of Daniel 2.

The Four-headed Leopard

"After this I beheld, and lo another, like a leopard, which had upon the back of it four wings of a fowl; the beast had also four heads; and dominion was given to it." Verse 6.

The leopard with four heads and four wings is Grecia. The extra wings indicated the rapidity of Alexander's conquests. He conquered Medo-Persia in five years, and in eight years marched his soldiers over 5,100 miles.

The four heads stand for the four divisions of the empire, made after Alexander's death, which followed a drunken debauch. His empire was soon divided among his four leading generals. Cassander took the western portion; Lysimachus, the northern; Seleucus, the eastern; and Ptolemy, the southern. (Read Daniel 8:8, 21, 22.) This is the brass kingdom of Daniel 2.

The Great and Terrible Beast

"After this I saw in the night visions, and behold a fourth beast, dreadful and terrible, and strong exceedingly; and it had great iron teeth: it devoured and brake in pieces, and stamped the residue with the feet of it: and it was diverse from all the beasts that were before it; and it had ten horns." Verse 7.

The dreadful beast represented Rome. The iron kingdom of Daniel 2 is here a beast with great iron teeth. Compare the statements of Daniel 2:40 and Daniel 7:7, 19, 23.

The ten horns are spoken of in these words: "And the ten horns out of this kingdom are ten kings that shall arise." Verse 24.

The ten horns represent ten kings. The king stands for a kingdom. (Daniel 7:17, 23.) So ten main kingdoms were to arise out of Rome's empire. These were named in the preceding chapter. The main modern nations of Europe are the outgrowth of these divisions. They can never be permanently united by men. (Daniel 2:43.)

THE LITTLE HORN

"And I considered the horns, and, behold, there came up among them another little horn, before whom there were three of the first horns plucked up by the roots: and, behold, in this horn were eyes like the eyes of man, and a mouth speaking great things." Verse 8.

The little horn represents papal Rome, or the Papacy. All students of history know that Rome had two phases: pagan (heathen) Rome and papal Rome.

When pagan Rome fell under the invasion of the barbarian tribes the Bishop of Rome picked up the scepter. Christianity was nominally accepted by the barbarians in general, and the pope became the chief power in Europe. No one can read a history of this period without reading a chapter entitled "The Rise of the Papacy."

The Papacy is the government of the *papa,* pope. For more than twelve hundred years the threads of European history are interwoven with those of the Papacy and its court.

James P. Conroy, in the *American Catholic Quarterly Review,* April, 1911, said: "Long ages ago, when Rome through the neglect of the Western emperors was left to the mercy of the barbarous hordes, the Romans turned to one figure for aid and protection, and asked him to rule them; and thus . . . commenced the temporal sovereignty of the popes. And meekly stepping to the throne of Caesar, the vicar of Christ took up the scepter to which the emperors and kings of Europe were to bow in reverence through so many ages."

All historians, both Catholic and Protestant, know that, following the breakup of pagan Rome, the Papacy, or papal Rome, became the outstanding force among the ten kingdoms of Europe. There simply is no other power which answers to the ten points set forth by Daniel concerning the little horn. Each point will be briefly touched.

Ten Points of the Papal Horn

1. *It came up after the ten horns.*

"And another shall rise after them." Daniel 7:24.

The little horn was to come up after the ten horns were in evidence. So it did. The roots of the Papacy were there, but it rose to power and prominence after Rome's division.

2. *It came up among the ten horns.*

"There came up among them another little horn." Verse 8.

This power must come up among the ten horns, that is, in the European region. The Papacy rose with its seat at Rome itself.

3. *It was to uproot three horns.*

"Before whom there were three of the first horns plucked up by the roots." Verse 8.

The three horns uprooted are generally recognized to be the Heruli, the Ostrogoths, and the Vandals. They were opposed to some of the teachings and claims of the papal hierarchy. Suffice it to say, the Papacy triumphed over them.

4. *It was to be different from the other horns.*

"And he shall be diverse from the first, and he shall subdue three kings." Verse 24.

It was a religio-political power, persecuting the saints. It was a mixture of religion and politics. It was also a mixture of Christianity and paganism, of Christian and heathen rites and ceremonies and philosophy.

Cardinal Newman (Roman Catholic), in his *An Essay on the Development of Christian Doctrine,* says: "Confiding then in the power of Christianity to resist the infection of evil, and to transmute the very instruments and appendages of demon-worship to an evangelical use, . . . the rulers of the Church from early times were prepared, should the occasion arise, to adopt, or imitate, or sanction the existing rites and customs of the populace, as well as the philosophy of the educated class."—Pages 371, 372.

The Easter number of the *Catholic World,* March, 1895, stated, "The church took the Pagan philosophy and made it the buckler of faith against the heathen."

So Mourant Brock truly wrote, "And indeed all writers who are acquainted with antiquity—be they lay or clerical, Protestant or papal, Italian or foreign—agree as to the pagan origin of Rome's present usages and ceremonies."—*Rome, Pagan and Papal,* p. 31.

One need only read the Holy Scriptures to know beyond any doubt that a veritable multitude of teachings and practices of the Papacy are not found in the Sacred Volume.

5. *It was to be a leading power.*

"Whose look was more stout than his fellows." Verse 20.

The little horn was to be the leading power. So it was. Emperors, princes, and rulers were crowned by the pope. They kissed his feet and held his saddle stirrup.

Said Henry Edward Manning (Roman Catholic),

"The vicar of the incarnate Son of God, anointed high priest and supreme ruler [the pope], sat in his tribunal, impartially to judge between nation and nation, between people and prince, between sovereign and subject."—*The Temporal Power of the Vicar of Jesus Christ,* p. 46.

King Henry IV of Germany defied Pope Gregory VII and told him "to come down from the throne." Gregory deposed the king. Henry hastened across the Alps in midwinter to meet Gregory, who was coming to Germany. At the Castle of Canossa, where the pope had stopped, King Henry stood outside for three days, barefoot in the snow, clothed in coarse garments of penance, before the pope would even talk to him. Truly the Papacy had "a look more stout than his fellows."

6. *It was to speak great words against God.*

"And he shall speak great words against the most High." Verse 25.

The pope is given titles which belong only to the Godhead.

The Council of Trent defines his power thus: "We define that the Holy Apostolic See and the Roman Pontiff holds the primacy over the whole world."—LABBE AND COSSART, *The Most Holy Councils,* vol. 13, col. 1167.

Pope Leo XIII wrote, "We hold upon this earth the place of God Almighty."

The *Catholic Encyclopedia* says, "This judicial authority will even include the power to pardon sins."—Volume 12, p. 265.

Volumes could be produced to prove that the Papacy makes claims belonging only to the Godhead. The Papacy is either what it claims to be, or the real Antichrist. Both Catholics and Protestants admit this.

7. *It was to make war on God's saints.*

"And shall wear out the saints of the most High." Verse 25.

It was to persecute dissenters. The noted Catholic Thomas Aquinas said that convicted heretics should be put to death just as surely as other criminals, because they were counterfeiters.

During the dark days of papal persecution unnumbered millions died on the gallows, at the stake, by the sword, through privation, et cetera, and were tortured in ways too numerous to be mentioned. This is one of the periods of "great tribulation."

"That the Church of Rome has shed more innocent blood than any other institution that has ever existed among mankind, will be questioned by no Protestant who has a competent knowledge of history. The memorials, indeed, of many of her persecutions are now so scanty that it is impossible to form a complete conception of the multitude of her victims, and it is quite certain that no powers of imagination can adequately realize their sufferings."—W. E. H. LECKY, in *History of the Rise and Influence of the Spirit of Rationalism in Europe* (1910 ed.), vol. 2, p. 32.

8. *It would think to change God's times and laws.* "And think to change times and laws." Verse 25.

Ferraris, a noted Roman Catholic writer, says, "The pope is of so great authority and power that he can modify, explain, or interpret even divine laws. . . . The pope can modify divine law, since his power is not of man, but of God, and he acts as vicegerent of God upon earth."—Translated from LUCIUS FERRARIS, *Prompta Bibliotheca* (Ready Library), "Papa," art. 2.

From Pope Nicholas' time we have this: "The pope has authority and has often exercised it, to dispense with the commands of Christ. . . . The pope's will stands for reason. He can dispense above the law; and of wrong make right, by correcting and changing the laws."

If you will read the Ten Commandments in a Catholic

catechism, you will note that the fourth commandment is made to teach something entirely different from Bible truth. This power was to "think to change" God's law. (See 2 Thessalonians 2:3, 4.) A power that changes God's law exalts itself above God.

The fourth of the Ten Commandments concerns the weekly Sabbath. Thus, if the little horn power was to change the "time" of God's law, we would expect some tampering with the Sabbath commandment, which deals with time. "The seventh day is the sabbath of the Lord thy God." Exodus 20:10.

From the *Catholic Mirror,* September 23, 1893, we quote: "The Catholic Church for over one thousand years before the existence of a Protestant, by virtue of her divine mission, changed the day from Saturday to Sunday."

From the Reverend Peter Geiermann's *Convert's Catechism of Catholic Doctrine* we take this:

"Q.—*Which is the Sabbath day?*

"A.—Saturday is the Sabbath day.

"Q.—*Why do we observe Sunday instead of Saturday?*

"A.—We observe Sunday instead of Saturday because the Catholic Church transferred the solemnity from Saturday to Sunday."—Page 50.

It is interesting to note that in Canon 29 the Council of Laodicea decreed: "Christians shall not Judaize and be idle on Saturday, but shall work on that day." Not only did the papal little horn power insist that Christians keep Sunday, the first day of the week, but it decreed that they should work on Saturday, the seventh-day Sabbath of the Ten Commandments. Said the prophetic voice, "And he shall . . . think to change times and laws."

9. *It would be in supremacy 1260 years.*

"And they shall be given into his hand until a time and times and the dividing of time." Daniel 7:25.

Read Revelation 12:6, 14 and note that "a time, and times, and half a time" are 1260 days. In prophetic time a day stands for a year. (Numbers 14:34; Ezekiel 4:6.) This method is Biblical and proves itself in practice.

The legally recognized supremacy of the pope began in A.D. 538, when there went into effect a decree of Emperor Justinian making the Bishop of Rome head over all the churches, the definer of doctrine, and the corrector of heretics. It was to continue 1260 years, or to A.D. 1798.

10. *Its dominion was to be taken away.*

"And they shall take away his dominion." Daniel 7:26.

Yes, the little horn's dominion was to be taken away. In 1798, just 1260 years from A.D. 538, the French general Berthier took the pope prisoner, and he died in French exile eighteen months later. The Papacy received a "deadly wound." (Revelation 13:3.) This was later to be healed. The Papacy will come back into power again.

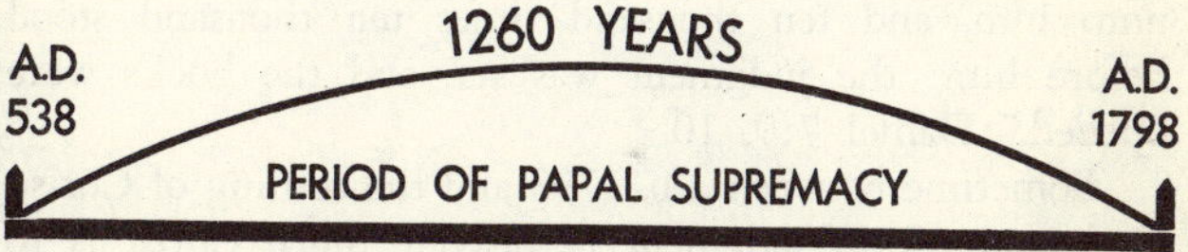

THE REFORMERS TESTIFY

John Wycliffe is called the "Morning Star" of the Protestant Reformation. "In chapter 2 of *De Papa* [On the Pope] he asserts that 'the pope is antichrist here in earth,' and in chapter 7 that the cardinals 'are hinges to the fiend's [devil's] house.'"—L. E. FROOM, *Prophetic Faith of Our Fathers,* vol. 2, p. 52.

"Wyclif regarded the pope, in bloodstained garments at the high altar of the central church of Christendom, as the Man of Sin, the Little Horn, and the true Antichrist of prophecy."—*Ibid.,* p. 53.

Martin Luther, mighty leader in the movement out of darkness into the light of the Scriptures, said, "I rejoice in having to bear such ills for the best of causes. Already I feel greater liberty in my heart; for at last I know that the pope is Antichrist, and that his throne is that of Satan himself."—D'AUBIGNE, *History of the Reformation,* book 6, chap. 9.

THE JUDGMENT CALLED IN HEAVEN

After the 1260 years of supremacy of the papal church, temporarily broken in A.D. 1798, God was to convene His court in heaven.

"I beheld till the thrones were cast down [placed], and the Ancient of days [God] did sit, whose garment was white as snow, and the hair of his head like the pure wool: his throne was like the fiery flame, and his wheels as burning fire. A fiery stream issued and came forth from before him: thousand thousands ministered unto him, and ten thousand times ten thousand stood before him: the judgment was set, and the books were opened." Daniel 7:9, 10.

Sometime between A.D. 1798 and the coming of Christ, God is to sit in judgment in heaven. Since Christ is to bring His reward with Him, all cases must be decided before He comes.

CHRIST'S KINGDOM TO BE SET UP

In connection with the judgment work and the setting up of God's kingdom, these words appear in verses 13 and 14:

"I saw in the night visions, and, behold, one like the Son of man came with the clouds of heaven, and came to the Ancient of days, and they brought him near before him. And there was given him dominion, and glory, and a kingdom, that all people, nations, and languages, should serve him: his dominion is an everlasting dominion, which shall not pass away, and his kingdom that which shall not be destroyed."

Thus in the seventh chapter of Daniel we have the same powers of Babylon, Medo-Persia, Greece, Rome, and the ten divisions of the Roman Empire as the main modern nations of Europe, and the setting up of God's everlasting kingdom—all just as in the second chapter.

However, in chapter 7 we view the 1260-year supremacy of the papal little horn, and note that God's great judgment day is to begin. Here it all is in diagram:

B.C. 605	B.C. 538	B.C. 331	B.C. 168	A.D. 476	A.D. 538	A.D. 1798		
BABYLON	MEDO-PERSIA	GRECIA	ROME	DIVISION	PAPAL SUPREMACY 1260 YEARS		JUDGMENT	GOD'S KINGDOM

Christ and the Saints

Not only is Christ set forth here as receiving the kingdom, but His faithful followers are to possess it with Him. We read it in verse 18: "The saints of the most High shall take the kingdom, and possess the kingdom for ever, even for ever and ever."

And again in verse 27: "The kingdom and dominion, and the greatness of the kingdom under the whole heaven, shall be given to the people of the saints of the most High, whose kingdom is an everlasting kingdom, and all dominions shall serve and obey him."

Who Are the Saints?

Who are the saints? What are the qualifications for entrance into this glorious and eternal kingdom? Will you not take your Bible and look up the references here given?

1. Those in Christ. (Philippians 1:1.)
2. Those who love the Lord. (Psalms 31:23.)
3. Praying people. (Revelation 5:8.)

4. Those willing to sacrifice. (Psalms 50:5.)

5. Those willing to suffer persecution. (Daniel 7:25.)

6. Those who keep the faith of Jesus. (Revelation 14:12.)

7. Those who keep the commandments of God. (Revelation 14:12.) (One version says, "Cling to the commandments of God and the faith of Jesus.")

Shut Out or Shut In

It has been said that when Admiral Piet Hein returned home after bringing in the captive Spanish ships loaded with silver from the mines of America, his wife called out, "Don't come in, Piet, until you've cleaned your shoes on the door mat."

Concerning that eternal home of Christ and the Redeemed we read, "There shall in no wise enter into it any thing that defileth, neither whatsoever worketh abomination, or maketh a lie: but they which are written in the Lamb's book of life." Revelation 21:27.

We must choose between the sin of earth and the righteousness of heaven. Calvary washes away the one and provides the other.

It has been said, "The more of earth we want, the less of heaven we'll get."

"All to Jesus I surrender,
All to Him I freely give;
I will ever love and trust Him,
In His presence daily live."

CHAPTER 29

The Battle of the Beasts

BASED ON DANIEL 8

WHEN A man builds a house he first lays the foundation. Then he builds the superstructure upon it.

The foundation for the study of historical prophecy is the second chapter of Daniel, with its great image of gold, silver, brass, iron, and clay. This image represented the kingdoms of Babylon, Medo-Persia, Grecia, Rome, and the ten main divisions of the Roman kingdom, most of which divisions grew up into the modern nations of Europe. God's kingdom, yet to come, was symbolized by the stone cut out of the mountain without hands.

The seventh chapter of Daniel is built directly upon the second chapter. Its four great beasts symbolize the same four kingdoms of Babylon, Medo-Persia, Grecia, and Rome. The ten horns stand for the ten divisions of Rome's empire, and correspond to the ten toes of Daniel 2. The little horn was the papal Roman power, in supremacy for 1260 years, from A.D. 538 to A.D. 1798. Sometime after 1798 God's judgment was to sit and His kingdom was to be set up.

Nebuchadnezzar's dream of the image was about the year 602 B.C. Daniel's vision of the four beasts was some sixty years later, or about 540 B.C. His visions of chapters 8 and 9 were both given at the time of Babylon's fall

 Lester Quade

Daniel was "astonished" at the vision of two mighty beasts in mortal combat symbolic prophecy is one of the most important in the Holy Scriptures.

to Medo-Persia, one in the last year of Belshazzar and the other in the first year of Darius.

We are now ready to build these two additional chapters into the prophetic structure. In all our study we seek not only to know prophecy but to know in person the Christ of prophecy.

Daniel's Vision of Chapter 8

Thus it was that two years after his vision of the four beasts, Daniel had another vision. Babylon was to fall that very year, so this dream begins with Medo-Persia, her conqueror.

Any child with ability to read well can understand the first part of this vision. Let us read it.

The Two-horned Ram

"I saw in a vision; and it came to pass, when I saw, that I was at Shushan in the palace, which is in the province of Elam; and I saw in a vision, and I was by the river of Ulai. Then I lifted up mine eyes, and saw, and, behold, there stood before the river a ram which had two horns: and the two horns were high; but one was higher than the other, and the higher came up last. I saw the ram pushing westward, and northward, and southward; so that no beasts might stand before him, neither was there any that could deliver out of his hand; but he did according to his will; and became great." Daniel 8:2-4.

What nation is represented by this mighty ram? Here is the answer in verse 20: "The ram which thou sawest having two horns are the kings of Media and Persia."

As the Medo-Persian bear of Daniel 7:5 raised himself up on one side, so one of the ram's horns was higher than the other, indicating that one of the powers of this dual monarchy was to be stronger than the other. Daniel

8 adds the point that the higher horn came up last. "The Medes were at first the leading people."—PHILIP V. MYERS, *General History,* p. 59. (See also Daniel 5:30, 31 and Jeremiah 51:11.) Later the Persians were in the ascendancy.

THE RAM AND HE-GOAT BATTLE

The female sheep is quite docile, but the ram loves a good fight. We next see a contest between this prophetic ram and a he-goat, also noted for battle instinct.

"As I was considering, behold, an he goat came from the west on the face of the whole earth, and touched not the ground: and the goat had a notable horn between his eyes. And he came to the ram that had two horns, which I had seen standing before the river, and ran unto him in the fury of his power. And I saw him come close unto the ram, and he was moved with choler [anger] against him, and smote the ram, and brake his two horns: and there was no power in the ram to stand before him, but he cast him down to the ground, and stamped upon him: and there was none that could deliver the ram out of his hand." Daniel 8:5-7.

It is needless to ask who is represented by this goat, for you are well aware that the Grecians overcame the Medo-Persians, as foretold in both chapters 2 and 7. However, let us read the Bible explanation in verse 21: "And the rough goat is the king [kingdom] of Grecia: and the great horn that is between his eyes is the first king."

Alexander the Great, first or most important king of Grecia, about two hundred years after Babylon's fall, overcame the Persians under Darius III at the Battle of Arbela in 331 B.C. The rough goat of Grecia gave the Medo-Persian ram a rough time. He was rightly described.

The four-winged leopard of Daniel 7 was swift. The he-goat, representing the same power, "touched not the ground." Both symbols for Grecia are fitting. Medo-Persia was to be "great" and Grecia "very great." (Verses 4 and 8.)

GRECIA'S GREAT HORN BREAKS

Concerning the goat's great horn, Alexander the Great, we read, "When he was strong, the great horn was broken; and for it came up four notable ones toward the four winds of heaven." Verse 8.

Again, you already know from chapter 7 what the four horns are. They are the same as the four heads of the leopard. But let us read the record of the broken horn in verse 22: "Now that being broken, whereas four stood up for it, four kingdoms shall stand up out of the nation, but not in his power."

The four horns represent the four divisions of Alexander's realm. The historian Rawlinson says, "A quadripartite division of Alexander's dominions was recognized." This took place twenty-two years after his death, when after the Battle of Ipsus (301 B.C.) his warring generals divided the kingdom into four parts—east, west, north, south—"toward the four winds of heaven." This conflict is also known as the Battle of the Kings. The tide of battle was turned by a large herd of war elephants.

THE "EXCEEDING GREAT" LITTLE HORN

We now read of what happens to one of those four horns, or divisions, of the Grecian kingdom.

"And out of one of them came forth a little horn which waxed exceeding great, toward the south, and toward the east, and toward the pleasant land." Verse 9.

In order to conserve space, let us outline *this* little horn's career:

The little horn is Rome, the next power in order. (168 B.C.)

a. The little horn of Daniel 7 is papal Rome.

b. This little horn of Daniel 8 is pagan Rome (with papal element).
c. It came out of one of the horns. (Daniel 8:9.) (Macedonia, 168 B.C.)
d. It was a fierce, mighty, destructive power. (Verses 23, 24.)
e. It was "exceeding great." (Verse 9.)
f. It went southward. (Verse 9.) (Took Egypt, 30 B.C.)
g. It went eastward. (Verse 9.) (Took Syria, 65 B.C.)
h. It went toward the pleasant land. (Verse 9.) (Took Judea, 63 B.C.)
i. It stood up against Christ. (Verse 25.)

The Medo-Persian ram was great. The Grecian goat was very great. This little horn was exceeding great.

The horn came forth from one of the four horns. The Romans defeated the Macedonians in 168 B.C. This was the western division, or horn, of Grecia. From this beginning Rome went on to conquer all. Pagan Rome became "exceeding great." It was under Roman rule that Jesus, the "Prince of princes," was crucified.

It can be said that papal Rome also became "exceeding great." She exalted herself to the place of Christ and above God in thinking "to change [His] times and laws." Daniel 7:25.

This Vision Reached to the Last Days

That the little horn of Daniel 8 took in the papal as well as the pagan phase of Rome seems clear from the fact that the vision was to include the last days. The angel Gabriel, in beginning his interpretation to Daniel, said, "Understand, O Son of man: for at the time of the end shall be the vision." Verse 17. At the close of chapter 8 he says, "For it shall be for many days." Verse 26. Since we live in the time of the end, there must be something here for us.

Daniel Faints

"And I Daniel fainted, and was sick certain days." Verse 26.

Under the glory of the heavenly teacher Daniel fainted. The prophecy had been carefully explained to him, with the exception of verse 14, "Unto two thousand and three hundred days; then shall the sanctuary be cleansed." The saints were interested in the matter. (Verse 13.) What could the meaning be?

Gabriel, the angel of prophecy, was gone. The Medes and Persians were soon to come and overthrow Babylon. Daniel was deeply concerned. "I was astonished at the vision, but none understood it." Verse 27. Would the holy angel return? We shall see.

Lester Quade, Artist

The prophecy of the 2300 years stretches across the centuries from the days of ancient Persia to our own times.

457 B.C.—Artaxerxes issued the final decree for the restoration of Jewish national life and the rebuilding of Jerusalem. (Daniel 9:25; Ezra 6:1, 6-12.) Beginning of seventy weeks and therefore of 2300 years.

A.D. 27—Jesus was baptized and began His ministry after being anointed by the Holy Spirit for His work. (Matthew 3:16; Acts 10:38.)

A.D. 31—Messiah was "cut off" in the midst of the seventieth week.

A.D. 34—With the stoning of Stephen the Jewish period ended and the apostles turned to the Gentiles.

CHAPTER 30

The Master Key to Bible Prophecy

THE IMPORTANT vision of Daniel 9, which we are now to study, was given in the first year of Darius the Mede, just a few months at most after the vision we have just considered in Daniel 8. Babylon had fallen to the Medo-Persians and Belshazzar had perished. But Daniel continued to function at the court of the new government.

DANIEL SEEKS UNDERSTANDING

Since the angel Gabriel had given no explanation of the 2300 days and the sanctuary question of Daniel 8:13, 14, Daniel now set himself to a study of the Scriptures, to earnest prayer and confession of sins, saying, "O our God, . . . cause thy face to shine upon thy sanctuary." Daniel 9:17.

THE ANGEL GABRIEL RETURNS

Gabriel is an angel. (Luke 1:26.) He seems to have special responsibility in revealing the plans of God to man.

We read, in Daniel 9:21-23: "Yea, whiles I was speaking in prayer, even the man Gabriel, whom I had seen in the vision at the beginning, being caused to fly swiftly, touched me about the time of the evening oblation. And he informed me, and talked with me, and said, O Daniel, I am now come forth to give thee skill and understanding. At the beginning of thy supplications the commandment came forth, and I am come to shew thee; for thou art greatly beloved: therefore understand the matter and consider the vision."

Consider *what* vision? It seems most evident that it must be the vision of a few weeks before, a portion of which had been unexplained, and had left Daniel "astonished."

What was the subject of the unexplained part of the vision? It was "time"—the 2300 days and the sanctuary. As we give study to Gabriel's immediate discussion of time periods we shall recall that in prophecy a day stands for a year. (Numbers 14:34; Ezekiel 4:6.) Thus 2300 days are actually 2300 years.

Gabriel Begins Explanation of Time Prophecy

The angel's very first words made unmistakably clear that he proposed to deal with this great time prophecy. We read Daniel 9:24:

"Seventy weeks are determined upon thy people and upon thy holy city, to finish the transgression, and to make an end of sins, and to make reconciliation for iniquity, and to bring in everlasting righteousness, and to seal up the vision and prophecy, and to anoint the most Holy."

How many days would seventy weeks be? With seven days to the week, seventy weeks would be seven times seventy, 490 prophetic days, or 490 *literal years.*

The next point is that the 490 years were to be determined, or "cut off," which is the basic meaning. From what were they to be "cut off"? Most naturally from the 2300 years of the vision, for did not Gabriel say, "Consider the vision"? Thus we have the following simple diagram:

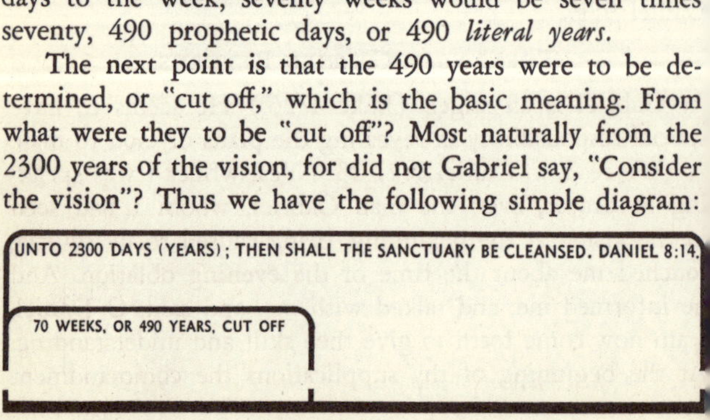

UNTO 2300 DAYS (YEARS); THEN SHALL THE SANCTUARY BE CLEANSED. DANIEL 8:14.

70 WEEKS, OR 490 YEARS, CUT OFF

During this 490 years, cut off from the 2300 years, and allotted to the Jewish people, certain things were to take place (verse 24):

1. Jewish transgression was to reach its limit.
2. Christ was to end sin offerings and make reconciliation for iniquity.
3. He was to bring His everlasting righteousness to men.
4. The vision was to be sealed and the Most Holy anointed.

The Starting Date for the Seventy Weeks

If we can find the date for the beginning of the seventy weeks, or 490 years, we shall also have the date for the beginning of the 2300 years, of which the 490 years are the first part.

Reading directly on, we find these words in verse 25, which give us the *date* we wish, as well as a division of the seventy weeks into yet smaller parts:

"Know therefore and understand, that from the going forth of the commandment to restore and to build Jerusalem unto the Messiah the Prince shall be seven weeks, and threescore and two weeks: the street shall be built again, and the wall, even in troublous times."

Follow this closely. Seven weeks plus threescore and two weeks would be sixty-nine weeks, or 483 prophetic days or literal years.

This would be all but seven years of the full 490 years allotted the Jewish people.

When were these 483 years to begin? "From the going forth of the commandment to restore and to build Jerusalem." Verse 25.

How far would these 483 years reach? "Unto the Messiah the Prince." "Messiah" means "the anointed one." Jesus was anointed by the Holy Spirit at the time of His baptism (Matthew 3:13-17; Acts 10:38), and went forth as the Messiah. This was in the year A.D. 27.

Now, let any school boy or girl figure it. Subtract 27 from 483 and that gives us 456. Since the year A.D. 27 was not fully gone when Jesus was baptized, we really would have 456 plus, or 457 B.C.

What happened in 457 B.C.? Just exactly what the Bible said would happen—the commandment was issued to restore Jerusalem. The Babylonians had destroyed it. The Medo-Persians were to help restore it. Here it is in Ezra 6:14:

"They builded, and finished it, according to the commandment of the God of Israel, and according to the commandment of Cyrus, and Darius, and Artaxerxes king of Persia."

It was God's commandment that counted, and it took the commands of three kings before God counted it as the *one commandment,* and so it is recorded in Scripture. Thus it was in 456 plus, or 457 B.C., that the final command of Artaxerxes was given in his seventh year. "For ever, O Lord, thy word is settled in heaven." Psalms 119:89.

Our diagram now looks like this:

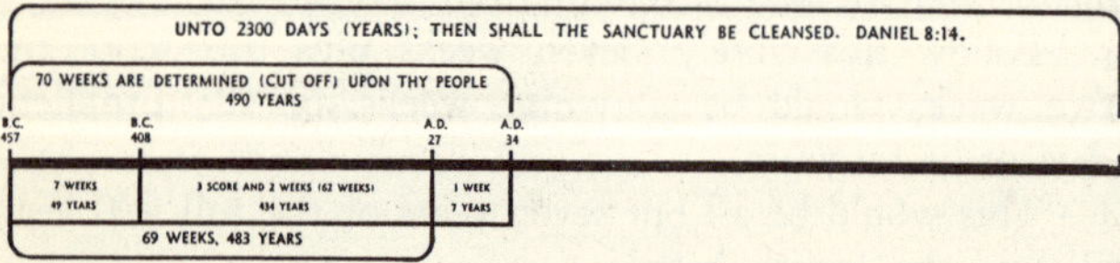

The year 457 B.C. is the beginning date of the 490 years, the 483 years, and the 2300 years. There is only one of the seventy weeks left, one week, or seven years, which would end in A.D. 34 as we see.

Why did the angel Gabriel break this seventy weeks,

or 490 years, into three parts, and make it a little more complicated?

His reason seems quite clear. Humphrey Prideaux says: "In the fifteenth year of Darius Nothus ended the first seven weeks of the seventy weeks of Daniel's prophecy. For then the restoration of the church and state of the Jews in Jerusalem and Judea was fully finished, in that last act of reformation, which is recorded in the thirteenth chapter of Nehemiah, from the twenty-third verse to the end of the chapter, *just forty-nine* years after it had been first begun by Ezra in the seventh year of Artaxerxes Longimanus."—*The Old and New Testament Connected in the History of the Jews,* vol. 1, p. 322. This is why we have the seven weeks, or forty-nine years, listed separately.

THE SEVENTIETH WEEK OF JEWISH TIME—A.D. 27 TO A.D. 34

We now turn to the last seven years of the 490 years, the seventieth week. The 69 weeks, or 483 years, were to bring us to Christ the Messiah in A.D. 27. When the date came He stood on the bank of the Jordan River and requested baptism of John the Baptist. Coming up out of the water, He received the Holy Spirit in the form of a dove, and God said, "This is my beloved Son, in whom I am well pleased." Matthew 3:17. "When the fulness of the time was come, God sent forth his Son." Galatians 4:4. Thus ends the sixty-ninth week, and the seventieth week begins. What happens in this last week of seven years?

We read, "And after threescore and two weeks [that is after the seven weeks and the threescore and two weeks, or sixty-nine weeks] shall Messiah be cut off, but not for himself." Daniel 9:26.

In the poorer section of a large city a frame apartment

house caught fire. On the top floor a father and three small sons were trapped. The father rushed to a window and discovered another window open in the nearby building. Here was a possible way of escape for the little boys. He planted his feet firmly on the window ledge and stretched himself across the gulf between the two buildings, placing his hands on the ledge of the window across the way. One by one the boys crawled over his body to safety. Just as the last one had crossed over, the father's strength gave way, and he plunged far below to his death. He died for his sons. The Messiah was "cut off" for us—"to make reconciliation for iniquity." Verse 24.

Go stand before Calvary, and see the Son of God dying of a broken heart for your own personal sins, and you will feel the deep stirrings of repentance. If you do not resist the call, you will find the salvation of God.

It was to be in A.D. 31 that Jesus would die, for we read in verse 27: "In the midst of the week he shall cause the sacrifice and the oblation to cease." The midway point of the last seven years from A.D. 27 to A.D. 34 would be in A.D. 31. That is the date of the crucifixion.

When Jesus died upon the cross as the Lamb of God, the Jewish sacrifices and offerings were to cease in the sanctuary at Jerusalem. Heaven gave signal notice of this fact by a supernatural rending of the heavy temple veil from top to bottom. Matthew gives the record: "Jesus, when he had cried again with a loud voice, yielded up the ghost. And, behold, the veil of the temple was rent in twain from the top to the bottom." Matthew 27:50, 51. A human hand would have torn it from bottom to top if it could have been torn at all.

The remaining three and one-half years of the seventieth week, or the 490 years, reach to A.D. 34. Stephen was stoned to death by the Jews, and the great persecution of the church at Jerusalem followed. (Acts 7:59; 8:1.)

The Jewish nation had rejected the Messiah, and now He left their house desolate. The 490 years allotted to the Jewish nation were finished.

The 70 weeks, or 490 years, were part of the 2300 years. Since the 490 years reach to A.D. 34, the remaining 1810 years of the 2300 years would reach to 1844. At this time the sanctuary was to be cleansed. Many interpreters of prophecy at that time thought the world would end. But the expression, "cleansing of the sanctuary," had a different meaning. We shall seek to find the truth of this important matter in the next chapter.

Here is the complete diagram:

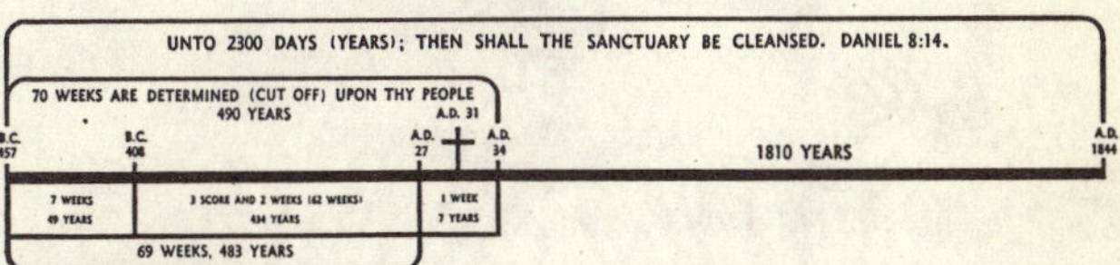

This year, 1844, is the Bible date for the cleansing of the sanctuary. It follows closely after 1798, the end of the 1260 years of papal supremacy. The judgment work was to begin sometime after 1798. Could there be a connection between the cleansing of the sanctuary and the judgment?

NOTE.—Many may wonder how Christ could be baptized in A.D. 27 when the Bible states that He was about thirty years of age. (Luke 3:23.) The answer is that Christ was born three or four years before A.D. 1, the date later erroneously set for the beginning of the Christian Era. See fuller explanation on page 213 of *Daniel and the Revelation,* 1944 edition.

Lester Quade, Arti

God said, "Let them make me a sanctuary; that I may dwell among them." T
illustration shows the sanctuary, the roof partially removed to show the interi

CHAPTER 31

The Cross Discovered in a Jewish Sanctuary

The Cleansing of the Sanctuary

THROUGH THE center of every inch of British Navy rope there runs an identifying colored thread. From cover to cover of the Bible there runs a scarlet thread of thought: "Salvation from sin is by blood sacrifice." Remove this thread, and Heaven's identification mark of the true gospel is gone. "Without shedding of blood is no remission." Hebrews 9:22. The blood stands for life. (Leviticus 17:11.) Take away the blood, and you take away salvation. Eliminate the cross, and man is left to die in his sins.

"The cleansing stream I see, I see,
I plunge, and O it cleanseth me!
O praise the Lord! it cleanseth me,
It cleanseth me, yes, cleanseth me."

Ancient Family Sacrifices

Abel, the second son of Adam, offered a blood sacrifice in the very shadow of Paradise lost, and God accepted it. The bloodless offering of Cain, Adam's first-born, was rejected. (Genesis 4:3-5.) It is clear beyond all doubt that God must have given them instruction regarding proper offerings. Otherwise He could not justly have held Cain in an act of sin for not complying. (Verses 6, 7.)

Then there was Noah. Concerning that thrilling though awesome experience when he came forth from the ark onto the desolate earth after the Flood, we read, "Noah builded an altar unto the Lord; and took of every clean beast, and of every clean fowl, and offered burnt offerings on the altar." Genesis 8:20.

Just four chapters further on in this first book of the Bible we come to the patriarch Abraham, "friend of God." He regularly offered sacrifices. "The Lord appeared unto Abraham . . . : and there builded he an altar unto the Lord. . . . And he removed from thence unto a mountain on the east of Bethel . . . : and there he builded an altar unto the Lord." Genesis 12:7, 8.

Abraham was ready to offer up his only son Isaac under a test God gave him. The voice of an "angel of the Lord called unto him out of heaven. . . . And he said, Lay not thine hand upon the lad." Genesis 22:11, 12. Abraham looked up, and there he saw a ram caught in the thicket. He offered it upon the altar "in the stead of his son." Verse 13.

Christ the Lamb of God

Jesus, speaking of this experience, said, "Your father Abraham rejoiced to see my day: and he saw it, and was glad." John 8:56. Jesus Christ deliberately walked into the thorny thicket of this world, and allowed Himself to be caught and crucified. John the Baptist, looking upon Jesus, said, "Behold the *Lamb of God,* which taketh away the sin of the world." John 1:29.

Christ is "the Lamb slain from the foundation of the world." Revelation 13:8. He stood in readiness to do this even before the foundation of the world. (1 Peter 1:18-20.) None but Christ, one equal to God's holy law, against which man had sinned, could redeem him from its curse. "For it is not possible that the blood of bulls and of goats should take away sins." Hebrews 10:4. Such blood could serve only as a type of Christ's blood.

When a man sacrifices his life, he sacrifices but a few days or years; he merely lays it down earlier instead of later. But Christ did not choose between dying at one time rather than at another time. He chose between dying and not dying. "I lay it [my life] down of myself," He said. John 10:18.

"Saviour, I lift my trembling eyes
  To that bright seat, where placed on high,
The great atoning sacrifice,
  For me, for all, is ever nigh."

From the days of Adam to Moses, some twenty-five hundred years, the coming sacrifice of Christ was typified by sacrificial offerings presented by responsible heads of families or others appointed. The family was the main unit of organization, save for the service of Melchizedek, "priest of the most high God," to whom Abraham paid tithe. (Genesis 14:18-20.)

Sacrificial Service Centers in Jewish Sanctuary

When Moses led Israel from Egyptian slavery, about fifteen hundred years before Christ, God said, "Let them make me a sanctuary; that I may dwell among them." Exodus 25:8. With hundreds of thousands of people together some center of worship was indeed most reasonable. The entire sacrificial work was now organized about the sanctuary, or tabernacle. The tribe of Levi was appointed for this service, and the descendants of Aaron, Moses' brother, were priests. All priests were Levites.

In the early years the sanctuary was a portable affair, housed under a type of tent roof with an open-air court. Later King Solomon built a magnificent Temple on the spot at Mount Moriah where Abraham had presented Isaac to God. This beautiful Temple housed the sanctuary. Destroyed centuries later by Nebuchadnezzar, it was afterward rebuilt under the Medo-Persian decree. This later Temple, embellished by the Romans, was the proud possession of the Jews when Jesus was upon earth. The Mohammedan Mosque of Omar now occupies the site of the actual Temple.

The sanctuary which Moses built was inside an open-air court about 75 by 150 feet. The walls of the court were made of linen screens suspended from upright brass pillars. The entrance was at the eastern end. Also in the court were the altar of burnt offering, and the brass laver, at which the priests washed their hands and feet before entering the sanctuary.

The First, or Holy, Place

The sanctuary stood at the western end of the oblong court. It had two rooms, or apartments, the holy and the most holy, separated by a beautiful veil, or heavy curtain. (Exodus 26:33.)

The *first* apartment, as Paul speaks of it, or the holy place, had three articles of furniture: the golden candlestick, with seven lamps (Exodus 25:37), the table of shewbread, and the golden altar of incense (Hebrews 9:2; Exodus 40:26, 27). On the altar of incense the priest burned sweet incense morning and evening. The service in this apartment was carried on daily. (Hebrews 9:6.)

The morning and evening sacrifices were for all the people, and offerings were brought by individuals for specific sins.

The Second, or Most Holy, Place

In the second, or most holy, apartment, separated from the first by a veil, was the ark, the central figure of the entire sanctuary. Made of shittim wood, it was in the form of a chest four feet long, with a width and depth of about two and one-half feet. It was overlaid with pure gold within and without, and had a crown of gold around the top edges. (Exodus 25:10, 11.)

The cover of the ark was made of solid gold and was called the mercy seat. At each end of this cover stood a cherub made of pure, beaten gold, with wings outstretched and face looking toward the mercy seat. (Verses 17-19.)

Between the cherubim and above the mercy seat was the Shekinah, or the holy presence of God. "There I will meet with thee, and I will commune with thee from above the mercy seat, from between the two cherubims." Verse 22.

What was in this sacred ark? After God had in trumpet tones proclaimed the Ten Commandments from Mount Sinai, He wrote them upon two tables of stone. (Deuteronomy 5:22.) Concerning the second and final writing God said to Moses: "I will write on the tables the words that were in the first tables which thou brakest, and thou shalt put them in the ark." Deuteronomy 10:2. Then Moses gives us this inspired record: "And he wrote on the tables, according to the first writing, the ten commandments, which the Lord spake unto you in the mount out of the midst of the fire in the day of the assembly: and the Lord gave them unto me. And I turned myself and came down from the mount, and put the tables in the ark which I had made; and there they be, as the Lord commanded me." Verses 4, 5.

All services of the sanctuary centered in the fact that man had transgressed the everlasting principles of the Ten Commandments, now engraved on tables of stone lying in the sacred ark of the sanctuary. All men needed mercy. So above the holy law was the mercy seat. And above the mercy seat was God, the author of His law, the dispenser of mercy, the Saviour of sinners.

God's law decreed death. His mercy provided life. Pardon was proffered by virtue of the atoning blood. Shining through all the ceremonies of spilled blood, gleamed the saving letters of everlasting life—C-A-L-V-A-R-Y. No Jew was ever saved in any other way than by God's eternal grace. The price of his salvation was the coming sacrifice on Calvary.

"Marvelous grace of our loving Lord,
Grace that exceeds our sin and our guilt,
Yonder on Calvary's mount outpoured,
There where the blood of the Lamb was spilt."

—"Grace Greater Than Our Sin." Copyright, 1938, renewal. Hope Publishing Company, owner. Used by permission.

Up in Yosemite Park an eleven-year-old boy dropped his canteen into the swollen Merced River just above beautiful Vernal Falls. Seeking to retrieve it, he fell in. The turbulent waters carried him swiftly toward the falls.

A twenty-one-year-old youth, just out of the Navy and still in uniform, leaped over the railing, swam rapidly, and about fifteen feet from the edge of the falls caught hold of the boy's shirt. He lost his hold, and when he had regained his grip it was too late. Both were swept over and down the roaring cataract, to be broken on the jagged rocks 317 feet below.

The noble Navy youth was willing but unable to save. Jesus is able to save to the uttermost, whether we be young or old, Jew or Gentile, free or bond! Declared Paul the Jew, "I am not ashamed of the gospel of Christ: for it is the power of God unto salvation to every one that believeth; to the Jew first, and also to the Greek." Romans 1:16. "For unto us was the gospel preached, as well as unto them." Hebrews 4:2. In the heart of the Jewish sanctuary God's grace planted the saving cross of Jesus.

"Sin and despair like the sea waves cold,
Threaten the soul with infinite loss;
Grace that is greater, yes, grace untold,
Points to the refuge, the mighty cross."
—Used by permission.

THE EARTHLY SANCTUARY A FIGURE OF THE HEAVENLY

The earthly sanctuary was patterned after the sanctuary, or temple, of heaven. (Hebrews 8:5.)

Both had the same articles of furniture. Centuries after the days of Moses, John the revelator in vision was shown the articles of furniture in the heavenly sanctuary. He saw the golden candlesticks. (Revelation 1:12, 13; 4:5.) He saw the golden altar of incense. (Revelation 8:3, 4.) As he viewed the future he saw the "ark of his testament" in the temple of heaven. (Revelation 11: 18, 19.)

Christ is the high priest of the heavenly sanctuary. There He ministers in our behalf. "Christ is not entered into the holy places made with hands, which are the figures of the true; but into heaven itself, now to appear in the presence of God for us." Hebrews 9:24.

As Israel had the morning and evening sacrifice, so should we make daily confession and daily consecration of our all to God, trusting His atoning grace. As the incense ascended daily, so should our prayers ascend to God as a sweet fragrance of gratitude. (Revelation 8:3, 4.) As the priest daily looked by faith beyond the veil to the mercy seat he could not see, so should we by faith look to Jesus as He ministers for us in the sanctuary above.

THE EARTHLY SANCTUARY CLEANSED ONCE A YEAR

The tenth day of the seventh month was called the "day of atonement." (Leviticus 23:27.) Atonement by blood was made for the sanctuary and for the people.

(Leviticus 16:16, 30.) Atonement means reconciliation, or the bringing of at-one-ment. This Day of Atonement was also, in a sense, a day of judgment. It was God's last call for His people to repent of sin and come under the atoning blood. (Leviticus 23:29.)

As the people confessed their sins day by day and sacrifices were offered, and the blood placed on the horns of the altar, the sins were in symbol transferred to the sanctuary. Then, once a year, on the tenth day of the seventh month, final opportunity was given for full disposition of sin. It was a solemn day indeed! It was "now or never." It was the annual day of judgment.

A Gentile consul of Jerusalem gives us the charge of the oldest priest to the high priest preceding the Day of Atonement.

"Take it to heart, that thou art going to appear before the King of all kings, who sits upon the throne of judgment."—*The Babylonian Talmud* (new ed.), translated by Michael L. Rodkinson, vol. 6, p. 146.

A modern Hebrew poet writes:

"What mandate gave the day to you and me?
It is the Judgment Day of all the year!"

The noted Dean Farrar wrote, "So awful was the Day of Atonement that we are told in a Jewish book of ritual that the very angels run to and fro in fear and trembling, saying, 'Lo, the Day of Judgment has come!' "—*The Early Days of Christianity,* p. 238.

So the cleansing of the earthly sanctuary had definitely connected with it the idea of the judgment day.

Cleansing of the Heavenly Sanctuary

How could the heavenly sanctuary need cleansing? Is there sin in heaven? No, there is no sin in heaven, though that is where sin first arose, and where the problem is to be forever settled.

Note the following points:

1. The service of the earthly sanctuary came to an end. (Matthew 27:50, 51.)

2. Christ entered the heavenly holy place after the cross. (Hebrews 9:24.)

3. In 1844 the time came to cleanse the heavenly sanctuary. (Daniel 8:14.)

4. This was the great antitypical judgment in the most holy place.

5. There is no sin in heaven, but there are records of sin. (Revelation 20:11, 12.)

6. "The judgment was set, and the books were opened." (Daniel 7:9, 10.)

7. John saw the ark of the testament (in the most holy place). (Revelation 11:18, 19.)

8. After the final decree is issued, Christ will soon come. (Revelation 22:11, 12.)

9. A worldwide judgment message is to be given before then. (Revelation 14:6, 7.)

This judgment message is here announced: "I saw another angel fly in the midst of heaven, having the everlasting gospel to preach unto them that dwell on the earth, and to every nation, and kindred, and tongue, and people, saying with a loud voice, Fear God, and give glory to him; for the hour of his judgment is come." Revelation 14:6, 7.

That judgment hour was to begin sometime between the close of papal supremacy in A.D. 1798 and the second coming of Christ. Here is a diagram of the main dates that belong to the prophetic story we have been studying:

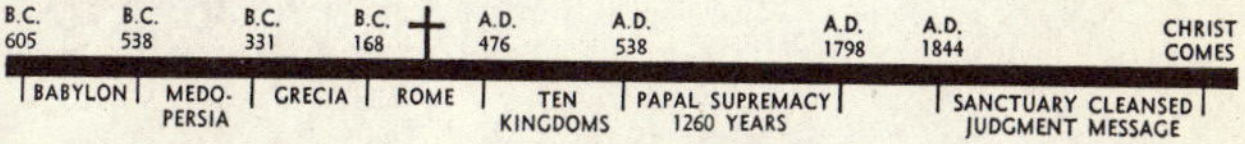

B.C. 605 | B.C. 538 | B.C. 331 | B.C. 168 † | A.D. 476 | A.D. 538 | A.D. 1798 | A.D. 1844 | CHRIST COMES

BABYLON | MEDO-PERSIA | GRECIA | ROME | TEN KINGDOMS | PAPAL SUPREMACY 1260 YEARS | SANCTUARY CLEANSED JUDGMENT MESSAGE

 Arlo Greer, Ar

The moment our Lord surrendered His life on the cross of Calvary the Temple curt was rent from top to bottom, indicating the end of the ceremonial sacrificial syst

When Jesus died on the cross the sacrificial system, which was a type of His sacrifice, ended as far as God was concerned. Christ rose from the dead and ascended to heaven to begin His work as our High Priest.

In 1844 some sanctuary was to be cleansed. It could not be the earthly, because its work was over. Some thought it meant the earth, and that the earth would be purified by fire at that time, when Christ would return. But this was a mistake. The earthly sanctuary was a type of the heavenly, and in 1844 the hour struck for the beginning of that cleansing. It was the beginning of Heaven's judgment.

God plans His work and works His plans. "When the fulness of the time was come, God sent forth his Son." Galatians 4:4. At the end of the 483 years of Daniel 9, Jesus was baptized, and anointed by the Holy Ghost, just as predicted. That was A.D. 27. He was also crucified at the stroke of the prophetic clock, in A.D. 31.

We may rest assured that in 1844, when the work of cleansing the heavenly sanctuary was to begin, Jesus entered the most holy apartment of the heavenly sanctuary and began that work. There is no sin in heaven, but a work of judgment is being done in connection with the records of sin.

As the cleansing of the earthly sanctuary was the final day to get right with God, a day of judgment, so the cleansing of the heavenly sanctuary is God's appointed time for the final judgment. "He hath appointed a day, in the which he will judge the world." Acts 17:31.

This judgment was future in Paul's day. (Acts 24:25.) It was "judgment to come." It did not come before death or at death but after death. "It is appointed unto men once to die, but after this the judgment." Hebrews 9:27. Only those living in the closing days of earth's history will be judged before death.

This is the investigative judgment. All cases must be decided before Christ comes, since He brings His reward with Him.

The judgment-hour message of Revelation 14:6, 7 must go to the whole world, and a people will be prepared to meet God. They will "keep the commandments of God, and the faith of Jesus." Revelation 14:12.

That message, which began on time, is now on its way to the remotest parts of the earth and will be finished on time. God alone knows the final hour.

Every reader of these lines may heed God's present-day message, the everlasting gospel in the judgment-hour setting.

As the children of Israel, ready to flee the slavery of Egypt, placed the blood on the doorposts and lintel of every home before the death angel passed over, so today, in Heaven's final judgment hour, we may find at Calvary the blood of Jesus for the door of our heart. May we permit it to cleanse every sin and stain.

"Dark is the stain that we cannot hide,
What can avail to wash it away?
Look, there is flowing a crimson tide;
Whiter than snow you may be today."
—Used by permission.

In ancient Greece many men were executed by being given a drink of the poison hemlock. Socrates is about the only man we remember who died in this manner.

Thousands of persons have been crucified upon crosses. But only one died upon a cross to save sinners. He will be remembered by the redeemed throughout all eternity.

"Blessing, and honour, and glory, and power, be unto him that sitteth upon the throne, and unto the Lamb for ever and ever." Revelation 5:13.

CHAPTER 32

Man's Case at God's Court

SOMEONE HAS said that we judge ourselves in our Sunday clothes, while our neighbors judge us in our shirt sleeves. That is an important distinction. It is more important to remember that God will judge our naked souls.

"He hath appointed a day, in the which he will judge the world." Acts 17:31.

Will that court call my name, or could it be that in my lowly place I might be overlooked? In time they will get around to everyone. "We must all appear before the judgment seat of Christ; that every one may receive the things done in his body, according to that he hath done, whether it be good or bad." 2 Corinthians 5:10. Daniel Webster said, "Gentlemen, the most serious question which has ever engaged my thoughts is my personal accountability to God."

The Time of the Investigative Judgment

When Jesus Christ comes to earth the second time, He will bring His reward with Him, "to give every man according as his work shall be." Revelation 22:12.

This being true, it is clearly evident that a work of judgment must take place before He comes again.

Therefore we are not surprised at what we have already learned, that the Bible paints a most magnificent though solemn picture of this very judgment work. After the 1260 years of papal church supremacy (the little horn of Daniel 7) from A.D. 538 to 1798, the judgment was to sit. We have discovered that A.D. 1844 is the Bible date for the beginning of that work. At that time the cleansing of the heavenly sanctuary began—the examination of the records of sinful man.

Following the Bible principle that "judgment must begin at the house of God" (1 Peter 4:17), we would expect Adam's name to be called first, and eventually the last name will be reached.

This work was future in Paul's day, for "he reasoned of . . . judgment to come." Acts 24:25. As the years of Jesus' baptism and death were specifically foretold, so did God set the clock of eternity to strike the hour for earth's investigative judgment to begin. The judgment-hour message is to be heralded to all nations. (Revelation 14:6, 7.) The time of its close has not been revealed, and is known to God alone. (Matthew 24:26.)

The Celestial Scene of the Judgment

Human pen cannot adequately portray the glory and solemnity of the heavenly court. But the Bible gives us an accurate account of the opening day. (Daniel 7:9-11, 13.) Four points are made clear:

1. "I beheld till the thrones were cast down." Verse 9. The expression "cast down" really means "placed," or "arranged." Since God's throne is in heaven (Psalms 103:19), it is evident that lesser thrones were placed in position about the throne of God.

2. God is the presiding judge, for "the Ancient of days did sit." Daniel 7:9. That the Ancient of Days is God the Father is clear from verse 13. God and His throne are pictured in these words: "Whose garment was white as snow, and the hair of his head like the pure wool:

 Frederic R. Gruger, Artist

, our high priest, "is able also to save them to the uttermost that come unto
by him, seeing he ever liveth to make intercession for them." Hebrews 7:25.

 Russ He

God has "appointed a day, in the which he will judge the world." Acts 17:31
who accepts the Saviour now has a divine Advocate at the judgment bar of he

his throne was like the fiery flame, and his wheels as burning fire. A fiery stream issued and came forth from before him." Verses 9, 10.

3. Angels and elders are in attendance, since "thousand thousands ministered unto him, and ten thousand times ten thousand stood before him." Verse 10. These are the angels and the elders. (Revelation 5:11.)

4. Christ came "to the Ancient of days, and they brought him near before him." Daniel 7:13. "We have an advocate with the Father, Jesus Christ the righteous." 1 John 2:1.

God the Father created all things by Jesus Christ. (Ephesians 3:9.) He reconciled the world to Himself by Jesus Christ. (2 Corinthians 5:18.) He will judge the world by Jesus Christ. (Acts 17:31.) Jesus is our Creator, our Redeemer, and our Friend at the judgment bar of God.

"He who has given the light, He who has followed the soul with tenderest entreaty, seeking to win it from sin to holiness, is in one its Advocate and Judge. . . . It is He who has encountered the deceiver, and who through all the ages has been seeking to wrest the captives from his grasp, who will pass judgment on every soul."—MRS. E. G. WHITE, *The Desire of Ages,* p. 210. He will accept and win our cases if we will only let Him.

The finishing touch to the judgment scene is given in these words: "The judgment was set, and the books were opened." Daniel 7:10.

THREE SOURCES OF TESTIMONY

Did you ever look carefully at the pyramid on the back of a United States one-dollar bill. If not, do so. You will notice that in the tip of the pyramid and encircled by a glow of light is an eye. This represents the all-seeing eye of God, which keeps watch over men.

The first and most fundamental source of testimony at God's court is His own knowledge of all things. "The eyes of the Lord are in every place, beholding the evil and the good." Proverbs 15:3. This testimony God need not bring forth Himself, since it is available from other sources as we shall see. It is well to remember that "as a shield from temptation and an inspiration to purity and truth, no other influence can equal the sense of God's presence."—MRS. E. G. WHITE, *Education,* p. 255. "Thou God seest me." Genesis 16:13.

The second source of testimony for God's court is taken from certain records in books. "The dead were judged out of those things which were written in the books, according to their works." Revelation 20:12.

One very special book is the "Lamb's book of life." (Revelation 21:27.) In this book the names of professed followers of Christ are entered. (Philippians 4:3.) Their names are to be retained or blotted out of the book of life as the full records may indicate. Revelation 3:5 says that the overcomers' names will not be blotted out. Of another we read, "God shall take away his part out of the book of life." Revelation 22:19.

Another special book is the "book of remembrance." (Malachi 3:16.) This contains a record of the kind words and gracious deeds of those who love and reverence God.

Some have considered that the following words indicate a special book of sin records: "For though thou wash thee with nitre, and take thee much soap, yet thine iniquity is marked before me, saith the Lord God." Jeremiah 2:22. We do not go beyond the Scriptures, and must be content with the information that Heaven keeps books of record, and we are to be judged by those records.

The third source of testimony is the angels who keep the records. The Bible indicates that angels do this work. "Suffer not thy mouth to cause thy flesh to sin; neither ay thou before the angel, that it was an error." Ecclesiastes 5:6. The Bible here reminds us that angels make no mistakes in their recording. Jesus also suggests that even each child has a guardian angel. (Matthew 18:10.)

Let us settle it in our minds and hearts that as men record their words on records and play them back again, so angels keep records of our lives, and those records will be opened in the judgment, and we shall be judged thereby.

It would not be necessary for God to keep records for His own information. The heavenly records are His evidence that He has dealt faithfully and mercifully with every soul.

The Scope of the Testimony

What does the judgment take in? Into how much detail does God go?

We will be judged by the following:

1. Our works. (Revelation 20:11, 12.)
2. Our words. (Matthew 12:36, 37.)
3. Our thoughts. (1 Corinthians 4:5.)
4. Our motives. (Proverbs 16:2.)
5. Every secret thing, good or bad. (Ecclesiastes 12:14.)

The X-ray photometer is said to detect counterfeit coins, spurious diamonds, and impurities in solid, liquid, or gaseous materials.

Someone tells of a maid in a Paris hotel who picked up an apple belonging to a guest. Biting into it, her teeth struck what proved to be the famous "rose diamond." The guest, taken into custody, proved to be a notorious jewel thief.

God's eye sees the hidden motive of every word and deed. He knows the "counsels of the heart," with "every secret thing, whether it be good, or whether it be evil."

We might conceivably fool others all the time, and deceive ourselves half the time, but we can deceive God none of the time. The X-ray telescope promises doctors living movies of our internal organs. God's X-ray gives a living movie of our inmost thoughts.

In this world we are often wrongly judged. Men suffer for what they have not done, and blindly reverse the process and misjudge others. But in God's court all the facts will be in the record.

Someone has said that if the most respected man's faults were written on his forehead, he would pull his hat over his eyes. Another has pointed out that there never was a man who, in his own opinion, got all the good things he deserved; or who, in the opinion of his neighbors, deserved all the good things he got. In any case and in every case, God will have the record straight. "Shall not the Judge of all the earth do right?" Genesis 18:25.

The Standard of the Judgment

Since God is to conduct a judgment of all men, He must have a law that is for all men. There can be no government without law. So we read these words: "For the Lord is our judge, the Lord is our lawgiver." Isaiah 33:22.

God's ten-commandment moral law was spoken by God and written with His finger on tables of stone at Mount Sinai. (Deuteronomy 4:12, 13.) The principles of this holy law were, of course, known by our first parents and were handed down by word of mouth.

If God's court is to be a court of justice, His law must be just. So we read, "Wherefore the law is holy, and the commandment holy, and just, and good." Romans 7:12.

This is the law whereby we are to be judged. James makes this clear when he writes: "For whosoever shall keep the whole law, and yet offend in one point, he is guilty of all. For he that said, Do not commit adultery, said also, Do not kill. Now if thou commit no adultery, yet if thou kill, thou art become a transgressor of the law. So speak ye, and so do, as they that shall be judged by the law of liberty." James 2:10-12. James, speaking of the Ten Commandments, presents this divine law not only as the standard of judgment but also as the "law of liberty." The psalmist says, "I will walk at liberty: for I seek thy precepts." Psalms 119:45.

Yes, the holy, eternal, immutable, unchangeable Ten Commandments will be the standard of that heavenly court. Thus it was that Solomon, summing up wisdom, said, "Let us hear the conclusion of the whole matter: Fear God, and keep his commandments: for this is the whole duty of man. For God shall bring every work into judgment, with every secret thing, whether it be good, or whether it be evil." Ecclesiastes 12:13, 14.

Solomon was simply saying, "Since we are to be *judged* by the law, let us *live* by the law. Let us obey its precepts."

In similar view does John the revelator write of Heaven's judgment-hour message, now due and hastening to all the world: "I saw another angel fly in the midst of heaven, having the everlasting gospel to preach unto them that dwell on the earth, and to every nation, and kindred, and tongue, and people, saying with a loud voice, Fear God, and give glory to him; for the hour of his judgment is come: and worship him that made heaven, and earth, and the sea, and the fountains of waters." Revelation 14:6, 7. God's judgment "is come." It is now going on. Men are called to worship the Creator and Judge, the Lawgiver.

A police officer picked up a law offender. The man objected and blustered. "All right," said the cop, "you can tell it to the judge." So he took the man to the police court, led him to the bench, and said, "Meet the judge." The man's attitude underwent a swift change. There is something about going to court that creates dread and fear. But where there is crime there must be courts. In God's universe, when there is sin, there must be a settlement.

Four Ways We Shall Be Judged

First of all, we shall be judged *by the law of God* as we have already read, but particularly as that law is interpreted in the life and teachings of Jesus. That means that we may be killers in heart, though we never took a life. We may be adulterers in thought, though not in deed. (Matthew 5:27, 28.) We may even do right for the wrong reason. And "there is nothing covered, that shall not be revealed; and hid, that shall not be known." Matthew 10:26.

The second point is that we are to be judged *by the light we have.* Said Jesus, "If ye were blind, ye should have no sin: but now ye say, We see; therefore your sin remaineth." John 9:41. Jesus advised the rejectors of His gospel preached in Capernaum, "It shall be more tolerable for the land of Sodom in the day of judgment, than for thee." Matthew 11:24.

A small schoolboy tarried long on his way home from school on short winter days. Why? He hoped his mother would already have the chickens fed; then he would not be asked to do it. He was an unwilling boy at heart. Like the schoolboy was the man who said, "We had better not get too concerned about religion. That way we will avoid the responsibility."

Jesus answered that in these words: "Every one that doeth evil hateth the light, neither cometh to the light, lest his deeds should be reproved." John 3:20. And in connection with that He also said, "This is the condemnation, that light is come into the world, and men loved darkness rather than light." Verse 19.

We shall therefore be judged by the light we have had and by that which we could have had.

Another principle of the judgment will be: *"With what judgment ye judge,* ye shall be judged." Matthew 7:2. It is said that the Sioux Indians had a prayer: "Great Spirit, help me never to judge another until I have walked two weeks in his moccasins." The Bible concludes: "Therefore judge nothing before the time, until the Lord come, who both will bring to light the hidden things of darkness, and will make manifest the counsels of the hearts." 1 Corinthians 4:5.

Finally, we shall be judged in mercy. We have all sinned. (Romans 3:23.) The wages of sin is eternal death. (Romans 6:23.) "He that covereth his sins shall not prosper: but whoso confesseth and forsaketh them shall have mercy." Proverbs 28:13.

Aquilla Webb tells the story of a boy who, attending a country school, just drifted along, making very bad marks. About Christmas time his teacher spoke some kind words to him, and after the holidays he took a sharp turn for the better. Final examinations were passed in flying colors, to the great joy of his parents.

The children's copybooks used through the year were laid on a large table for parents and friends to see. The boy saw his parents pick up his book, and his heart sank within him. They would see the bleary mess of blots and poor work of the first semester. However, to his surprise they smiled and seemed highly pleased.

Afterward the boy discovered that his kind teacher had torn out all the miserable, blotted leaves, and made his book begin where he had started to do better.

So God covers with His mercy the blotted pages of our unworthy lives and lets us start all over again. "It is God's glory to encircle sinful, repentant human beings in the arms of His love, to bind up their wounds, to cleanse them from sin, and to clothe them with the garments of salvation."—MRS. E. G. WHITE, *Prophets and Kings,* p. 668.

We should not flee from God to escape justice, but come to Christ for mercy. The farther away from his teacher an erring schoolboy stands, the sharper the bite of the lash.

"'Tis vain to flee; till gentle Mercy show
Her better eye, the farther off we go,
The swing of Justice deals the mightier blow."
—QUARLES.

When we feel the sting of the whip in the hand of God's justice, let us flee into the open arms of mercy, and find refuge close against His breast of love. The deserved lashings of holy law can be escaped no other place. Then from out the very womb of love shall our hearts be born anew, and upon their fleshy tablets shall the finger of God trace the precepts of His divine and holy law.

"Precept and promise, law and love combining,
Till night shall vanish in eternal day."

Several years ago the public press reported the following story of the mayor of New York City:

La Guardia, former mayor of New York, presided occasionally in police court. One cold day a trembling old man was brought before him, charged with stealing a loaf of bread. His family, he said, was starving. "I've got to punish you," said La Guardia. "The law makes no exception. I sentence you to a fine of ten dollars." But the Little Flower was reaching into his pocket as he added, "Here's ten dollars to pay your fine. And now I remit the fine." He tossed the bill into his famous sombrero. "Furthermore," he declared, "I'm going to fine everybody in this room 50 cents for living in a town where a man has to steal bread in order to eat." The hat was passed, and an incredulous old man, with the light of heaven in his eyes, left the courtroom with a stake of $47.50.

God too will consider the background of men's lives, and deal accordingly. "The Lord shall count, when he writeth up the people, that this man was born there." Psalms 87:6.

"As snow blots out the blackened roof,
The weary, brown-leaved sod—
So, upon the burdened heart,
Falls the forgiveness of God."

—VIRGINIA SCOTT MINER.

SECTION SIX

GOD SPEAKS CONCERNING HEAVEN'S GOVERNMENT FOR MAN

Heaven's Law for Man

Who Nailed What to the Cross?

Saved by Grace

Men Testify on the Ten Commandments

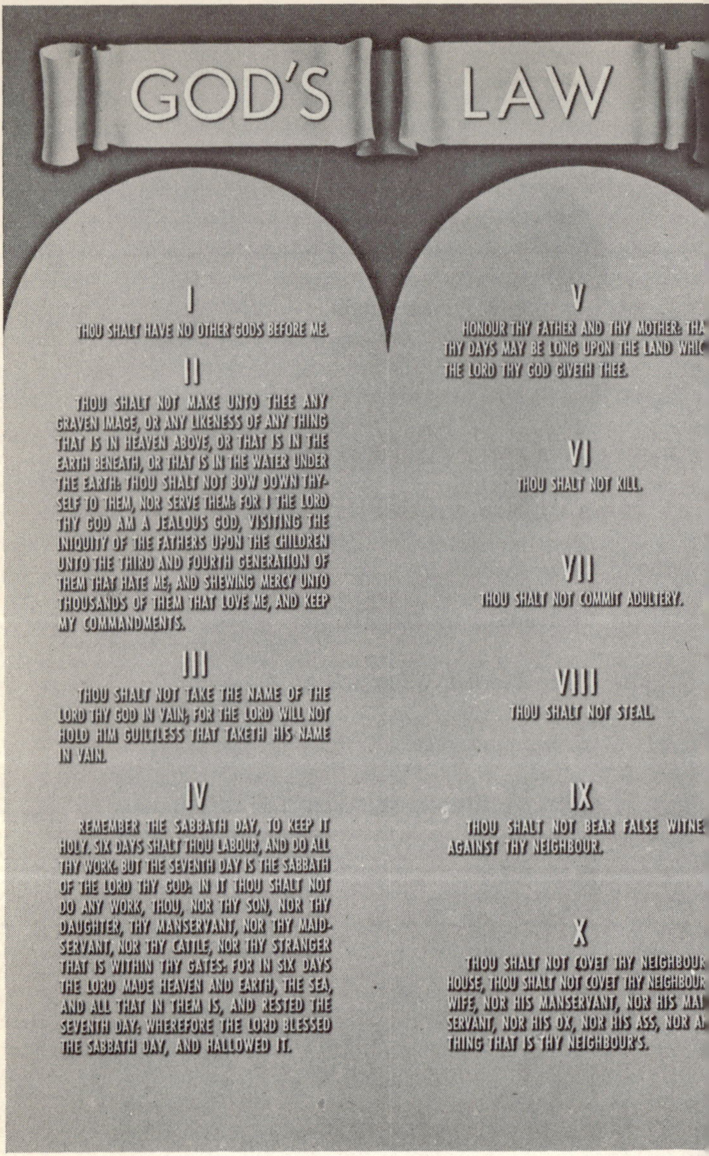

GOD'S LAW

I

THOU SHALT HAVE NO OTHER GODS BEFORE ME.

II

THOU SHALT NOT MAKE UNTO THEE ANY GRAVEN IMAGE, OR ANY LIKENESS OF ANY THING THAT IS IN HEAVEN ABOVE, OR THAT IS IN THE EARTH BENEATH, OR THAT IS IN THE WATER UNDER THE EARTH: THOU SHALT NOT BOW DOWN THYSELF TO THEM, NOR SERVE THEM: FOR I THE LORD THY GOD AM A JEALOUS GOD, VISITING THE INIQUITY OF THE FATHERS UPON THE CHILDREN UNTO THE THIRD AND FOURTH GENERATION OF THEM THAT HATE ME; AND SHEWING MERCY UNTO THOUSANDS OF THEM THAT LOVE ME, AND KEEP MY COMMANDMENTS.

III

THOU SHALT NOT TAKE THE NAME OF THE LORD THY GOD IN VAIN; FOR THE LORD WILL NOT HOLD HIM GUILTLESS THAT TAKETH HIS NAME IN VAIN.

IV

REMEMBER THE SABBATH DAY, TO KEEP IT HOLY. SIX DAYS SHALT THOU LABOUR, AND DO ALL THY WORK: BUT THE SEVENTH DAY IS THE SABBATH OF THE LORD THY GOD: IN IT THOU SHALT NOT DO ANY WORK, THOU, NOR THY SON, NOR THY DAUGHTER, THY MANSERVANT, NOR THY MAIDSERVANT, NOR THY CATTLE, NOR THY STRANGER THAT IS WITHIN THY GATES: FOR IN SIX DAYS THE LORD MADE HEAVEN AND EARTH, THE SEA, AND ALL THAT IN THEM IS, AND RESTED THE SEVENTH DAY: WHEREFORE THE LORD BLESSED THE SABBATH DAY, AND HALLOWED IT.

V

HONOUR THY FATHER AND THY MOTHER: THA
THY DAYS MAY BE LONG UPON THE LAND WHIC
THE LORD THY GOD GIVETH THEE.

VI

THOU SHALT NOT KILL.

VII

THOU SHALT NOT COMMIT ADULTERY.

VIII

THOU SHALT NOT STEAL.

IX

THOU SHALT NOT BEAR FALSE WITNE
AGAINST THY NEIGHBOUR.

X

THOU SHALT NOT COVET THY NEIGHBOUR
HOUSE, THOU SHALT NOT COVET THY NEIGHBOUR
WIFE, NOR HIS MANSERVANT, NOR HIS MAI
SERVANT, NOR HIS OX, NOR HIS ASS, NOR A
THING THAT IS THY NEIGHBOUR'S.

Martin J. Weber, A

God's unchangeable moral code for man was written by the divine finger. It was g
by God to mankind for all generations, and has never been revoked or annu

CHAPTER 33

Heaven's Law for Man

ACCORDING TO the Bible, God is a king. (Jeremiah 10:6, 7.) His throne is in heaven, "and his kingdom ruleth over all." Psalms 103:19.

God shares this rulership with Christ. The Old Testament testifies: "The government shall be upon his shoulder." Isaiah 9:6. The last book in the Bible pictures Him coming as "KING OF KINGS, AND LORD OF LORDS." Revelation 19:16.

Government Requires Law

There can be no orderly government without law, and no happy, ordered society without *accepted* laws.

Boys cannot play a peaceful marble game, or one-old-cat-bat, or two-old-cat-bat, or baseball, football, or any other game without rules.

A six-year-old boy started to school. His kind parents had trained him on the idea that he should mostly do as he pleased. So he got the idea that the world was created mainly for his pleasure. We watched him break up marble games by running away with a handful of marbles. He interrupted the ball game by throwing the ball away. Needless to say, via the hard way, he learned to play by the rules. Even school grounds must have laws.

Men cannot do business without rules. There must be yardsticks, scales, measures of gallons, bushels, et cetera.

Belief in, and obedience to, good laws are the very foundation of human society, the very warp and woof of happy, ordered existence. If men are to live together in peace and decency, there can be no program of every man's doing only what he may choose to do without respect to law. He who drives his automobile down the left-hand side of the street is bound to have at least one collision, and it might be his last.

The Laws of God's Government

Human rulers have often enacted cruel and oppressive laws. In God's government He issues the laws. (Isaiah 33:22.) Since these laws are naturally a reflection of His character, we are not surprised to find that "righteousness and justice are the foundation of thy throne." Psalms 89:14, A.R.V. The Ten Commandments are God's fundamental, moral law. They are holy, just, good, and spiritual. (Romans 7:12-14.)

"All his commandments are sure. They stand fast for ever and ever." Psalms 111:7, 8. Said Christ, "It is easier for heaven and earth to pass, than one tittle of the law to fail." Luke 16:17.

The Law Reigned From Adam to Moses

The Ten Commandments were not in written form in those days. Adam lived 930 years. Methuselah was two hundred years old when Adam died, therefore he had received from Adam the knowledge of God's will. Methuselah lived 969 years, dying the year of the Flood. Thus Noah received by word of mouth the truth of God, and became a preacher of "righteousness." (2 Peter 2:5.) Say the Scriptures: "All thy commandments are righteousness." Psalms 119:172.

Can we be sure that Adam knew the principles of the law? Yes, very sure. Because "sin is the transgression of the law." 1 John 3:4. And "where no law is, there is no transgression [or sin]." Romans 4:15. Since Adam sinned (Romans 5:12) he therefore transgressed the law of God, of which he had knowledge.

Just one step more. Men are not held accountable for sin when there is no law. "Sin is not imputed when there is no law." Romans 5:13. That is, it is not charged up to man. But sin was charged against men from Adam to Moses, because "the wages of sin is death" (Romans 6:23), and "death reigned from Adam to Moses" (Romans 5:14). So men knew of the commandments of God, even though they had no written law. The expression in Romans 5:13, "Until the law sin was in the world," means until the *written* law.

James M. Gillis, C.S.P., writing in *The Catholic Bulletin,* September 22, 1945, page 6, said: "It would be childish to imagine that lying and stealing and killing were no sin until Moses came. . . . To think that the law of God didn't bind the race in those twenty centuries would be to put oneself in a class with the child who asked the teacher what the world was like 'before the law of gravitation was passed.'"

Adam's son Cain sinned. (Genesis 4:6, 7.) Noah and Lot lived among lawbreaking men. (2 Peter 2:4-8.) Abraham knew God's commandments, statutes, and laws. (Genesis 26:5.) Paul sums it up when he says, "So death passed upon all men, for that all have sinned." Romans 5:12.

Law Reigned From Moses to Christ

When Moses led Israel out of Egyptian bondage God Himself spoke the Ten Commandments and "wrote them upon two tables of stone." Deuteronomy 4:13.

Because these stone tablets contained the written testimony of God, they are called the "two tables of testimony." Exodus 31:18. Moses was instructed to place them in the sacred golden ark in the most holy place of the sanctuary. (Deuteronomy 10:2; Hebrews 9:3, 4.) His own record reads, "I turned myself and came down from the mount, and put the tables in the ark which I had made; and there they be, as the Lord commanded me." Deuteronomy 10:5. The ark is therefore called the ark of the testimony, or the ark of the testament. (Exodus 25:22; Revelation 11:19.) The testimony, or the written will of God, was based upon His spoken word.

Israel sang of this holy law. (Psalms 119:97. See the entire psalm.)

Solomon said, "He that turneth away his ear from hearing the law, even his prayer shall be abomination." Proverbs 28:9.

Isaiah declared the law of God to be the divine test of all teaching. (Isaiah 8:20.)

The Law Reigned in Jesus' Life

One prophet predicted that Jesus would "magnify the law, and make it honourable." Isaiah 42:21. Another, that God's law would be in His heart. (Psalms 40:7, 8; Hebrews 10:7.)

When Christ Himself came He had spoken less than two minutes of His wonderful sermon on the mount when He declared before the multitudes: "Think not that I am come to destroy the law, or the prophets: I am not come to destroy, but to fulfil." Matthew 5:17.

In order to fulfill prophecy, He must do what the prophets predicted. This He did, asserting in Nazareth, "This day is this scripture fulfilled in your ears." Luke 4:21.

To fulfill God's moral ten-commandment law, He must needs do what it requires. This He did, for as He approached the hour of Gethsemane, He declared, "I have kept my Father's commandments." John 15:10. These He obeyed with delight, for God Himself testified, "Thou hast loved righteousness, and hated iniquity." Hebrews 1:9.

In His teaching He magnified the law, making it apply not only to outward deeds but to inward thoughts. (Matthew 5:21, 22, 27, 28.) In His life He fulfilled the law. Indeed, He was the living law. Of His enemies He asked, "Which of you convinceth me of sin?" John 8:46. Concerning Him the apostle Peter said that He "did no sin." (1 Peter 2:22.) He died, not because *He* sinned, but because *we* sinned.

The Law Reigned in the Time of the Apostles

The apostle Paul proclaimed the law holy, just, good, and spiritual. (Romans 7:7, 12-14.) In strong language he asserted that through faith "we establish the law." Romans 3:31. Finally he testified in a Roman court at his own trial: "So worship I the God of my fathers, believing all things which are written in the law and in the prophets." Acts 24:14.

It is a device of the devil to quote the apostles of Christ as being against the law of God. Paul was a great theologian, but the unlearned misunderstood him at times, as Peter says, and the deceivers and antilaw people misinterpret and misapply his words. (2 Peter 3:15, 16.)

Had Paul turned against the law of God, he himself would thereby have become a leader of apostasy, paving the way for the man of sin to "think to change times and laws." Daniel 7:25. (See 2 Thessalonians 2:3, 4.)

James declared in his unequivocal manner that we are to be "judged by the law," and "whosoever shall . . . offend in one point, he is guilty of all." James 2:12, 10.

John goes so far as to say that "he that saith, I know him, and keepeth not his commandments, is a liar, and the truth is not in him." 1 John 2:4. He further insists that "all liars" shall perish in the second death (Revelation

21:8), and that all who make "lies" will be barred from entrance into the city of God (verse 27).

He also agrees with James that the law of God is to be the standard of the judgment. Note the report of his vision: "The nations were angry, and thy wrath is come, and the time of the dead, that they should be judged. . . . And the temple of God was opened in heaven, and there was seen in his temple the ark of his testament." Revelation 11:18, 19.

Here is the clearest indication that the judgment work takes place in the most holy place of the heavenly sanctuary, since the "ark of his testament" is there. Within that ark is the ten-commandment law, as we have learned. This is the law of the judgment.

When the final fiat of that judgment goes forth, and the righteous and wicked are forever separated, commandment keeping will be part of the passports to Paradise. "Blessed are they that do his commandments, that they may have right to the tree of life, and may enter in through the gates into the city." Revelation 22:14. As a commandment keeper you may serve God among the minority here, but you will unite with a one hundred per cent majority there, including the angels. "Bless the Lord, ye his angels, . . . that do his commandments." Psalms 103:20.

Jesus on Nature of God's Law

On one occasion when Jesus had silenced a group of Jewish Sadducees with His wise words, the Pharisees tried their hand. One of their company, a lawyer, asked this question: "Master, which is the great commandment in the law?" Matthew 22:36.

In answer Jesus said, "Thou shalt love the Lord thy God with all thy heart, and with all thy soul, and with all thy mind. This is the first and great commandment.

And the second is like unto it, Thou shalt love thy neighbour as thyself. On these two commandments hang all the law and the prophets." Verses 37-40.

You will recall that God wrote the Ten Commandments on *two* tables of stone. It is generally understood that the first four commandments belong to the first table, and the last six to the second table. The reason is clear. Jesus divided the Ten Commandments into two main principles: love to God and love to man. A reading of the commandments in Exodus 20:3-17 will quickly reveal that the first four commandments show our duty to God, and the last six our duty to man. Thus all ten commandments hang on the two principles of love to God and love to man.

Of these two principles, the first is comprised of the "great" commandments. Therefore the first four commandments should never be considered of *minor importance.* It is interesting to note that God used almost three times as many words in giving the first four commandments as He did in giving the last six. And when Jesus answered the lawyer's question, He used three times as many words for the "*first and great*" commandment as for the second.

Two things emerge from all this. One is that only when God is made first in our lives can we meet His mind and fulfill our true destiny. The other is that God's ten-commandment law is a law of love.

"'God is love.' His nature, his law, is love. It ever has been; it ever will be. 'The high and lofty One that inhabiteth eternity,' 'whose ways are everlasting,' changeth not. With him 'is no variableness, neither shadow of turning.'"—MRS. E. G. WHITE, *Patriarchs and Prophets,* p. 33.

THE TWOFOLD MESSAGE OF CALVARY

Christ's death on the cross definitely settled two things.

First, it declared to all intelligent beings in the universe that God's law is eternal and unchangeable, and that sin against its holy precepts brings death. The Son of God had not sinned, but He had taken the sinner's place. Therefore He must die.

God's law and His character are inseparable. He did not and will not change either. Calvary is God's final and unanswerable argument in favor of His eternal law. Destroy the law, and Calvary becomes a meaningless tragedy.

The second thing that Calvary proved is that God is love. "God so loved the world, that he gave his only begotten Son, that whosoever believeth in him should not perish, but have everlasting life." John 3:16.

The charges of Satan against God's law, against His Son, and against His character, were all fully answered at the cross. God is love. His law is love. His Son is entitled to an undisputed place in the Godhead of the universe.

War on Commandment Keepers

In these final testing days of the age-old conflict between Christ and Satan, this enemy of Heaven will bring persecution upon commandment keepers.

Here is the prophecy: "The dragon [Satan] was wroth with the woman [the church], and went to make war with the remnant of her seed, which keep the commandments of God, and have the testimony of Jesus Christ." Revelation 12:17.

While there is yet a remnant of human time, we all have a choice to make. On God's side are Calvary and the commandments and life. On Satan's side are sin and self and death.

To every one of us God sends this urgent, personal appeal:

"I call heaven and earth to record this day against you, that I have set before you life and death, blessing and cursing: therefore choose life, that both thou and thy seed may live: that thou mayest love the Lord thy God, and that thou mayest obey his voice." Deuteronomy 30:19, 20.

CROWN OR CRUCIFY

"I stood alone at the bar of God,
In the hush of the twilight dim,
And faced the question that pierced my heart:
'What will you do with Him?
Crowned or crucified—which shall it be?'
No other choice was offered to me.

"I looked on the face so marred with tears
That were shed in His agony.
The look in His kind eyes broke my heart—
'Twas so full of love for me.
'The crown or the cross,' it seemed to say:
'For or against Me—choose thou today.'

"He held out His loving hands to me
While He pleadingly said, 'Obey.
Make Me thy choice, for I love thee so';
And I could not say Him Nay.
Crowned, not crucified—this must it be;
No other way was open to me.

"I knelt in tears at the feet of Christ,
In the hush of the twilight dim,
And all that I was or hoped or thought,
Surrendered unto Him.
Crowned, not crucified—my heart shall know
No king but Christ, who loveth me so."

—FLORENCE JOHNSON.

CHAPTER 34

Who Nailed What to the Cross?

MARTIN LUTHER, a Roman Catholic monk, was professor of Biblical literature at the Catholic University of Wittenberg, Germany. On October 31, 1517, as the festival of All Saints was approaching, he tacked on the Castle church door a paper containing ninety-five propositions of protest which he had written against what he believed to be unholy practices of the Catholic Church.

Luther's bold act was a world-shaking event. It set into rapid movement the forces of Protestantism. Such was the good result of posting a paper on a church door.

More than nineteen hundred years ago Roman soldiers nailed, not a holy protest to a church door, but a holy Man to a tree. These men did not realize who the Man was or what they were really doing. And the Man prayed, "Father, forgive them; for they know not what they do." Luke 23:34.

The crucifixion of Jesus Christ was a universe-shaking event, opening a new era of world history and assuring a day of universal good will—a time when all the intelligent creation will worship the true God and obey the precepts of His holy law.

The Mysterious Manuscript of the Cross

The dying Son of God Himself is said to have nailed something to the cross. The apostle Paul speaks of it in these words:

"Blotting out the handwriting of ordinances that was against us, . . . and took it out of the way, nailing it to his cross." Colossians 2:14.

This does not mean that Jesus took a hammer and nailed a roll of ordinances to the cross. But it does signify to all of us that some law or set of laws ended then.

Paul again speaks of it in Ephesians 2:15: "Having abolished in his flesh the enmity, even the law of commandments contained in ordinances."

It is clear to all that there must be more than one type, or kind, of law in the Bible. We know that the ten-commandment, moral law of God did not end at the cross. This we have already learned. It is just as wrong today for one to steal, kill, commit adultery, or break any of the Ten Commandments as it ever was.

Christ did not come to destroy this law; He came to fulfill it. Consider also that had God desired to abolish this law, Christ need not have died to meet its holy demands. God's holy moral law is as enduring as His own character.

Three Types of Laws

First and foremost, there is the moral, ten-commandment law, written by God on tables of stone. (Exodus 31:18.) "Think not that I am come to destroy the law," said Christ. Matthew 5:17.

Second, there are the ceremonial, sacrificial sanctuary laws—the ritual laws of worship.

Third, there are the civil laws of the Jewish nation. These regulated the multitude of matters pertaining to health, sanitation, disease, crime, court procedure, and so forth.

What Laws Were Nailed to the Cross?

With the ending of the Jewish nation as God's chosen instrument, the civil laws naturally lapsed. For instance, by the law of Exodus 22:1, one who stole an ox was, if apprehended, required to give to the owner five oxen. Though this law was a good one, it would not of necessity be followed in a nation today. However, the principles underlying the civil laws remain unchanged. For instance, it is just as obligatory upon a Christian to abide by the principles of health as it ever was for a Jew.

But more specifically, the ceremonial laws were nailed to the cross. "The law of commandments contained in ordinances." "The handwriting of ordinances that was against us."

Gone were the blood offerings, the meat and drink offerings, the special holy days and yearly sabbath days "which are a shadow of things to come; but the body is of Christ." Colossians 2:17. The typical services and their yearly holy days (not the weekly Sabbath of the Ten Commandments) pointed forward to Christ and His death on the cross.

When He died the great veil of the Jewish Temple at Jerusalem was torn from top to bottom. (Matthew 27:51.) This signified the end of the ceremonial system and laws.

In the figure of Paul's speech they had been nailed to His cross. (See the delineation at the close of this chapter for a comparison of the moral and ceremonial laws.)

WHAT MEN SAY

Prominent Bible students have always recognized these different types of laws in the Bible.

The great Dr. Barnes writes, when commenting on Matthew 5:18: "The ceremonial laws are such as are appointed to meet certain states of society, or to regulate the religious rites and ceremonies of a people. These can be changed when circumstances are changed, and yet the moral law be untouched."—*Notes, Explanatory and Practical, on the Gospels* (1860 ed.), vol. 1, p. 65.

Methodist Articles of Religion, article 6, says, "Although the law given from God to Moses, as touching ceremonies and rites, doth not bind Christians, nor ought the civil precepts thereof of necessity be received in any commonwealth, yet, notwithstanding, no Christian whatsoever is free from the obedience to the commandments which are called moral."—Cited in PHILIP SCHAFF, *The Creeds of Christendom,* vol. 3, p. 808.

A Lutheran catechism states:

"Ques.—How many kinds of law are given in the Old Testament?

"Ans.—Three. (1) The ceremonial, or church, law, which God gave to the Jews for the regulation of their worship, sacrifices, festivals, and other ceremonies; (2) the civil law, or that which regulated their political affairs; (3) the moral law, or that which related to their duties to God and man, which is summarily comprehended in the Ten Commandments.

"Ques.—Are we under obligation to keep the ceremonial, or church, law of the Jews?

"Ans.—No, the ordinances which it enjoined were only types and shadows of Christ; and when they were fulfilled by His death, and the distinction between Jew and Gentile was removed, the ceremonial law was abolished, because it was no longer necessary.

"Ques.—Are we under obligation to keep the moral law?

"Ans.—Yes, because that is founded on the nature of God and cannot be changed; it is of universal application, which was impossible with respect to the ceremonial and civil laws. Christ demands obedience to His law."

This special emphasis we have placed on the distinction between the moral law and other laws in order that you may be well armed to meet deceptions that would distort the teaching of God's Holy Word against His holy law.

The ceremonial laws are like the scaffolding of a building, to be removed when the building is finished. The moral law is like the foundation of the building.

Throwing away the Ten Commandments with the abolition of the ceremonial law is like tearing down the building when removing the scaffolding.

Said Jesus: "Therefore whosoever heareth these sayings of mine, and doeth them, I will liken him unto a wise man, which built his house upon a rock: and the rain descended, and the floods came, and the winds blew, and beat upon that house; and it fell not: for it was founded upon a rock." Matthew 7:24, 25.

Many years ago a bridge was to be built across the Conemaugh River in Pennsylvania. The contract for the job was given out, and the contractor set to work. On each side of the river he dug down and down to bedrock. Friends said it was too expensive, but he was building solidly. Finally his bridge was finished, and the matter forgotten.

In the late spring of 1889 melting snows in the mountains and heavy rains brought more and more water down the streams. The South Fork Reservoir was surely filling to the very top. Its walls were weak, and finally gave way, permitting a mighty avalanche of water to sweep down the valley. Trees, houses, buildings—everything was swept before the gigantic liquid wall.

What would happen when all this water and wreckage would strike the bridge built many years before? With awful impact it struck. The bridge staggered, groaned, shivered, and shook; but it stood! The flood swept on, spreading death and desolation in one of America's greatest disasters—the Johnstown Flood. That bridge, built on the solid rock, stood like a lone and mighty stronghold in the midst of ruin and desolation. It had stood the test of storms and floods because it was fastened to the rock.

Let us build upon the rock Christ Jesus and upon the foundation of His unchangeable, everlasting law.

"We are building every day
A temple the world may not see,
Building, building every day,
Building for eternity."

Moral and Ceremonial Law Compared

Moral Law

Ten Commandments

1. *A perfect law.*

"The law of the Lord is perfect, converting the soul." Psalms 19:7.

"All thy commandments are righteousness." Psalms 119:172.

"Thy righteousness is an everlasting righteousness, and thy law is the truth." Verse 142.

"Wherefore the law is holy, and the commandment holy, and just, and good." Romans 7:12.

2. *A law in itself spiritual.*

"For we know that the law is spiritual." Romans 7:14.

Ceremonial Law

Commandments Contained in Ordinances

1. *An imperfect law.*

"For there is verily a disannulling of the commandment going before for the weakness and unprofitableness thereof. For the law made nothing perfect, but the bringing in of a better hope did." Hebrews 7:18, 19.

"For the law having a shadow of good things to come, . . . can never with those sacrifices which they offered year by year continually make the comers thereunto perfect." Hebrews 10:1.

2. *A law not in itself spiritual.*

"Which stood only in meats and drinks, and divers washings, and carnal ordinances, imposed on them until the time of reformation." Hebrews 9:10.

3. *Spoken by Jehovah.*

"And the Lord spake unto you out of the midst of the fire. . . . And he declared unto you his covenant, which he commanded you to perform, even ten commandments." Deuteronomy 4:12, 13. (Exodus 20:1.) "He added no more." Deuteronomy 5:22.

3. *Spoken by Moses.*

"And the Lord called unto Moses, . . . saying, Speak unto the children of Israel, and say unto them, If any man of you bring an offering unto the Lord, ye shall bring your offering of the cattle, even of the herd, and of the flock." Leviticus 1:1, 2.

"This is the law of the burnt offering, of the meat offering, and of the sin offering, . . . which the Lord commanded Moses in mount Sinai, in the day that he commanded the children of Israel to offer their oblations unto the Lord." Leviticus 7:37, 38.

4. *Written by the Lord upon two tables of stone.*

"These words the Lord spake unto all your assembly in the mount out of the midst of the fire, of the cloud, and of the thick darkness, with a great voice: and he added no more. And he wrote them in two tables of stone." Deuteronomy 5:22. (Exodus 31:18.)

4. *Written by Moses in a book.*

"And the Lord said unto Moses, Write thou these words." Exodus 34:27.

"And Moses wrote this law, and delivered it unto the priests the sons of Levi." Deuteronomy 31:9.

"And they spake unto Ezra the scribe to bring the book of the law of Moses." Nehemiah 8:1. (2 Kings 22:8-16.)

5. *Eternal, therefore requiring obedience from all.*

"Do we then make void the law through faith? God forbid: yea, we establish the law." Romans 3:31.

"Think not that I am come to destroy the law, or the

5. *Abolished, therefore not requiring obedience from any.*

"Having abolished in his flesh the enmity, even the law of commandments contained in ordinances." Ephesians 2:15.

prophets: I am not come to destroy, but to fulfil." Matthew 5:17.

"But it is easier for heaven and earth to pass away, than for one tittle of the law to fall." Luke 16:17, R.V.

"If thou wilt enter into life, keep the commandments." Matthew 19:17.

"Circumcision is nothing, and uncircumcision is nothing, but the keeping of the commandments of God." 1 Corinthians 7:19.

"Blessed are they that do his commandments, that they may have right to the tree of life." Revelation 22:14.

"Blotting out the handwriting of ordinances that was against us, which was contrary to us, . . . nailing it to his cross. . . . Let no man therefore judge you in meat, or in drink, or in respect of an holyday, or of the new moon, or of the sabbath days: which are a shadow of things to come; but the body is of Christ." Colossians 2:14-17.

"Certain which went out from us have troubled you with words, subverting your souls, saying, Ye must be circumcised, and keep the law: to whom we gave no such commandment." Acts 15:24.

Vernon Nye, Artist

CHAPTER 35

Saved by Grace

IN THE early days a band of explorers gave an Indian chief a sundial. He was so thrilled with it that he had a shelter built over it. Thus it became a useless object of admiration, which could no longer indicate the time of day, being hidden from the rays of the sun. The Indians did not use it according to its purpose.

Perfect as is the holy ten-commandment law, there are some things that it cannot do.

What the Law Does for the Sinner

First, the law gives a knowledge of sin. "For by the law is the knowledge of sin." "Nay, I had not known sin, but by the law: for I had not known lust, except the law had said, Thou shalt not covet." Romans 3:20; 7:7. The law that does this is the ten-commandment law, of which the tenth command is, "Thou shalt not covet."

Second, the law brings a sense of guilt. "Now we know that what things so ever the law saith, it saith to them who are under the law: that every mouth may be stopped, and all the world may become guilty before God." Romans 3:19.

A motorist races through a stop sign, and suddenly hears the screaming of a siren. The traffic officer motions him to the curb. The presence of the law intensifies guilt and fear in the heart of the violator. In this case he may argue innocence, offer excuse, or plead guilty. Before God's law all the world must plead guilty, "for all have sinned." Verse 23.

The third thing the law does is to act as a spiritual mirror. This is but another way of saying what has already been said. A mirror reveals what one looks like.

James, the apostle, tells us about this heavenly mirror. "If any be a hearer of the word, and not a doer, he is like unto a man beholding his natural face in a glass: for he beholdeth himself, and goeth his way, and straightway forgetteth what manner of man he was." James 1:23, 24.

What was this mirror? James answers this in verse 25, "But whoso looketh into the perfect law of liberty, and continueth therein, he being not a forgetful hearer, but a doer of the work, this man shall be blessed in his deed."

The "perfect law of liberty," then, is the heavenly mirror into which men may look. That this is the ten-commandment law James makes plain in chapter 2, verses 10-12. He states that we are to be "judged by the perfect law of liberty," and presents this law as the one which says, "Do not commit adultery," and, "Do not kill."

This perfect law is Heaven's perfect mirror. David sang, "The law of the Lord is perfect." Psalms 19:7.

Abraham Lincoln said, "It seems to me that nothing short of infinite wisdom could by any possibility have devised and given to man this excellent and perfect moral code."

As the polished mirror of the dentist reveals the cavities of decaying teeth, so does the perfect law of God disclose the spots where sin is eating away at our souls. The sinner may go away and deliberately, or through simple neglect, forget about the spots he has seen, but sin will keep on working if it is not stopped.

In a fruit warehouse where apples were sorted, a sign for the workers read, "*A spot today means rot tomorrow.*"

The law of God says, "Sinner, see that spot of sin. It will be larger tomorrow."

God uses the law to do for the sinner just what needs to be done. The sinner must realize that he is a sinner. The heavy hand of the law must be laid upon him, and he must be arrested in his course.

Without the law the sinner is like a man afflicted with a deadly disease who does not know that he has it. Paul said, "I had not known sin, but by the law." Romans 7:7.

Evangelist John Brown once said, "The human heart cannot receive the healing thread of the gospel unless it is first pierced by the needle of the law."

F. B. Meyer, in *Elijah, and the Secret of His Power,* wrote: "There is an alarming lack amongst us of the sense of sin. Our vast populations are indifferent to the message of mercy, because they have not been aroused with the message of the holy wrath of God against sin. . . . The crying need of our times is a deeper conviction of sin. And if this shall be ever brought about, it must be by the religious teachers being led to study the law as well as the Gospel."—Page 176.

What the Law Cannot Do for the Sinner

Two things that the sinner needs desperately the law cannot provide.

First, the sinner needs *forgiveness,* or *justification.* He needs to be counted as just. That is justification. The publican cried for forgiveness, and went down to his house "justified." (Luke 18:13, 14.) But "by the deeds of the law there shall no flesh be justified." Romans 3:20.

Perfect as the law of God is, it cannot forgive. It keeps saying, "You are a sinner. You are *under condemnation."* This is what "under the law" means. Only the *Lawgiver* can forgive. The needle of the law alone can never sew up the wound that sin has made.

The *second* thing the sinner needs is *power over sin*, or *sanctification.* This the law, though ever so holy, cannot provide. The sinner must be changed, and law cannot do this.

Paul says, "If there had been a law given which could have given life, verily righteousness should have been by the law." Galatians 3:21. Thus do we all agree that the law will not make a sinner righteous. Paul further asserts, "The carnal mind . . . is not subject to the law of God, neither indeed can be." Romans 8:7. Yesterday, today, and tomorrow the sinner's case is hopeless as far as law alone is concerned. A mirror may reveal a dirty face, but it cannot cleanse it or keep it clean.

Saved by Grace

When the law of God and the Spirit of God have made the sinner *conscious of his sin,* let him come to Christ. The forgiveness that the law could not provide, Christ will freely give. The publican found it so. The woman taken in adultery Christ did not condemn, for she already felt condemned and ashamed. She needed sympathy and forgiveness, and Christ was ready to grant it to her.

"God sent not his Son into the world to condemn the world; but that the world through him might be saved." John 3:17. Unbelievers are "condemned already." (Verse 18.) The law attended to that.

"By grace are ye saved through faith." Ephesians 2:8.

"If we confess our sins, he is faithful and just to *forgive* us our sins." 1 John 1:9.

This is God's grace, or unmerited favor. This gracious love of God, through Christ, awakens love in the heart of the forgiven sinner. If he does not resist this love, he will both desire and choose to serve and obey God. Forgiveness of sin and power over sin come through exercise of faith in God's promises and a full surrender of the heart to Him.

"For what the law could not do, in that it was weak through the flesh, God sending his own Son in the likeness of sinful flesh, and for sin, condemned sin in the flesh: that the righteousness of the law might be fulfilled in us, who walk not after the flesh, but after the Spirit." Romans 8:3, 4.

This is just another picture of blessed Calvary, where we sinners condemned by law may go, be forgiven, and pray, "Create in me a clean heart, O God; and renew a right spirit within me." Psalms 51:10. Thus Christ is "made unto us . . . sanctification and redemption." 1 Corinthians 1:30.

"In the early days of '49, when the gold rush was on in California, an eastern miner crossed the continent to seek his fortune in the gold fields of the Far West.

"He 'struck it rich' very soon after his arrival, and immediately wrote to his wife, asking her to join him in California, and to bring with her their eight-year-old son.

"The wife took passage on a boat leaving New York for San Francisco, which meant in those days going around Cape Horn, the southern part of South America.

"The voyage was very favorable for the greater part of the way going south. But when they neared Cape Horn, a great storm arose, and the ship was unable to withstand the fury of the gale. Finally, the passengers and the crew were ordered to take to the lifeboats, as the ship was about to sink. For some reason, the wife of the miner and her little boy were detained below, but came rushing to the deck just as the last lifeboat was leaving.

"She soon discovered that the lifeboats were filled to capacity; but in the last one to leave there was room for just one more person. As the mother stood there looking at the one lone place of security, which meant a choice between herself and her boy, she did not hesitate a moment. She kissed the boy, and dropped him into the place of safety. As she did so, she said to him, 'My boy, when you see your father, tell him Mother died for you,' and she went down with the ship."—C. T. EVERSON, *Saved by Grace,* pp. 7, 8.

Exclaimed the beloved John, "Herein is love, not that we loved God, but that he loved us, and sent his Son to be the propitiation for our sins." 1 John 4:10. And then sensing that it was this divine love which awakens love, he wrote, "We love him, because he first loved us." Verse 19.

WHAT THE LAW DOES FOR THE SINNER SAVED BY GRACE

After the sinner has been forgiven and cleansed, and born again, what does the law now do for him? Let the Bible answer:

"Now the righteousness of God without the law is manifested, being witnessed by the law." Romans 3:21.

How beautiful! How simple! How plain! We look into the mirror of God's law and see our sins. Then we flee to the fountain of wonderful Calvary. There we plunge beneath that flood and are made clean—forgiven and cleansed. Turning again to look into the very depths of divine law, we hear it speak to us, saying: "I, the law of God, bear testimony to the righteousness of God, which I could not give to you. Behold, you are clean."

Once we stood before the holy law and saw reflected there our wayward self, clothed in garments filthy and tattered and old. Now we return to look again! And lo, we are arrayed in a garment of purest white, even the spotless robe of the righteousness of Jesus Christ, woven in the loom of heaven by the hand of love, and brought to earth by the way called Calvary.

"Through the gates to the city, in a robe of spotless white,
He will lead me where no tears shall ever fall;
In the glad song of ages I shall mingle with delight;
But I long to meet my Saviour first of all.

"I shall know Him, I shall know Him
As redeemed by His side I shall stand,
I shall know Him, I shall know Him
By the print of the nails in His hands."
—FANNY J. CROSBY.

WHAT SHALL WE SAY THEN?

Standing in the presence of God our Father, of Jesus our Saviour, and before the holy, imperishable Ten Commandments, what shall we say?

Having been delivered from under *the condemnation* of the law, cleansed and restored to favor with God, what shall we say? May we deliberately disobey the law because grace has freed us from its condemnation? Let the apostle Paul ask and answer this question.

"What then? shall we sin, because we are not under the law, but under grace? God forbid. Know ye not, that to whom ye yield yourselves servants to obey, his servants ye are to whom ye obey; whether of sin unto death, or of obedience unto righteousness?" Romans 6:15, 16.

Wholehearted obedience to the law of God is the supreme responsibility and privilege of the sinner saved by grace. Asks one, "If God's grace is greater than the vilest sin, why can it not cover 'continued' sin?"

Let Paul again speak: "Where sin abounded, grace did much more abound. . . .What shall we say then? Shall we continue in sin, that grace may abound? God forbid. How shall we, that are dead to sin, live any longer therein?" "Let not sin therefore reign in your mortal body." Romans 5:20; 6:1, 2, 12.

GRACE, FAITH, LOVE, AND LAW

Grace is like a governor's pardon to a prisoner. It forgives him, but it is not a license to violate one law on the statute books.

Faith is like a man's hand. It reaches out and accepts

the pardon. It also reaches up to God for power to obey law. "This is the victory that overcometh the world, even our faith." 1 John 5:4.

"*Love* is the fulfilling of the law." Romans 13:10. "This is the love of God, that we keep his commandments." 1 John 5:3.

John Wesley wrote in his *Sermons on Several Occasions* (1833-36 ed.), volume 1, pages 314, 315: "I cannot spare the law one moment, no more than I can spare Christ: seeing I now want it as much, to keep me to Christ, as I ever wanted it to bring me to him. . . . Indeed each is continually sending me to the other,—the law to Christ, and Christ to the law. On the one hand, the height and depth of the law constrain me to fly to the love of God in Christ; on the other, the love of God in Christ endears the law to me 'above gold or precious stones.' . . . This is perfect freedom; thus to keep his law, and to walk in all his commandments blameless."

The doctrine of grace without obedience to God's law is a doctrine of disgrace.

New Hampshire Confession of Faith, article 12, says: "We believe the Scriptures teach that the law of God is the eternal and unchangeable rule of His moral government; that it is holy, just, and good; and that the inability which the Scriptures ascribe to fallen men to fulfill its precepts arises entirely from their love of sin; to deliver them from which, and to restore them through a mediator to unfeigned obedience to the holy law, is one great end of the gospel."—Quoted by O. C. S. Wallace, in *What Baptists Believe* (1934), p. 79.

FOOLISH, VAIN, OR BLESSED?

The foolish man seeks salvation by his own works in keeping the law. He looks into the spiritual mirror of God's law and sees that he is a sinner. Then he straightway takes the mirror and tries to wash himself with it. From Cain, the son of Adam, to this day, many have sought peace with God by works of penance. The apostle Paul wrote, "O foolish Galatians. . . . This only would I learn of you, Received ye the Spirit by the works of the law, or by the hearing of faith?" Galatians 3:1, 2.

The sinner can begin his fellowship with God only by knocking in simple faith on the door marked "Mercy."

The vain man thinks he does not need good works. He looks into the spiritual mirror of God's law, and seeing that it condemns him, straightway takes unto himself a hammer and breaks the mirror to pieces. Or more strangely still he may say: "Christ took the law out of the way, nailing it to His cross. I am now free indeed. I can do as I please and still be a Christian."

Listening to this superficial consideration of the gospel, James the apostle cries out, "But wilt thou know, O vain man, that faith without works is dead?" James 2:20.

Then There Is the Blessed Man

The blessed man, looking into the same spiritual mirror as the other two men, and sensing himself to be a lost sinner, flees to Christ. Receiving forgiveness by grace through faith, he exclaims with David, "Blessed is he whose transgression is forgiven, whose sin is covered." Psalms 32:1.

This is justification, and it is accomplished without the deeds of the law. (Romans 3:28.) Good deeds today cannot pay for evil deeds yesterday.

What does this blessed, forgiven man now do? He straightway draws the door of his heart wide open, and says, "O Spirit of God, come in and take control. Write the precepts of thy law upon my heart. Put within me the spirit of obedience, for 'to be spiritually minded is life and peace.'" (Romans 8:6.)

Of such a man the psalmist sang: "Blessed is the man that walketh not in the counsel of the ungodly, nor standeth in the way of sinners, nor sitteth in the seat of the scornful. But his delight is in the law of the Lord; and in his law doth he meditate day and night." Psalms 1:1, 2.

Here is the true, understanding, genuine Christian. He receives all that God offers, then places upon God's altar all that he has, is, or hopes to be.

CHAPTER 36

Men Testify on the Ten Commandments

A UNIVERSITY professor is quoted as saying: "It is stated that God wrote the Ten Commandments on two tables of stone. I will show you how they can be demolished in ten minutes."

Leaving this learned commandment demolisher for the moment (we have all done enough commandment breaking), let us examine the testimony of great men and movements.

LUTHERANS

"22. *Why are the laws of God binding upon all men?*

"Because they are based upon the nature of God and his relations to man, and were reaffirmed by Christ, and can, therefore, neither lose their binding authority nor be changed. . . .

"26. *Where is the moral law of God found?*

"In the Decalogue or Ten Commandments."—FREDERICK W. CONRAD, *Luther's Small Catechism, Explained and Amplified* (1886), pp. 22, 23.

Martin Luther said, "He who destroys the doctrine of the law, destroys at the same time political and social order. . . . As to the law in itself, I never rejected it."—M. MICHELET'S *Life of Luther* (Hazlitt translation, 2d ed.), p. 315.

PRESBYTERIANS

"The moral law doth forever bind all, as well justified persons as others, to the obedience thereof. . . . Neither doth Christ in the gospel in any way dissolve, but much strengthen, this obligation."—*Presbyterian Confession of Faith,* chap. 19, art. 5.

John Calvin, the father of Presbyterianism, wrote, "We must not imagine that the coming of Christ has freed us from the authority of the law; for it is the eternal rule of a devout and holy life, and must, therefore, be as unchangeable as the justice of God."—CALVIN, *Commentary on a Harmony of the Gospels,* vol. 1, p. 277.

Albert Barnes, noted Presbyterian Bible scholar, wrote: "We learn hence, 1. That *all* the law of God is binding on Christians. Comp. James ii. 10. 2. That all the commands of God should be preached, in their proper place, by Christian ministers. 3. That they who pretend that there are any laws of God so small that they need not obey them, are unworthy of his kingdom. And 4. That true piety has respect to *all* the commandments of God, and keeps them. Ps. cxix. 6."—*Notes, Explanatory and Practical, on the Gospels* (1868), comment on Matthew 5:19.

METHODISTS

John Wesley said: "The moral law, contained in the Ten Commandments, and enforced by the Prophets, he [Christ] did not take away. It was not the design of his coming to revoke any part of this. . . . The moral law stands on an entirely different foundation from the ceremonial or ritual law. . . . Every part of this law must remain in force upon all mankind, and in all ages."—JOHN WESLEY, "Upon Our Lord's Sermon on the Mount," Discourse 5, in *Works,* vol. 5 (1829 ed.), pp. 311, 312.

Articles of Religion, article 6, "Of the Old Testament": "Although the law given from God by Moses as touching

Ceremonies and Rites doth not bind Christians . . . ; yet, notwithstanding, no Christian whatsoever is free from the obedience of the commandments which are called Moral." —Quoted in Thomas Benjamin Neely, *Doctrinal Standards of Methodism,* pp. 190, 191.

Baptists

"Q. 46. Where is the moral law summarily comprehended?

"A. The moral law is summarily comprehended in the Ten Commandments. . . .

"Q. 49. What doth the preface to the Ten Commandments teach us?

"A. The preface to the Ten Commandments teacheth us that because God is the Lord, and our God, and Redeemer, therefore we are bound to keep all His commandments."—*The Baptist Catechism,* p. 9.

Spurgeon, the prince of Baptist preachers, wrote in his *Sermons*: "The law of God is a divine law, holy, heavenly, perfect. . . . There is not a commandment too many; there is not one too few; but it is so *incomparable,* that its *perfection* is a proof of its divinity."—Volume 2, sermon 18, "The Curse Removed."

There were two tables of the law. On the first were the first four commandments, showing our duty to God. On the second were the last six commandments, showing our duty to man.

As Spurgeon said, "If you love God with all your heart, you must keep the first table of the law; and if you love your neighbor as yourself, you must keep the second table."

In a sermon delivered in London, and widely published in Australia in 1898 (first in the Melbourne *Age*), he said: "First, the law of God must be perpetual. There is no abrogation of it, nor amendment of it. It is not to be toned down or adjusted to our fallen condition; but every one of the Lord's righteous judgments abideth forever."

The Christian Church

"God's ten words: which not only in the Old Testament, but in all revelation, are the most emphatically regarded as the synopsis of all religion and morality. . . . The only instrument in the universe that he wrote with his own hand!"—ALEXANDER CAMPBELL, *Debate on the Roman Catholic Religion, Between Alexander Campbell and John B. Purcell,* p. 214.

The Episcopal Church

"No Christian whatsoever is free from the obedience of the commandments which are called moral."—*The Book of Common Prayer,* "Articles of Religion," p. 260.

Dwight L. Moody

This mighty evangelist of the nineteenth century wrote:

"The law that was given at Sinai has lost none of its solemnity. Time cannot wear out its authority or the fact of its authorship. . . . Men may cavil as much as they like about other parts of the Bible, but I have never met an honest man that found fault with the Ten Commandments. . . .

"We call it the 'Mosaic' Law, but it has been well said that the commandments did not originate with Moses, nor were they done away with when the Mosaic Law was fulfilled in Christ. . . . The commandments of God . . . are as binding to-day as ever they have been. . . .

"Jesus never condemned the law and the prophets, but He did condemn those who did not obey them. Because He gave new commandments it does not follow that He abolished the old. Christ's explanation of them made them all the more searching. . . .

"The people must be made to understand that the Ten Commandments are still binding, and that there is a penalty attached to their violation. We do not want a gospel of mere sentiment. The Sermon on the Mount did not blot out the Ten Commandments."—DWIGHT L. MOODY, *Weighed and Wanting,* pp. 11-16.

A MODERN RELIGIOUS JOURNAL

An editorial in the *Christian Advocate* quotes this simple but significant statement from an Oxford scholar: "The road to the promised land runs past Sinai."

This comment is added:

"So says Clive S. Lewis of Oxford University, and no prophet of the Old Testament ever proclaimed a greater truth. There can be no postwar world worth all the sacrifices now being made if that world after the conflict ignores the simple and basic code of Sinai, which calls for reverence toward God and respect toward man."—November 11, 1943.

The *Wall Street Journal* years ago put it in these words: "There is one code and constitution, with some thousands of years' continuous test, which has never been repealed or even amended. This is called the Ten Commandments."—May 28, 1921, p. 1.

Let us be assured that all these statements of men and church creeds do not of themselves prove that the Ten Commandments are eternal. But they do prove that these men and church organizations agree with the Bible, the Word of God; and "thy word is truth." John 17:17.

In fact, the law of God is the simplest of all tests in dividing the false from the true. "To the law and to the testimony: if they speak not according to this word, it is because there is no light in them." Isaiah 8:20. Shall any man judge the law that is the judge of truth, and by which law he himself must be judged?

How shocking will be the disappointment of those who exalt themselves to think they may exercise a power to dispense with or change God's ten eternal words, when He Himself will not for all eternity entertain one such thought.

As long as God lives, His law lives. There is no way to abolish the Ten Commandments.

When a minister visited a prison quarry, one of the prisoners preached him a sermon on this wise: "Parson, do you see them stones? They're just like the Ten Commandments; you can keep on breaking 'em, but you can't get rid of 'em." That is an old story, but it isn't as old as the Ten Commandments.

There is another story that is older than the human race. Before the tree of life ever bore its precious fruit in the garden eastward in Eden, there was a council of salvation in heaven. There, redemption by the precious blood of Christ was "foreordained before the foundation of the world." 1 Peter 1:20. This insurance policy was written then, and when the fire of sin broke out, the premium was paid by God Himself; in Christ, who signed the document with His own blood on the cross. This is the old, old story.

"Thou shalt have no more gods but Me,
Before no idol bow the knee,
Take not the name of God in vain,
Nor dare the Sabbath to profane,
Give both thy parents honor due,
Take heed that thou no murder do.
Abstain from words and deeds unclean;
Nor steal, though thou be poor and mean;
Nor make a wilful lie, nor love it,
What is thy neighbor's dare not covet."

—From *Now.*

"Surely the people is grass. The grass withereth, the flower fadeth: but the word of our God shall stand for ever." Isaiah 40:7, 8. "For ever, O Lord, thy word is settled in heaven." Psalms 119:89.

Countless laws have been enacted by men, but there is only one perfect law—God's law.

Countless crosses have carried their victims into the dim shadows of death, but only one cross bore the perfect sacrifice.

The justice of perfect law was met with God's own perfect sacrifice—"a lamb without blemish and without spot."

"Nor silver nor gold hath obtained my redemption,
No riches of earth could have saved my poor soul;
The blood of the cross is my only foundation,
The death of my Saviour now maketh me whole."

—JAMES MCGRAY.

SECTION SEVEN

GOD SPEAKS CONCERNING HEAVEN'S TRADEMARK AND SIGN

Rumpel, Artist

made traditions and regulations

CHAPTER 37

Heaven's Trademark for This World

SOMEONE HAS said that "craftsmen are men who cannot help doing whatever is given them to do better than others think worth while."

Ask any informed carpenter about a good handsaw, and he may say, "A Henry Disston & Sons D-95 saw is top quality." On that saw you will see a trademark with the name of the manufacturer, the date 1840, and the place Philadelphia. That trademark stands for the skill and integrity of the manufacturer.

Ask a hardware man for a high-grade carpenter's hammer, and it might carry the name "MAYDOLE" stamped in the steel. Back of that name stands a stirring story of perseverance, talent, precision, and character.

Years ago George Graham, a London watchmaker, said to his customer who had just purchased a watch, "Sir, it is a watch that I have made and regulated myself. Take it with you wherever you please. If after seven years you come back to see me, and can tell me that there has been a difference of five minutes, I will return your money."

Seven years later the man came back and said, "The watch has varied five minutes." "Here is your money," responded Mr. Graham. The man replied, "No, I would not sell it for ten times the price." But Mr. Graham said, "I gave you my word, here is your money." He then took this remarkable watch and used it for a regulator.

The Architect and Craftsman of the Universe

God is the great architect and supercraftsman of the universe. "To whom then will ye liken me, or shall I be equal? saith the Holy One. Lift up your eyes on high, and behold who hath created these things, that bringeth out their host by number: he calleth them all by names by the greatness of his might, for that he is strong in power; not one faileth." Isaiah 40:25, 26.

The starry wheels of God's huge and intricate clock never fail. At the United States Naval Observatory at Washington, D.C., men check the stars of God to ascertain the correct time for men. From their observations they set the nation's standard clock. At noon every day a time signal is telegraphed to the Western Union Telegraph Company. Their regulator clock is set. Then this time information is distributed to the public. In England the Royal Observatory at Greenwich maintains a similar service.

The source of time accuracy is the Creator's clock of the universe. "Hast thou not known? hast thou not heard, that the everlasting God, the Lord, the Creator of the ends of the earth, fainteth not, neither is weary?" Isaiah 40:28. His clock never runs down, because He keeps it running.

Everyone honors a man who puts skill and effort and conscience into the creation of superior products. Let all men honor the Craftsman of all craftsmen, the Creator of the vast, intricate, mysterious universe.

The Creation of the World

What does the Bible teach concerning the creation of our world and its forms of life?

In the first verse of the Bible we read: "In the beginning God created the heaven and the earth." Genesis 1:1. Following immediately is the story of how God brought order and life out of chaos: the first day, light;

the second day, atmosphere; the third day, dry land and vegetation; the fourth day, the light of the sun, moon, and stars; the fifth day, fish and fowl; the sixth day, animals and man.

Many have difficulty in believing that God has existed forever. Our minds can understand how future existence could be eternal, but it is not so easy to see how a being could have always existed. This problem is not solved by the fool who simply says, "There is no God." Psalms 14:1. Nor is it solved by simply forgetting the whole matter. It is a vital question. "Without faith it is impossible to please him [God]: for he that cometh to God must believe that he is." Hebrews 11:6.

There are four things that we could believe about the past:

1. God the Creator must have existed forever.
2. The earth and life in its approximate present forms must have always been.
3. Mere matter must have existed from eternity.
4. Sometime in the hoary ages of the past, all of a sudden something must have come into existence from nothing, with no one to make it happen.

The farther we get from the Bible theory of Creation as the definite act of a creator, the less reasonable do our theories become, and the more do faith and reason conflict. The order, system, and intelligence that we ourselves observe make the theory of a self-existent God appear as the most rational explanation of all things. Without God men have never yet been able to solve the riddle of which came first—the hen or the egg.

"Through faith we understand that the worlds were framed by the word of God, so that things which are seen were not made of things which do appear." Hebrews 11:3. "For he spake, and it was done; he commanded, and it stood fast." Psalms 33:9.

"The heavens declare the glory of God." Psalms 19:1. "For the invisible things of him from the creation of the world are clearly seen, being understood by the things that are made, even his eternal power and Godhead; so that they are without excuse." Romans 1:20. The everlasting God is the Creator. (Isaiah 40:28.) "From everlasting to everlasting, thou art God." Psalms 90:2.

Long before the modern scientist declared that the earth has no visible means of support, Job said, "He . . . hangeth the earth upon nothing." Job 26:7. Having made the world of nothing, He hung it upon nothing tangible. This world and all worlds are upheld "by the word of his power." Hebrews 1:3.

This is the God who declared, "Thus shall ye say unto them, The gods that have not made the heavens and the earth, even they shall perish from the earth." Jeremiah 10:11. The Creator God "is not like them." (Verse 16.) Thus does God make the act of creation to distinguish Himself from false gods.

God's Trademark for His Works

As men choose a particular trademark for their products, so has the Creator chosen a trademark, or sign, for His works. Men may print, stamp, etch, or chisel their trademarks upon their goods. God chiseled His mark out of that intangible something we call time.

Let us read: "God saw everything that he had made, and, behold, it was very good. And the evening and the morning were the sixth day. Thus the heavens and the earth were finished, and all the host of them. And on the seventh day God ended his work which he had made; and he rested on the seventh day from all his work which he had made. And God blessed the seventh day, and sanctified it: because that in it he had rested from all his work which God created and made." Genesis 1:31; 2:1-3.

What a beautiful story. Not a legend! Not a tradition! But the simple, glorious truth about God's trademark. On the seventh day of creation week He made His trademark. He made it *on* the seventh day, *out of* the seventh day, by *resting* on that day, *blessing* that day. This is the plain, unmistakable record of this Book.

Edgar J. Goodspeed, prominent Bible scholar and translator, says:

"Taken together, the story of the seven days is, of course, the story of the Institution of the Sabbath, which is thus made to appear wrought into the *very fabric of the universe.*"—"In the Beginning," *Religion in Life,* winter number, 1947-48, p. 18. (Italics ours.)

Only God could make His own trademark. Only God could make a particular day holy, by blessing it with His own hallowed presence. Only God would have the right to "sanctify" a day, which means to "set it apart for a holy use." So it is that we read, "The sabbath was made for man." Mark 2:27. It was a sign to man that God was his Creator.

"In Eden, God set up the memorial of His work of creation, in placing His blessing upon the seventh day. The Sabbath was committed to Adam, the father and representative of the whole human family. Its observance was to be an act of grateful acknowledgment, on the part of all who should dwell upon the earth, that God was their creator and their rightful sovereign; that they were the work of His hands, and the subjects of His authority. . . . God saw that a Sabbath was essential for man, even in Paradise."—*Patriarchs and Prophets,* p. 48.

Thus God created the world, placed man in dominion (Genesis 1:26), and gave to him the holy sign that He had made. This was before our first parents had sinned. The Sabbath and marriage are the two holy institutions that came from Eden to bless the world.

Engraving the Trademark

There came a thrilling time when the divine law of God was to be written for man. God wrote it. With His finger He traced it upon two tablets of stone. (Exodus 31:18.)

And behold, there in the very heart of the Ten Commandments, He engraved the eternal trademark of His creative craftsmanship. This Sabbath sign He set as the fourth of the Ten Commandments in the following words: "Remember the sabbath day, to keep it holy. Six days shalt thou labour and do all thy work: but the seventh day is the sabbath of the Lord thy God: in it thou shalt not do any work, thou, nor thy son, nor thy daughter, thy manservant, nor thy maidservant, nor thy cattle, nor thy stranger that is within thy gates: for in six days the Lord made heaven and earth, the sea, and all that in them is, and rested the seventh day: wherefore the Lord blessed the sabbath day, and hallowed it." Exodus 20:8-11.

Six days God created. On the seventh day He rested. "Wherefore, the Lord blessed the sabbath day, and hallowed it." The Sabbath may not be disconnected from God, the Creator.

Again we read: "It is a sign between me and the children of Israel for ever: for in six days the Lord made heaven and earth, and on the seventh day he rested, and was refreshed." Exodus 31:17.

The Sabbath is thus the sign of God's creatorship. This is clearly stated. The Sabbath is not God's sign because Jews are Jews, but because God is God and He is the Creator. And He created in six days and rested on the seventh day 2,500 years before the Jewish nation existed. This is God's own stated reason for making the Sabbath a sign. All the inhabitants of all God's worlds combined could not erase these facts.

James G. Murphy, in *A Critical and Exegetical Com-*

mentary on the Book of Exodus, says, "The act of creation is the origin of all title to the creature and to the obedience of the intelligent creation. The creation of man is commemorated in the fourth commandment. Hence it contains the fountain-head of all authority in God and all duty in man."—Page 144.

The Sabbath is not merely a day of physical rest. We need that, but any day would do for that. It is not a day merely for spiritual refreshment, sorely and surely as we need that. It is both these and more. It is the sign of God as Creator.

On His part it is the sign of His creatorship, with all the obligations to usward that devolve upon Him because of the act and fact of creation. It is the sign of His right to rule over us, the symbol of His gracious and timeless sovereignty.

On our part it is the sign that we gratefully acknowledge Him as our Creator and accept His right of title to and rulership over us and all things. It is a sign that as His creatures we assume the obligations that naturally come to us in this relationship.

It is God's flag, the symbol of His sovereignty, woven in the loom of heaven out of that intangible and precious something men call time, and raised over His fair earthly dominion in the freshness of creation's morning. The Sabbath is a matter of holy duty and a thing of infinite beauty.

"My Maker and my King, to Thee my all I owe;
Thy sovereign bounty is the spring whence all my blessings flow.

"The creature of Thy hand, on Thee alone I live;
My God, Thy benefits demand more praise than I can give.

"Lord, what can I impart when all is Thine before?
Thy love demands a thankful heart; the gift, alas! how poor.

"O! let Thy grace inspire my soul with strength divine;
Let every word and each desire and all my days be
Thine."

The Seal of His Law

This Sabbath sign God made the seal of His holy law. The seal of a law gives the name of the lawgiver, his official title, and the extent of his dominion. For instance, "Elizabeth II [name], Queen [title] of England [extent of dominion]."

The fourth, or Sabbath, commandment is the only one of the Ten Commandments that qualifies as a seal. Read it carefully (Exodus 20:8-11), and there you will discover God's seal: *"The Lord thy God* [name], *Creator* [title] *of heaven and earth* [dominion]." Thus when God wrote His law upon tables of stone He wrote His seal in the law itself. His name is "The Lord thy God." His title is "Creator." His dominion is "heaven and earth."

Since God created all things from nothing (Hebrews 11:3), and hung the earth upon nothing (Job 26:7), and upholds all things (Hebrews 1:3), and sustains life (Acts 17:28), He therefore has undisputed, final, and absolute right to ownership and rulership. The Sabbath is the Creator's sign of His right to rule. It therefore became the seal of His law.

The Sign of Redemption

Consider for a moment two things we have learned thus far: (1) The Sabbath is the sign of God's creative power and of His right to rule; (2) it is the seal of His holy law.

Where, now, does that place the sinner?

Consider the sinner. All have sinned. We have all transgressed the law of the Creator, sealed by His own hand. The wages of sin is eternal death.

The sinner needs redemption. And the Sabbath, though

made before sin entered, becomes a sign of redemption. "Verily my sabbaths ye shall keep: for it is a sign between me and you . . . that ye may know that I am the Lord that doth sanctify you." Exodus 31:13.

Redemption from sin to sanctification requires creative power. Paul so states it in 2 Corinthians 5:17: "Therefore if any man be in Christ, he is a new creature." Nothing less than the power of God can bring about this new creation in us. The Sabbath is the sign of that creative power.

The Sabbath and the Cross

The glorious cross of Christ has become, as it were, a symbol of the love of God, the sacrifice of Christ, and the crucifixion of the old man of sin.

The Sabbath is the sign of God's power to raise us up to a new life in Christ Jesus, to a new fellowship of love and holiness, to an experience of rest and peace. As God rested from His works, so the believer rests from his works and enters into the rest of God. The Sabbath is the sign of this rest. (Hebrews 4:4-10.)

The Sabbath is the sign of creatorship, rulership, and fellowship; the sign of peace and rest and power. It is inextricably and forever bound up in all that involves fellowship between the Creator and His creatures. It is the golden clasp that binds God's children to Himself.

He who would abolish the Sabbath must challenge God the Creator and Redeemer, for whom the Sabbath stands.

God's Remarkable Promise

Did you ever consider what this world would be like if all churches were gone? not one spire or steeple pointing heavenward? seven days of work and no Sabbath of rest and worship?

So important did God consider the Sabbath that He made a most remarkable promise to the Jewish people. On condition that they properly honor His holy day, He gave them the bold assurance that the throne of David and the city of Jerusalem should stand forever. (Jeremiah 17: 21-25.)

"Safely through another week
  God has brought us on our way;
Let us now a blessing seek,
  Waiting in His courts today;
Day of all the week the best,
  Emblem of eternal rest."

Had the Jews sincerely joined in the spirit of that song Sabbath by Sabbath, and accepted the Saviour of the world, they would today be the chosen church of God.

The Jews failed. They chose the path of disobedience. They substituted the wisdom of man for the wisdom of God. When their beautiful city was destroyed, they remembered the words of warning:

"If ye will not hearken unto me to hallow the sabbath day, and not to bear a burden, even entering in at the gates of Jerusalem on the sabbath day; then will I kindle a fire in the gates thereof, and it shall devour the palaces of Jerusalem, and it shall not be quenched." Jeremiah 17:27.

Gazing upon the broken and smoldering ruins, they sorrowed at the sight of sin's wages. Some who were carried away to Babylon hung their harps upon the willows by the river Euphrates and wept when they remembered Zion. (Psalms 137:1, 2.)

They saw that their love of money and their affection for this world had caused them to forget the God for whom the Sabbath stands, and to disobey His law. How they wished that they had been faithful, honoring the Creator in spirit and in deed.

"While we seek supplies of grace
　　Through the dear Redeemer's name,
Show Thy reconciling face,
　　Take away our sin and shame;
From our worldly cares set free
　　May we rest this day in Thee."

From the Jews and their failure we turn to a consideration of Christ and the Lord's day.

CHAPTER 38

Christ and God's Sign

NATIONS OF earth send ambassadors to represent them at the capitals of other nations.

Christ came to this world as Heaven's ambassador to declare God (John 1:18), that is, to make God really known to men.

"The earth was dark through misapprehension of God. . . . To know God is to love Him; His character must be manifested in contrast to the character of Satan. This work only one Being in all the universe could do. Only He who knew the height and depth of the love of God could make it known."—*The Desire of Ages,* p. 22.

CHRIST HAS A DAY

The truth that Christ, who came to reveal God, has a special day, is clearly taught in Holy Scripture. Consider three Bible statements.

First let us read Revelation 1:10, written by the apostle John: "I was in the Spirit on the Lord's day." This makes it plain that the Lord has a particular day set apart as His day.

We wish next to discover who this Lord is and what day is His day. Jesus gives us the answer in Mark 2:28: "Therefore the Son of man is Lord also of the sabbath." Thus we see that Jesus is Lord and that the Sabbath is His day.

Our third scripture will instruct us as to which day of the week is the Sabbath. The fourth commandment gives us the specific answer: "But the seventh day is the sabbath of the Lord thy God." Exodus 20:10.

Let us now put these three facts together and reach a conclusion.

1. The Lord has a day—the Lord's day.
2. Jesus is Lord of the Sabbath day.
3. The Sabbath day is the seventh day.
4. Therefore the seventh day is the Lord's day.

How Christ Became Lord of the Sabbath

It immediately becomes of great interest for us to find out why Christ claimed that He is Lord of the seventh-day Sabbath. There are two most valid reasons for this.

The first is found in Ephesians 3:9: "To make all men see what is the fellowship of the mystery, which from the beginning of the world hath been hid in God, who created all things by Jesus Christ." In other words, the Christ who came to this earth to redeem man was Himself the active agent of God in creating all things in the beginning. This truth of Christ the Creator is taught again and again in the Bible. (See Colossians 1:15, 16; Hebrews 1:1, 2; John 1:1-3, 10, 14.) Christ's position as co-Creator with God makes Him Lord of creation. It was right and proper for Him to say, "Therefore the Son of man is Lord."

The second reason why Christ claims that He is "Lord also of the sabbath" is that He made the Sabbath.

Since the Son performed the work of creation in six days it must be that it was He who rested on the seventh day, blessed the seventh day, and sanctified it. (Genesis 2:2.) That made it His rest day, His Sabbath day, His blessed day, His sanctified day. The seventh day is therefore the Sabbath of Christ—the Christian Sabbath—the Lord's day.

THE LORD SHARES HIS DAY

Since God's children are members of His family (Ephesians 3:14, 15), we would expect that they would have special fellowship with Him on His rest day. The seventh-day Sabbath would be the Sabbath not only of God and Christ but of man.

Said Jesus, "The sabbath was made for man." Mark 2:27. That man was Adam, the head of the human race. Through him the Sabbath comes to all men. Like a golden clasp it binds heaven and earth in spiritual fellowship.

The Son of God became the Son of man, born of woman. Indeed He became the second Adam, head of the redeemed from among men. As such He proclaimed, "The Son of man is Lord also of the sabbath." Verse 28.

As Son of God, at creation He became Lord of the Sabbath. He made it. As the Son of man He continued to claim lordship of the Sabbath. Did He keep His own day holy?

THE SON OF MAN IN HIS HOME TOWN

Jesus was a carpenter. His home was in Nazareth, where He dwelt until the age of thirty. What was His customary practice with reference to the Sabbath?

"He came to Nazareth, where he had been brought up: and, as his custom was, he went into the synagogue on the sabbath day, and stood up for to read." Luke 4:16.

Jesus, the carpenter, honored the golden clasp of God. He kept the Sabbath habitually.

AN ARGUMENT OVER THE SABBATH

Little is accomplished by argument. Much is gained by honest search for truth.

In Matthew 12:1-12 is recorded the criticism by the Pharisees of Christ and His disciples. They criticized the disciples for snapping off a few heads of wheat as they walked through a field on the Sabbath. They accused these men of working, threshing, on the Sabbath. They criticized Jesus for healing a man on the Sabbath.

In both instances Christ insisted that the acts were permissible on the Sabbath. He was Lord of the Sabbath. The Sabbath was His day. He was the Son of man, and the Sabbath was made for man.

The Jews sometimes dishonored the Sabbath by trampling it under the feet of business. (Nehemiah 13:15-19.) When Jesus was here, however, they were very strict in Sabbath observance. They had added so many man-made laws to the Sabbath commandment that it was no longer a "delight" but was more and more becoming an unwelcome burden. As such it misrepresented the God whom Jesus came to "declare," or to reveal and interpret. No one was permitted to eat an egg that was laid on the Sabbath, because the hen violated the fourth commandment in doing work on the Sabbath. One must not carry with him a needle and thread or a piece of cloth on Friday afternoon for fear he might continue to carry it with him on the Sabbath, and therefore he would be bearing a burden on the Sabbath day. People were prohibited from walking on the grass for fear they might thresh out a few seeds. If they wore shoes with nails, it was considered as bearing a burden. They were permitted to write one letter of the alphabet but not two letters. They could not carry a mouthful of food two steps on the Sabbath without bearing a burden. Such laws Jesus ignored.

Jesus magnified the Sabbath. He refused to pay heed to the many burdensome laws the Jewish leaders had enacted, making God's holy day of delight a wearisome day of dismal don'ts. Christ told the Pharisees that had they understood the Scriptures they "would not have condemned the guiltless." (Matthew 12:7.) Therefore the disciples had not broken the Sabbath commandment.

The great preacher G. Campbell Morgan, on page 50 of his book *The Ten Commandments,* wrote: "Much has been made of the attitude of Christ in speech and deed toward the Sabbath. Some have imagined that by words He uttered and by deeds He did He relaxed the binding nature of the old command. This view, however, is to absolutely misunderstand and misinterpret the doing and the teaching of Jesus."

Concerning Himself Jesus said, "I have kept my Father's commandments." John 15:10. Therefore He did not break the fourth commandment. Jesus polished and brightened the golden clasp of God in His teaching, ministry, and example.

The Golden Clasp and Calvary

On the sixth day of creation week "the heavens and the earth were finished, and all the host of them." Genesis 2:1. Then Christ, co-Creator with God, rested on the seventh day and was refreshed. This holy day was to be a sign between God and His people. (Exodus 31:17.)

This same Son of God came among men—Immanuel, "God with us." Misled and bigoted religious leaders clamored for His execution on a cross. Hanging there in His last moments of agony, He cried, "It is finished." John 19:30.

That also was the sixth day of the week. There was barely time to bury Him before the sun went down and the holy hours of the Sabbath came. (Luke 24:54-56.) As He had finished creation's work on the sixth day and rested on the Sabbath, so at Calvary on the sixth day of the week He cried, *"It is finished,"* and rested in the tomb on the Sabbath.

Consider thoughtfully the following words of Jesus, prayed to His Father concerning the disciples. It is an early hour of the day before the crucifixion.

"Sanctify them through thy truth: thy word is truth. . . . And for their sakes I sanctify myself, that they also might be sanctified through the truth." John 17:17-19.

Jesus sanctified Himself—set Himself apart for the salvation of sinners, submitted Himself to Calvary, that men might be redeemed and sanctified, created anew in Christ Jesus. (2 Corinthians 5:17.)

Not only is the Sabbath the memorial of the original creation, but it is God's own appointed sign of redemption and sanctification—the symbol of the new birth, the spiritual creation. We read His words: "Verily my sabbaths ye shall keep: for it is a sign between me and you . . . ; that ye may know that I am the Lord that doth sanctify you." Exodus 31:13.

The cross of Jesus Christ cast the glorious rainbow of Heaven's redeeming love around the Sabbath of God on that holy day of rest nearly two thousand years ago.

The Sabbath, emblem of creative power, and the Creator's gift of peace, unfurled its folds of sacred time over a rugged cross and a rock-bound tomb wherein lay the world's Redeemer, who died that men might live.

The Lord of creation, who made the Sabbath a memorial of His creative power, says to us, "My day, the Lord's day, the seventh day, the Sabbath day, is the sign of My creative, redeeming, sanctifying power. It is at Calvary that you will find that saving power. The Sabbath and Calvary stand together for My creative, redeeming power. What I have joined together, let no man put asunder."

The Lord of Creation Creates Again

In the future there is to dawn a new day. Sin and sinners will be no more. What then? Let Isaiah the prophet give us the picture:

"As the new heavens and the new earth, which I will make, shall remain before me, saith the Lord, so shall your seed and your name remain. And it shall come to pass, tha from one new moon to another, and from one sabbath t another, shall all flesh come to worship before me, sait the Lord." Isaiah 66:22, 23.

In that land where we will never grow old and wher sorrows will never come, we shall keep the Sabbath as sign of God's peace and power, while we sing, "Worth is the Lamb that was slain." Revelation 5:12.

The Christ of Calvary is therefore Lord of the Sabbat for all time. "If ye love me," said He, "keep my command ments." John 14:15. "Ye are my friends, if ye do whatso ever I command you." John 15:14. "Why call ye me, Lor Lord, and do not the things which I say?" Luke 6:46.

"Don't forget the Sabbath,
The Lord our God hath blest,
Of all the week the brightest,
Of all the week the best;
It brings repose from labor,
It tells of joy divine,
Its beams of light descending,
With heavenly beauty shine."

CHAPTER 39

The Sign of God to His Disciples

IT HAS been thought by some that though Jesus honored the Sabbath as a sign of creative power, His disciples laid aside this practice. It seems fitting for us to examine the New Testament record for its testimony in this matter.

THE WOMEN AT THE CROSS AND TOMB

Among the followers of Christ none were more faithful than certain women. Four of them with the apostle John stood at the cross in sad vigil as Jesus suffered and died. (John 19:25-27.)

Concerning these faithful women we read: "That day was the preparation, and the sabbath drew on. And the women also, which came with him from Galilee, followed after, and beheld the sepulchre, and how his body was laid. And they returned, and prepared spices and ointments; and rested the sabbath day according to the commandment." Luke 23:54-56.

The picture is clear. By the time Nicodemus and Joseph of Arimathea had arranged the burial of Jesus, the sun had almost set on that fateful sixth day of the week. "The sabbath drew on." By Bible reckoning each day begins at evening, or sundown. (Genesis 1:5, 8, 13, 19, 23, 31; Leviticus 23:32; Mark 1:32.)

These women who loved Christ so deeply prepared

J. D. Penrose, A

After their Lord's burial the holy women prepared spices and rested over the Sabb Early Sunday morning they returned to the tomb to find the Lord risen.

spices that they might anoint His body. But lo, the sacred hours of the Sabbath were drawing nigh. So they "rested the sabbath day according to the commandment."

And when the Sabbath was past, they brought the spices which they had prepared. (Mark 16:1.) So sacred did they consider the Sabbath that they waited until its hours were past, and then came to the sepulcher to anoint His body.

The Apostle to the Gentiles

Paul was God's special chosen messenger to the Gentiles. As such he would take care to set before them the right example on Sabbath observance. What was his practice?

At Antioch the followers of Christ were first called Christians. (Acts 11:26.)

Coming to this city, Paul and his company "went into the synagogue on the sabbath day." Acts 13:14. There he delivered a fervent and powerful appeal for men to accept Christ, the seed of David, as the Saviour of the world.

Then came the Gentiles, and "besought that these words might be preached to them the next sabbath." Verse 42.

There is no thought, word, or intimation that the acceptance of the gospel disturbed the practice of keeping Christ's holy Sabbath, which He had made for man.

Called to Philippi in Macedonia by special vision, Paul and his company "on the sabbath . . . went out of the city by a river side, where prayer was wont to be made." Acts 16:13. Here was a regular Sabbath service that Christ's followers sought out. There is no word of controversy about the Sabbath, no effort to get people to keep another day.

Thessalonica was the next stop. "Paul, as his manner was, went in unto them, and three sabbath days reasoned with them out of the scriptures." Acts 17:2. He preached Christ crucified and risen. No argument about the Sabbath. No new day proposed. "As his manner was," he went to church on the Sabbath. Persecution drove him to Berea and thence to Athens.

At Corinth, Greece, he was able to settle down for eighteen months, preaching Sabbath after Sabbath. (Acts 18:1-4, 11.) There is no word concerning another holy day, no voice raised against the holy Sabbath.

In these few scriptures we have indicated eighty-four Sabbaths when Paul preached the gospel. It was his custom to keep the Sabbath as it was the custom of Jesus, who called him to preach to the Gentiles.

A Reasonable Conclusion

From the record of Paul's life it seems beyond all question that his burden was the preaching of salvation by grace, which forgave men and restored them to obedience to holy law. (Acts 13:38, 39; 24:14; Romans 3:31; 6:1, 2, 15, 16.) There was no controversy over which day of the week was the Sabbath. There was no discussion of setting up a new day.

In fact, the general council of the Christian leaders at Jerusalem, convened to study the question of what to teach the Gentiles, issued this closing statement: "For Moses of old time hath in every city them that preach him, being read in the synagogues every sabbath day." Acts 15:21. There was no problem over the weekly Sabbath. The discussion was over circumcision and other matters of the "law of Moses," referring to the ceremonial law, as is clearly indicated.

The holding of meetings on a certain day does not make that day holy. No man, yea, not all men, can make any day holy. Christ sanctified the seventh day. He hallowed it. "He hath blessed; and I cannot reverse it."

Numbers 23:20. No man can bless a day or remove God's blessing from that day. But let it be always remembered that we may bring God's blessing upon our souls by choosing His holy will, or His curse by refusing obedience.

"I call heaven and earth to record this day against you, that I have set before you life and death, blessing and cursing: therefore choose life, that both thou and thy seed may live: that thou mayest love the Lord thy God, and that thou mayest obey his voice." Deuteronomy 30:19, 20. The disciples kept the Sabbath because it was the will of God that they should do so.

The great European preacher Karl Barth said, "What is required of us is that we should be watchful, willing and ready to make Christian decisions in the midst of an evil world."

This is precisely what Jesus did, and He was "obedient unto death, even the death of the cross." Philippians 2:8. "The disciple is not above his Master, nor the servant above his lord. It is enough for the disciple that he be as his Master, and the servant as his lord." Matthew 10:24, 25.

"More like the Master I would ever be,
More of His meekness, more humility;
More zeal to labor, more courage to be true,
More consecration for work He bids me do.

"Take Thou my heart, I would be Thine alone;
Take Thou my heart and make it all Thine own;
Purge me from sin, O Lord, I now implore,
Wash me and keep me Thine forevermore."

—CHARLES H. GABRIEL.

CHAPTER 40

A Reward for the Missing Text

SOME YEARS ago a prominent Catholic priest offered one thousand dollars to anyone who would prove from the Bible that Sunday, the first day of the week, was to be observed as a holy day. This challenge created widespread comment. No one ever claimed the reward.

It is with no small interest that we proceed to examine the New Testament with reference to the possible sacredness of the first day of the week, commonly called Sunday.

Jesus and the First Day of the Week

Matthew, Mark, Luke, and John each wrote a book recording events of Jesus' life from birth to death, resurrection, and ascension. No other disciple wrote such an account in the New Testament.

According to these first four books of the New Testament, which present His teachings, what did Jesus have to say about the first day of the week? How many times did He mention it? To many it comes as a surprise that, in the record, Jesus utters no word regarding the first day of the week. The Christ of the Gospels is completely silent.

He who came to declare God, declared nothing at all about the first day of the week. He who came to magnify the law did indeed reveal its deep spiritual meaning but exalted no new holy day.

At creation He worked on the first day and rested on the seventh. As a carpenter He worked on the first day and rested on the seventh. As the Redeemer He finished His earthly redemptive ministry on the sixth day and rested in the tomb on the Sabbath. Concerning the first day He makes no statement either before His death or after His resurrection. First-day sacredness, if it have any, comes not from the lips of Christ.

But is not the first day of the week mentioned in the New Testament? Yes, eight times. These references we shall now examine.

MATTHEW'S ONE RECORD

"In the end of the sabbath, as it began to dawn toward the first day of the week, came Mary Magdalene and the other Mary to see the sepulchre." Matthew 28:1.

Here we see that the Sabbath ends before the first day of the week begins. Therefore the two days are distinct one from the other. There is no slighest hint of any sacredness being attached to the first day of the week. Matthew wrote his record several years after the resurrection of Christ.

MARK'S TWO RECORDS

"When the sabbath was past, Mary Magdalene, and Mary the mother of James, and Salome, had brought sweet spices that they might come and anoint him. And very early in the morning the first day of the week, they came unto the sepulchre at the rising of the sun." Mark 16:1, 2.

"Now when Jesus was risen early the first day of the week, he appeared first to Mary Magdalene, out of whom he had cast seven devils." Verse 9.

Here again is no word from Christ, but only Mark's record of the resurrection. The Sabbath was past before the first day came. They are two different days. One is holy; the other, one of the six working days. Years after the resurrection Mark knew of no first-day sacredness.

Luke's One Record

"Now upon the first day of the week, very early in the morning, they came unto the sepulchre, bringing the spices which they had prepared, and certain others with them." Luke 24:1.

Luke likewise gives no record that Jesus ever referred to the first day of the week. He does point out (in the two preceding verses) that some of Jesus' most ardent followers "rested on the Sabbath day according to the commandment." Naturally this was according to the fourth commandment. These friends of Jesus had never heard of any change, nor had Luke.

John's Two Records

"The first day of the week cometh Mary Magdalene early, when it was yet dark, unto the sepulchre." John 20:1. John gives the same story, a simple record of the early morning experience.

"Then the same day at evening, being the first day of the week, when the doors were shut where the disciples were assembled for fear of the Jews, came Jesus and stood in the midst, and saith unto them, Peace be unto you." John 20:19.

Here again John's record gives no account that Jesus ever mentioned the first day of the week.

What John does say is that the disciples were gathered together *"for fear of the Jews."* And there Jesus appeared before them. This was at the close of this same resurrection day.

Some have thought that the disciples may have been celebrating Christ's resurrection. This is completely in error, because the disciples did not believe Jesus had risen.

Mark makes this unmistakably clear. Mary Magdalene, having seen the resurrected Christ, told the disciples, but they "believed not." (Mark 16:11.) And again, "After that he appeared in another form unto two of them, as they walked, and went into the country. And they went and told it unto the residue: neither believed they them." Verses 12, 13.

Luke writes of these same two men who saw Christ, and states: "They rose up the same hour, and returned to Jerusalem, and found the eleven gathered together, . . . saying, The Lord is risen indeed. . . . And as they thus spake, Jesus himself stood in the midst of them, and saith unto them, Peace be unto you." Luke 24:33-36.

This is the same meeting of which John wrote. What was the reaction of the disciples who had thus far refused to believe He had risen? We read on: "They were terrified and affrighted, and supposed that they had seen a spirit." Luke 24:37. Here is conclusive proof that the disciples gathered in the upper room were not celebrating the resurrection. They did not believe that He was risen, and were frightened when they saw Him.

Jesus invited these doubting disciples to feel of His body and behold His wounded hands and feet. Then He asked for food and ate before them. Thomas, one of the twelve, was absent from the gathering. Hearing of it, he refused to believe until he might actually feel of the wounded flesh of the Saviour's hands and side. Some days later Jesus invited him to do this. Then, and then only, did Thomas believe that Jesus had actually risen from the dead.

To the honest seeker of truth it seems clear beyond all question that Matthew, Mark, Luke, and John, the recorders of Jesus' life and teachings, knew nothing of any Sunday sacredness. They maintain a significant silence on the sanctity of any day save the Sabbath.

One Record in Acts

"Upon the first day of the week, when the disciples came together to break bread, Paul preached unto them, ready to depart on the morrow; and continued his speech until midnight. And there were many lights in the upper chamber, where they were gathered together." Acts 20:7, 8.

Luke wrote the book of Acts, giving an inspired historical account of the early New Testament church. He recorded eighty-four Sabbath services (after Christ's ascension) and only one first-day meeting, the one referred to in the text above.

Paul and his missionary company had spent seven days at Troas. (Verse 6.) Their farewell gathering was held at night, since there were lights in the upper chamber. Paul preached until midnight.

The first day of the week (Bible time) begins Saturday night at sundown and ends Sunday night at sundown. Inasmuch as this meeting was held on the first day of the week and at night, it must therefore have been on what we call Saturday night, the first day having begun at sundown. Had it been held on what we call Sunday night (after sundown on Sunday), it would then have been on the second day of the week. That is why Conybeare and Howson, in their work *The Life and Epistles of St. Paul,* say, "It was the evening which succeeded the Jewish Sabbath."—Volume 2, p. 206.

It is interesting to note what followed. Paul having preached, conversed, and eaten, found that day was breaking. His company had already set sail Saturday night (the first day of the week). Sunday morning the apostle walked nineteen miles across a point of land to Assos, where his company took him on board ship. (Verses 11-14.) Neither Paul nor any of the believers attached any sacredness to the first day of the week. They had spent seven days at Troas. Then on Saturday night (after the

Sabbath) they had a farewell gathering with the believers, "ready to depart on the morrow."

What does the expression "to break bread" mean? They came together to break bread. Does this signify the Lord's supper? There is nothing to infer this. It is the common Bible expression to indicate partaking of food.

Jesus broke bread with two of His disciples. It was at a meal. (Luke 24:30-35.) The disciples broke bread daily from house to house. (Acts 2:46.) If breaking bread means the Lord's supper, then the disciples celebrated it every day. It is evident that this is not the true meaning of the record, since the statement is added that they "did eat their meat with gladness." Verse 46.

In the case of Paul at Troas, they came together "to break bread." (Acts 20:7.) Paul launched into preaching and did not stop until a young man went to sleep and fell out of the window at midnight. The apostle went down and helped revive the youth.

Note carefully the record: "When he [Paul] therefore was come up again, and had broken bread, and eaten, and talked a long while, even till break of day, so he departed." Verse 11.

Nothing is said about a Lord's supper or any wine to represent the blood of Christ. The whole tenor of the record is that of a farewell gathering where Paul preached and they had a meal together.

However, even had they held the actual communion service on the first day of the week, this would in no way make Sunday a holy day. The Lord's supper may be celebrated on any day. (1 Corinthians 11:26.) And, in any case, it commemorates Christ's death, not His resurrection. "Ye do shew the Lord's death till he come." Verse 26.

So we may honestly and fairly conclude that the entire book of Acts is as silent on first-day sanctity as are Matthew, Mark, Luke, and John.

 Arlo Greer, Ar

The apostle Paul urged that Christians make up their accounts on the first day of week, and in doing so to lay aside an amount for needy Christians in Jerusal

Paul's One Mention of the First Day

This is the eighth and final mention of the first day of the week in the New Testament. In all Paul's fervent epistles he writes of it but this one time.

"Now concerning the collection for the saints, as I have given order to the churches of Galatia, even so do ye. Upon the first day of the week let every one of you lay by him in store, as God hath prospered him, that there be no gatherings when I come." 1 Corinthians 16:1, 2.

Several things are here worthy of notice. First, a general order had gone out to most of the Gentile churches to the effect that a collection of money be gathered for the poor saints at Jerusalem. Paul found considerable satisfaction in seeing his Gentile converts give needed assistance to poor believers at Jerusalem, mostly Jews.

It is evident also that the apostle was one of those preachers who do not enjoy putting on financial drives in person or in making this work too prominent in the pulpit. "That there be no gatherings when I come," he said. Gatherings of money, of course. He evidently had observed that if people do not give systematically, on a basis of income, there must be not only a gathering of money but gatherings (plural).

To avoid this, he specifically instructs this church, as he had others, "Let every one of you lay by him in store." The Revised Standard Version says, "Put something aside and save." Thus this plan had no connection with a weekly collection at a church service. Quite to the contrary, the money was to be laid aside at home.

Furthermore, it was to be on a basis of "as God hath prospered." How simple and clear is the picture. A church member runs a small shop all week, let us say. Friday afternoon he closes early enough to prepare for the Sabbath. There is no time to figure accounts. But when the Sabbath is past, and the first day of the week comes, he is to check his net earnings and lay aside a proper sum, not at church, but at home.

This last of the eight New Testament first-day texts, like the other seven, gives no shred of evidence for a new holy day or a regular first-day church gathering.

The Bible, as Chillingsworth wrote, "is the religion of Protestants." It speaks of seventh-day rest, Sabbath holiness, and Lord's-day sacredness. But it is silent on first-day sanctity.

What Men Say

Gibbons, the brilliant Roman Catholic cardinal, wrote: "You may read the Bible from Genesis to Revelation, and you will not find a single line authorizing the sanctification of Sunday. The Scriptures enforce the religious observance of Saturday."—*Faith of Our Fathers* (110th ed.), pp. 72, 73.

Protestants say there is no Bible text. Smith and Cheetham's *Dictionary of Christian Antiquities:* "The notion of a formal substitution by apostolic authority of the Lord's Day [meaning Sunday] for the Jewish Sabbath, and the transference to it, perhaps in a spiritual form, of the Sabbatical obligation established by the promulgation of the Fourth Commandment, has no basis whatever, either in Holy Scripture or in Christian antiquity."—Article "Sabbath."

R. W. Dale (British Congregational) in *The Ten Commandments,* pages 104-106, writes: "It is quite clear that however rigidly or devoutly we may spend Sunday, we are not keeping the Sabbath. . . . The Sabbath was founded on a specific Divine command. We can plead no such command for the obligation to observe Sunday. . . . There is not a single sentence in the New Testament to suggest that we incur any penalty by violating the supposed sanctity of Sunday."

Edward T. Hiscox, in a paper read before a New York ministers' conference, November 13, 1893, says: "There was and is a commandment to keep holy the Sabbath day, but that Sabbath day was not Sunday. It will be said, however, and with some show of triumph, that the Sabbath was transferred from the seventh to the first day of the week. . . . Where can the record of such a transaction be found? Not in the New Testament, absolutely not."

Canon Eyton (of Westminster) in the *Ten Commandments* writes: "There is no word, no hint, in the New Testament about abstaining from work on Sunday. . . . Into the rest of Sunday no divine law enters. . . . The observance of Ash Wednesday or Lent stands exactly on the same footing as the observance of Sunday."—Pages 62, 63, 65.

Historians testify likewise. *Chambers' Ecyclopaedia* says: "Unquestionably the first law, either ecclesiastical or civil, by which the sabbatical observance of that day is known to have been ordained, is the edict of Constantine, 321 A.D."—Page 401, art. "Sabbath." This Roman emperor had not yet professed Christianity at the time of this edict, and he speaks of Sunday as "the venerable day of the sun."

Neander, celebrated historian, states: "The festival of Sunday, like all other festivals, was always only a human ordinance, and it was far from the intentions of the apostles to establish a Divine command in this respect, far from them, and far from the early apostolic Church, to transfer the laws of the Sabbath to Sunday."—*The History of the Christian Religion and Church,* Rose's translation, p. 186.

The apostle John wrote, "Sin is the transgression of the law." 1 John 3:4. Paul declared, "Where no law is, there is no transgression." Romans 4:15.

There is a Bible Sabbath law. There is no Bible Sunday

law, no law setting aside the day as a holy day, no law of instruction on how to keep it, no law of penalty for not keeping it. The only Bible law governing Sunday, the first day, is "Six days shalt thou labour."

How, then, does it come that the Sabbath of the law of God has been so fully set aside in Christendom, and Sunday, the first day, one of God's prescribed working days, exalted as the weekly day of rest and worship?

The answer to this question will be of great interest and importance to every reader.

CHAPTER 41

Who Tampered With God's Trademark?

GOD DID not change His own Sabbath trademark of creation. We are certain of this because the Bible says, "Surely the Lord God will do nothing, but he revealeth his secret unto his servants the prophets." Amos 3:7.

The Bible gives no record of God's changing the day. On the contrary the prophet predicts that the Sabbath will be kept in the new earth. (Isaiah 66:23.)

If the Sabbath change is valid, where should the record be found? In the Holy Scriptures. With Bible Christians this goes without saying. To them the Bible is more authoritative in spiritual matters than is a dictionary for spelling and definition of words. Dictionaries change, but "the word of our God shall stand for ever." Isaiah 40:8.

What of the Early Church Fathers?

In the first and second centuries, after the days of the apostles, there arose such men as Clement, Polycarp, Justin Martyr, Irenaeus, and Tertullian. These men are called the early church fathers. Shall we build our faith on the writings of such men? Shall tradition take the place of Holy Scripture? You who are Bible believers will say No, and very emphatically. All will do well to read the following estimates of the value of the writing of these fathers.

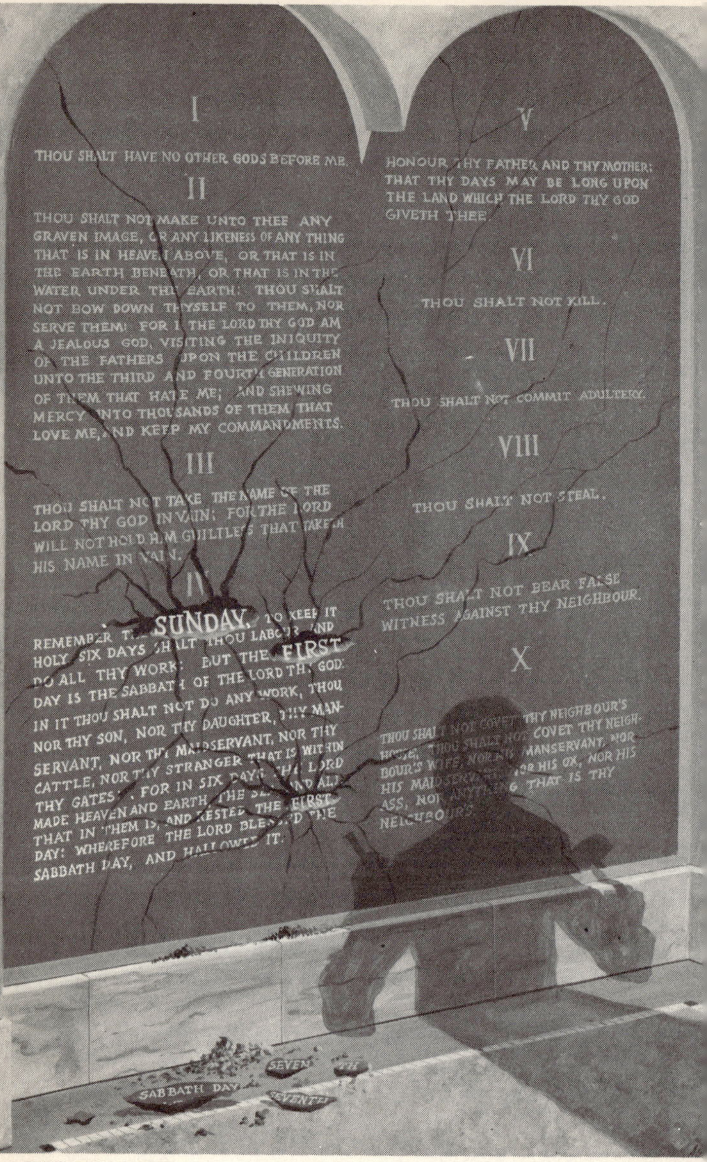

 Arlo Greer, Art

God, speaking through the prophet Daniel, foresaw a human attempt to change
law, of which Christ said, "One jot or one tittle shall in no wise pass from the la

Archdeacon Farrar says, "There are but few of them whose pages are not rife with errors—errors of method, errors of fact, errors of history, of grammar, and even of doctrine. This is the language of simple truth, not of slighting disparagement."—*History of Interpretation,* pp. 162, 163.

Martin Luther speaks thus: "When God's Word is by the Fathers expounded, construed, and glossed, then, in my judgment, it is even as when one strains milk through a coal-sack, which must needs spoil and make the milk black; God's Word of itself is pure, clean, bright and clear; but, through the doctrines, books, and writings of the Fathers, it is darkened, falsified, and spoiled."—*The Table-Talk of Martin Luther* (Hazlitt trans., Philadelphia, 1868), p. 281.

Neander writes: "The writings of the so-called Apostolic Fathers have unhappily, for the most part, come down to us in a condition very little worthy of confidence, partly because under the name of these men, so highly venerated in the church, writings were early forged for the purpose of giving authority to particular opinions or principles." —*General History of the Christian Religion and Church,* vol. 1, p. 657.

Dr. Adam Clarke (Methodist) says: "But of these [the Fathers] we may safely state, that there is not a truth in the most orthodox creed, that cannot be proved by their authority, nor a *heresy* that has disgraced the Romish Church, that may not challenge them as its abettors. In points of *doctrine,* their authority is, *with me* nothing. The word of GOD alone contains my creed."—*Commentary,* comments on Proverbs 8, vol. 3, p. 725.

Archibald Bower wrote: "To avoid being imposed upon, we ought to treat tradition as we do a notorious and known liar, to whom we give no credit, unless what he says is confirmed to us by some person of undoubted veracity. . . . False and lying traditions are of an early date, and the greatest men have, out of a pious credulity, suffered themselves to be imposed upon by them."—*The History of the Popes,* vol. 1, p. 1.

There is no safety save in a "Thus saith the Lord." And the simplest of all tests is the Ten Commandments. "To the law and to the testimony: if they speak not according to this word, it is because there is no light in them." Isaiah 8:20. The Ten Commandments are heaven's constitution. All Christian laws must conform to this fundamental, everlasting code.

The Ten Commandments are like a carpenter's square. By laying the square on a board the carpenter can tell in an instant whether the end is cut on the square. No one argues with a true square. But would it not be a wicked deed for some other carpenter to spring that square out of true, and cause lumber for a building to be cut untrue? We are being cut and squared for God's spiritual building.

Someone has been tampering with God's eternal square. Somebody has been chiseling on Heaven's constitution, the one which God wrote with His own finger on tables of stone. An effort has been made to change Christ's eternal trademark, the seal of His law.

The Reverend George Elliot said: "Long should pause the erring hand of man before it dares to chip away with the chisel of human reasonings one single word graven on the enduring tables by the hand of the infinite God. What is proposed? To make an erasure in a heaven-born code; to expunge one article from the recorded will of the Eternal! Is the eternal tablet of his law to be defaced by a creature's hand? He who proposes such an act should fortify himself by reasons as holy as God and as mighty as his power."—*The Abiding Sabbath* (Prize Essay), part 2, p. 128. New York: American Tract Society, 1884.

Did Prophecy Foretell This Attempted Change?

God is never taken unawares. "I am God, and there is none like me, declaring the end from the beginning, and from ancient times the things that are not yet done." Isaiah 46:9, 10.

We, His followers, are sometimes slow to believe what the prophets have predicted. Said Jesus to two of His disciples: "O fools, and slow of heart to believe all that the prophets have spoken." Luke 24:25. We are prone to believe some things but "slow of heart at times to believe *all*."

Here is the prophecy. Let us believe it.

"He shall speak great words against the most High, and shall wear out the saints of the most High, and think to change times and laws." Daniel 7:25.

This little-horn power of Daniel 7 would "think" to change times and laws. The Catholic Douay Version reads: "He shall think himself able to change times and laws."

The prophecy is clear on two points. This little horn power would make a deliberate effort to change God's law, and in particular the time of the law. The fourth commandment is the only one dealing with time. "Six days shalt thou labour, . . . but the seventh day is the sabbath of the Lord thy God." Exodus 20:9, 10.

Does the papal little horn "think himself able" to change the Sabbath? Does it admit to making this deliberate attempt?

Note these statements from Catholic sources:

Catholic Mirror, September 23, 1893: "The Catholic Church for over one thousand years before the existence of a Protestant, by virtue of her divine mission, changed the day from Saturday to Sunday."

Rev. Peter Geiermann, *Convert's Catechism* (Catholic), page 50:

"Q.—*Which is the Sabbath day?*

"A.—Saturday is the Sabbath day.

"Q.—*Why do we observe Sunday instead of Saturday?*

"A.—We observe Sunday instead of Saturday because the Catholic Church, in the Council of Laodicea (A.D. 336), transferred the solemnity from Saturday to Sunday."

American Sentinel (New York), June 1, 1893, page 173, quotes Father T. Enright, C.Ss.R., of Redemptorist College, Kansas City, Missouri: "The Bible says, 'Remember that thou keep holy the Sabbath day.' The Catholic Church says, 'No! By my divine power I abolish the Sabbath day, and command you to keep holy the first day of the week.' "

The Change a Gradual Process

The influence of Mithraism and sun worship, the existence of the heathen festival Sunday, the rising anti-Jewish sentiment among Christians, the fact that Christians had a tendency to think of the resurrection of Christ with a certain holy joy, the interest of Roman rulers to bind together all religious elements of the empire, and the gradual apostasy of the church—all combined to bring about a gradual change from God's holy Sabbath to Sunday.

Thus the Roman emperor Constantine passed the first-known Sunday law A.D. 321. A few years later the apostatizing church at the Council of Laodicea transferred the solemnity from Sabbath to Sunday as noted above. That council in Canon 29 decreed: "Christians shall not Judaize and be idle on the Sabbath, but shall work on that day."

This definitely indicates that many Christians were keeping the Sabbath more than three hundred years after Christ's ascension, as scholars have always known.

Pagan Background of Sundaykeeping

Scholars freely admit that Sundaykeeping came to the church from the pagans.

"The early Christian church adopted, as far as possible, the *sacred days* of the older cults, and *grafted* on to them Christian commemorations."—WILBERFORCE, Archdeacon of Westminster, in *Sunday Circle,* London, Feb. 1, 1908.

"Sunday being the day on which the Gentiles solemnly adored that planet [the sun], . . . the Christians thought fit to keep the same day and the same name of it, that they might not appear causelessly peevish, and by that means hinder the conversion of the Gentiles."—T. H. MORER, *Discourses on the Lord's Day,* p. 23.

Dr. Edward T. Hiscox summarizes the matter in these lines: "I quite well know that Sunday did come into use in early Christian history as a religious day, as we learn from the Christian Fathers and other sources. But what a pity that it comes branded with the mark of paganism, and christened with the name of the sun god, when adopted and sanctioned by the papal apostasy, and bequeathed as a sacred [?] legacy to Protestantism!"—In a paper read before a New York ministers' conference, Nov. 13, 1893.

Four facts now stand out in bold relief: (1) The change from Sabbath to Sunday is not found in the Bible; (2) God predicted that the Papacy would "think to change" His times and laws; (3) the Papacy openly declares that it has changed God's law; (4) the Papacy thus exalts itself above God, as forecast by the apostle Paul. (2 Thessalonians 2:3, 4.)

THE CHANGELESS GOD

"For I am the Lord, I change not." Malachi 3:6.

"Jesus Christ the same yesterday, and to day, and for ever." Hebrews 13:8.

A wooden cross bore a changeless Christ,
On the face of Golgotha's hill,
Where He died for my sins 'gainst a changeless law,
And fulfilled His Father's will.

What shall I do with this changeless Christ and His changeless law?

"I will follow Thee, my Saviour,
Wheresoe'er my lot may be.
Where Thou goest I will follow;
Yes, my Lord, I'll follow Thee.

"I will follow Thee, my Saviour,
Thou didst shed Thy blood for me;
And though all men should forsake Thee,
By Thy grace I'll follow Thee."

—J. LAWSON.

CHAPTER 42

Seven Questions

MORE EASILY asked than answered are questions. Jesus taught the Jews that lesson (Mark 11:27-33), yet He always appreciated sincere questions (Mark 12:28-34; Matthew 24). He soon silenced insincere quibblers. (Matthew 22:35-46.)

Let us consider seven proper questions relating to the matter of the weekly Sabbath.

1. After His Resurrection Did Christ Appear Only on Sunday?

His first appearance to His disciples as a group was at the close of the first day of the week, the day on which He rose. (John 20:19.)

His second appearance was "after eight days," when Thomas was present. (Verse 26.) This is an idiomatic expression which indicates that the meeting occurred the following Sunday.

The third time He found the disciples fishing, and instructed them how to catch fish. (John 21:1-6.) The record gives no information on what day of the week it was. If it were the first day, then both the disciples and Jesus approved of Sunday fishing.

Christ appeared to His disciples at other times during a period of forty days. (Acts 1:3.) But we are not told the day or days of the week. The time of Christ's appearance to His disciples has no possible bearing on the question of the weekly rest day based on the spoken and written command of God. The identity of God's holy day does not rest on such irregularities as occasional meetings. This will be accepted by all.

2. May Not Each One Select His Own Day?

Is not every day alike? What does Paul mean when he says: "One man esteemeth one day above another: another esteemeth every day alike. Let every man be fully persuaded in his own mind. He that regardeth the day, regardeth it unto the Lord; and he that regardeth not the day, to the Lord he doth not regard it"? Romans 14:5, 6.

That this could not refer to the weekly Sabbath is clearly evident. God never gave to man the right to decide the Sabbath of the fourth commandment. No man, yea, not even all men, could make any day holy. Christ sanctified the seventh day. "He hath blessed; and I cannot reverse it." Numbers 23:20. No man can bless a day or remove God's blessing from that day. What then does Paul intend by his words in Romans 14:5, 6?

Paul was seeking to divorce the Jewish Christians from continuing to attach duty to the observance of the special yearly holy days of the ceremonial system. He also sought to lead them not to judge one another on the matter of observing these ceremonial laws. (See Leviticus, chapter 23, for yearly sabbaths.)

3. Does Paul Say the Sabbath Was Nailed to the Cross?

Let us read Colossians 2:14, 16, 17: "Blotting out the handwriting of ordinances that was against us, which was contrary to us, and took it out of the way, nailing it to his cross. . . . Let no man therefore judge you in meat or in drink, or in respect of an holyday or of the new moon, or of the sabbath days: which are a shadow of things to come; but the body is of Christ."

This could not possibly refer to the weekly Sabbath of the fourth commandment for the following reasons that will be clear to all:

The commandments here are not the Ten Commandments, else Christ would have destroyed the very foundation of God's government. "Think not that I am come to destroy the law," He said. Matthew 5:17.

It was the "handwriting of ordinances" that was nailed to the cross; that is, the ceremonial law, with its bloody sacrifices and its multiplied yearly sabbath days. (Leviticus 23.)

These "ordinances" were "against us, . . . contrary to us." But the weekly Sabbath is not so. God blessed it, and pronounced a blessing on all men who keep it. (Genesis 2:1-3; Isaiah 56:1-7.) To such the Sabbath would be a "delight," not a yoke of bondage. (Isaiah 58:13, 14.)

The ceremonial system with its blood, meat, drink offerings, and special yearly holy days was a "shadow of things to come"; that is, of the "body of Christ," who in the flesh died for us.

This ceremonial system developed after Adam sinned. The weekly Sabbath was made before sin. It was for "man," for all time.

Dr. Adam Clarke, the Methodist commentator, in his notes on Colossians 2:14-17, says: "The apostle speaks here in reference to some particulars of the *handwriting of ordinances,* which had *been taken away,* viz., the distinction of *meats* and *drinks,* what was *clean* and what *unclean,* according to the law; and the necessity of observing certain *holydays* or *festivals,* such as the *new moons* and particular *sabbaths. . . .* There is no intimation here that the *Sabbath* was done away, or that its moral use was superseded, by the introduction of Christianity."

Dr. Albert Barnes, Presbyterian, writes: "The use of the term in the plural number [sabbaths], and the connection, show that he [Paul] had his eye on the great number of days which were observed by the Hebrews as festivals, as a part of their ceremonial and typical laws, and not to the *moral* law, or the ten commandments. No part of the moral law—no one of the ten commandments could be spoken of as '*a shadow* of good things to come.'"—*Notes, Explanatory and Practical, on the Epistles of Paul to the Ephesians, Philippians, and Colossians* (1851 ed.), p. 307.

All informed students should agree with these correct statements.

4. Does God Speak of "Another Day"?

Some have wondered about Hebrews 4:1-9. Just read it prayerfully. The first day is not mentioned. The Sabbath is presented as a symbol of spiritual rest. Most of the Jews did not enter this spiritual rest. Joshua (verse 8, see margin) could not give spiritual rest just by taking them to Canaan. So God keeps calling to men not to harden their hearts, but to come and find rest. The conclusion in verse 9 is, "There remaineth therefore a rest ["keeping of a sabbath," margin] to the people of God." God still gives people rest, and someday we shall have our heavenly rest, and then as now, the seventh day on which God rested will continue to be the beautiful symbol of spiritual rest.

5. Are We Not Told to Assemble on the First Day?

Many earnest persons have thought the Bible has a verse which reads something like this: "Forsake not the assembling of yourselves together on the first day of the week."

However, here is the exact wording of the actual text

in Hebrews 10:25: "Not forsaking the assembling of ourselves together, as the manner of some is; but exhorting one another: and so much the more, as ye see the day approaching." No mention is here made of any particular holy day. If the weekly rest day was what Paul had in mind, that day would be the Sabbath.

6. Has Time Been Lost?

Some have asked, "Has time been lost?" We probably would all agree that the only way we could prove that such an element as time had been lost would be to locate when and where it was lost, and in that act we would have found it. For anyone to say that time has been lost is merely to suppose something he cannot prove.

If the weekly cycle were lost between the time of Adam and Moses, this certainly would have been rectified when God wrote the Ten Commandments, with the Sabbath as the fourth.

For 40 years, or 2,080 weeks, God worked a number of miracles every week, thereby pointing out the identical seventh day 2,080 times. In the wilderness the manna fell on each of the first five days of the week. That was one miracle. Any portion kept over one day would spoil. Then on the sixth day a double portion fell. This was another miracle. The unused portion kept over to the seventh day did not spoil. This was a third miracle. To this we might add the fact that on the seventh, or Sabbath, day no manna fell. And this could be called a fourth miracle. God thus emphasized the sacredness of the Sabbath, and clearly marked the identical seventh day. (See Exodus 16.)

If the Sabbath were lost between Moses' time and Jesus' day, we have the example of the Saviour, which is indeed sufficient. "He that saith he abideth in him ought himself also so to walk, even as he walked." 1 John 2:6.

Has the Sabbath been lost since Jesus' time? On this

there can be no question. The Jews, scattered over the earth, have kept strict account of time, and wherever you find the orthodox Jew, you find the seventh-day Sabbath, Saturday. This leaves us the final question about the calendars.

7. Have Calendar Changes Disturbed the Sabbath?

The answer is No. Here is the true account, the facts of which can be verified in any authoritative encyclopedia.

The Julian Calendar was in use when Jesus was upon the earth. Its originator, Julius Caesar, died forty-four years before the Christian Era. The week in use in the East at that time is precisely the same as the week of our calendar today, which is the Gregorian. The days of the month are different, but the days of the week were never changed. On the following page is a calendar illustrating how the change was effected.

The change from the Julian to the Gregorian Calendar was on this wise. The Julian Calendar used for sixteen centuries was not accurate in the length of its year, being nearly one quarter of an hour too long. By 1582 the vernal equinox had receded, and fell on March 11, ten days earlier than the March 21 date to which the Catholic Church had, in A.D. 321, anchored the computation of Easter.

Pope Gregory XIII led out in a change, and the Gregorian Calendar began to function at Rome on Friday the fifth of October, 1582. Friday the fifth was changed to Friday the fifteenth. The week remained untouched, and the days of the week were undisturbed.

Some nations began the use of the new calendar at once. Others began later—England waited 170 years until 1752. Yet these different states and nations with dif ferent calendars had the same week. Just remember that the seventh day of the week today is the same as when Christ was here, and calendar changes have not affected it.

It is true that in connection with the French Revolution the French tried a ten-day week, but it did not endure.

It is well known also that Soviet Russia introduced a five-day week, then a six-day week, and forbade the printing of a seven-day-week calendar. All this is a modern attempt to banish the weekly rest day. But Russia failed.

1582		OCTOBER			1582	
SUN	MON	TUE	WED	THU	FRI	SAT
	1	2	3	4	15	16
17	18	19	20	21	22	23
24	25	26	27	28	29	30
31						

How the Calendar Was Changed

The world blank-day calendar idea, of which we hear much today, would, if accepted, cause the true Sabbath to occur on a different day of the calendar week each year. The same would be so of the true first day, for that matter. All persons who believe in honoring any regular weekly day should oppose the adoption of such a calendar under whatever name it may appear. Meantime, our regular Gregorian Calendar has the true weekly cycle. Sunday is the first day of the week and Saturday is the seventh day.

The Young Man and the Calendar

A consecrated Christian young man was taught the Ten Commandments. He memorized them according to the suggestion of his Sunday school teacher.

One day he looked at the calendar and noticed that the seventh day of the week is Saturday and that the first day of the week is Sunday. He recalled that the fourth commandment says, "The seventh day is the sabbath of the Lord thy God." Exodus 20:10. Thus, since Saturday is the seventh day of the week, Saturday is the Sabbath of the fourth commandment. This is the logical way he reasoned.

He asked his mother about it. She could not explain it. She just had never thought about it.

Next time he inquired of his Sunday school teacher. Said he, "Oh, the Sabbath has been changed from the seventh to the first day of the week." It seemed strange that the teacher had his pupils memorize the wrong commandment. So the young man wanted to know where to find the first-day commandment. The teacher was positive it was in the Bible, but said he would have to look it up.

Then the young man visited the head deacon. The deacon said, "Oh, the calendar has been changed. Time was lost 'way back there, and so we can't tell which is the seventh day. The seventh day is the Sabbath, but we don't really know which is the seventh day." This was confusing.

So in desperation the young man went to see his pastor. Here he would surely get it straight. The kindly pastor said, "Don't let it worry you, because one day is just as good as another. All days are holy." Said the young man, "Has the Sabbath been changed on the calendar?" "Oh, no," came the reply. "Calendar adjustments have had nothing to do with the weekly cycle. Only uninformed people ever say that. Saturday is the seventh day, and Sunday is the first day of the week."

The young man went away. His mother could give no help, and his teacher, the deacon, and the pastor gave him these contradictory explanations. He put it all together, began to study, sought God for guidance, and reached his own conclusion. He became a minister who preached "the commandments of God, and the faith of Jesus." Revelation 14:12. He lived to see this message reach out into some eight hundred languages and dialects of the world.

SECTION EIGHT

GOD SPEAKS CONCERNING DIVINE HEALING AND HEALTHFUL LIVING

Divine Healing

Ten Commandments of Health

The Case of Liquor and Nicotine

Gabriel Max,

Jesus came to set men free, not only from sin, but from sickness. The touch o
hand brought healing and health to many, both old and young.

CHAPTER 43

Divine Healing

WHEN GOD created man He looked upon His work and saw that it was "very good." (Genesis 1:31.) A tree of life was provided, the fruit of which would perpetuate life. (Genesis 3:22-24.) Even when removed from access to this tree, Adam was so strong and vigorous that he lived to the age of 930 years.

It was never God's intention that any person should at any time be sick, languish in pain, or die.

It was sin that brought the curse of sickness, suffering, and death. Eve, doubting God's love, and disbelieving His word, was led to reject His authority. Adam followed. The deed was small, the sin great. The results were devastating and far reaching, costing man everything, and costing heaven its greatest gift—the Son of God. Let none be persuaded that sin, sickness, sorrow, suffering, and death are but figments of human imagination. They are very real and should be met in God's own way.

God's Provision for the Curse of Sin and Death

Into this sin-cursed world came the Saviour. "Thou shalt call his name JESUS: for he shall save his people from their sins." Matthew 1:21. To sinners everywhere God says, "Look unto me, and be ye saved, all the ends of the earth." Isaiah 45:22.

Those who confess and forsake their sins He will

pardon. (Proverbs 28:13.) Those who in times past have "made their hearts as an adamant stone, lest they should hear the law" may, if they choose, accept this offer: "A new heart also will I give you . . . and I will take away the stony heart out of your flesh, and I will give you an heart of flesh." Zechariah 7:12; Ezekiel 36:26.

Into this new heart and mind God will put the spirit of obedience to His law. The newborn Christian will grow in grace and in harmony with divine law, reach up toward the "measure of the stature of the fulness of Christ." Ephesians 4:13. From the curse of sin God restores us to increasing spiritual health.

But what of death? Does not God say, "I have no pleasure in the death of the wicked; but that the wicked turn from his way and live"? Ezekiel 33:11. Did not Christ die for us, and redeem us from the curse of the law? (Romans 5:8; Galatians 3:13.) Why is it, then, that all, both good and bad, die on every hand?

Saith the Scriptures, "In Adam all die." 1 Corinthians 15:22. And again, "It is appointed unto men once to die." Hebrews 9:27. Therefore the gospel does not save men from the first death but from the second death. (Revelation 20:6, 14.)

It is the privilege of every reader of these lines to escape the second death and everlasting destruction by the simple expedient of coming to Jesus Christ, accepting His gracious pardon, and in faith making an unconditional surrender of the heart to God to do His holy will.

God's Provision for the Curse of Sickness

The Bible expresses interest in our physical health. "Beloved, I wish above all things that thou mayest prosper and be in health." 3 John 2. "He doth not afflict willingly nor grieve the children of men." Lamentations 3:33. He does bring good out of our afflictions if we let Him. "Now no chastening for the present seemeth to be joyous, but grievous: nevertheless afterward it yieldeth the peaceable fruit of righteousness unto them which are exercised thereby." Hebrews 12:11.

We must always remember that Satan often afflicts men, as we have studied before. Men also bring suffering upon themselves by sinning against the laws of the body. "Whatsoever a man soweth, that shall he also reap." Galatians 6:7. We need also to be reminded that some are born with a richer heritage of health than others. The sins of our forefathers are felt by us. As the law of God says, "Visiting the iniquity of the fathers upon the children unto the third and fourth generation." Exodus 20:5.

God forgives our sins and heals our diseases. (Psalms 103:3.) There is a distinction that should be clearly made here. Christ died because of sin. He died for sin. He did not die because of man's sickness. Sin is a root cause. Sickness is an effect, a result. It may be a result of our sins or of our forefathers' sins. Even Adam's sin affects us. The tree of life was taken away, and it was necessary for continued existence. "In Adam all die."

In this life we are not fully freed from all the results of sin. Sickness, suffering, and death are the common lot of all. Our own violation of God's moral and physical laws will increase our difficulties and hasten death.

God heals supernaturally at times. Jesus often left an entire village without one sick person, one body racked with pain, one blind eye, one deaf ear, one stammering tongue, or one lone cripple in it. He can do the same today.

The healing processes of nature are also of God. The more we learn of the intricate workings of the infinite God as revealed in these human bodies of ours, the more fully do we understand that we are "fearfully and wonderfully made," and that within us are the forces of God combining in grand and harmonious array to fight for the preservation of our lives. Space forbids the giving of specific details, but let us never forget to thank God daily that "in him we live, and move, and have our being."

Does God Heal All Christians?

Jesus healed Peter's mother-in-law. The apostle Paul was not healed. Therefore God does not always heal Christians. We know that He could, but we know also that He does not. In fact, only those true Christians who live to see Christ come can escape the swinging scythe of Father Time as he mows us down and lets us fall as tall grain into his spacious cradle.

Many of the noblest Christians of all times have lived under the burden of almost constant infirmity. Does God permit you to suffer through many weary days or years? Will you not today hear a still small voice saying in sweet tenderness, "My grace is sufficient for thee: for my strength is made perfect in weakness." 2 Corinthians 12:9. Then say with Paul, "Therefore I take pleasure in infirmities." Verse 10.

It is more important to trust God than to be healed. He who makes bodily healing the first of all desires makes a grievous mistake. Of him it may be said, "He that loveth his life shall lose it." Satan is on the hunt to catch in his snare those who do not make the will of God the first thing in their lives. Let us remember that sickness is not necessarily a sign of weak faith and Christian experience.

Are Miracles a Test of True Religion?

Shall one seek a religion that makes healing and miracle working the mark of its genuineness?

The great John the Baptist did no miracle. (John 10:41.) The recorded miracles of the apostles are few.

According to Christ, Satan bound a woman in infirmity for eighteen long years. Would it not be probable that he could also loose her from her sickness?

Jesus warned against false christs and false prophets who in the last days would do "great signs and wonders." (Matthew 24:24.) Devils will work miracles to deceive even the world leaders and stir up the whole world to Armageddon. (Revelation 16:14.) Fire will be brought down from heaven to deceive men. (Revelation 13:13, 14.)

There are four reasons why it is wholly unsafe to make miracles a test of true religion.

First, the miracle worker himself may be false. Satan is a miracle worker. He transforms himself into an angel of light. "Therefore it is no great thing if his ministers also be transformed as the ministers of righteousness." 2 Corinthians 11:14, 15. Jesus said there would be many in the last days.

Second, there may be healing without salvation, as in the case of the ten lepers cleansed by Jesus. Only one returned to give glory to God. To him Jesus said, "Thy faith hath made thee whole." He received soul healing also, but the other nine did not.

Third, there may be salvation without healing, as witnessed in the case of Paul already mentioned.

Fourth, God does not always work in the same manner. Moses said, "I have led you forty years in the wilderness: your clothes are not waxen old upon you, and thy shoe is not waxen old upon thy foot." Deuteronomy 29:5. God also fed them with manna from heaven for forty years. We have no evidence that the clothing and the shoes of Jesus and the disciples did not wear out. And normally they were not fed miraculously.

In Jesus' day the Jews sought for a sign. "What sign shewest thou . . . ? what dost thou work?" John 6:30.

God knew that in the last days people would judge

truth by miracles and that they would be deceived thereby. Therefore Jesus gave His urgent warning.

Furthermore, God's remnant church, His special people of the last days, are clearly pictured in Revelation 12:17; 14:12, and they have three special characteristics: (1) They keep the commandments of God; (2) they keep the faith of Jesus; and (3) they have the testimony of Jesus. Miracles are not mentioned. Faith that obeys God's law is paramount. This does not exclude miracles, but they are not a particular sign of God's remnant people. Signs and wonders were forecast to be especially common with false religion.

The Ten Commandments and the testimony of Scripture must ever be the test for us. (Isaiah 8:20.)

Prayer for the Sick

It is always proper for any child of God to pray for himself or others. It is right for a sinner to turn to God in prayer, though he should also turn from his sin.

What of special prayer for the sick? Here is the Scriptural answer: "Is any sick among you? let him call for the elders of the church; and let them pray over him, anointing him with oil in the name of the Lord: and the prayer of faith shall save the sick, and the Lord shall raise him up; and if he have committed sins, they shall be forgiven him. Confess your faults one to another, and pray one for another, that ye may be healed. The effectual fervent prayer of a righteous man availeth much." James 5:14-16.

The steps are simple. The sick man confesses his sins and faults. He calls for the church elders. Prayer is made in faith, and he is anointed with oil, a symbol of God's Spirit. The sincerity and righteousness of all concerned is involved also. "The prayer of a righteous man availeth much."

After special prayer for the sick is it then proper to continue remedial agencies? The following is helpful:

"Those who seek healing by prayer should not neglect to make use of the remedial agencies within their reach. It is not a denial of faith to use such remedies as God has provided to alleviate pain and to aid nature in her work of restoration. . . .

"We have the sanction of the word of God for the use of remedial agencies. Hezekiah, king of Israel, was sick. . . . Now one word from God would have healed Hezekiah instantly; but special directions were given, 'Let them take a lump of figs, and lay it for a plaster upon the boil, and he shall recover.' "—MRS. E. G. WHITE, *The Ministry of Healing,* pp. 231, 232.

What if the healing we so much desire does not occur?

"In prayer for the sick, it should be remembered that 'we know not what we should pray for as we ought.' We do not know whether the blessing we desire will be best or not."—*Ibid.,* p. 229.

"When we have prayed for the recovery of the sick, whatever the outcome of the case, let us not lose faith in God. If we are called upon to meet bereavement, let us accept the bitter cup, remembering that a Father's hand holds it to our lips. But should health be restored, it should not be forgotten that the recipient of healing mercy is placed under renewed obligation to the Creator. When the ten lepers were cleansed, only one returned to find Jesus, and give him glory. Let none of us be like the unthinking nine, whose hearts were untouched by the mercy of God."—*Ibid.,* p. 233.

No Christian could ever forget the words of Jesus when He prayed His Father to let the bitter cup of suffering and death pass Him by. Said He, "Nevertheless not as I will, but as thou wilt." Matthew 26:39.

CHAPTER 44

Ten Commandments of Health

WHY ARE we morally obligated to obey the laws of health? There are four good reasons:

1. *We owe it to ourselves.* A man may drive his car hard, but he gives it good care. He has it greased regularly, the oil kept at proper level, and changed at the proper time. He uses the best gas and oil he can afford to buy and keeps the tires inflated. He accepts the fact that the builders of the car perhaps knew more about the care of the car than he does, and so he follows the manufacturer's instruction. We owe it to ourselves to treat our bodies just as intelligently. Cars can have new parts put in, but with our bodies this is not generally true, except for false hair, false teeth, artificial limbs, or glass eyes. Said Paul, "No man ever yet hated his own flesh; but nourisheth and cherisheth it." Ephesians 5:29.

2. *We owe it to our families and to society.* True, if a husband dies, his wife might find another and better one, and then again she might not or might not wish to. Every man and woman owes it to his home to live in love and decency just as long as possible. The same is true for society. The possession of the gift of life carries with it the high responsibility to live it well in every way. "None of us liveth to himself." Romans 14:7.

3. *We owe it to God.* To Him, the Creator, in whom "we live . . . and have our being," we shall render an account

of the use made of life and its countless blessings and opportunities. All His laws are for our good. Obedience to them brings the greatest good to us and to others and brings honor to God. "Present your bodies a living sacrifice, holy, acceptable unto God, which is your reasonable service." Romans 12:1. Our bodies are the temple of God's Spirit. They are not our own. They have been bought with a price. We are obligated to glorify God in our bodies. (1 Corinthians 6:19, 20.)

4. *If we defile our bodies, God will destroy us.* We really destroy ourselves. "O Israel, thou hast destroyed thyself, but in me is thine help." Hosea 13:9. If we have been defiling our bodies, God will forgive us and help us to get the victory. As a captive in ancient Babylon, "Daniel purposed in his heart that he would not defile himself with the portion of the king's meat, nor with the wine which he drank." Daniel 1:8.

THE TEN COMMANDMENTS OF HEALTH

1. *Come out in the sunshine.*

This gift of God "is the strongest stimulant, the mightiest vitalizer in all nature." It is a great purifier. It is a destroyer of germs. Mold and the germs of typhoid, cholera, and tuberculosis perish in the direct rays of the sun. "The sun extends its vitalizing activity to all nature, destroying disease elements, and energizing all other forms of life."

"Come out in the sunshine! O gather its wealth!
There's joy in the sunshine, and beauty and health.
Why stay in the shadow? Why weep in the gloom?
Come out in the sunshine, and let your soul bloom."

—FANNIE BOLTON.

Little wonder the ancients worshiped the sun when they forgot God. If the sun suddenly burned out, life on this planet would cease. Thank God that sunlight is free.

2. *Partake freely of fresh air.*

Proper air is an immediate necessity of life. Deep breathing is a lifegiver and lifesaver. Good ventilation is essential to good health. Many gas stations have signs reading, "FREE AIR." Rejoice that we still have price-free and tax-free air. Use it freely.

3. *Eat wisely of proper foods.*

The provisions of nature in various parts of the world, supplying each locality with a family's adequate supply of starches, proteins, fats, mineral salts, and vitamins, are marvelous. However, every individual, and particularly the housewife, should be intelligent on the subject of diet and food preparation.

In the beginning God gave to Adam fruits, nuts, grains, and vegetables. (Genesis 1:29; 3:18.) Under this ideal plan there was no flesh food to be eaten. Men lived to be almost one thousand years old.

After the devastating Flood, Noah was given permission to eat meat. (Genesis 9:3-5.) He knew the difference between clean and unclean animals. In the ark he had housed only one pair of unclean beasts as compared to seven pairs of clean beasts. (Genesis 7:2; 8:20.) This gave him the flesh of clean animals for offerings to God and for food. It is interesting to note that after the Flood man's life span rapidly declined. Even Abraham died at the age of 175. (Genesis 25:7.)

In Moses' day the distinction between clean and unclean animals was put in writing. (See Leviticus, chapter 11.) However, the facts were known by Noah centuries before Abraham, the father of the Jews, was born. The distinction is not of Jewish origin; it came from God.

A sharp prohibition was registered against eating swine's flesh, or pork. This was, we understand, for man's benefit.

Pork eating is a prolific cause of the disease trichinosis. Tiny parasites enter the human system and infest the body until death results. Dr. Maurice Hall says that about one in every seven Americans probably has it. There are at least forty diseases one may think he has and yet the real disease may be trichinosis. Don't let anybody lead you to believe that Jesus Christ made hogs clean. A pigsty is just as filthy, and pork as unclean as ever.

Time, for December 3, 1945, page 77, says that Dr. S. E. Gould, of Detroit, suspects that from 25 per cent to 36 per cent of U.S. citizens now contract trichinosis. The encysted worms "much prefer hogs, rats and men." That means women and children too, of course. Dr. Gould warns that the words, "U.S. inspected and passed," do not mean much on roasts and chops. "The government stopped making microscopic examination of meat in 1906." It has been estimated by Dr. Norman R. Stoll, of Rockefeller Institute, that 21,000,000 Americans are infested with these worms. They produce spots on the skin, swellings, nausea, pains all over the body, wasting, and general weakness. Some patients die of damaged hearts after about a month of painful spasms.

Not only may man pay now for eating swine's flesh, but there is also a future punishment. (Read Isaiah 66: 15-17.)

The vision of Peter recorded in Acts 10:9-35 does not teach that unclean animals are clean but that Gentiles as well as Jews may be cleansed by the gospel. In the vision Peter did not "kill, and eat." (Verse 13.) Coming out of the vision, he "doubted" what it meant. (Verse 17.) Later he said, "God hath shewed me that I should not call any man common or unclean." Verse 28. The swine is not ceremonially unclean, but physically as unclean for food as ever it was in the days of Israel.

It is well to note that orthodox Jews, who use no pork, rarely, if ever, contract the disease of trichinosis.

To those who use the flesh of even the "clean animals"

it is well to say a few things. Increasing disease among stock, the practice of marketing animals with disease, and inability to determine the presence of disease germs and worms in cut meat, make it wise to cook all flesh foods thoroughly. Rare-cooked meat is dangerous.

Many find it better to discard flesh foods altogether. Dr. V. E. McCollum states: "I have not the slightest hesitation in saying that a vegetarian diet, supplemented with fairly liberal amounts of milk, is the most satisfactory type of diet that a man can take."

Circumstances, a person's state of health, and medical counsel may vary one's practice with reference to diet. One authority wrote: "A meat diet is not the most wholesome of diets, and yet I would take the position that meat should not be discarded by every one. Those who have feeble digestive organs can often use meat, when they cannot eat vegetables, fruit, or porridge."—E. G. WHITE, *Youth's Instructor,* May 31, 1894. The same writer says, "To eat largely of porridge would not insure health to the digestive organs." In other words, persons forced perhaps temporarily to a soft, bland diet may find meat of the "clean" animals to be helpful.

"Select the best food you can, eat regularly, moderately, and dine peacefully and happily while you masticate thoroughly."

4. *Drink plenty of pure water.*

Water is a necessity of life most of us need to use more liberally. It composes four fifths of our bodies. It has much to do with the digestion of food and the maintenance of the body.

5. *Take reasonable exercise.*

Physical work normally would provide exercise, but today life with many of us gives only mental exercise. Playful exercise is the way for many under modern conditions. Exercise tones the muscles, stimulates deep breathing, good circulation, and proper elimination, not to mention appetite and digestion.

6. *Get proper rest.*

This comes naturally under normal conditions to those who have sufficient exercise. "The sleep of a labouring man is sweet." Ecclesiastes 5:12.

7. *"Be ye clean."* Isaiah 52:11.

"Cleanliness is next to godliness," is often quoted as being a Bible saying. It happens that this is one of those texts not in the Bible. Some think it should be, and some are glad it isn't. Nevertheless the Bible teaches sanitation and order. Israel's community was under strict sanitary rules. Order is one of heaven's first laws.

A professed Christian has a solemn obligation to be clean in heart, mind, body, and premises. Filth breeds disease and contempt. To be unclean is a disgrace for those who profess the name of the Son of man, who neatly folded His own graveclothes on rising from the dead. A prude is a pity, but a dirty, unkempt church member is a shame.

8. *Stand up and sit up.*

Proper posture when one is standing places the weight primarily on the front of the feet and toward the outside —the small toes. This relieves pressure on the bony arches of the feet and strain from the small of the back. Stand with feet parallel, chest up, chin in, and think that you are very tall. Don't let the organs of the lower abdomen sag. That is bad for health and appearance. Keep the shoulders, arms, and the knees fairly relaxed. Stand tall but not stiff.

Sit well back in your chair, with feet squarely on the floor. Walk erect and sprightly.

9. *Dress properly.*

Clothing should be modest, suited to climatic conditions, supported from the shoulders, and comfortable in fit. It should protect the extremities properly, and be clean and appropriate.

10. *Have peace of mind and joy of spirit.*

Peace and joy have a marvelous influence on every organ and function of the body. As Christians we need to ask God for a larger measure of them. "The kingdom of God is . . . righteousness, and peace, and joy in the Holy Ghost." Romans 14:17. "The fruit of the Spirit is love, joy, peace." Galatians 5:22. "A merry heart doeth good like a medicine." Proverbs 17:22. "Godliness with contentment is great gain." 1 Timothy 6:6. "Great peace have they which love thy law." Psalms 119:165. "There is no peace, saith the Lord, unto the wicked." Isaiah 48:22. Worry, anger, and jealousy poison the system.

"If you cannot help worrying, remember that worrying cannot help you either."

Put these two texts together, and you will have a happy combination.

"Therefore take no thought, saying, What shall we eat? or, What shall we drink? or, Wherewithal shall we be clothed?" Matthew 6:31.

"Whether therefore ye eat, or drink, or whatsoever ye do, do all to the glory of God." 1 Corinthians 10:31.

The first text spells trust; the second, purposeful obedience.

CHAPTER 45

The Case of Liquor and Nicotine

WHEN ABRAHAM LINCOLN said that "liquor has many defenders, but no defence," he uttered a simple statement of fact.

Solomon, the wise man of long ago, took a turn at the tavern. He made of himself a laboratory, a test tube. Said he, "I sought in mine heart to give myself unto wine, . . . till I might see what was that good for the sons of men, which they should do under the heaven all the days of their life." Ecclesiastes 2:3.

He had seen others drink. Now he would try it himself. Would it make him wise or foolish? Strong or weak? Happy or unhappy? Good or bad? Would it cure worry, relieve tension, drown trouble? He promised himself that he would not go too far. "I searched my mind how to pamper my body with wine (keeping control of myself wisely all the time)." Ecclesiastes 2:3, Moffatt. Solomon would be a temperate drinker—take it or leave it, just as he chose—and he would find out the facts. He did.

Fact I. Alcohol Is a Drug and a Poison

"It biteth like a serpent, and stingeth like an adder." Proverbs 23:32. A little alcohol is like a little rattlesnake without much sting. A lot of alcohol is like a big snake.

Haven Emerson, M.D., of Columbia University, wrote: "Alcohol as commonly used by modern man here and

 Lester Quade, Ar

One cannot play with fire and not expect to get burned. The long, evil record liquor in accidents, wrecked homes, and families is witness to its destructive nat

abroad deteriorates the cells of the body, degrades the man, and degenerates the race."—Foundation for Narcotics Research and Information, New York.

The great Dr. Johns Hopkins condemned it even as a medicine. In fact, alcohol used in quantity has a definite connection with almost anything from hobnailed livers to pneumonia. It increases the risk of damage and death. It decreases the chances for life and health. The epitaph of an old Egyptian tomb is reported to read, "His earthly tenement was shattered by wine, and his spirit departed before it was called for."

Fact 2. Alcohol Is a Deceiver

Solomon reached this sharp conclusion: "Wine is a mocker, strong drink is raging: and whosoever is deceived thereby is not wise." Proverbs 20:1.

Alcohol attacks the highest brain centers first. It dulls your powers of discernment first. You are ready for deception.

Alcohol says, "I'll drown your troubles." But for every trouble it drowns, two more come up.

Alcohol says, "I'll make you smart and gay and bright." Life says, "Liquor makes you a fool with a babbling mouth." Solomon discovered that. (Proverbs 23:29.)

Alcohol says, "I'll make you strong." When it is all over, a man wonders where he got his black eyes and bruised body.

Alcohol in a man makes him think he is the best driver on the road. But he is the highway's greatest menace. A glass or two of beer will slow up the reaction time of the nervous system. Taken in any quantity alcohol makes a man a less skillful driver while making him believe that he is a better driver. It also lessens his sense of responsibility. Hence the widespread admonition, "If you drive, don't drink. If you drink, don't drive." One might wisely inquire, "Why drink at all?" After a man drinks it is too late to tell him not to drive. He thinks he can drive better than ever. Alcohol is a deceiver.

The Chicago Motor Club tested two experienced drivers. After two mint juleps neither felt intoxicated nor showed signs of it. In test driving one's score of efficiency was reduced 31 per cent and the other 39 per cent. Liquor deceives the driver.

Alcohol makes one feel warm when he is cold. It relaxes the nerves that control the blood vessels near the surface of the body. Thus the warm blood is kept in larger quantity at the surface and is exposed to the cold. The temperature of the body is lowered, though the drinker does not look as blue or feel as chilly as the nondrinker. In the latter's case the nerves cause the surface blood vessels to shrink, forcing the blood to the inward parts of the body away from the cold. Scientific tests prove that the drunkard will freeze to death more quickly than the nondrinker.

Alcohol says, "You can drink without being a drunkard." There are two things wrong with that statement.

One is that some people are highly sensitive to alcohol, and once they take to drinking the road leads straight to alcoholism. They become alcoholics, pitiful wrecks, and slaves. Robert S. Carrol, M.D., Highland Hospital, Asheville, North Carolina, says: "It is startling to think that in our land one out of three whom we meet is incapable of continuing any form of alcoholic usage without courting a very present danger of being damaged or wrecked by its potency."—*Signs of the Times,* Sept. 21, 1948.

The other point is that any so-called moderate drinker may move right on to alcoholism. The deceptive nature of alcohol keeps him from being aware of his danger until he has reached his alcoholic Niagara. Millions have gone over this Niagara in their liquor barrel, and few have been redeemed.

As the Japanese proverb says, "At the first cup, man drinks wine; at the second cup, wine drinks wine; at the third cup, wine drinks man." In 1930, Hack Wilson of the National League hit fifty-four home runs—six under Babe Ruth's record of 60. Hack drank liquor. Then liquor drank Hack out of the big leagues. He died broke at forty-eight.

It is estimated that there are some 4,000,000 excessive drinkers in America and 750,000 alcoholics. Most of them began drinking in early youth. They were deceived.

Alcohol Advertising

In the theatre,
On the radio,
On the signboard,
In the papers and magazines
  I say what I'm paid to say.
But in the laboratory,
In the wrecked automobile,
In the city jail,
In the roadhouse,
In the veins of the drunks,
  I tell the truth.

—Maryland *News*.

Fact 3. Alcohol Is Expensive

In recent years the liquor per person consumption has doubled in the U.S. In Canada it has increased 400 per cent in twenty-five years according to Dr. John Colburn in a report to the Canadian Temperance Federation.

In a recent year the people of the United States spent ten dollars for liquor for each one dollar for religion. They spent five times as much for booze as for education.

Sidney Katz tells of a man who passed by a saloon

and the proprietor called, "You never come in any more. Have you quit drinking?"

"Yes," said the man, "and I'm getting a big lump in my side."

"Well," said the proprietor, "you had better start again or it may get worse."

"Yes," replied the man, "it's getting bigger all the time." And so saying he reached into his pocket and pulled out a fat purse.

Americans could grow a lump of nine billions if they would stop drinking. That's what it costs. Crime costs fifteen billions, and liquor has a lot to do with that. Even these figures will be too small by the time you read this. Insanity, venereal disease, Monday morning hangovers, accidents, irresponsibility, and inefficiency cost additional untold billions. Liquor is mixed up in much of this.

Dr. Roy L. Smith is quoted in the *Watchman Examiner*, June 26, 1947: "The chemist defines it [alcohol] as poison; the biologist defines it as a hazard; the pathologist calls it a narcotic; the sociologist calls it a waste; the economist calls it a parasite; the psychologist calls it a deceiver; the criminologist calls it an accessory after the fact in crime."

The key to the tavern, saloon, bar, and night club, whether public or private, opens the door to utter deception. Drink mocks and deceives the drinker. It makes him think he is wise when he is foolish, strong when he is weak, and right when he is wrong. It is harmful, deceptive, expensive, and corruptive. It is a pal of tobacco and narcotics, a cause of crime, an aggravation of disease, and a curse unto all men. He who uses it pays in money and health. He who supports it with his influence becomes responsible for its tragic results in the lives of others.

Nicotine, the Narcotic

Tobacco contains a narcotic poison, nicotine. The cigarette is the worst form in which to use tobacco. Yet the production of cigarettes in the United States has passed the astonishing total of one billion per day. This is about seven times the entire population and more than 125 packs a year for every man, woman, and child in the land.

Having made cigarette smoking popular among women, the tobacco companies turn now to capture the school children in their teens. One survey indicated that women smoke three times as many cigarettes as men. If the boys and girls can be roped in, we will become a nation of nicotine addicts.

Americans in a recent year spent some four billion dollars for tobacco, or about three times as much as for religion. In a year of financial crisis Britons spent one tenth of their income for tobacco.

Great Leaders Speak

The noted Luther Burbank is quoted as saying:

"'You have seen pictures of military cemeteries near great battlefields.

"'Upon every headstone is chiseled the inscription, "Killed in action."

"'If one knew nothing about war, these headstones would be sufficient to impress upon him that war is deadly,—that it kills.

"'How much would you know about tobacco if upon the tombstone of everyone killed by it were inscribed, "Killed by tobacco"?

"'You would know a lot more about it than you do now, but you would not know all, because tobacco does more than kill. *It half kills*. It has its victims in the cemeteries and in the streets. It is bad enough to be dead, but it is a question if it is not sometimes worse to be half dead,—to be nervous, irritable, unable to sleep well, with efficiency cut in two and vitality ready to snap at the first great strain.

"'This seems like exaggeration. It isn't. It is well within the truth. You do not know the facts because you are not permitted to know them.

"'Let me tell you how tobacco kills. Smokers do not all drop dead around the cigar lighters in tobacco stores. They go away and, years later, die of something else. From the tobacco trust's point of view, that is one of the finest things about tobacco. The victims do not die on the premises, even when sold the worst cigars. They go away and, when they die, the doctors certify that they died of something else,—pneumonia, heart disease, typhoid fever, or what not. In other words, tobacco kills indirectly and escapes the blame.

"'Always remember that the tendency of tobacco is to destroy.

"'Don't be fooled by newspaper stories inspired by the tobacco interests about gentlemen one hundred four years old who attribute their multitude of years to the use of tobacco.

"'When whisky selling was a legal method of getting a living, you used to read the same kind of stories about centenarians who had drunk whisky since they were nine years old.

"'There is no doubt that some men have lived to be very old, notwithstanding the use of tobacco and whisky.

"'But they are entirely mistaken in believing that it was the tobacco or the whisky that helped them to live long. Here is one proof: Look for all those who were boyhood chums of these aged survivors of tobacco and whisky and who, like them, smoked and drank. Where are they? In graveyards. Tobacco and whisky helped put the finishing touches upon them.

" 'Nicotine, after you have used it awhile, puts you in a condition to be "bumped off" by the first thing that hits you. If you saw some men undermine a building until it was ready to topple into the street, and then saw a woman hit the building with a baby carriage and make it topple, you would not say the woman wrecked the building, would you? Yet when a smoker dies of pneumonia, the doctor's death certificate gives pneumonia, and not tobacco, as the cause of death. And the tombstone man with his chisel says nothing at all.

" 'What a shock people would get if they went through cemeteries and saw tombstones declaring the fact that this man died of typhoid made fatal by a tobacco-weakened heart, and that man succumbed to nervous prostration because tobacco had shot his nerves to pieces, and another one gave up the ghost because tobacco had ruined his stomach.' "—D. H. KRESS, M.D., *The Cigarette as a Physician Sees It,* pp. 6, 7.

Tests prove that tobacco cuts down scholarship, and even one or two cigarettes make a pilot's eyes less capable of night flying. Up to the age of fifty the death rate of heavy smokers is double that of nonsmokers. Among babies born to smoking mothers there are more immature infants, more miscarriages, and more stillbirths.

A Dallas, Texas, throat specialist reports he has treated 150 patients for cancer of the mouth, throat, and vocal cords. Of these, 149 used tobacco.

Dr. David Starr Jordan says, "Cigarette-smoking boys are like wormy apples; they drop long before harvest time."

Judge Griffith, of Tacoma City Court, said, "A growing boy can't smoke cigarettes without warping his moral nature; and it is a fact that nine tenths of the young cigarette smokers will steal. Cigarettes cause a boy to lose all self-respect, to become listless, shiftless, and less ambitious, and start him on the road to the reform school or state prison."

The great Edison in his day declared, "No man or boy who smokes cigarettes can work in my laboratories."

The eminent Dr. William Mayo said, "No surgeon can afford to smoke."

Former President Herbert Hoover gave this word: "There is no agency in the world that is so seriously affecting the health, efficiency, education, and character of boys and girls as the cigarette habit. . . . Nearly every delinquent boy is a cigarette smoker. . . . Cigarettes are a source of crime. To neglect crime at its source is a shortsighted policy, unworthy of a nation of our intelligence."

Yet tobacco merchantmen would have us believe that it is a mark of distinction to smoke their brand of cigarettes. A better mark of distinction is not to smoke.

Great Athletes Speak

Red Grange, the noted football star, says, "You cannot drink, and smoke, and expect to succeed as an athlete."

Walter Johnson, famed pitcher of baseball, said, "I strongly advise any boy who hopes to become an athlete to let cigarettes alone. They are bad for the wind. It is true that some great ball players have smoked cigarettes, but my answer to that is that they would have been still greater ball players had they not used cigarettes."

Ty Cobb, one of America's greatest ball players, insisted, "Too much cannot be said against the evils of cigarette smoking. It stupefies the brain, saps vitality, undermines one's health, and lessens the moral fiber of man."

Gene Tunney won the heavyweight boxing championship of the world. Over his own signature he declared that he "never used liquor or tobacco."

Connie Mack, the grand old leader of baseball, says, "We do everything in our power to discourage the use of cigarettes among our baseball boys. . . . Every one should have will power enough to overcome the tobacco habit."

Tobacco and Discourtesy

The tobacco smoker often makes himself a nuisance, and disregards signs which forbid smoking in certain places. One such sat down by a woman in a train coach. She pointed to the no-smoking sign, but he paid no heed. She took out a pair of scissors, and as he looked out the window, clipped off the end of his cigarette.

Tobacco is injurious to the body and mind, is a waste of money, a filthy, breath-fouling habit, which dulls the sense of courtesy and respect for others. A woman will use body deodorants, expensive perfume, then foul her breath with tobacco, and blow it into the air for others to breathe. What causes her to be so inconsistent? Tobacco!

The apostle admonishes us: "Let us cleanse ourselves from all filthiness of the flesh." 2 Corinthians 7:1. "Know ye not that ye are the temple of God? . . . If any man defile the temple of God, him shall God destroy." 1 Corinthians 3:16, 17.

Increasing numbers of people are learning that even coffee contains a narcotic poison, caffeine, and that tea has this poison, as well as tannic acid. Many are turning to harmless drinks.

The Christian will wish to heed this counsel: "Whether therefore ye eat, or drink, or whatsoever ye do, do all to the glory of God." 1 Corinthians 10:31.

Living a Temperate Life

It is natural for man to do evil and then to justify himself in his course. Evil habits should be broken off with dispatch, and right habits established to take their place. This can be done by our choosing to let God work in us "both to will and to do of his good pleasure." Philippians 2:13.

It may bring some discomfort to stop evil habits, but it will result in good. Christ died on the cross *for* our sins. We must die *to* sin. What shall it profit a man to know the 500,000 words of a dictionary if he cannot say "No"?

"He said to them all, If any man will come after me, let him deny himself, and take up his cross daily, and follow me." Luke 9:23.

When the yoke of evil habits is broken the yoke of Christ will be found much lighter. Said He, "My yoke is easy."

It has been said that on the wall of an ancient temple there was the picture of a king forging from his crown a chain. Nearby a slave was making his chains into a crown.

Link your life with Christ, and let Him help you forge a crown of success for today and a crown of eternal life for tomorrow.

SECTION NINE

GOD SPEAKS CONCERNING DEATH AND IMMORTALITY

STAY THE ANGEL

"Never quite ready the parting words to say;
When comes the hour, I'm prone to pray
Not now, dear Lord,
Let Thy hand stay the angel of death
Yet one more day."

Review Pictures *Daniel Chester French, Scul*

Somewhere along life's way everyone has to meet the unwelcome angel of death. cannot escape it. Only through Christ is there hope of life after death.

CHAPTER 46

Man, Mortal or Immortal?

"I'LL GIVE a million dollars for each year you can add to my life," a noted American is reported to have said to his medical advisers when he was eighty years old.

Most people, if in good health and circumstances, wish to keep right on living. Days of mental depression have overtaken the majority even as in the experience of the great Elijah when he said, "It is enough; now, O Lord, take away my life." 1 Kings 19:4. Yet, when the time of departure comes, men tend to prefer life.

As Dr. William W. Booth has paraphrased the old poem, "Lives there a man with soul so dead, who never to himself has said, 'I wish I could live forever'?"

The word *mortal* is defined: "subject to death; destined to die."

The word *immortal* means "not mortal; exempt from liability to die; imperishable; everlasting."—*Webster's New International Dictionary.*

Did God purpose that sinless man, created in the image of God, should die? We think all will agree that He did not. God created man to live. But God did not purpose that man should live if he sinned. This is the way it was presented to Adam: "Of the tree of the knowledge of good and evil, thou shalt not eat of it: for in the day that thou eatest thereof thou shalt surely die."

Genesis 2:17. The marginal reading is, "dying thou shalt die." The sentence of death would be pronounced the day man sinned, and the process of dying would begin.

Satan, in the form of a serpent, said to Eve, "Ye shall not surely die." Genesis 3:4. (Christ said that the devil was a liar. John 8:44.) This more pleasing promise of Satan, Eve believed, then disobeyed God. Adam followed in her footsteps of sin, though he was not deceived. (1 Timothy 2:14.) God closed His conversation with them over the incident in these words: "Dust thou art, and unto dust shalt thou return." Genesis 3:19.

What would happen now if Adam and Eve, having sinned, should continue to eat of the "tree of life"?

This tree was planted in the midst of the garden, as was the tree of the knowledge of good and evil. (Genesis 2:9.) To partake of the latter meant death. To partake regularly of the tree of life would perpetuate life. What now?

We read, "The Lord God said, . . . lest he put forth his hand, and take also of the tree of life, and eat, and live for ever: therefore the Lord God sent him forth from the garden of Eden, to till the ground from whence he was taken. So he drove out the man; and he placed at the east of the garden of Eden Cherubims, and a flaming sword which turned every way, to keep the way of the tree of life." Genesis 3:22-24. God did not propose that sinners should live forever.

From this clear Biblical picture of the matter we conclude two things: (1) Man was created with the *possibility* of immortality before him on condition that he meet the test of obedience. (2) Man was not created with *inherent* immortality. He was "subject unto death" if he should sin, and in this sense was "mortal."

Thus we are not shocked to find the Bible reference to man as "mortal." We quote, "Shall mortal man be more just than God?" Job 4:17. Nor are we surprised to find this very sweeping statement regarding God, "who only hath immortality." 1 Timothy 6:16.

In other words, God is immortal and man is mortal. In fact, the word *immortal* is found but once in the Bible and is applied to God. "Now unto the King eternal, immortal, invisible, the only wise God." 1 Timothy 1:17.

Did God Give Man an Immortal Soul?

Once upon a time King Charles II stood before a group of scientists and scholars at a meeting of the Royal Society of England. He said something like this, "Suppose I take a pail of water, set it on a scale, and it tips the beam at ten pounds. Then I drop into the water five pounds of live fish. This would make, we would suppose, a total weight of fifteen pounds. Why is it that after I add the five pounds of fish, the scale still stands at ten pounds?"

Various wise men rose and made deep and sometimes inexplicable explanations—everything from air-filled fish sacs to theoretical vacuum and ungravitating gravitation.

Finally the king closed the discussion. Said he, "You are all wrong, and for this reason: when you take a pail of water weighing ten pounds and add to it five pounds of fish, the pail, water, and fish will weigh fifteen pounds, as you learned gentlemen should all right well know." These men had been misled by trusting too much to a prominent man.

The Bible presents the following:

1. Man is mortal. (Job 4:17.)
2. God is immortal. (1 Timothy 1:17.)
3. God *only* has immortality. (1 Timothy 6:16.)
4. Man must seek for immortality. (Romans 2:7.)
5. Immortality is brought to light in the gospel. (2 Timothy 1:10.)

6. It will be bestowed at Christ's second coming. (1 Corinthians 15:51-55.)

Is it not strange, with this array of Bible teaching, that some should believe that man has something immortal about him that even God cannot destroy? This is more strange than the reasoning of the king's scientists, who would have ten plus five equal ten.

With this background we may examine the record of man's creation in Genesis 2:7: "The Lord God formed man of the dust of the ground, and breathed into his nostrils the breath of life; and man became a living soul."

Let us follow the steps:

First God made Adam's body from the dust of the ground. The substantial part of man's body is composed of dust, as the Bible says. As a matter of interest and fact, he is almost 80 per cent gas, most of which is oxygen, some 10 per cent hydrogen, with a trifle of nitrogen. Of the heavier elements, carbon leads, then calcium, phosphorus, potassium, sodium, chlorine, sulfur, magnesium, iron, and traces of iodine and other elements. In this respect men and animals are alike.

Second, God breathed into Adam's nostrils the breath of life. Here is no indication of any "immortal soul" being put into Adam. No such "spirit" Adam had ever existed. None was here created. God simply breathed into Adam's nostrils the breath of life. Do we have any reasonable right to assume anything more?

The third point is thus stated, "Man became a living soul." Body plus breath of life equals a living soul. Note carefully that God did not breathe into man a living soul, but He breathed into his nostrils the breath of life, and man *became* a living soul. An electric light bulb of itself gives no light. But when an electric current is sent through its inner wiring, light is produced. Thus Adam's body, perfect as it was, could not perform any function or fulfill any purpose. So God switched on the current of life, and Adam then became a living, active, functioning soul. The living soul did not exist before Adam was made, and it was not breathed into Adam, but came as a result of the union of his body and the breath of life, or "the breath of the spirit of life," as it is called in one place.

The Hebrew and Greek words from which we translate our English words *soul* and *spirit* are found some 1,700 times in the Bible. Actually the word *soul* as used in the Bible does not always have exactly the same meaning. The same holds true of the word *spirit.* We should therefore avoid being dogmatic on any one definition.

This much let us know of a surety. In not one of the 1,700 appearances of these original words for *soul* and *spirit* is either of them said to be immortal, never dying, imperishable, indestructible, everlasting, eternal, or in possession of immortality. Nor are the dead represented to be capable of a consious existence apart from the body.

MAN AND THE LOWER ANIMALS

Man belongs to the animal kingdom. Do animals, as well as man, have the "breath of life"? The answer is given in Genesis 7:15, where is recorded the entrance of animals into Noah's ark at the time of the Flood. "They went in unto Noah into the ark, two and two of all flesh, wherein is the breath of life." Therefore animals also possess the breath of life ("the breath of the spirit of life," Genesis 7:22, margin). An animal may have a perfect body, but it may be perfectly dead. It must have the current of life switched on just as man must have it.

Do the animals become living souls when the breath of life enters their bodies? In Genesis 1:30 we read, "To every beast of the earth, and to every fowl of the air, and to every thing that creepeth upon the earth, wherein there is life." The marginal reading of "life" is "a living soul." In Revelation 16:3 the animals of the sea are called living souls. The original expression for "living soul" is *nephesh hayyah*. This expression is used in Genesis 1:20, 21, 24, 30, in referring to the animals as "the moving creature that hath *life*," "every *living creature*," and "the *living creature*." Thus an animal is called a "living soul," or *nephesh hayyah*. This is the identical expression used in Genesis 2:7, when man became a "living soul," or "*nephesh hayyah*."

A Different Organism

Is man then a mere animal? No, indeed! Such a conclusion is entirely unwarranted. In your garden is a green-leafed bush bearing beautiful blushing roses. Close by is an ugly weed. They are both of the same kingdom, and receive the same kind of sunshine and rain, and grow in identical soil. But no one calls a rose a weed, or a weed a rose. The difference does not lie in the sunshine, soil, or rain, but in the plant organism. When God put life into Adam's organism He produced different results from those that occurred when He put life into animal organisms.

A boy fills a gallon bucket two thirds full of water, solders the lid fast, sets it on two bricks, and builds a fire under it. After the steam pressure comes up he punches a small hole in the lid and lets a jet of steam strike the paddles of a wheel attached to a small shaft. On the shaft is a pulley with a string belt running to a spool fastened in place with a nail. The fire burns, the water boils, the steam issues forth, the paddle wheel turns, and the boy's mill runs. But what a far cry from a glorious modern steam engine with its great connecting arm, its silent slides, its gleaming oil cups, its rocking eccentric, its giant flywheel, and its surging power, fed into it from a high-pressure boiler. Yes, a great difference. But it is the same kind of fire, water, and steam that the boy used in his play mill.

When God put the vitalizing energy of life into Adam, it was the same life as that of the animal kingdom, but how different the results!

An electric current passes into a light bulb filament, and we get light. It passes into the heavy coils of an electric heater, and heat is the chief product. The current is connected with an electric motor, and a revolving motion is the result. We get power. Whether we get light, heat, or power depends on what the current goes into. But it is the same current.

So when God breathed life into Adam He was putting that life into the masterpiece of earthly creation. Said the psalmist, "I am fearfully and wonderfully made." Psalms 139:14. Man was made only a "little lower than the angels." Psalms 8:5. As poetically expressed by one writer, "What a piece of work is man! how noble in reason, how infinite in faculty! in form and moving how expressive and admirable! in action how like an angel! in apprehension how like a god!"

Sin and Salvation

This glorious masterpiece of God's earthly creation sinned, and became subject to death.

"God so loved the world, that he gave his only begotten Son, that whosoever believeth in him should not perish, but have everlasting life." John 3:16.

The appearance of Jesus Christ "hath brought life and immortality to light through the gospel." 2 Timothy 1:10.

"He that hath the Son hath life; and he that hath not the Son of God hath not life." 1 John 5:12.

We may all conclude that man does not by nature possess an immortal soul. Souls so small that ten thousand of them may dance on the point of a needle are but a fancy. A soul that is the same size as the body, and which has all the senses of touch, taste, smell, sight, and hearing; the feelings of love and hatred, joy and sorrow; and which exists apart from the body is but a figment of man's imagination. It takes the body and the spirit of life together to make a *living soul.*

Job said, "The spirit of God is in my nostrils." Job 27:3. Paul writes, "The very God of peace sanctify you wholly; and I pray God your whole spirit and soul and body be preserved blameless unto the coming of our Lord Jesus Christ." 1 Thessalonians 5:23. The body and the spirit of life make man a living soul.

Christ came to save all there is of man. For this to be done we must let Him sanctify all there is of us—body, soul, and spirit.

Christ died to save us, to sanctify us. "Wherefore Jesus also, that he might sanctify the people with his own blood, suffered without the gate." Hebrews 13:12.

Seeing that the Saviour was willing to suffer in order to save us, Paul says, "Let us go forth therefore unto him without the camp, bearing his reproach. For here have we no continuing city, but seek one to come." Verses 13, 14.

About five hundred years ago there lived a great preacher by the name of Savonarola. In the city of Florence, Italy, he spoke fearlessly against sin and evil, and lifted up the Man of Calvary. The ruler of Florence threatened him with punishment and torture. The pope offered him a high church position if he would cease talking about the corruption in the church. But Savonarola had heard the voice of God, and would not be disobedient unto the heavenly vision. They took him prisoner, tortured him, and finally publicly burned him to death.

It is the way of the cross that leads to immortality. "Be thou faithful unto death, and I will give thee a crown of life." Revelation 2:10.

"Whosoever will save his life shall lose it: and whosoever will lose his life for my sake shall find it." Matthew 16:25.

Christ is trying to say to us, "You cannot save yourselves. Come to My cross, and give yourselves completely over to the will of God as I did on Calvary. Accept the sacrifice that I have made. Choose rather to die than to sin. This is the only road to holiness, heaven, and immortality."

"The love-lighted cross points the way to the sky,
And tells of a home in the sweet by and by,
Where we shall see Jesus ascended on high;
I'll cling to the love-lighted cross.

"The blessed old cross, the Calvary cross,
The love-lighted cross of Jesus;
Through gain or through loss, I'll cling to the cross,
The love-lighted cross of Jesus."

—A. H. ACKLEY.

CHAPTER 47

Five Minutes After Death

MEDICAL SCIENCE has succeeded in bringing the modern generation in America right up against the Biblical life length of threescore and ten years. But this is a very brief span for man. Only 7 per cent of Americans are over sixty-five years of age.

Some say that man should live to be 150 years old. Dr. Alexander Bogomoletz, Russian scientist, agreed to this, and prepared a serum designed to retard the aging of the body's connective tissues. It is known scientifically as "ACS," or "anti-reticular cyto-toxic serum." The doctor died at the age of sixty-four, or eighty-six years short of the mark. His heart did not permit him to take his medicine.

Whether a man lives to be 70 or 170 he is short of what God designed. FOREVER!—that was heaven's plan for man.

Yet because of sin "it is appointed unto men once to die." Hebrews 9:27. Most men will die twice; Christians, but once. Questioned the psalmist, "What man is he that liveth, and shall not see death?" Psalms 89:48. Said Job, "I know that thou wilt bring me to death, and to the house appointed for all living." Job 30:23.

The death rate in the United States is more than a million a year; in China, a million a month, it is said. The "man with the sickle" gets around to all of us, because "there is no man" who has "power in the day of death." Ecclesiastes 8:8.

"Ten thousand human beings set forth together on their journey. After ten years one third at least have disappeared. At the middle point of the common measure of life but half are still upon the road. Fast and faster as the ranks grow thinner, they that remained till now become weary and lie down to rise no more. At three score and ten a band of four hundred struggles on. At ninety these have been reduced to a handful of trembling patriarchs. . . . One lingers, perhaps, a lonely marvel till the century is over. We look again and the work of death is finished."—BURGESS.

"One dieth in his full strength, being wholly at ease and quiet. . . . Another dieth in the bitterness of his soul." Job 21:23-25. Death's sharpest impact comes to those with plenty, yet who are unprepared.

> "How shocking must thy summons be,
> O Death,
> To him that is at ease in his possessions;
> Who counting on long years of pleasure here,
> Is quite unfurnish'd for that world to come!"
> —ROBERT BLAIR, "The Grave."

It has been said that Alexander the Great came upon Diogenes as he searched among a pile of human bones.

"What are you doing?" inquired Alexander.

"I am looking for your father's bones," said Diogenes, "but I cannot tell them from the bones of his slaves."

WHAT HAPPENS WHEN MAN DIES?

When man was created his body was first formed of dust. Then God "breathed into his nostrils the breath of life; and man became a living soul." Genesis 2:7. He became a living, thinking, feeling, active being. He had not existed before.

When man dies the simple opposite of the creative process takes place.

First, "his breath goeth forth." Psalms 146:4. Said Job, "The breath of the Almighty hath given me life." Job 33:4. And again, "The spirit of God is in my nostrils." Job 27:3. This is the "spirit of life" which God gives to all men, and at death "the spirit shall return unto God who gave it." Ecclesiastes 12:7.

What happens to the body? This we all know. "His breath goeth forth, he returneth to his earth." Psalms 146:4. "Then shall the dust return to earth as it was." Ecclesiastes 12:7. "Dust thou art, and unto dust shalt thou return." Genesis 3:19.

There was a popular notion in the days of Solomon that a man's spirit went up to heaven at death, and an animal's spirit went downward into the earth. Solomon said, "Who knoweth the spirit of man whether it goeth upward, and the spirit of the beast, whether it goeth downward to the earth?" Ecclesiastes 3:21, A.R.V. Solomon insisted that "as the one dieth, so dieth the other" (verse 19), and "all go unto one place," and that the bodies of all "turn to dust again" (verse 20). (See also Psalms 104:26-29.)

How Much Does One Know After Death?

In Psalms 146:4, referred to several times, we find the simple answer, "His breath goeth forth, he returneth to his earth; in that very day his thoughts perish."

Solomon declares, "The living know that they shall die: but the dead know not any thing." Ecclesiastes 9:5.

What of the feelings, or emotions? Do they also cease at death? "Also their love, and their hatred, and their envy, is now perished." Verse 6.

The scripture is plain. When death comes all thinking and feeling end. If they do not, the Bible is false and unreliable. Thinking and feeling did not exist before God breathed life into man, and they stop entirely when the man dies. When the electric current is turned off, the bulb is there, but light is gone. Thinking and feeling come as a result of the current of life operating in conjunction with the body and brain of man. When the body gets too much out of order, or the current of life is turned off, or both, all thinking and feeling cease.

Origin of the Natural Immortality Theory

Who started the theory of the natural immortality of man, of his soul? The Egyptians believed in the immortality of the soul, and passed the doctrine on to the Greeks and Romans, who in turn gave it to Christianity. But this belief did not originate with the Egyptians, but with the devil himself. God said, "Thou shalt surely die." Genesis 2:17. The devil said, "Ye shall not surely die." Genesis 3:4. The devil deceived Eve and nearly the entire world. Countless millions live in fear, dread, and superstition and under religious tyranny because of the devil's lie and by reason of the multiplied horrible theories that have been built upon this original falsehood.

After man sinned God removed him from the tree of life, lest he live forever. (Genesis 3:22, 23.) God did not propose to have everlasting sinners.

Death Is Like Sleep

Death is like sound sleep. There is no consciousness of the passing of time. When David is resurrected it will seem but the next instant after he died—"the twinkling of an eye," as it were. In the Bible death is called "sleep" fifty-four times. Said Paul, "I would not have you to be ignorant, brethren, concerning them which are asleep [dead]." 1 Thessalonians 4:13.

In sound sleep there is no thought or remembrance. A man lies on a bed in a complete coma. His heart beats, his blood circulates, and his breathing is regular. Yet he knows absolutely nothing about anything. Someone hits him over the head and kills him. Then, lo, he knows everything, some say. Says the Bible, "The dead know not any thing." Ecclesiastes 9:5.

It was Thomas Gray, in his well-known "Elegy Written in a Country Churchyard," who wrote:

"The boast of heraldry, the pomp of power,
And all that beauty, all that wealth e'er gave,
Await alike the inevitable hour:
The paths of glory lead but to the grave.

. . . . .

"Can storied urn or animated bust
Back to its mansion call the fleeting breath?
Can Honor's voice provoke the silent dust
Or Flattery soothe the dull cold ear of Death?"

"If a man die, shall he live again?" Job 14:14. That was the question raised by suffering Job as his body wasted away and his bones stared at him through his dry and wrinkled skin and the breath of life seemed ready for silent departure.

A friend of mine preached at a funeral in Hollywood, California. When he had finished, one of the bereaved daughters stepped to the casket and said:

"Now the doctor has made his speech; I will make mine. Up at the university the professors have shot the Bible full of holes. We no longer believe in traditional religion; in this twentieth century that is passé.

"Mamma never recalled any events of her life before she was born into this world; neither do we, for there is no previous life. And when she dies that's the end of everything for her. Of course she still lives in our hearts as a beautiful memory, but that's all. And since there is no previous life and no hereafter for any of us, even a funeral service is useless and senseless. Now, I do not know what you will think of my speech, but this is what I believe."

The young woman stated some truth. But here are two things she ought to consider: (1) Death does not end all, because "it is appointed unto men once to die, but after this the judgment." Hebrews 9:27. (2) "There shall be a resurrection of the dead, both of the just and unjust." Acts 24:15.

The Bible Picture of the Resurrection

1. Christ said that He would "be raised again on the third day." Matthew 16:21.
2. Afterward Jesus said, "It is I myself." Luke 24:39.
3. The angel said, "He is risen." Mark 16:6.
4. Again, "All that are in the graves shall . . . come forth." John 5:28, 29.
5. Paul said, "Christ . . . the firstfruits of them that slept." 1 Corinthians 15:20.
6. Again, "Afterward they that are Christ's at his coming." Verse 23.
7. "The Lord himself shall descend from heaven with a shout, with the voice of the archangel, and with the trump of God: and the dead in Christ shall rise first: then we which are alive and remain shall be caught up together with them in the clouds, to meet the Lord in the air: and so shall we ever be with the Lord. Wherefore comfort one another with these words." 1 Thessalonians 4:16-18.

From this we see that the resurrection from the dead is the real hope of those who "sorrow not, even as others." Verse 13.

Furthermore, Paul makes it clear that Christians who live to see the second coming of Christ will go to heaven "together with" the resurrected righteous. They will "not

 Russ Harlan, Art

"The Lord himself shall descend from heaven with a shout, with the voice of archangel, and with the trump of God: and the dead in Christ shall rise firs

prevent [go before] them which are asleep." Verse 15. And those who have died will not reach heaven before those who live to see Christ come. "God having provided some better thing for us, that they without us should not be made perfect." Hebrews 11:40. Paul will receive his reward at Christ's coming. (2 Timothy 4:8.) Even one thousand years after David's death Peter declared that the patriarch was not yet in heaven. (Acts 2:29, 34.)

Paul goes so far as to say that if the dead do not rise, then those who have died believing in Christ are perished, and that is the end of it all. (1 Corinthians 15:16-18.) Thank God, the dead shall rise.

The Hope of Both Old and New Testaments

Not only does the New Testament set forth this resurrection hope, but the Old Testament does also.

In fact Job answers his own question, "If a man die, shall he live again?" Job 14:14.

Follow his thoughts. "All the days of my appointed time will I wait, till my change come." Verse 14.

Where would he wait? "If I wait, the grave is mine house." Job 17:13.

When would the "change" come? "Thou shalt call, and I will answer thee: thou wilt have a desire to the works of thine hands." Job 14:15. Yes, this is as Jesus put it, "All that are in the graves shall hear his voice, and shall come forth." John 5:28, 29.

What would be the nature of the change?

For one thing, there would be an actual, bodily resurrection. Said Job, "I know that my redeemer liveth, and that he shall stand at the latter day upon the earth: and though after my skin worms destroy this body, yet in my flesh shall I see God." Job 19:25, 26.

The apostle Paul adds this: "We shall not all sleep [die], but we shall all be changed, in a moment, in the twinkling of an eye, at the last trump: . . . the dead shall be raised incorruptible, and we shall be changed. . . . This mortal must put on immortality." 1 Corinthians 15:51-53.

Speaking of Christ and His second coming, Paul finishes with these words: "Who shall change our vile body, that it may be fashioned like unto his glorious body, according to the working whereby he is able even to subdue all things unto himself." Philippians 3:21.

The Mystery

Yes, it is a mystery. "Behold, I shew you a mystery; . . . we shall all be changed."

Michael Faraday was a great scientist. "One of Faraday's workmen by accident dropped a little, highly valued silver cup in a strong acid bath. In a little while it utterly disappeared.

"But when Faraday came in and learned of it, he said nothing, cast another acid into the jar, and the silver soon precipitated—a shapeless mass, indeed, but every grain was there. A few days later it came back from the silversmith a more beautiful cup than ever. May not God as readily restore our bodies after the decay and disorganization of death?"

The Hope

Death is an enemy. (1 Corinthians 15:26.) Mother Eve chose to believe that she would not die, but rather enter upon a higher plane of experience, and become as a god. How many millions have since been misled as she was, believing that death is not real at all but just the gateway of release into a higher realm!

However, dark as death is, it is not hopeless. It does not end all for the Christian. "God so loved the world, that he gave his only begotten Son, that whosoever believeth in him should not perish, but have everlasting life." In Christ we have hope of life, and without Him we can anticipate only everlasting destruction at the time of the second death. The voice of Jesus at His second coming will open the tomb of every saint, and with the righteous living they shall be rewarded together.

"At the sounding of the trumpet, when the
saints are gathered home,
We will greet each other by the crystal sea;
When the Lord Himself from heaven to His
glory bids them come,
What a gathering of the faithful that will be!"

Today we may but see some picture of a loved one gone, touch some trinket made sacred by his contact, feel some garment hallowed by his hands, hear some sacred strains he always loved, cherish a heartful of memories from the yesteryears.

With all of these there is a mingling of joy and sorrow, of peace and pain. But on some tomorrow there shall be life and joy and love forever.

I Know

"Although I grieve now you are gone,
Black night precedes the fairest dawn.

"The flowers bloom, then fall asleep,
And buried lie in earth beds deep,
Then rise anew when comes the spring
To prove a resurrectioning.

"Some day the angels' reveille
Will call you back again to me.

"Then we shall share eternal spring,
And view its glorious blossoming,
And all the stars shall shine anew
When love supreme comes smiling
through."

—Helen M. Johnston.

CHAPTER 48

What the Bible Teaches About Hell

IN RELIGIOUS instruction for children some years ago is found this word picture of hell and its tortures.

"Look into this little prison. In the middle of it there is a boy, a young man. He is silent; despair is on him. He stands straight up. His eyes are burning like two burning coals. Two long flames come out of his ears. His breathing is difficult. Sometimes he opens his mouth and a breath of blazing fire rolls out of it. But listen! there is a sound just like that of a kettle boiling. Is it really a kettle which is boiling? No; then what is it? Hear what it is. The blood is boiling in the scalded veins of that boy. The brain is boiling and bubbling in his head. The marrow is boiling in his bones! Ask him, put the question to him, why is he thus tormented? His answer is, that when he was alive, his blood boiled to do very wicked things, and he did them, and it was for that he went to dancing-houses, public-houses, and theatres. Ask him, does he think the punishment greater than he deserves? 'No,' he says, 'my punishment is not greater than I deserve, it is just. I knew it not so well on earth, but I know now that it is just. There is a just and a terrible God. He is terrible to sinners in hell—but He is just!' "—J. FURNISS, "The Sight of Hell," *Tracts for Spiritual Reading*, sec. 27, p. 20.

It is indeed astonishing what people may be led to believe in the name of religion. It is yet more unbelievable how responsible high churchmen feel free to pass favorable judgment upon such teaching as the above. One leader wrote, "I have carefully read over this Little Volume for Children and have found nothing whatever in it contrary to the doctrines of Holy Faith; but, on the contrary, a great deal to charm, instruct and edify our youthful classes, for whose benefit it has been written."—WILLIAM MEAGHER, Vicar General, Dublin, December 14, 1855.

What far-reaching responsibility does man take upon himself!

THE TRUTH ABOUT THREE WORDS FOR HELL

In the Bible our English word *hell* has three meanings:

1. Hell sometimes means the "grave." The Hebrew word widely used for "grave" is *sheol.* In Psalms 16:10 we have it rendered "hell," referring to the grave. "Thou wilt not leave my soul in hell; neither wilt thou suffer thine Holy One to see corruption." In Acts 2:27 this scripture is quoted by Peter. In this verse the Greek word for "hell" is *hades.* Its meaning is "grave," the same as *sheol* in the Hebrew. As you know, the New Testament was originally written in Greek. In Acts 2:31, Peter definitely says that Psalms 16:10, the verse we speak of, refers to Christ's resurrection. Christ was not left in "hell," that is, not in the grave, but was raised from the dead. The word *hades* is used eleven times in the New Testament. In 1 Corinthians 15:55 it is translated "grave." Otherwise it is translated "hell," signifying the grave or "state in the grave."

2. Hell also signifies a "place of burning." In the New Testament the word is "Gehenna," or the "Valley of Hinnom," described as "a deep, narrow glen south of Jeru-

salem, where, after the introduction of the fire gods of Ahaz, the idolatrous Jews offered their children to Moloch." In this Valley of Hinnom the bodies of dead animals and the refuse of the city were cast. Fires burned continuously, and worms infested the carcasses of animals. What the fire did not destroy the worms consumed. It thus was a type of complete annihilation. *Gehenna,* the place of burning, is used twelve times, being translated "hell."

3. The third meaning of the word "hell" is found in 2 Peter 2:4. "God spared not the angels that sinned, but cast them down to hell, and delivered them into chains of darkness, to be reserved unto judgment." The Greek word here is *tartaroō,* not *Gehenna* or *hades.* The text above pictures it as a place of darkness, a fit representation of the darkness that enshrouded Satan and his angels when they were separated from God and heaven.

Where Do All Men Go at Death?

All men go to the grave at death, that is, to *hades* or *sheol.* Said Job, "I know that thou wilt bring me to death, and to the house appointed for all living." Job 30:23. This house of death is the grave. "If I wait, the grave is mine house." Job 17:13.

This hell is an impartial one. "There is one event to the righteous, and to the wicked." Ecclesiastes 9:2. "What man is he that liveth, and shall not see death? shall he deliver his soul from the hand of the grave [*sheol*]?" Psalms 89:48.

The rich and poor, the high and low, the righteous and the wicked—all meet in that abode.

Into the grave have gone the vilest characters who have ever lived, and its portals have opened to receive the loveliest and sweetest mortals who ever graced the earth. Of these latter Isaac Watts sang:

"Unveil thy bosom, faithful tomb;
Take this new treasure to thy trust
And give these sacred relics room
To slumber in thy silent dust."

Yes, death is an enemy (1 Corinthians 15:26), and the grave is not a comforting consolation, but we thank God that "blessed are the dead which die in the Lord from henceforth: Yea, saith the Spirit, that they may rest from their labours; and their works do follow them." Revelation 14:13. And we may also rejoice that the wicked slumber in silence rather than scream in torture and agony. There is no pain in the grave.

When Will the Righteous Dead Come Out of Hades?

The righteous dead will come out of their graves at the sound of the "last trump: for the trumpet shall sound, and the dead shall be raised incorruptible." 1 Corinthians 15:52. This is at the second coming of Christ when "the Lord himself shall descend . . . with the trump of God: and the dead in Christ shall rise first." 1 Thessalonians 4:16.

Christ's promise of His glorious return to gather His chosen ones unto Himself (John 14:1-3) will someday be fulfilled. At the sound of the "trump of God" the saints who have slept in silence, unconscious of the passing of time, will suddenly be wakened. Some have slumbered for thousands of years; others have had only a brief rest in the grave. To all, the time will seem the same—just as a moment, or as the "twinkling of an eye." They will come forth with their faces glowing with joy, health, and immortality, and go to their heavenly home.

When Will the Wicked Dead Come Out of Hades?

There is to be, as Paul states, "a resurrection of the dead, both of the just and unjust." Acts 24:15.

The wicked, or unjust, do not rise from their graves until one thousand years after the resurrection of the righteous. "The rest of the dead lived not again until the thousand years were finished." Revelation 20:5.

WHERE WILL THE WICKED BE CAST?

When the wicked are resurrected, they together with the devil, death, and the grave, will be cast into the lake of fire. (Verses 10-15.) This is the "Gehenna," the burning hell.

Peter declares that the Lord knows how to "reserve the unjust unto the day of judgment to be punished." 2 Peter 2:9. Also that the earth itself is "reserved unto fire against the day of judgment" (2 Peter 3:7), and that "the elements shall melt with fervent heat" (Verse 10).

According to John the revelator fire comes down from God out of heaven and devours the wicked (including the devil, death, and the grave) in a "lake of fire." This is called the "second death." (Revelation 20:9-14.)

Since the wicked perish in this burning Gehenna, and the earth itself becomes a molten lake of fire, we understand more clearly the Bible statement that the wicked will be recompensed in the earth (Proverbs 11:31), and also that "they shall be brought forth to the day of wrath" (Job 21:30). Jesus Himself said that "the tares are the children of the wicked one," and "as therefore the tares are gathered and burned in the fire; so shall it be in the end of this world." Matthew 13:38, 40.

This gives us ample evidence to believe that the fiery hell is yet future, and at this present moment not a single, solitary sinner is burning in hell.

HOW MUCH OF A MAN WILL BE CAST INTO THIS FIRE?

Nine times Jesus warns of the "burning" hell, the "Gehenna" hell.

In Matthew 10:28 He said, "Fear him which is able to destroy both soul and body in hell." Again he counseled, "It is better for thee to enter into life halt or maimed, rather than having two hands or two feet to be cast into everlasting fire," or "having two eyes to be cast into hell fire." Matthew 18:8, 9.

This makes it clear that the whole man, soul and body, is cast into hell-fire. Since the body goes into the grave at death, and since there is no fire in the grave, again we see that the burning hell is yet future. If God takes "no pleasure in the death of the wicked" (Ezekiel 33:11), and has reserved them unto the day of judgment to be punished, why should we wish to rush them off to hell as soon as they die? Why are some so bent on believing that God has literally billions of wicked souls roasting in a fiery coffin of hell?

How Long Will the Gehenna Hell Burn?

The Gehenna hell will burn until "both soul and body" are destroyed. "Fear him which is able to destroy both soul and body." Matthew 10:28.

"The day that cometh shall burn them up, saith the Lord of hosts, that it shall leave them neither root nor branch. . . . For they shall be *ashes*." Malachi 4:1-3.

This hell will burn until the wicked are devoured. (Revelation 20:9.) This is the "second death," not everlasting, burning life. (Verse 14.)

It is perfectly plain that the wicked are going to be completely destroyed. This will be the second death. At the first death the wicked go into the grave. The second death marks the end of the sinner, the end of death, and the end of the grave. God is forever through with sin, sinners, death, and the grave.

When the work of burning and complete destruction is over, the fire does not necessarily keep burning for all time. The expression "for ever and ever" in Revelation 14:11 and Revelation 20:10 means "continuous, with no cessation," and may signify a long time or a shorter time. These are two texts that must be understood, in the light of the abundant testimony of the Bible, to mean that the wicked will be annihilated. Eternal life endures forever. Eternal death (the second death) lasts forever. Those who suffer the second death will be destroyed by eternal fire. Jesus declared, "These shall go away into everlasting punishment." Matthew 25:46. Notice, it does not say "punishing," but "punishment," and has reference to the result rather than to the method.

If you will read Exodus 21:2-6, you will find that "for ever" may mean only as long as man lives. Jonah said that he was shut up in the great fish and "the earth with her bars was about me for ever." Jonah 2:6. Yet he was in this strange abode only three short days.

What Is This Kind of Fire Called?

The fire of this future hell is called "everlasting," or eternal. "These shall go away into everlasting punishment." Matthew 25:46.

Sodom and Gomorrah are examples of how this kind of fire works. We read Jude 7, "Even as Sodom and Gomorrha, . . . are set forth for an example, suffering the vengeance of eternal fire."

How did this eternal, or everlasting, fire affect these cities? Please note, "And turning the cities of Sodom and Gomorrha into ashes, . . . making them an ensample unto those that after should live ungodly." 2 Peter 2:6.

What more could be said! Both Jude and Peter set forth the destruction of Sodom and Gomorrah as an example of destruction by "eternal" fire. The result was "ashes." Are the fires of these cities still burning? No.

The fire of hell is also spoken of as being unquenchable. "Where their worm dieth not, and the fire is not quenched." Mark 9:44.

Because of continued Sabbath desecration by the Jews, God threatened the destruction of Jerusalem by a fire that "shall not be quenched." (Jeremiah 17:27.) The record of the destruction is found in Jeremiah 52:12, 13.

Jerusalem is not still burning today. "Unquenchable" fire is fire that cannot be put out until it has consumed everything. It burns everything up and then burns out. In the same way shall the wicked be destroyed.

The "worm that dieth not" is a figure taken from the refuse dump in the Valley of Hinnom before mentioned. What the fire did not destroy the worms devoured. It is a symbol of complete and final destruction—total annihilation of sinners.

The wicked "shall be as though they had not been." Obadiah 16. "For yet a little while, and the wicked shall not be: yea, thou shalt diligently consider his place, and it shall not be." Psalms 37:10. When hell has burned out there will be less left of sinners than there is of Sodom and Gomorrah today. Their ashes will become a part of the very ground upon which the righteous tread. (Malachi 4:3.)

God's Better Way

God never intended that any man should ever suffer in hell. It was "prepared for the devil and his angels." Matthew 25:41. If we are ever cast into that place of final destruction, it will be because we did not cast ourselves upon the mercy and grace of God or because we held back the full surrender of our hearts to Him.

God never purposed for men to believe that He operates a brimstone concentration camp, under the direction of the devil.

The dead, good and bad, rest in silent slumber. There

is no consciousness, no pain. Resurrection day is coming. Those who sleep in Christ will be raised to reign with Him. The wicked will be raised for the execution of final penalty. Then sin and sinners will be no more.

A woman who was sharply denouncing the Bible said, "I'm going to heaven whether God wants me there or not."

The simple truth is that God will not close the door of heaven to any soul who could be happy there. All who reach hell would be dissatisfied in heaven. That is why we must prepare for heaven *now*.

In a foxhole, by a hidden light, a soldier wrote, "The shells are exploding so near they shake my paper as I write. . . . Sometimes I wonder if my world will ever again be filled with peace and quiet, with laughter and love. I want to go home once more. If only for a little while, I want to go home."

In the human breast God has planted a deep desire for the heavenly home. The warfare of earth will one day be past, and Christ will come again.

When darkness overshadowed the cruel cross, and the outlook was black, the suffering Saviour took time to say to a repentant thief, "Thou shalt be with me in paradise."

"Through the gates to the city, in a robe of spotless white,
He will lead me where no tears shall ever fall;
In the glad song of ages I shall mingle with delight;
But I long to meet my Saviour first of all."

—FANNY J. CROSBY.

ʻH Pub. Assn. Vernon Nye, *Artist*

ıing man of the dust of the ground, God breathed into his nostrils the breath of life, and he became a living soul made in the image of God.

Russ Harlan

Standing at the foot of the cross, we see the love of God demonstrated, "that whoever believeth in him should not perish, but have everlasting life."

CHAPTER 49

Can the Dead Communicate With the Living?

SPIRITUALISM, OR Spiritism, is the belief that living persons may communicate with the spirits of those who have died. The method may be anything from ouija boards, table tipping, rapping, snapping, slate-writing, and music, to trances, seeming ghostly apparitions, occult voices, and the touch of invisible hands.

Modern Spiritism

In Christian lands modern manifestations of psychic phenomena as connected with Spiritism are more or less recent. It is generally agreed that 1848 is the time, Hydesville, New York, the place, and the Fox sisters the first participants.

M'Clintock and Strong's Cyclopaedia, under the topic "Spiritualism," quotes Mr. Dale Owen as follows:

"'In the month of January, 1848, the noises assumed the character of distinct knockings at night in the bedrooms, sounding sometimes as from the cellar below, and resembling the hammering of a shoemaker. These knocks produced a tremulous motion in the furniture and even in the floor. The children (Margaret, aged 12 years, and Kate, aged 9 years) felt something heavy, as of a dog, lie on their feet when in bed; and Kate felt, as it were, a cold hand passed over her face. Sometimes the bed-

Paul Remmey, Ar

It has long been a master stroke of Satan to promote the theory that the living communicate with the dead. Thousands today are deceived on this point.

clothes were pulled off. Chairs and the dining-table were moved from their places. Raps were made on doors as they stood close to them, but on suddenly opening them no one was visible. On the night of March 13 (or 31), 1848, the knockings were unusually loud,' whereupon 'Mr. Fox tried the sashes, to see if they were shaken by the wind. Kate observed that the knockings in the room exactly answered the rattle made by her father with the sash. Thereupon she snapped her fingers and exclaimed, "Here, old Splitfoot, do as I do." The rap followed. This at once arrested the mother's attention. "Count ten," she said. Ten strokes were distinctly given. "How old is my daughter Margaret?" Twelve strokes. "And Kate?" Nine.' Other questions were answered, When 'she asked if it was a man? No answer. Was it a spirit? It rapped. Numbers of questions were put to the spirit, which replied by knocks that it was that of a travelling tradesman [Charles B. Rosma], who had been murdered by the then tenant, John C. Bell, for his property. The peddler had never been seen afterwards; and on the floor being dug up, the remains of a human body were found.' "

In fact, the rappings indicated just where to dig in order to find the body. It was afterward ascertained that a man answering the description of the mudered Rosma had been seen to enter the house of Mr. Bell, and had not been seen again.

Neighbors at first scorned the rapping idea. However, when their secrets were revealed and lost articles found it was a different story.

Margaret Fox developed unusual occult powers. The next year she and sister Kate gave public exhibitions, and proceeded to New York the following year. Three years later there were thirty thousand spiritualists, it is said, and the movement spread like wildfire. They claim fifty million believers.

Believers in Spiritism come from the ranks of scientists, literary leaders, prominent preachers, and political figures, as well as from nearly all walks of life.

Sir Arthur Conan Doyle, literary genius and creator of the fictional Sherlock Holmes, was a vigorous promoter of the faith.

Sir Oliver Lodge, great scientist, was certain that his son, killed in World War I, returned in spirit form. He claimed to have many times seen a figure appear and glide about the room, playing an accordion.

Rev. A. J. Callahan, S.J., is quoted in the *Western Watchman* (Catholic), March 12, 1920: "The dead can come back to life, but only through God's extraordinary permission. . . . There are cases where a dead mother has come to her wandering boy, but always for the best of reasons and for the boy's welfare."

Dean Welldon, of Durham, at a congress of the Church of England, held at Leicester back in 1919, said, "Spiritualism has come to fill a void in church practice because of the coldness of the old services."—Cited in *Current Opinion,* December, 1919, p. 317.

The noted Dr. Russell H. Conwell, pastor of Baptist Temple in Philadelphia, believed that his deceased wife held converse with him on several occasions. (See *Public Ledger,* Philadelphia, Dec. 22, 1919, p. 1.)

Dr. Isaac Funk quotes the *War Cry* of November 27, 1897, to the effect that General Booth, founder of the Salvation Army, spoke of regular communion with his dead wife.

The former Russian minister of war in World War I, General Sukhomlinoff, is quoted in the Washington *Post,* July 2, 1918, page 4, as saying concerning Grand Duke Nicholas: "In addition to his weaknesses as commander-in-chief, he was so influenced by his passion for spiritualism, in which his wife, Anastasya Nikolayevna, believed blindly, that he frequently sought in spiritualism solutions for some of the most serious military problems."

The Kaiser of Germany during the same war is reported to have followed the same practice, consulting the famous German medium Augusta Schoen and others. He purportedly contacted the spirit of his grandfather, founder of the German Empire.

Sir William Crookes, famous chemist and physicist of his day, said, "I have talked with the spirit of Katie King scores and scores of times, saw her form appear and disappear, and photographed her many times."

Flammarion, the celebrated French astronomer, asserted that "any scientific man who declares spiritualistic phenomena to be impossible is one who speaks without knowing what he is talking about."

Emperor Hirohito, of Japan, went from his palace in Tokyo to the tomb of his father, Emperor Yoshihito, to tell him that Japan lost the war in 1945.

How Old Is Spiritism?

That Spiritism is not actually new or modern in origin is attested by all. Dr. James H. Hyslop, in his *Contact With the Other World,* writes, "Ancestor-worship, in most cases simply the Spiritualism of the East, survives as the exponent of immortality."—Page 14.

Sir Arthur Conan Doyle says, "The thing itself, in one form or another, is as old as history."—*The Vital Message,* p. 30.

Why Does the Bible Condemn Spiritism?

The Bible condemns Spiritism for three reasons: First, Spiritism's belief in establishing contact with supposed spirits of the dead is unsound. The Bible says that "the dead know not any thing. . . . Neither have they any more a portion for ever in any thing that is done under the sun." Ecclesiastes 9:5, 6.

This is in full agreement with Psalms 146:4, that "his breath goeth forth, he returneth to his earth; in that very day his thoughts perish." It is evident to all that since the Bible teaches the cessation of thought at death, so much so that the dead know not anything, and since they have nothing more to do with earthly affairs, it is indeed reasonable that the Bible should condemn Spiritism, which claims communication with the dead.

The second reason why the Bible is against Spiritism is that Satan, the archenemy of God, claims that death is not real. To Eve, mother of all, he said, "Ye shall not surely die: for God doth know that in the day ye eat thereof, then your eyes shall be opened, and ye shall be as gods." Genesis 3:4, 5. In the eternal conflict between Christ and Satan here is an issue. God says *death;* Satan says *life.* Satan says a higher plane—ye shall be as gods. Satan's lie about death led the human race into sin and woe. The God of truth is against Satan, "for he is a liar, and the father of it." John 8:44.

The third reason the Bible opposes all forms of Spiritism is that its general influence is not good.

It uproots faith in the Bible. They call up John Wesley, and he renounces his Bible preaching. It teaches that infidels and saints share everlasting life and honor alike. They call up Thomas Paine, and he says he lives with John Bunyan.

Talmage is reported to have said, "First it makes a man quarter of an infidel; then it makes him half an infidel; then it makes him a whole infidel."

Dr. L. S. Forbes Winslow, lecturer on mental diseases, once wrote, "I could quote many . . . instances where men of the highest ability have, so to speak, neglected all, and followed the doctrines of spiritualism, only to end their days in a lunatic asylum."—*Spiritualistic Madness,* p. 29.

In one State four persons were committed to an insane asylum after a twenty-four-hour steady siege at the ouija board.

J. Godfrey Raupert, K.S.G., Catholic specialist on Spiritism, stated, "Let it once be clearly and fully known that these 'dear ones' on the other side of life ruin and desolate homes, that they drive men and women to destruction and to the madhouse, that they undermine religious faith and confidence, and that in a thousand instances, they bring about an utter weariness and detestation of the duties of the present life. . . . I have, during the last ten years, spent much of my time in answering the inquiries of persons whose lives have been shipwrecked by spiritistic practices, and it is upon painful facts and incontrovertible evidence that I base my conclusions and opinions."

What Does the Bible Say?

In the Old Testament strictest command was given against the practice of spiritist mediums or the consulting of the same by the people.

"When thou art come into the land which the Lord thy God giveth thee, thou shalt not learn to do after the abominations of those nations. There shall not be found among you any one that maketh his son or his daughter to pass through the fire, or that useth divination, or an observer of times, or an enchanter, or a witch, or a charmer, or a consulter with familiar spirits, or a wizard, or a necromancer. For all that do these things are an abomination unto the Lord: and because of these abominations the Lord thy God doth drive them out from before thee." Deuteronomy 18:9-12.

Sweeping condemnation is here passed upon astrology, fortune-telling, charms, spiritist mediums (consulters of familiar spirits), and all pseudoprophets and pretended wise ones. "I will come near to you to judgment; and I will be a swift witness against the sorcerers." Malachi 3:5.

In the New Testament the prophecy is made that in our day there would be a special manifestation of this work of Satan. "Now the Spirit speaketh expressly, that in the latter times some shall depart from the faith, giving heed to seducing spirits, and doctrines of devils." 1 Timothy 4:1.

We have already noted how leaders of nations have given heed to such seducing spirits in the conduct of war. One cannot resist quoting Revelation 16:14, "They are the spirits of devils, working miracles, which go forth unto the kings of the earth and of the whole world, to gather them to the battle of that great day of God Almighty."

The Bible clarifies the whole issue. The dead are unconscious; therefore they cannot make intelligent contact with anyone. The purported communications from the dead are fakery. They are the fakery of the medium or fakery performed by the "spirits of devils," "seducing spirits." Concerning the Jews, who were deluded in ancient time, the Bible says, "They sacrificed their sons and their daughters unto devils." Psalms 106:37.

Satan and his angels, who were "cast out into the earth," have great power. They possess information that may be known only to the dead loved ones and their kin or friends. When such is revealed through mediums people are deceived. They believe the messages actually come from the dead. Evil angels may conceivably appear in the form of a deceased loved one.

Whether these things are faked by mediums or by "seducing spirits," through mediums or apart from mediums, it is well to remember that "the dead know not any thing."

It is also wise to recall that even the most intelligent may at times suffer from hallucinations, and all of us have a way of seeing what we *want* to see and hearing what we *want* to hear.

Consider these four Bible verses:

"Satan, which deceiveth the whole world." Revelation 12:9.

"Take heed that no man deceive you." Matthew 24:4.

"We deceive ourselves." 1 John 1:8.

"Let no man deceive himself." 1 Corinthians 3:18.

He who plays with Spiritism is like a man who puts his head in a crocodile's mouth. Not long ago a young man, putting on his regular act at a circus, thrust his head into an alligator's mouth before a body of spectators. Suddenly the alligator's mouth snapped shut as his powerful jaws went into action. The father rushed out with a crowbar, inserted it, and finally succeeded in prying the mouth open. The boy was rushed off to the hospital.

There is a lot of show business in spiritistic séances, but it is no place for a Christian to seek counsel, show his face, or risk his soul.

"Wherefore if they shall say unto you . . . Behold, he is in the secret chambers; believe it not." Matthew 24:26.

Americans spend literally hundreds of millions of dollars with fortunetellers of one kind or another. "Wherefore do ye spend money for that which is not bread?" Isaiah 55:2.

"When they tell you to consult mediums and ghosts that cheep and gibber in low murmurs, ask them if a nation should not consult its God. Say, 'Why consult the dead on behalf of the living?'" Isaiah 8:19, Moffatt.

Then Isaiah adds, "To the law and to the testimony: if they speak not according to this word, it is because there is no light in them." Verse 20.

Arthur Greenwalt tells of a Sunday school teacher who asked a class of boys, "Where do you keep your Bible at home?" One lad, quick on the draw, chirped, "In the cellar." "What a place for the Bible," replied the teacher. "Oh, the Bible," the lad replied; "I thought you said bottle."

"Many men today, trying to find an answer for their problems and troubles, make the same mistake. They try to answer with a bottle instead of the Bible."—*Pulpit Digest,* September, 1948.

Thousands have tried the spiked wine of Spiritism to comfort the soul, to stimulate a lagging interest in life, to reach the solution of riddles, and to solve the mystery of the grave.

What the world needs today is with open heart to look within an open Bible.

"An open Bible for the world!
May this our glorious motto be!
On every breeze the truth unfurled
Shall scatter blessings rich and free.

. . . . .

"It tells of Jesus and His death,
Of life for dying men;
And to each soul of humble faith,
Gives sonship with the Lord again.

"It offers rest to weary hearts;
It comforts those who sit in tears;
To all who faint it strength imparts;
And gilds with hope the eternal years."

—HENRY M. KING.

CHAPTER 50

Puzzling Questions About Death

THE LATE Clarence Darrow, famous criminal lawyer, once held a debate with a rabbi, a priest, and a minister on the subject of immortality. The clergymen, with no mean skill, summoned similes and allegories to set forth the theory that the soul of man is indestructible, not subject unto the power of death. When the lawyer rose he said, "These gentlemen never once used the Bible to prove their assertions, much less did they quote from its pages."

We who preach from a Bible text often wander a long way from Biblical teaching. Yet in all fairness it may be said that there are some things in the Good Book "hard to be understood." (2 Peter 3:15, 16.) When there is apparent contradiction or seeming difference of meaning two things should be borne in mind. One is that difficult texts should be studied in the light of the general teaching of the Bible on that particular topic; the other, that all lines of Bible doctrine should run parallel. For instance, if, as the Bible teaches, judgment takes place after death, then we would be out of harmony if we believed God took good people to heaven at death and consigned bad people to hell at death, when as yet they had not been judged.

The Thief on the Cross

Did not Jesus on the cross say to the penitent thief, "Verily I say unto thee, Today shalt thou be with me in paradise"? Luke 23:43. The answer is Yes. But it must also be noted that Jesus did not go to Paradise that day. Paradise is where the tree of life is. (Revelation 2:7.) That is in heaven at the throne of God. (Revelation 22:1, 2.) Jesus did not ascend to heaven until the day of His resurrection. To Mary He said at that time, "Touch me not; for I am not yet ascended to my Father." John 20:17.

What, then, did Jesus mean by His promise to the thief?

Only this: "You ask me to remember you in my kingdom. I say to you today (in this dark hour), thou shalt be with me in paradise." The comma in this verse should be after *today,* not before it. When Luke wrote the record there were no punctuation marks at all. Men have supplied these. In this instance the comma is not in the proper place.

"Me thought beneath the lurid sky
I saw three crosses lifted high;
And round one cross I saw the light
Of heaven's own glory beaming bright,
And from the patient Sufferer's side
A trembling voice in anguish cried:
'O Lord, and must I be forgot?
Thou pitying Christ, forget me not!'

"And then above the din I heard
The Godlike Sufferer speak the word:
'Thou shalt be with me by and by,
Beneath the star-bespangled sky,
When in my kingdom bright and fair
I reign in endless glory there.'"

—Mrs. L. D. Avery Stuttle.

Shall Never Die

What did Jesus mean when He told Martha that those who believed in Him would never die? The full text makes it clear:

"Jesus said unto her, I am the resurrection, and the life: he that believeth in me, though he were dead, yet shall he live: and whosoever liveth and believeth in me shall never die." John 11:25, 26.

Both righteous and wicked will be resurrected, but only those who believe in Christ will live forever. The rest will die the second death. (Revelation 20:13-15.)

The Spirits in Prison

Some have thought that Peter believed that Christ, while His body hung on the cross, went and preached to human spirits in some mysterious prison or purgatory.

The scripture reads, "By which also he went and preached unto the spirits in prison; which sometime were disobedient, when once the longsuffering of God waited in the days of Noah." 1 Peter 3:19, 20.

This is a simple statement that Jesus preached unto the wicked people in the days of Noah, who were in the prison house of sin. (Isaiah 61:1.) Christ preached to them by the same Spirit of God that raised, or quickened, Him from the dead. (1 Peter 3:18.)

Saul and the Witch of Endor

Did not King Saul consult a spirit medium, and did she not bring up the dead prophet Samuel? The account is found in 1 Samuel 28.

God no longer heard the prayers of Saul. (Verse 6.) The king disguised himself and sought counsel of a spirit medium at Endor. (Verses 7, 8.) The medium was suspicious, but on promise that the inquirer would not tell King Saul she agreed to do business. (Verses 9, 10.)

The woman asked, "Whom shall I bring up?" Saul said, "Bring me up Samuel." Verse 11.

Now if Samuel went to heaven when he died, why not call him down from heaven and not up from the grave?

Samuel was a man of God. But this medium said, "I saw gods ascending out of the earth." Verse 13. And when Saul asked, "What form is he of?" she said, "An old man cometh up; and he is covered with a mantle." Verse 14. Saul accepted that as Samuel.

You clearly see that Satan's old original lie was at work. "Ye shall not surely die: . . . ye shall be as gods." Genesis 3:4, 5. The spirit medium saw "gods" coming up, and one of them was Samuel, she said. Yes, this is the devil's work.

The message came through, "To morrow shalt thou and thy sons be with me." 1 Samuel 28:19. That is, one day you and your sons will die and come where I am. If righteous Samuel were in heaven, how could rejected Saul go there?

Again, if Samuel were actually in heaven, would God permit him to go talk to the God-rejected Saul, and at the request of a spirit medium that Saul knew was condemned of the same God? Hardly, we think.

The simple fact is that Samuel was dead, and knew not anything. Saul went to a medium and received a mixture of truth and error. He heard what God had already told him, and he no doubt believed that Samuel was actually sending a message. Saul was deceived.

The Rich Man and Lazarus

In the parable of Luke 16:19-31 the rich man died and went to hell. "Being in torments," he called to the beggar Lazarus, who had also died and was in Abraham's bosom. Read the account.

First, let us observe that God sometimes speaks of the future as present. "God . . . quickeneth the dead, and calleth those things which be not as though they were." Romans 4:17.

However, the story of the rich man and Lazarus is a parable, and cannot be regarded as literal. It comes in a long series of parables. Parables often teach some main lesson but should not be held to every detail. (See Judges 9:6-20.) Jesus sought to rebuke the covetous Pharisees (Luke 16:14) by showing that the rich may fare well here but not hereafter. He used one of their own traditions.

Let us first consider Lazarus and then the rich man.

Lazarus is represented as being carried by angels to Abraham's bosom. However, it is at the second coming of Christ, not at death, that the angels gather the elect. (Matthew 24:31.) Furthermore, Abraham would find it difficult to hold all the redeemed in his bosom. So this cannot possibly be literal.

There was another Lazarus, a literal one, who died. (John 11:14-44.) He was the brother of Mary and Martha. For four days he lay dead. When Jesus called him to life He said, "Lazarus, come forth." He did not say, "Come from Abraham's bosom." Jesus simply gave this literal Lazarus life, and he came forth from the grave. We note also that this literal Lazarus had nothing to say about Abraham's bosom. He had nothing to say about anything that occurred during those four days. "The dead know not any thing." It is perfectly clear that when a literal Lazarus dies "his thoughts perish." It is evident that the Lazarus of the parable cannot be taken literally.

Of the rich man we read, "The rich man also died, and was buried; and in hell he lift up his eyes, being in torments." He further stated, "I am tormented in this flame." The word "hell" used in this connection is the word "hades," or the grave. Since there is no fire in the grave, we here have still further evidence that this parable cannot be taken literally.

The real lesson of the parable is that prosperity here does not guarantee prosperity hereafter. And also this life is the only time we shall ever have to prepare for the next. "For the grave cannot praise thee, death can not celebrate thee: they that go down into the pit [grave] cannot hope for thy truth." Isaiah 38:18. There is no second chance. "Behold, now is the accepted time; behold, now is the day of salvation." 2 Corinthians 6:2. The little boy who wanted to be the rich man while he lived and Lazarus when he died, expressed the wish of many, but it is a wish that can never come true.

The story is told that when a maiden of the Seneca Indians died, her family imprisoned a young bird and held it captive until it began to sing. Then, loading it with caresses and messages, they released it over the maiden's grave. They believed that the bird would fly directly to spirit land and deliver its messages of affection to the loved maiden.

Now is the time to speak words of kindness. Today is the day to do deeds of love. This is the life in which decision is to be made as to where we shall spend eternity. All who would live forever with God must now learn to enjoy the things of God.

Susan Ertz, in *Anger in the Sky,* has aptly said, "Millions long for immortality who do not know what to do with themselves on a rainy Sunday afternoon." How miserable such people would be if penned up in heaven for endless ages. It would be a prison house of eternal longing for the whirl of a sinful world. We make our own bed for the future.

Someone has said, "The more of earth we want, the less of heaven we'll get."

In World War II Col. Warren J. Clear was asked by his superior officer to leave Corregidor just before it fell. He was to board a submarine at midnight. In his orders were these words, "Be ready to go aboard. No personal baggage."

When we embark for heaven we can take only our character. That is the righteous character of Jesus Christ, imputed to us in forgiveness (justification) and imparted to us through the Holy Spirit and the Word of God in sanctification.

SECTION TEN

GOD SPEAKS CONCERNING THE PROPHECIES OF REVELATION

The Drama of the Dragon and the Woman

The Mysterious Number 666

The Divine Forecast of America

The Mark of the Beast

God's Last Warning Message to the World

The Seven Last Plagues

The Battle of Armageddon

Living a Thousand Years! When? Where?

Where Will the Righteous Spend Eternity?

Russ Harlan, Ar

The book of Revelation vividly portrays a religio-political power as a richly ador
woman riding on a seven-headed beast, which will endeavor to dominate the ea

CHAPTER 51

The Drama of the Dragon and the Woman

BASED ON REVELATION 12

MORE PEOPLE are interested in drama than in abstract theology and philosophy. An actor said that he spoke lines that were not true as if they were true, but preachers often speak words of truth as though they were not true.

The Bible dramatizes and symbolizes in order to create interest and deliver a sharper effect.

To understand this study more clearly, you would do well to read the entire twelfth chapter of Revelation. In vision John saw a woman in the sky, standing on the moon, clothed with the sun, and having a crown of twelve stars upon her head. She was in the travail of childbirth.

Before her stood a great red dragon with seven heads, seven crowns, and ten horns. His tail drew a third of the stars. He waited in readiness to devour the babe as soon as it was born. But the child, which was a boy destined someday to rule all nations, was later caught up to God on His throne.

Then the woman fled into the wilderness for many years. The dragon persecuted her. He sought to overwhelm her. But God kept watch, and angels maintained a ceaseless vigil through that long period of tribulation.

The dark night of persecution ended. The morning of freedom came. The torch of liberty was lighted. For a season men were free.

Then comes the final scene. The spiritual descendants of the woman appear. They are called the "remnant of her seed." Faithful to the "testimony of Jesus," they "keep the commandments of God." The dragon that had been wroth with the woman now goes forth in final fury "to make war" on God's remnant, commandment-keeping people.

Let us examine in more detail this vital and interesting drama, for we live in the time of the last act.

Act 1—The Woman, the Dragon, and the Child

Who was this woman? What did she symbolize? In Bible language a symbolic woman stands for a church.

A corrupt woman indicates a corrupt church. For instance, the harlot Aholibah stood for backslidden Jerusalem, center of Jewish worship in the days of Ezekiel the prophet. (Ezekiel 23:1-4.) John the revelator foresaw a highly bedecked harlot sitting on the back of a scarlet beast. He thus depicted corrupt religion riding high in worldly affairs. (Revelation 17:3-6, 15, 16.)

In contrast, a pure woman represents a pure church, God's church, Christ's church. Paul wrote, "I have espoused you to one husband, that I may present you as a chaste virgin to Christ." 2 Corinthians 11:2. This agrees with the same comparison as beautifully represented by Jeremiah of old, "I have likened the daughter of Zion [the church] to a comely and delicate woman." Jeremiah 6:2. In Hosea 2:19 we read, "I will betroth thee unto me for ever." Again we read in Isaiah 62:5, "As the bridegroom rejoiceth over the bride, so shall thy God rejoice over thee."

The sun that clothed the woman aptly represents the glory of the New Testament church, the moon the lesser glory, the reflected light of the Old Testament. The twelve stars suggest the twelve tribes of Israel and the twelve apostles.

The Old Testament days had their glory of types and shadows and the glory of the majesty of law. This glory was as the shining of the moon. The ministration of love and grace and the Spirit of God, as more fully revealed in the New Testament, is like the shining of the sun. Justice is deep and abiding, but love and mercy are warm, kind, and gracious. Their rays bring life and light, and warm the heart with an overwhelming desire to do the will of God and keep His commandments.

That the man child born of the woman is Christ would seem to admit of no question. He was to rule with a rod of iron. Of Christ it is said in Revelation 2:27, "He shall rule them with a rod of iron." The Son of the woman was to be caught up to God and His throne. In Ephesians 4:8 Paul speaks of "when he [Christ] ascended up on high." And in Hebrews 8:1 is the following: "We have such an high priest, who is set on the right hand of the throne of the Majesty in the heavens."

The great red dragon is a symbol of pagan, or heathen, Rome. The red dragon had ten horns, as did the great and terrible beast of Daniel 7, which also represented pagan Rome. The dragon was a common symbol on old Roman ensigns.

Rome, under Augustus, brought Joseph and Mary to Bethlehem to register. (Luke 2:1-5.) Rome, through King Herod, sought to destroy Christ as a babe. (Matthew 2: 3-18.) Rome, under Pilate, put Christ to death. (Matthew 27:26.) The tomb of Jesus was sealed with a Roman seal. (Verse 66.) It was guarded by a Roman watch, or guard. (Verses 62-65.)

Satan is called the "great dragon" and "that old serpent" in Revelation 12:9. It is he who works through the "great red dragon." It seems beyond all controversy that the "great red dragon" is pagan, or heathen, Rome. This was the legally constituted power, which became the tool for the devouring of the man child. Of pagan Rome we read in Daniel 8:25, "He shall also stand up against the Prince of princes." As a general rule, we find the nations of earth brought to view in the Bible when they have some connection with God's work and people.

The tail drawing the third part of the stars of heaven would aptly fit the picture of the Jewish nation and its relation to the Roman power. Judea became a Roman province in 63 B.C. Leading prophetic commentators point out that the Jews had three classes of rulers. These were kings, priests, and the Sanhedrin. One third of these, or the kings, were shorn of their real power.

In Isaiah 7:16 we read, "Before the child shall know to refuse the evil, and choose the good, the land that thou abhorrest shall be forsaken of both her kings."

It is said that when Herod died he made two wills—the first making Herod Antipas his successor and the second naming Archelaus. The people preferred Archelaus, but later revolted. Thereupon, Antipas and Archelaus went to Rome for Caesar's decision. Neither appointment was confirmed. Archelaus was given the title of ethnarch, with promise of the crown later. He never received the crown. So the land was "forsaken of both her kings."

The conflict between the church and the powers of the earth is really the conflict between Christ and Satan. This is presented in Revelation 12:7-10. Satan is here called the "great dragon . . . , that old serpent, called the Devil." Michael is Christ. (See Jude 9; 1 Thessalonians 4:16; John 5:28.) "And there was war in heaven: Michael and his angels fought against the dragon; and the dragon fought and his angels. . . . He [the dragon] was cast out into the earth, and his angels were cast out with him." Revelation 12:7-9.

W. A. Spicer writes, "This picture of the original conflict in heaven is evidently thrown in here to show the animus of Satan in his warfare against the man child, the Son of man. They had met before. Jesus was not only Son of man, but He was the eternal Son of God. As Commander of heaven's hosts He had expelled Satan and the rebellious angels from heaven." This would be considered the first casting down of Satan.

When Christ came to earth Satan assaulted Him again. He sought to have Him slain as a babe. He tried in vain to conquer Him in the wilderness of temptation. He trailed the Saviour day and night, seeking to lead Him to sin against God's law or to give up His plan of saving man. Satan rested not until Jesus was nailed fast to the cross. Here Satan was again cast down.

"The cross of Calvary, while it declares the law immutable, proclaims to the universe that the wages of sin is death. In the Saviour's expiring cry, 'It is finished,' the death-knell of Satan was rung. The great controversy which had been so long in progress was then decided, and the final eradiction of evil was made certain. The Son of God passed through the portals of the tomb, that 'through death He might destroy him that had the power of death, that is, the devil.'"—*The Great Controversy,* p. 503.

With this victory of Calvary in mind John wrote, "Now is come salvation, and strength, and the kingdom of our God, and the power of his Christ: for the accuser of our brethren is cast down." Revelation 12:10. Thus does it seem reasonable to speak of this as a second step in the casting down of Satan. Jesus humbled Himself to the death of the cross, but was then exalted "far above all principality, and power, and might, and dominion, and every name that is named." Ephesians 1:21. Satan sought to exalt himself and was cast down.

At the end of the millennium Satan will be cast down for the third and last time.

Act 2—Satan's Fury Against the Early Church

Satan, having failed to defeat Christ, sensed anew that both God and time were against him. "He knoweth that he hath but a short time." Some four thousand years of battle lay behind him, with only some two thousand years ahead, and every passing year brought him nearer to the day of awful retribution.

In fury Satan turned upon the followers of Jesus. The apostles drank of the cup of sacrifice and martyrdom as Jesus had predicted. Paganism, Satan's carefully constructed system of error, was now headed by the pagan Roman power, the great red dragon. Under the emperors Nero, Domitian, Trajan, Marcus Aurelius, Septimius Severus, Maximinus, Decius, Valerian, Aurelian, and Diocletian the early church suffered the tortures of persecution and the pangs of cruel death. Multitudes sealed their testimony with their own blood, "and they loved not their lives unto the death." Not the least of these was the great apostle Paul, who early died a martyr's death outside the walls of Rome.

Act 3—Persecuting the Woman in the Wilderness

"The woman fled into the wilderness, where she hath a place prepared of God, that they should feed her there a thousand two hundred and threescore days." Revelation 12:6.

A day stands for a year in Bible prophecy. (Numbers 14:34; Ezekiel 4:6.) The 1260 days previously mentioned symbolize 1260 years, a day for a year. A comparison of Revelation 12:6 with verse 14 indicates that the 1260 years are the same as a "time, and times, and half a time."

Thus we rightly conclude that this 1260-year persecution is the same as that which the "little horn" of Daniel 7:25 inflicted upon the "saints of the most High," for a "time and times and the dividing of time." This is the period of papal persecution—the 1260 years from A.D. 538 to A.D. 1798. This was made clear in the section on the prophecies of Daniel.

Satan was somewhat successful in his assault on the early church. Persecution is not easy to endure, and popularity is often preferred. The church began to take on the color and complexion of heathen Rome's religion.

Out of this mixture of Judaism, Christianity, and paganism came the Papacy, or papal Rome. Satan, having filled the church itself with error, brought about the exaltation of the "man of sin" to rule over even the kings and princes. The long, dismal night of the Dark Ages came and dragged on for century after century. The noonday of the Papacy was indeed the midnight of the world.

We shall refrain from discussing the horrors of the torture and death of its millions of victims. On the illustrious roster of martyrs are such names as Huss, Jerome, Latimer, Cranmer, Tyndale, and many others. The great Wycliffe justly should be placed with them. Only the account of heaven can ever number them all or adequately portray their exquisite tortures and sufferings. To Heaven must be left the final accounting yet to be made in terms of vengeance.

The earth helped the woman. She fled into the wilderness. In the mountain fastnesses, the Alpine retreats, and the Piedmont valleys the faithful of God sought refuge.

Act 4—War on the Remnant

Satan persecuted Jesus Christ through pagan Rome. Then he persecuted the early church through pagan Rome. Next he persecuted the faithful through papal Rome. Finally, he makes war upon the remnant church. Said

Jesus, "He was a murderer from the beginning." John 8:44.

The Protestant Reformation stirred the wrath of Satan deeply, but as time has gone by apostasy has been making its inroads into this great movement. Moreover, the Reformation was unable to eradicate all the errors of the papal system. The change in God's law was not remedied.

God has set His hand to gather His remnant people. As the remnant of cloth is the last piece from the bolt, so the remnant church is the church of the last days. This church will keep God's commandments—all of them.

Satan, knowing that his time now is truly short, is stirred to "make war with the remnant of her seed, which keep the commandments of God, and have the testimony of Jesus Christ." Revelation 12:17. Yet "the Lord knoweth them that are his." 2 Timothy 2:19. And "the Lord knoweth how to deliver the godly out of temptations." 2 Peter 2:9.

There was a sincere woman who after careful study decided to walk in the way of all God's commandments. She began to attend church. Satan, not pleased to see anyone obey God's law, stirred up her erstwhile kind husband to say many mean, ugly things to her, calling her fanatical and foolish, and accusing her of bringing reproach upon him. From time to time he tried in vain to turn her from God's way.

Finally he threatened to break their marital relations completely. We recall that Jesus said, "A man's foes shall be they of his own household." Matthew 10:36. Satan, of course, was as happy as a devil can be. Said the man to his wife, "If you go to church another time, you will find your suitcase on the front steps when you return home, the door will be locked, and you may go forever."

Howbeit, the woman with Bible in hand went to church. It was with some misgivings that she returned home. Sure enough, there it was—the suitcase on the steps.

She tried the door. It was locked. What should she do? Was obedience to God worth such a grave risk and consequence?

She slowly turned, picked up her suitcase, and descended the steps. There was a sound of an opening door, and the husband emerged, hastening down the steps toward his vanishing wife. He had no difficulty in persuading her to return, for he said to her, "I decided that a woman who would risk her home to obey God was too good to lose." We think so too!

In the agelong conflict between Christ and Satan we are all involved. Each one is, beyond all doubt, on one side or the other. "He that is not with me is against me." Matthew 12:30.

There are Captain Christ and Captain Satan. There are Mount Calvary and Mount Sin. There are the church of Christ and the synagogue of Satan. There are right and wrong, life and death, heaven and hell. "Choose you this day whom ye will serve." Joshua 24:15.

Tom M. Olson reports in *Now* how a druggist filled a prescription for barium sulphate with barium sulphite—just one letter different. The woman who took the medicine died.

There is just one letter different in *Son* and *sin.* Choose the Son, and you choose life. Choose sin, and you choose death. "Therefore choose life, that both thou and thy seed may live." Deuteronomy 30:19.

"Not for weight of glory,
Not for crown and palm,
Enter we the army,
Raise the warrior psalm;
But for love that claimeth
Lives for whom He died;
He whom Jesus nameth,
Must be on His side."

—F. R. HAVERGAL.

CHAPTER 52

The Mysterious Number 666

READ REVELATION 13

ARITHMETIC MAY be said to begin with addition. Subtraction is addition in reverse. It really is a form of addition. Multiplication is but a short-cut method of adding. Division is a combination of multiplication and subtraction.

All learning proceeds from the simple to the complex, with considerable repeating. Bible truth is the same. "But the word of the Lord was unto them precept upon precept, precept upon precept; line upon line, line upon line; here a little, and there a little." Isaiah 28:13. Especially is this true of Bible prophecy.

In Daniel 2 is presented the great image, representing human history from Babylon (600 B.C.) through Medo-Persia, Grecia, Rome, and her breakup into ten main kingdoms, to the second coming of Christ and the setting up of God's kingdom of glory on earth.

In Daniel 7 the same period is embraced by the four great beasts: the lion, bear, leopard, and the dreadful beast. The great and dreadful beast stood for Rome and had ten horns for the ten divisions. Another "little horn" came up among the ten. This was the papal power, standing in supremacy for 1260 years from A.D. 538 to A.D. 1798. It spoke words against God, made war on the saints of God, and thought to change the law of God. This chapter also brings to view the judgment day, Christ's coming, and the rise of His kingdom.

The eighth and ninth chapters present again Medo-Persia and Grecia, and establish the date A.D. 1844 as the time for the beginning of the cleansing of the sanctuary. This is the work of the investigative judgment in heaven.

The Compound Leopard Beast

In Revelation 13 we have a beast composed of parts of the three former beasts of Daniel 7. It is sometimes called the composite beast. Coming up out of the sea, it had seven heads and ten crowned horns. It looked like a leopard with a bear's feet and a lion's mouth. "The dragon [pagan Rome] gave him his power, and his seat, and great authority." Revelation 13:2.

This compound beast would partake of the nature of the lion (Babylon), the bear (Medo-Persia), and the leopard (Grecia), and was to take over the reins of power following the dragon of pagan Rome.

Concerning the composite nature of the beast, we quote from *Beacon Lights of Prophecy,* pages 279, 280: "History traces the passage of the old Babylonian system of religion straight on through Medo-Persia to Grecia, and from Grecia into Rome, to leaven the religious life of the [pagan] Roman Empire. This, in turn, leavened the great apostasy in Christendom that grew into the Roman Papacy. The Papacy was the heir of the superstitions and false philosophies of all the ages, from Babylon down."

Since, in Daniel 7, the little horn papal power followed the terrible beast power of pagan Rome, it is not surprising to find this composite papal beast of Revelation 13 following the dragon power of pagan Rome.

Concerning the shift from papan to papal power, James H. Conry writes: "Long ages ago, when Rome through the neglect of the Western emperors was left to the mercy of barbarous hordes, Romans turned to one figure for aid and protection and asked him to rule them; and thus . . . commenced the temporal sovereignty of the Popes. And meekly stepping to the throne of Caesar, the Vicar of Christ took up the sceptre to which the emperors and kings of Europe were to bow in reverence through so many ages."—"Two Romes," *The American Catholic Quarterly Review,* April 11, 1911, p. 194. Thus the Papacy took over the seat of pagan Rome. The word "seat" means the "seat of government." The word "see" used in "Holy See" means the same. There the Pope sits today in the city of Rome, the seat of the ancient pagan empire. Pagan Rome gave papal Rome its seat, or see.

"And all the world wondered after the beast." Revelation 13:3. The Papacy is a world power.

This leopard beast had "a mouth speaking great things and blasphemies." Verse 5. By claiming to be the vicar of Christ on earth, he "sitteth in the temple of God, shewing himself that he is God." 2 Thessalonians 2:4. This is the very same power as the "little horn" of Daniel 7:8, 25, which had "a mouth speaking great things" "against the most High."

This power was "to continue forty and two months." Revelation 13:5. This is the same as 1260 days, or years, of the "little horn" power in Daniel 7.

It was to "make war with the saints" just as the little horn. (Revelation 13:7.)

Its power was to be broken. "He that leadeth into captivity shall go into captivity." Verse 10. One head was to be "wounded to death." Verse 3. This took place in 1798 (end of the 1260 years), when the French general Berthier took Pope Pius VI prisoner, and hastened him as a captive from prison to prison. He died in the French fortress of Valence eighteen months later.

In 1870 the Papacy head received another blow, when

Russ Harlan, Artist

v is the day of salvation. There may never be a tomorrow. When the sands of time run out, earth's history closes—eternity begins.

Harry Anderse

"I saw another angel fly . . . , having the everlasting gospel . . . , saying with a lo
voice, Fear God, . . . for the hour of his judgment is come." Revelation 14:6,

Rome was seized by Italy as its capital. The Pope became a voluntary prisoner of the Vatican. Hence in 1798 and 1870 he who had sent others into captivity went himself into captivity.

But the deadly wound was to be healed. In 1929 the Italian Government recognized the Vatican City as an independent state. The pope was again king. On March 9, 1929, the pope said, "The peoples of the entire world are with us." Today the Papacy is coming back into great power. In *The Modern Papacy* (edited by Joseph Rickaby, S.J.), page 1, we read, "Yet since then [A.D. 1798], the Papacy has been lifted to a pinnacle of spiritual power unreached, it may be, since earliest Christian history."—In *Lectures on the History of Religions,* vol. 3, lecture 24.

It is clearly evident that this beast power is the Papacy, or "little horn" power of Daniel 7. But one additional point of identification is given. "Here is wisdom. Let him that hath understanding count the number of the beast: for it is the number of a man; and his number is Six hundred threescore and six." Revelation 13:18.

The beast has a number—the number of a man's name. (Verse 17.) The man would naturally be the head of the Papacy, or the pope. A leading title for the pope is Vicar of the Son of God. In Latin this is *Vicarius Filii Dei.* Adding up the numeral letters in this title we have: *V*—5, *I*—1, *C*—100 (*A* and *R* no value), *I*—1, *V* (U)—5 (*S* and *F* no value), *I*—1, *L*—50, *I*—1, *I*—1, *D*—500 (*E* no value), *I*—1. This totals 666, the number the Bible gives for the beast. This follows the ancient custom of a person's having a name and a number also.

The Douay Bible (Catholic) gives this note on Revelation 13:18: "Six hundred sixty-six. The numeral letters of his name shall make up this number."

We would throw in this caution. The beast is not identified merely by the number 666. This is but one point in many. Other names will work out to the number 666, but this does not prove those persons to be the beast. The beast was in supremacy 1260 years and did many things which identify the Papacy, and the Papacy only, as the leopard beast of Revelation 13. The number 666 is just another point in favor of a position already proved.

The Image of the Beast

In concluding this chapter it may be well to take a brief look at the prophecy concerning an "image of the beast." "He had power to give life unto the image of the beast, that the image of the beast should both speak, and cause that as many as would not worship the image of the beast should be killed." Verse 15.

The leopard beast is the papal power. The Papacy was a religious power dominating the state, to the end that its own plans might be forwarded by civil laws and government influence. An image to the beast would be another religious force doing the same thing. Protestantism today is organizing its forces to play a conspicuous role in political, social, economic, and religious matters. Shall we develop a Protestant image of the Papacy? Shall church law be enforced by civil power? Shall union of church and state replace America's historic separation of church and state? Shall religious freedom continue to live, or shall it perish from the face of the whole earth? Shall we pay lip service to the rights of minorities while we sacrifice more rights upon the altar of the image to the beast?

Someone said to a boy, "You are the very image of your father." The boy was not his father. He was not exactly like his father, but there was a strong resemblance.

A Protestant federation of churches, seeking to save society by social reforms, and by enforcing religious dogma with civil law, surely would have strong resemblance to the Papacy. It would be the very image of its father.

CHAPTER 53

The Divine Forecast of America

GOVERNOR POWELL, English statesman of 1780, in speaking of America, said that "this country would become independent, and that a civilizing activity beyond what Europe could produce would animate it; and that its commercial and naval power would be found in every quarter of the globe." Then he refers to this experience as "a revolution that has stronger marks of divine interposition superseding the ordinary course of human affairs, than any other event which this world experienced."

That statement was made more than 150 years ago. What is the picture today?

General George Marshall is quoted in *Time,* March 29, 1948, "No nation in modern history has ever occupied a position of responsibility comparable to that of this country . . . thrust upon it in so short a time."

David L. Cohn, author, says: "America today is in a position of unparalleled physical, if not spiritual eminence. No other nation in all the history of the world has so towered over the other nations like a colossus."—*Quote,* April 11, 1948.

Hans Bendix, Danish commentator, was quoted in the *Reader's Digest,* of February, 1946: " 'The United States is the power house of civilization. . . . America is a battery from which radiate electric shocks.' "

History gives no record of a nation with such great

 Arlo Greer, A

The purpose of Bible prophecy is to warn God's people of coming world events.
United States is to play an important part in the closing scenes of earth's his

power yet with such little desire to use that power for selfish ends.

"Two thousand years ago, when Western civilization was bounded by the laws and legions of the Roman Empire, the proudest words a man could utter were: 'I am a citizen of Rome.' A century ago, when the world was girdled by the British Empire, the Englishman's voice sounded from the earth's far corners: 'I am a British subject.' Now in the middle of the 20th Century, the most arresting tones of history said something else: 'I am an American.'"—*Time,* May 10, 1948. Courtesy of *Time,* copyright Time Inc., 1948. In every corner of the world the Stars and Stripes wave as a banner, "not of conquerors, but of a people adventurous in brotherhood."

When Nations Are Brought to Light in the Bible

Nations are brought to view in the Bible for two main reasons.

One is to reveal the hand of God in history and prophecy, and verify the reliability of both. "The word of our God shall stand for ever." Isaiah 40:8. "I am God, and there is none like me, declaring the end from the beginning . . . : I have spoken it, I will also bring it to pass." Isaiah 46:9-11.

The other reason for national mention is contact with God's people, church, and work. Egypt fed Israel in famine, enslaved her in bondage, and later made war and alliances with her. Assyria battled her, captured her, released her, and made affinity with her. Babylon destroyed her city and Temple and took her captive. Medo-Persia gave her freedom and assisted in her recuperation. Greece furnished a universal language for the gospel. Rome subjected the Jews, crucified Christ, destroyed Jerusalem, and persecuted Christians. Papal Rome adulterated the gospel, persecuted the church, and ruled over the nations through union of church and state. The main national divisions of the old Roman Empire exist as the modern nations of Europe, all in direct contact with organized, professed Christianity. All these nations figure in Bible history or prophecy.

The United States in Prophecy

On a basis of world importance, and as a base from which the gospel is going to all the world, it would surely seem that the United States should be found in Bible prophecy. In fact, consistency would practically demand it.

We believe that America is depicted in prophecy. It is found in the same portion of prophecy we discussed in our previous chapter—Revelation 13. Immediately after verse 10, which pictures the temporary break of papal power in 1798 at the end of the 1260 years, we read these words: "I beheld another beast coming up out of the earth; and he had two horns like a lamb, and he spake as a dragon." Revelation 13:11. In order to get the clearest and most comprehensive understanding of this topic, ten points will be listed and briefly discussed.

1. *The Time of America's Rise.*—As previously indicated, this new power, symbolized as a beast with two lamblike horns, would be coming into power as the Papacy was declining in power. So it was. The pope was taken into captivity in 1798, shortly after George Washington finished his tenure as the first president of the United States. It is recorded that from 1817 to 1867, twenty-one governments disappeared, and only three new ones arose. The United States added nearly two million square miles of territory, and eight hundred thousand more than all other nations combined.

John Wesley, in his *Explanatory Notes Upon the New Testament,* written just twenty-two years before the

American Declaration of Independence, said concerning this two-horned beast power, "He is not yet come: tho' he cannot be far off. For he is to appear at the End of the forty-two Months of the first Beast." That is, near the end of the 1260-year supremacy of the papal leopard beast of this same chapter of Revelation (1798). How right Wesley was!

2. *The Age of the Power.*—"He had two horns like a lamb." A lamb is young. This power was not to be an old nation in a sudden burst of new life. It was to be young in 1798. It was.

3. *The Place of Its Rise.*—This power was seen "coming up out of the earth."

The composite, leopard, papal beast power was seen to "rise up out of the sea." This indicates the appearance of a power among multitudes of people. (Revelation 17: 15.)

But the two-horned beast came up out of the earth. This suggests a thinly populated area, removed from the old centers of habitation.

Comparing the United States with other regimes which European governments had sought to establish in America, George Alfred Townsend wrote, "The history of the United States was separated by the beneficent Providence far from this wild and cruel history of the rest of the continent."—*The New World Compared With the Old,* p. 635.

In the same century that Gutenberg produced the first printed Bible and Martin Luther was born, the daring Columbus set sail into the unknown and reached the Americas. God was laying the groundwork for the rise of a free nation for a free Protestantism with its free gospel for all the world.

For this work He chose a new land—truly the good earth. When the date 1798 came there was the new nation.

When Americans declared independence, there were only three million of them, but before them lay a potential continental area of three million square miles, or 640 acres (a full section, a square mile), for every person—man, woman, and child. Truly this nation came up out of the "earth."

4. *The Manner of Its Rise.*—John saw the two-horned beast "coming up" out of the earth. This phrase, "coming up," is from the original Greek word *anabainon,* one meaning of which is "to grow or spring up as a plant." Townsend aptly puts it, "Like a silent seed, we grew into empire."—*Ibid.*

A writer in the Dublin *Nation* depicted the United States as "emerging," and "amid the silence of the earth daily adding to its power." In Edward Everett's oration at Plymouth, Massachusetts, on the English exiles who fled to America for religious freedom, he spoke of their "peaceful conquest." So America came into power after the exact manner suggested by the Scriptures.

5. *Character of the Government.*—John said this power would have "two horns like a lamb." This would indicate a minimum of warlike spirit or disposition to conquer other nations. Since horns in prophecy stand for power, the lamblike horns suggest the basic character of American government. The Honorable J. A. Bingham presented the purpose of our forebears to be that of establishing "what the world has not seen for ages; viz., a church without a pope, and a state without a king."

In other words, our fathers sought civil and religious freedom. They wanted a government of their own choosing and the religion of their own choice. In the course of time they discovered that the only way they could have both of those inestimable blessings was to keep church and state separate. Church and state joined together produced oppression in America as elsewhere. Kept separate, the state was free and progressive, and the church was free and open to advancing light.

Article IV, section 4, of the Constitution says, "The United States shall guarantee every state in this union a Republican form of government." That means representative government—democracy.

Since every person has a right to choose his own religion without the price of discrimination, Article VI reads, "No religious test shall ever be required as a qualification to any office or public trust under the United States." Thus a citizen was free to profess any religion or no religion.

Then, in order to guard the future yet more securely, certain amendments were added. These are known as the Bill of Rights. The first of these vital amendments reads, "Congress shall make no law respecting an establishment of religion, or prohibiting the free exercise thereof."

These men lived with lingering memory of persecution in Europe. They had an acute memory and actual observation of the human tendency to civil and religious tyranny right in America. As the one and only remedy they took the civil power and the church, or religious power, and purposed forever to separate them. The lamb had two horns. They were separate.

Then our fathers placed in the Constitution certain specific limitations on the power of the majority to invade the inalienable, God-given rights of the minority. The masses must not tyrannize over one solitary man. Men were at long last free to think for themselves, learn for themselves, labor for themselves, bless God, and pray for themselves, just as long as they did not violate the equal rights of others. This is America, symbolized by a beast with two lamblike horns—civil and religious freedom, separation of church and state, and freedom of speech, press, and peaceable assembly.

The horns of this power had no crowns. It was not a

land of kings or popes. Since the Catholic Church fundamentally believes in union of church and state, and that the individual is not free either to believe or to publicly advocate his own independent religious ideas, this nation was not to be dominantly Catholic. The religious thought of America has been and is preponderantly Protestant.

6. *Great Wonders.*—"He doeth great wonders." Revelation 13:13. Surely America is the land of endless wonder; a land of science, invention, and mass production; a world of learning, healing, speed, and glamour unsurpassed.

But there were to be wonders in the religious realm. Fire would be brought down from heaven as a miracle to deceive men in spiritual things. Here false christs and prophets will yet perform astonishing things, as Christ foretold. (Matthew 24:24.) That some of this will come through the channel of Spiritism is clear. (1 Timothy 4:1; Revelation 16:13, 14.)

7. *An Image to the Beast.*—In this land of basic Protestant faith, an image of the composite, leopard, papal beast is to be set up. Our historic principle of separation of church and state is to be violated. Men are already crying that America is too secular, and they think the remedy is church federation and activity in social and state matters. The church, failing to save the people in the pews, would devise salvation in political halls.

America is represented as "saying to them that dwell on the earth, that they should make an image to the beast, which had the wound by a sword, and did live." Revelation 13:14. Forsaking the freedoms that finally came as a fruitage of the Protestant Reformation in America, men turn to the security and power of totalitarian religion. Churchmen say Protestantism is weak because it is divided, and Catholicism is strong because it is united. So the tide of ecumenical, federated Protestantism is rolling. When churches select a few tenets of faith upon which all may unite, and when they gain power to define and enforce their dogmas, we will have an image to the beast. Dominant Protestant religion in America will resemble the Papacy in purpose and work.

8. *The Voice of the Dragon.*—"He spake as a dragon. And he exerciseth all the power of the first beast before him [the papal leopard beast]. . . . And he had power to give life unto the image of the beast, that the image of the beast should both speak, and cause that as many as would not worship the image of the beast should be killed." Verses 11-15.

Note the three things here revealed:

First, the voice of the dragon is to be heard in America. That is the voice of persecution. Satan persecuted through pagan Rome, then through papal Rome, and finally he will bring persecution in our own nation.

Second, the same kind of power the leopard beast manifested is to be exercised. That means religious dogma enforced by civil law. The policeman's power supplements the preacher's persuasion.

Third, the government is to have power to give "life" to the image of the beast. Only when religionists can lead government to enact legislation to support their plans can the image live. When that legislation is secured, and to the extent it is made effective, we shall have the living image of the beast, the practical union of church and state. So vigorous is this image to become that "as many as would not worship the image of the beast should be killed."

9. *Wide Influence.*—In the nature of things this matter cannot be hidden. This power says "to them that dwell on the earth, that they should make an image to the beast." Verse 14. That direct power would be exercised in this nation that came up out of the earth is evident. That the influence will be worldwide seems clear. America is not

merely a world power but in a large sense the one world power, especially when it comes to those nations whose people hold belief in Christianity.

The gigantic world contest of contrary ideologies opens the door of temptation to swift church federation plus union of church and state in principle. Communism may destroy religious freedom within its own domain, and yet frighten other nations into totalitarian regimentation both in civil and in religious matters.

Society and the state are being considered more and more important and the individual less and less significant. Unity means more, conscience less. All this while freedom and democracy are words bandied all about the world as of prime importance. Well may freedom say in altogether too many nations and groups, "This people draweth nigh unto me with their mouth, and honoureth me with their lips; but their heart is far from me." Matthew 15:8.

In these momentous times what will America do with her world leadership and opportunity? Shall we continue in the path of freedom, or shall a kind of totalitarian religion join hands with the state to deny liberty to minorities? Bible prophecy predicts the latter.

10. *Enforcing Worship and Mark of Beast.*—The last point of the ten is that worship of the leopardlike beast and acceptance of its mark will be enforced in America. How in a Protestant America could worship of the Papacy be brought about? How could the mark of papal power be enforced in this land? What does worship of the beast involve? What is its mark? These things will be considered in the following chapter.

The question is raised: Does our country have to do these things just because the prophet predicted it? Not at all. Jonah the prophet proclaimed through the streets of Nineveh, capital city of Assyria, "Yet forty days, and Nineveh shall be overthrown." Jonah 3:4. The prophet spoke the message that God told him to speak. Was Nineveh destroyed at the end of forty days? No. How then is this explained? Simply by this. God's judgments, as well as His promises, are conditional. Nineveh's king led out in a city-wide repentance, and the judgment of God was avoided.

If in America we lose our God-given freedoms, it will be our fault, not God's. It was while men slept that the devil sowed tares. If we do not awake and remain awake, freedom will die in America as it has died or is dying elsewhere. "Eternal vigilance is the price of liberty." Political power and religious authority possessed by men tend quickly to take possession of them. Only the people can preserve their own freedoms. If we value anything more than our freedom to worship and serve God, we will lose both our freedom and our souls.

CHAPTER 54

The Mark of the Beast

"HE CAUSETH all, both small and great, rich and poor, free and bond, to receive a mark in their right hand, or in their foreheads: and that no man might buy or sell, save he that had the mark, or the name of the beast, or the number of his name." Revelation 13:16, 17.

Here the two-horned beast power, or the United States, enforces under civil penalty the mark of the leopardlike beast, or papal power. So stringent will the law be that one cannot buy or sell unless he accepts the papal mark.

God's Sign or Mark

We have already learned that God has a sign of His power and authority. That sign is the seventh-day Sabbath. (Exodus 31:14-17.) It was made at the close of creation week. It was based on the unchangeable facts of God's creation and rest. He created six days, and made the Sabbath on the seventh day by resting upon it, blessing it, and sanctifying it for man's use. "The sabbath was made for man." Mark 2:27.

This seventh-day Sabbath was placed in the very heart of the Ten Commandments as a sign or seal.

The fourth commandment is the only one which identifies the Giver of the law, the source of authority, and the extent of the law's application. The Law-giver's name is "the Lord thy God." His title is Creator, or Maker of heaven and earth. His territory or dominion is "heaven and earth." (Exodus 20:10, 11.)

God's law is to be sealed among His disciples. (Isaiah 8:16.) The law of God is to be in our hearts, and God wants to place His seal there.

The Predicted Change of God's Sign

Of the papal power we read, "He shall think . . . to change times and laws." Daniel 7:25.

In other words, this power, "shewing himself that he is God" (2 Thessalonians 2:4), would think himself able to change the fundamental, constitutional law of God. He would go so far as to change the seal of that law, the time element, the sign and mark of God's power and authority.

Admission of the Change

God gave us His seal, the Sabbath. He predicted the attempted change. What does the Papacy say? The Papacy claims the deed was hers, and one writer says it is a mark of papal power. Note these Catholic statements:

"Q. *Have you any other way of proving that the Church has power to institute festivals of precept?*

"*A.* Had she not had such power, she could not have done that in which all modern religionists agree with her; —she could not have substituted the observance of Sunday the first day of the week, for the observance of Saturday the seventh day, a change for which there is no Scriptural authority."—Rev. Stephen Keenan, *A Doctrinal Catechism,* p. 174.

From the office of Cardinal Gibbons, through Chancellor C. F. Thomas, came this statement: "'Of course the Catholic Church claims that the change was her act, . . . and the act is a *mark of her ecclesiastical power.*'" (Italics ours.)

Thus God's sign, or mark, or seal, was taken out of the law and the Sunday institution put in its place. How natural for this act to be set forth as a sign, or mark, of the papal authority.

The Papal Mark to Become Law

Through the prophet Daniel, God predicted the attempted change of the Sabbath. Then through the pen of John the revelator He forecast the exaltation of the papal mark by civil government. Sundaykeeping would be enforced by the power of civil law in America.

"No man might buy or sell, save he that had the mark, or the name of the beast, or the number of his name." Revelation 13:17.

That a commandment-keeping, Sabbathkeeping Christian would find himself in great difficulty goes without saying.

In the early history of this country Sunday blue laws were very rigid. Today most of the States in the Union have Sunday laws. There is perennial effort for a national Sunday law, or at least a law for the District of Columbia. This might bring quickly into action the State and city Sunday laws.

The Catholic power is for more emphasis on Sunday observance. An Associated Press dispatch from Vatican City, September 8, 1947, reporting the Pope's call for "action," said: "While a plane dropped thousands of leaflets bearing the Ten Commandments on the vast throng, the Pope, his voice transmitted over a series of loud speakers, declared that the battle in religious and moral fields hinged on five points:

"Religious culture, the *sanctifying of Sunday,* the saving of the Christian family, social justice and loyalty and truthfulness in dealings."—*The Evening Star* (Washington), Sept. 8, 1947, p. A 11. (Italics ours.)

Here then is the modern papal call for men to honor the day set apart, not by the command of God, but by the command of the church.

The Lord's Day Alliance and the International Reform Bureau have long labored for a national Sunday law. The Reform Bureau seeks to place our laws and Constitution on a religious basis, the laws of God to be the laws of the land. That means Sunday legislation.

Such things as this have been said: "Let those who will, remember the Sabbath [Sunday] to keep it holy, from motives of love and obedience; the remnant must be made to do so through fear of law. We have no option."—*The Christian Nation,* Sept. 28, 1887.

In *The Christian Statesman,* May 21, 1885, we read this: "We might add, in all justice, if the opponents of the Bible do not like our government and its Christian features, let them go to some wild, desolate land, and in the name of the devil, and for the sake of the devil, subdue it, and set up a government of their own on infidel and atheistic ideas; and then if they can stand it, stay there till they die."—REV. E. B. GRAHAM.

In calmer language but with greater force and import the Federal Council of the Churches of Christ in America set forth the following resolution at its first meeting: "That all encroachments upon the claims and the sanctities of the Lord's Day should *be stoutly resisted . . . by such legislation as may be secured to protect and preserve this bulwark of our American Christianity.*"

American religionists in general will place themselves squarely behind the Sunday sign, or mark, of papal power.

T. G. Wallace, canon of St. James (Westminster Church), London, Canada, wrote in *The Religious Digest,* November, 1942, "We say we shall observe one day a week as a day of rest and we agree on the first day of the week; then someone says 'no, we shall observe the seventh day';

. . . we can't do both as a community—it is a matter of convenience for the largest number, a matter of being able to act in common."

Now, as a matter of fact, it is God who commanded us to keep the seventh day. But men say, "We agree to keep the first day, the papal day. We must *all* do this." So turning away from God's law, they accept the papal law. And then they plead for a civil law, which would make a man a criminal against the community if he chooses to obey God by working six days and resting on the seventh-day Sabbath, Saturday.

How do you think God considers this? What would you do if you were in His place? And what do you propose to do in your situation? Will you obey God or man?

CHAPTER 55

God's Last Warning Message to the World

BASED ON REVELATION 14

THERE ARE probably more people living today who believe in the second coming of Christ than at any other time since Jesus made the promise: "I will come again."

Now that we believe in His coming we want to prepare for it. What message does God send for men today?

Said the prophet Amos, "Surely the Lord God will do nothing, but he revealeth his secret unto his servants the prophets." Amos 3:7. God sent a special message by Noah to the world of his day. (2 Peter 2:5.) He sent Moses to raise up the church in the wilderness. (Acts 7:37, 38.) He heralded a special message by the voice of John the Baptist, crying in the wilderness, and preparing the way for Christ's first coming. (Luke 1:17.) He gave His only-begotten Son to live and preach and die, and to found the New Testament church. Christ sent His followers into all the world with His gospel. Today, as we stand before the grand climax of the ages, the second coming of Christ, what special message does God send to us that we may be ready, and that the world may be without excuse? In Revelation 14 there are three worldwide messages to be given in our day.

To symbolize nations, God sometimes uses beasts, birds,

metals, and so forth. To represent a corrupt church, He presents a lewd woman; for the true church, a pure woman. In this chaper, to symbolize three special world messages, God uses three angels flying in the midst of heaven. Let us examine these messages.

Worldwide First Angel's Message

We have already learned that the investigative judgment is in session at the throne of God. We know that we live in a time of great and excessive wickedness, when men despair for civilization itself. What message would we expect? The very message of the first angel.

"I saw another angel fly in the midst of heaven, having the everlasting gospel to preach unto them that dwell on the earth, and to every nation, and kindred, and tongue, and people, saying with a loud voice, Fear God, and give glory to him; for the hour of his judgment is come: and worship him that made heaven, and earth, and the sea, and the fountains of waters." Revelation 14:6, 7.

The message has five characteristics.

1. *It is to go to every nation, kindred, tongue, and people.* It is not an offshoot of some denomination, but a mighty, invincible, worldwide movement, growing from a small beginning to envelop the earth—a movement organized for God's final work for fallen man.

2. *It calls men to "fear God."* Surely such a message is needed today, for the world has lost God from its thinking. Solomon wrote, "By the fear of the Lord men depart from evil." Proverbs 16:6. Thus God is calling men away from sin to righteousness, from transgression of His law to obedience. "Fear God, and keep his commandments." Ecclesiastes 12:13.

3. *It calls men to "give glory" to God.* We give glory to God when we "make confession unto him." (Joshua 7:19.) We give glory "for thy truth's sake." We withhold

glory when we do not thank Him for His blessings, as in the case of the lepers. (Luke 17:12-18.) Christ is "glorified in his saints." (2 Thessalonians 1:10.) His saints "keep the commandments of God, and the faith of Jesus." Revelation 14:12.

4. *It announces the hour of God's judgment.* This could not be done unless the time of the judgment were known. We discovered that the investigative judgment, symbolized by the cleansing of the sanctuary, began in 1844 at the end of the 2300-year period. "The hour of his judgment *is* come."

We are admonished to "fear God, and give glory to him; for the hour of his judgment is come." The judgment is a serious and solemn matter. The law of God is the standard, and Jesus Christ is our advocate. Surely it is high time that we accept the Saviour, and by His indwelling Spirit obey His law.

5. *It calls men to worship the Creator.* God is worthy of worship because He is the Creator. "Thou art worthy, O Lord, to receive glory and honour and power: for thou hast created all things." Revelation 4:11. The seventh-day Sabbath as taught in the fourth commandment is the sign of the Creator. "It is a sign . . . : for in six days the Lord made heaven and earth, and on the seventh day he rested, and was refreshed." Exodus 31:17. Since the Bible record of creation is today denied by many, and since God's Sabbath and sign of Creatorship has been set aside in the practice of mankind in general, it is vital that all men everywhere be called to worship the true God, and in doing so to accept the sign of His creative power, which is the Sabbath of the fourth commandment.

Again, since God's remnant people are distinguished as those who "keep the commandments of God," and since Jesus says, "In vain they do worship me, teaching for doctrines the commandments of men," a call to true worship and commandment keeping would demand a teaching of all God's commandments, with special emphasis on the fourth, which men have set aside.

WORLDWIDE SECOND ANGEL'S MESSAGE OF BABYLON'S FALL

"There followed another angel, saying, Babylon is fallen, is fallen, that great city, because she made all nations drink of the wine of the wrath of her fornication." Revelation 14:8.

There are seven points here to bear in mind.

1. *This is mystic Babylon, who persecuted the saints.* (Revelation 17:5, 6.) Babylon is called both a "great city," "which reigneth over the kings of the earth," and also a woman, "MOTHER OF HARLOTS." Revelation 14:8; 17:18, 5. Mystic Babylon is the Papacy, "drunken with the blood of the saints, and with the blood of the martyrs of Jesus." Revelation 17:6. In the Creed of Pope Pius IV we read, "I acknowledge the Holy, Catholic, Apostolic, Roman Church for the mother and mistress of all Churches."—JOSEPH FAA DI BRUNO, *Catholic Belief*, p. 253.

2. *She is the same power as the little horn of Daniel 7:25.* Like the little horn, she persecutes the saints and rules over the kings of the earth.

3. *She is the same as the leopard beast of Revelation 13.* We clearly saw that this beast is the same as the little horn of Daniel 7:25.

4. *Her false doctrines largely came from ancient Babylon.* The Church of Rome is called Babylon because its religion is a revival of the religion of ancient Babylon. Her priesthood, her dogma of the immaculate conception, and her denial that God in Christ dwelt in the same flesh as fallen man are relics of ancient Babylon. Both Babylons are alike in claiming universal spiritual jurisdiction and demanding submission under pains and penalties.

A careful examination of the ritual of ancient Babylon will reveal that the Papacy is largely an adaptation of this ancient pagan religion. It is not difficult to trace the connection between the two in the religious history of Rome.

"On the overthrow of Babylon by the Persians, who nourished a traditional hatred for its idolatry, the Chaldean priesthood fled to Pergamos in Asia Minor, and made it the headquarters of their religion. . . . The last Pontiff King of Pergamos was Attalus, III. who at his death bequeathed his dominions and authority to the Roman people, 133 B.C., and from that time the two lines of Pontifex Maximus were merged in the Roman one."—J. GARNIER, *The True Christ and the False Christ,* vol. 2, part II, *The False Christ,* pp. 94, 95. Thus did the religion of ancient Babylon become the religion of modern Babylon.

5. *All nations are made drunk with her wine.* Mystic Babylon holds a golden cup. (Revelation 17:4.) Ancient Babylon was likened to a golden cup. (Jeremiah 51:7.) "In 1825, on the occasion of the Jubilee, Pope Leo XII. struck a medal, bearing on the one side his own image, and on the other, that of the Church of Rome symbolised as a 'woman,' holding in her left hand a cross, and in her right a cup, with the legend around her, '*Sedet super universum* [the whole world is her seat].' "—ALEXANDER HISLOP, *The Two Babylons,* p. 6.

Multitudes have been drinking the wine of her false doctrines. When professed Protestant churches repudiate the fundamental principle of Protestantism by setting aside the authority of God's Word and accepting tradition and speculation and man-made laws, they adopt the principles of modern Babylon and may be regarded as the daughters of Babylon, deliberately choosing to drink of her cup.

6. *Practically all the world will wonder at her.* (Revelation 13:3.) The world stands in awe and wonderment at

the amazing revival of her power. This has been especially true since the independent sovereignty of Vatican City was recognized by Italy in 1929. (See *America,* January 4, 1930.) Said the Pope, "This moment, so historic, so important, that stands between the past and the future; which closes the past and opens the future."—*Codress,* June 27, 1929.

7. *She is scheduled for a final fall.* Though she says, "I sit a queen, and am no widow, and shall see no sorrow," yet God says, "Therefore shall her plagues come in one day, . . . for strong is the Lord God who judgeth her." Revelation 18:7, 8. Even the powers of the earth shall forsake her. (Revelation 17:16.)

The Fourfold Final Warning of the Third Angel

"The third angel followed them, saying with a loud voice, If any man worship the beast and his image, and receive his mark in his forehead, or in his hand, the same shall drink of the wine of the wrath of God, which is poured out without mixture into the cup of his indignation." Revelation 14:9, 10.

The warning of the third angel is given in a "loud voice," and there are four things in it to consider.

1. *It warns against the worship of the beast.* The first angel's message calls to "worship him that made heaven, and the earth." The third angel's message warns against the worship of the beast. There must be and is an essential difference. If we accept the teachings and commandments of the beast above God's Word and law, we worship the beast.

2. *It warns against worship of the image of the beast.* If we yield to the pressure of apostate Protestantism as it joins hands with civil power to enforce the mark of the beast, we cannot be judged as true worshipers of the Creator.

3. *It warns against receiving the mark of the beast.* In the last hours of the crisis the papal mark of Sunday-keeping will be enforced by civil law. God's warning is raised against this mark, and as He calls men to worship the Creator, the Sabbath-Sunday issue will be clearly drawn.

4. *It warns of God's wrath upon those who do not heed His warning.* Between the wrath of man and the wrath of God all must choose. Between obedience to man and obedience to God the decision must be made.

Would God not accept my worship, even though I choose under pressure to violate His Sabbath law and honor the papal Sunday? Let Jesus Himself answer: "In vain do they worship me, teaching for doctrines the commandments of men. . . . Full well ye reject the commandment of God, that ye may keep your own tradition." Mark 7:7, 9.

What do Catholics say? They say that Sundaykeeping Protestants "bow down" to the commands of the Papacy. Note the following:

Monsignor Louis Segur (Catholic), in *Plain Talk About the Protestantism of Today* (1868 ed.), page 213, writes, "The observance of *Sunday* by Protestants is an homage they pay, in spite of themselves, to the authority of the [Catholic] Church."

T. Enright, C.Ss.R. (a Catholic priest), in a letter dated Jan. 11, 1892, in *American Sentinel* (New York), June 1, 1893, page 173, said: "The Bible says, 'Remember that thou keep holy the Sabbath day.' The Catholic Church says: 'NO! By my divine power I abolish the Sabbath day, and command you to keep holy the first day of the week.' And, lo! the entire civilized world bows down in reverent obedience to the command of the holy Catholic Church."

How could we expect God to remain silent on such an issue as changing the only commandment that gives His sign and seal? God's wrath could not justly be visited upon men unless they had warning. So with the beginning of the judgment in 1844 the Sabbath truth began to go to the world. Around the circle of the earth and from north to south it is found today.

"The Sabbath will be the great test of loyalty; for it is the point of truth especially controverted. When the final test shall be brought to bear upon men, then the line of distinction will be drawn between those who serve God and those who serve Him not. While the observance of the false sabbath in compliance with the law of the state, contrary to the fourth commandment, will be an avowal of allegiance to a power that is in opposition to God, the keeping of the true Sabbath, in obedience to God's law, is an evidence of loyalty to the Creator. While one class, by accepting the sign of submission to earthly powers, receive the mark of the beast, the other, choosing the token of allegiance to divine authority, receive the seal of God."—*The Great Controversy,* p. 605.

God's Last Call

In connection with the three angels' messages God sends His final call to men. After special emphasis is placed on the fallen condition of modern Babylon, with her mixture of truth and error (Revelation 18:1-3), we read God's call: "I heard another voice from heaven, saying, Come out of her, my people, that ye be not partakers of her sins, and that ye receive not of her plagues. For her sins have reached unto heaven, and God hath remembered her iniquities." Verses 4, 5.

Note the following six things: 1. The voice is from heaven. 2. God has a people in the confusion of modern Babylon. 3. He is calling them to come out and be separate. 4. He does not wish His people to partake of the sins of Babylon. 5. He wishes them to avoid the plagues that are to fall on the apostate church and churches. 6.

Babylon's sins have reached unto heaven. Her cup of iniquity is full. Human probation is about to close.

A Commandment-keeping People

From the preaching of the three angels' messages in all the world, with the call, "Come out of her, my people," there is gathered God's last-day commandment-keeping church. They cling to the faith of Jesus and keep the commandments of God. They clasp to their hearts the cross of Christ and the law of God.

Here they are, in Revelation 14:12, in direct connection with these worldwide messages: "Here is the patience of the saints: here are they that keep the commandments of God, and the faith of Jesus."

It is clearly manifest that if we trust in Christ, and keep all the commandments of God, we will not receive the mark of the beast. As servants of God we will receive His seal. (Revelation 7:3.) We will have the Father's name written upon us. (Revelation 14:1.)

On the other hand, if we choose to obey man rather than God, we will be accounted as worshipers of the beast and his image, and will receive his mark.

The great issue will involve the world.

Making the Choice

If Moses were here, what would he do? He would choose "rather to suffer affliction with the people of God, . . . not fearing the wrath of the king." Hebrews 11:25-27.

What would Elijah do? He would say, "How long halt ye between two opinions? if the Lord be God, follow him: but if Baal, then follow him." 1 Kings 18:21.

What would Solomon say? "He that turneth away his ear from hearing the law, even his prayer shall be abomination." Proverbs 28:9.

What would Jesus say and do? "I have kept my

Father's commandments." "I do always those things that please him." "I have given you an example." "Whosoever will save his life shall lose it." John 15:10; 8:29; 13:15; Matthew 16:25.

What would Paul say? "Know ye not, that to whom ye yield yourselves servants to obey, his servants ye are to whom ye obey?" Romans 6:16. We will be marked as servants of men or sealed as servants of God.

What would Peter say? "Whether it be right in the sight of God to hearken unto you more than unto God, judge ye." "We ought to obey God rather than men." Acts 4:19; 5:29.

What would John the revelator say? "Blessed are they that do his commandments, that they may have right to the tree of life, and may enter in through the gates into the city." Revelation 22:14.

What shall we choose? Shall we choose the side of God and all the worthies of old and of His commandment-keeping people today? Or shall we choose the path of popularity and disobedience and the wrath of God?

"Choose you this day whom ye will serve; . . . but as for me and my house, we will serve the Lord." Joshua 24:15.

CHAPTER 56

The Seven Last Plagues

THE PRINCIPAL of the school had told us of the rules. He had explained why they were necessary. He had warned of the consequences of breaking them. The result? Five of us were kept after school, stood up one by one, and given a sound thrashing with a long willowy stick cut from a tree down on the creek. Those were the old-fashioned days, when people believed in the saying of Solomon, "Chasten thy son while there is hope, and let not thy soul spare for his crying." Proverbs 19:18.

Does God take pleasure in punishing us for our sins? Let Him answer:

"Repent, and turn yourselves from all your transgressions; so iniquity shall not be your ruin. . . . For I have no pleasure in the death of him that dieth, saith the Lord God: wherefore turn yourselves, and live ye." Ezekiel 18:30-32.

As long as there is hope we may be chastened for our profit. (Hebrews 12:9-11.) But it is possible for us to reach a point of hopelessness. "He, that being often reproved hardeneth his neck, shall suddenly be destroyed, and that without remedy." Proverbs 29:1.

Concerning Israel, God said, "I have hewed them by the prophets." Hosea 6:5. "But they mocked the messengers of God, and despised his words, and misused his prophets, until the wrath of the Lord arose against his people, till there was no remedy." 2 Chronicles 36:16. When there is no remedy, what then?

The Full Cup and God's Strange Act

When man's cup of iniquity runs over, God acts. His wrath against sin falls upon sinners. "Vengeance is mine; I will repay, saith the Lord." Romans 12:19.

As long as there is hope, chastisement is in mercy. When the cup of sin spills over, the cup of God's wrath overturns in vengeance. This is when God shall "bring to pass his act, his strange act. Now therefore be ye not mockers, lest your bands be made strong: for I have heard from the Lord God of hosts a consumption, even determined upon the whole earth." Isaiah 28:21, 22.

In the days of Noah wickedness became very great. God gave men 120 years of grace. They repented not. The Flood engulfed the world.

In the days of Abraham the Amorites were wicked, but the cup of their iniquity was not yet full. (Genesis 15:16.) God gave them over four hundred years. They repented not. Israel displaced them.

The Jews were the chosen of God for fifteen hundred years, even from Moses' day. But their cup overflowed. Said Jesus, "Behold, your house is left unto you desolate." Matthew 23:38. To the Jews, Paul announced, "We turn to the Gentiles." Acts 13:46.

When World Probation Closes

This world has had six thousand years to prove itself; that is, it has been on probation. The love of God and the law of God have been pitted against Satan's hate and his rebellion against God's law. The world has had and still has its chance to decide.

Someday erelong, according to Bible prophecy, man's probationary time will run out. The exact time no one knows. When that moment arrives, seven angels, having the seven last plagues, filled up with the wrath of God, come out of the most holy place of the heavenly temple—"the tabernacle of the testimony," or law, of God. (See Revelation 15:6, 7.) "And the temple was filled with smoke from the glory of God, and from his power; and no man was able to enter into the temple, till the seven plagues of the seven angels were fulfilled." Verse 8.

God's last warning message has already gone to the world. The ministry of the Son of man in the most holy place of the heavenly temple is finished; "no man was able to enter into the temple." Man's probation is over.

On earth the people of God have gotten the victory over the beast, his image, and his mark. (Verse 2.)

The Seven Last Plagues: Revelation 16

Now the angels go forth to pour out the seven last plagues upon the wicked. Christ has not yet come, but His people will be protected. (Psalms 91.)

Of the first plague we read, "The first went, and poured out his vial upon the earth; and there fell a noisome and grievous sore upon the men which had the mark of the beast, and upon them which worshipped his image." Revelation 16:2.

How plain! The people who chose to cling to the cross of Jesus and the commandments of God did not worship the beast or his image or receive his mark. They got the victory. Those who yielded, now receive of the plagues.

Please note that the wicked do not repent. (Verses 9, 11.) This is evidence that man's probation will be over.

As angels of God watch the awful ordeal one cries out, "Thou art righteous, O Lord, which art, and wast, and shalt be, because thou hast judged thus." Verse 5. Then another angel at the altar says, "Even so, Lord God Almighty, true and righteous are thy judgments." Verse 7.

Now Is the Day of Salvation

After the plagues begin to fall it will then be too late for any to get right with God. The Son of man, our Mediator, has left the temple. His priestly robes of intercession are then laid aside. He is to be crowned with the diadem of the universe. He is to come in the clouds of heaven as "KING OF KINGS, AND LORD OF LORDS." (Revelation 19:16.)

"Now is the accepted time." Before the plagues fall, those solemn words will sound forth: "He that is unjust, let him be unjust still: and he which is filthy, let him be filthy still: and he that is righteous, let him be righteous still: and he that is holy, let him be holy still. And, behold, I come quickly." Revelation 22:11, 12.

Surely this is the day of salvation, this is the time to accept Christ while He ministers in our behalf.

"Five bleeding wounds He bears,
Received on Calvary;
They pour effectual prayers,
They strongly speak for me.
Forgive him, O, forgive! they cry,
Nor let the contrite sinner die."
—Charles Wesley.

Up there in the judgment court of heaven He will plead your case if you will let Him. But they are nearing the end of that great ledger of names. "To day if ye will hear his voice, harden not your hearts." Hebrews 3:15.

Today Christ ministers for us in the most holy place in heaven. "Which hope we have as an anchor of the soul, both sure and stedfast, and which entereth into that within the veil." Hebrews 6:19.

Let us anchor our faith up there in that temple before He comes out and before the seven angels come out with the seven last plagues.

CHAPTER 57

The Battle of Armageddon

THE SIXTEENTH chapter of Revelation gives us the account of the coming seven last plagues. The sixth of these plagues involves the famous, and as yet unfought, battle of Armageddon. Since all seven plagues follow the close of human probation, none dare put off salvation until the opening barrage of Armageddon. It will then be too late.

WHAT IS ARMAGEDDON?

In his concluding address, following the Japanese surrender, General Douglas MacArthur said:

"Military alliance, balances of power, League of Nations all in turn failed. We have had our last chance. If we do not now devise some greater and more equitable system Armageddon will be at our door."—New York *Times*, Sept. 2, 1945, p. 3.

Here is the Bible prophecy of Armageddon under the sixth plague:

"The sixth angel poured out his vial upon the great river Euphrates; and the water thereof was dried up, that the way of the kings of the east might be prepared. And I saw three unclean spirits like frogs come out of the mouth of the dragon, and out of the mouth of the beast, and out of the mouth of the false prophet. For they are the spirits of devils, working miracles, which go forth unto the kings

 William Heaslip, Art

Great preparations for war signify great wars ahead—wars that will draw into th vortex all nations in the climactic battle of Armageddon.

of the earth and of the whole world, to gather them to the battle of that great day of God Almighty. . . . And he gathered them together into a place called in the Hebrew tongue Armageddon." Revelation 16:12-16.

In brief we may say that Armageddon involves the nations of the whole world. Particular mention is made of the "kings of the east." And the spirits of devils will work to incite the world to this conflict. Religion will be involved because the dragon, the beast, and the false prophet are prominent. Miracles will play a part.

WHERE IS ARMAGEDDON?

Some forty miles north of Jerusalem the town of Megiddo stood in the center of the tableland of Esdraelon. From the word *Megiddo* comes the word *Armageddon. A Dictionary of Religious Knowledge* says, "This name [Esdraelon] is given to the great plain of central Palestine which extends from the Mediterranean to the Jordan, separating the mountain ranges of Carmel and Samaria from those of Galilee. . . . It is the ancient plain of Megiddo, the Armageddon of Revelation."—Pages 326, 327, art. "Esdraelon."

WHY IS THIS REGION SO IMPORTANT?

It is a geographic center. This region, with Constantinople on the northwest, Egypt on the south, and the Persian Gulf on the east, has always been, and is destined yet to be, the tragic, strategic center of the world. This territory is the very geographic hub of the world wheel, the continents of the Old World stretching forth as spokes to the rim. Here is the great natural highway between East and West. This geographic fact has been written in creation itself and cannot be wished out of existence.

This region is also the great international political center. Here God placed the chosen Hebrews. On this battlefield Barak and Gideon did their exploits. Here Saul became a suicide by his own sword as his soldiers fell before the Philistines. Here Josiah was slain at the head of his armies.

The kings of Babylon, Medo-Persia, Greece, and Rome, as world rulers, held sway over this territory. At St. Jean d'Acre, within twenty miles of Megiddo itself, that fighting genius Napoleon Bonaparte met his first great military defeat as he fought his way toward fulfillment of his life's dream—rulership of the world. Looking back on his career, he said, "I missed my destiny at St. Jean d'Acre." That was in 1799. Eight years later, seated on a raft in the Niemen River, Napoleon bowed his imperial head with that of Alexander of Russia over the map of the world. Alexander asked for Constantinople, and Napoleon answered, "Never! He who holds Constantinople rules the world." He knew that if any great power got this northern point of the Armageddon region, that power would not rest until it had control of all the territory of this world hub, and such control would spell world leadership.

England's history has been one of constant guard with jealous and sleepless eye over this whole strategic territory. She has felt that it is the very lifeline of her dominions.

Russia looks with constant concern upon this region. Getting into political disagreement with Turkey in 1853, she found herself at war not only with Turkey but with England, France, and Piedmont. These powers did not love Turkey. But they would rather have Turkey in charge than to have a strong power like Russia in that strategic position. The Crimean War was fought as a result.

Germany grew friendly with the Turk, securing unusual concession from the Sick Man of the East. The German dream of the B.B.B. line—Berlin, Byzantium, Baghdad—a railway which would compete with Britain's sea route to India, was becoming a reality. Harbor, mining, and irrigation projects were boldly carried on in Turkey by Germany. Jealous eyes from all around about began to flash with fire. The end was war—war such as had never before been witnessed. That was World War I, from which the world staggered for twenty years, then reeled into World War II. The Armageddon territory is just as important now as ever.

Middle East oil is a center of interest for the great nations, including the United States. The nations think they need oil for Armageddon.

Then, too, this region is a religious center. It was the birthplace of Judaism, the cradle of Christianity, the nursery and control center of Mohammedanism—religions embracing more than half the human race. The Crusades were launched because of religious interest in this area. Zionism's purpose to put Jews in Palestine is stirring up the anger of 205,000,000 Mohammedans, and this with other considerations makes this territory important indeed from a religious viewpoint.

The Kings of the East

The kings of the East are to come to Armageddon, according to Revelation 16:12. Since the prophet Joel pictures the heathen peoples gathered to Palestine in the very close of earthly history, let us compare the two visions.

There are four distinct points to remember.

1. *Heathen are to be awakened.* "Let the heathen be wakened." This means that they were asleep.

Russia, half Eastern and half Western, was asleep. One historian says that they were "content to vegetate in indolence and obscurity. Out of this dull and laggard state they were destined to be roughly and emphatically roused by one of the most energetic rulers known to history." That was Peter the Great. Russia is awake and has been converted into one of the leading industrial and military nations of the world.

China was asleep. Content with her walls, her laborious and intelligent people devoted themselves to the peaceful pursuits of life. She sent out no ambassadors and received none. Canton was the only port on the entire coast open to trade with foreigners, and that trade was with vexation of spirit.

But China must be awakened. It was the English who took the primary, initial steps in arousing China. This was in 1840-42 in connection with the Opium War. Four more seaports were opened, and the island of Hong Kong was ceded to the British.

Two years later, in 1844, the United States sent Caleb Cushing as her representative to China. France, Belgium, Holland, and others followed, until more than forty ports were opened. China was being awakened.

Japan, the little island empire of the rising sun, was also asleep, and stubbornly so. For more than two hundred years her only foreign contact was a small trading station with the Dutch. Who would disturb the seclusion of this magic land of little but mighty people?

This role was played by Commodore Matthew Perry, of the U.S. Navy, in 1853. He sailed his American fleet into Japanese waters, demanding protection for American whale fishers cast ashore in storm. He sought permission for American vessels to put into port for supplies and to unload cargo. Perry departed with promise to return next year for an answer. Japan signed up, saying to herself, "I shall learn the secret of the military superiority of the white man."

It cost Japan a civil war to come out of sleep. But after 1868 she proceeded to appropriate Western ideas in a most revolutionary manner. Parliament, suffrage, schools, newspapers, railroads, et cetera, are pages in that astounding story of rapid change. Japan woke up, but had to be awakened as the prophet said. Funk and Wagnalls' *New Standard Encyclopedia,* volume 16, page 402, says, "In 1853 they were rudely awakened by Commodore Perry's steaming into the harbor of Uraga with a squadron of United States war vessels."

2. *The heathen are to prepare for war.* "Proclaim ye this among the Gentiles; Prepare war, wake up the mighty men, let all the men of war draw near." Joel 3:9.

Let us see how they have done this, just taking Japan as an example.

Japan, stirred from slumber, proceeded forthwith to arm herself, modeling her army on German lines, and her navy after the English. In 1894 she tested out her fighting skill and apparatus on China in a war over Korea. Success was easy. By the Treaty of Shimonoseki, April 17, 1895, her prizes were Port Arthur and the important Liaotung Peninsula, and an indemnity of $175,000,000 from China.

Russia, looking on with fear and jealousy, turned to Germany and France. The trio then approached Japan with their pious doctrine about the "Integrity of China." It would be an international sin for Japan to keep Port Arthur and Liaotung; world peace would be endangered. So Japan was forced to relinquish all but the island of Formosa.

Japan went home, saying to herself, "I will build up my army and navy, and bide my time."

Within two years Japan was to learn a lesson in the ways of Western diplomacy. Two German missionaries were killed in the Shantung Province of China in 1897. Germany dispatched a fleet to China and secured a ninety-nine-year lease on the fine harbor of Kiaochow (Q'cho) and special commercial privileges in Shantung. Russia leased Port Arthur for herself for twenty-five years. England and France got a port each. The powers forced open a dozen other ports, and secured spheres of influence here and there. It began to look as though the big butcher knives would not stop short of carving up all China to be served on the platters of hungry foreign nations.

The antiforeign Boxer Uprising was reaped from this selfish grasping, but more important was Japan's musing. She discovered that Western nations could practice hypocrisy almost as well as any Oriental, that they could take with holy hands what it was entirely wrong for her to take.

Japan waited, and continued to prepare. Russian activity in Manchuria increased. Japan finally opened hostilities, and the sizable Russo-Japanese War of 1904-5 began, with battles involving as many as five hundred thousand men. Mukden cost 120,000 killed and wounded in four days. Two Russian fleets were defeated, and another was annihilated. Japan won and took over Port Arthur and Liaotung—the prizes she had before won in war with China, but had been forced by great powers to give up.

Japan has gone right on in war preparation and in war, until the world has been utterly astonished at the long stride of her short legs. Defeated in World War II, she will undoubtedly be heard from again.

India, hot and sweltering, is bestirred as a long-sleeping giant roused to anger. War is one of China's chief occupations. The East is awake, and great things are in the offing.

3. *The kings of the East come west.* This is clear from Revelation 16:12, as well as from Joel 3:12, "Let the heathen be wakened, and come up to the valley of Jehoshaphat." This is in the region of Jerusalem.

4. *The way for this movement would be prepared.* "The sixth angel poured out his vial upon the great river Euphrates; and the water thereof was dried up, that the way of the kings of the east might be prepared." Revelation 16:12.

The drying up of the river Euphrates may fitly symbolize the weakening grip of the Turks on the territory drained by the Euphrates. For half a millennium Turkey has been in possession of strategic territory of this region.

Slowly but surely her position has weakened. In 1856 at the close of the Crimean War between Russia and Turkey, by the Treaty of Paris, the greater powers still left Turkey in possession. "Thus Turkey was *bolstered up* by the Christian powers of western Europe because they did not wish to see Russia installed in Constantinople. As a solution of the Eastern Question the war was a flat failure."—CHARLES D. HAZEN, *Modern European History* (Holt), p. 545. (Italics ours.)

Since then two world wars have been fought. Yet Turkey, the miracle Sick Man of the East, stays on.

The Jews have now won a place in Palestine. The fires of Mohammedan hatred are burning. Communism is slowly but surely rolling over the Orient. Russia still wants Constantinople and control of Palestine.

A possible conflict between East and West, forecast by statesmen and writers for decades, may be emerging before our eyes.

Ernest Bevin, British Foreign Secretary, is reported in *Quote,* January 8, 1949, as saying, "I am quite sure that before many years—I make this prophecy—you will find the defense ministers and finance ministers of the western world sitting down discussing a common budget, common cost, and common method of defense." This statement indicates belief that the East will unite against the West.

The British general, Sir Ian Hamilton, in an interview with Kingsbury Smith of International News Service, predicted that "the spot where Europe may attempt to halt Asiatic penetration will become the last battlefield of all time and mark the end of civilization." He added, "I have looked carefully at the map and the best spot for Europe to meet and throw back Asia is called Megiddo, or, in some maps, Armageddon."—New York *Journal and American,* Jan. 17, 1938, p. 2.

Little wonder that Brigadier General Charles King said years ago, " 'The Eastern Question' is one which the statesmen of Europe will probably wrangle over until the millennium."—*Decisive Battles of the World* (ed. 1895), p. 243.

The Time of the Judgment

Joel the prophet pictures the war preparations of the heathen as being in the time of great wickedness, of the judgment, and of the harvest. (Joel 3:12, 13.) Said Jesus, "The harvest is the end of the world." Matthew 13:39.

In this solemn hour of the judgment in heaven the judgment-hour message of Revelation 14:6, 7 is going to the world in about eight hundred languages.

As mercy yet lingers men may still make their choice for God and His Christ and their law, refusing to worship the beast and his image or receive his mark.

Said Joel, "Multitudes, multitudes in the valley of decision: for the day of the Lord is near in the valley of decision." Joel 3:14.

On her deathbed a woman told me the experience of two of her uncles. They were discussing the use of tobacco. Both of them had become convinced that if they were to be real Christians, they should break the habit. One of them said, "I have just enough tobacco left for a chew apiece. Let's chew it and then quit." The brother reasoned, "If it is wrong, why chew this piece? Throw it away." The one who said that quit. The other chewed tobacco until he died.

If you are friendly with sin, you will suffer. It is reported that in Bradford on Avon, England, Thomas Musty was bitten by a dog. Next day, in passing, he gave the dog a biscuit. The dog ate the biscuit and promptly bit Mr. Musty again.

If you play with sin, feed sin, procrastinate with sin, or do anything with sin but take it down to Calvary to be cleansed away, you will regret it. Until the angel of mercy uproots the cross and carries it away from this sinning world there is hope for all. But earth's shadows are lengthening. "Time is running out." "Therefore be ye also ready: for in such an hour as ye think not the Son of man cometh." Matthew 24:44.

CHAPTER 58

Living a Thousand Years! When? Where?

IT IS said that a cat, full grown at eighteen months, has a life expectancy of ten years. A dog, mature at two years, has an expectancy of twelve years. A horse, grown at four years, may expect to live twenty-five years.

On this basis a man, maturing at twenty-five years, should live 150 years, so said Dr. Edward L. Bortz, president of the American Medical Association, 1947-48. Other notables agree with him.

As a matter of fact, God desired man to live forever. In America right now he is averaging less than the Bible's seventy years.

We turn to consider a time when some men will live one thousand years. That time is soon. Armageddon comes under the sixth of the seven last plagues. The seventh plague is a violent hailstorm, with stones weighing a talent, or fifty-seven pounds each. The greatest earthquake of history will shake mountains to pieces and cause islands to disappear. From out of the temple of heaven a great voice calls, "It is done." (See Revelation 16:17-21.)

The millennium will then be ushered in. But let us read Revelation 20:1-9:

"I saw an angel come down from heaven, having the key of the bottomless pit and a great chain in his hand. And he laid hold on the dragon, that old serpent, which is the Devil, and Satan, and bound him a thousand years, and cast him into the bottomless pit, and shut him up, and set a seal upon him, that he should deceive the nations no more, till the thousand years should be fulfilled: and after that he must be loosed a little season. And I saw thrones, and they sat upon them, and judgment was given unto them: and I saw the souls of them that were beheaded for the witness of Jesus, and for the word of God, and which had not worshipped the beast, neither his image, neither had received his mark upon their foreheads, or in their hands; and they lived and reigned with Christ a thousand years. But the rest of the dead lived not again until the thousand years were finished. This is the first resurrection. Blessed and holy is he that hath part in the first resurrection: on such the second death hath no power, but they shall be priests of God and of Christ, and shall reign with him a thousand years. And when the thousand years are expired, Satan shall be loosed out of his prison, and shall go out to deceive the nations which are in the four quarters of the earth, Gog and Magog, to gather them together to battle: the number of whom is as the sand of the sea. And they went up on the breadth of the earth, and compassed the camp of the saints about, and the beloved city: and fire came down from God out of heaven, and devoured them."

This is the only place in the Bible where the thousand-year period, as such, is specifically set forth. It is here mentioned six times. The word *millennium* is not found in the Bible. It comes from two Latin words, *mille,* meaning "a thousand," and *annum,* meaning "a year"; thus we have *mille-annum,* or *millennium,* a thousand years.

Twice in the foregoing brief Bible record of the millennium we are informed that Satan is a deceiver. During the millennium he cannot deceive the nations. At its close, for a short time, he again deceives men. Today he works at his deceptive trade with great diligence, knowing that he has but a short time. But searching the Scriptures with the Spirit's aid we may know the truth of the millennium, and avoid deception.

Two Resurrections Mark the Millennium

Paul declares "that there shall be a resurrection of the dead, both of the just and unjust."

One of these resurrections will take place at the beginning of the one thousand years; the other, at the end. These two resurrections will be one thousand years apart. Which one comes first? The resurrection of the righteous or that of the wicked? We read Revelation 20:6: "Blessed and holy is he that hath part in the *first* resurrection." Referring to these same righteous ones in verse 4, the Revised Standard Version says, "They came to life again, and reigned with Christ a thousand years."

Thus it is crystal clear that the righteous dead are to be resurrected at the beginning of the millennium.

What then of the wicked dead, those who went into Christless graves? The answer is brief and plain. "But the rest of the dead lived not again until the thousand years were finished." Verse 5. That is to say, the wicked dead (the rest of the dead) will live again at the end of the thousand years.

Thus far a diagram of the one thousand years looks like this:

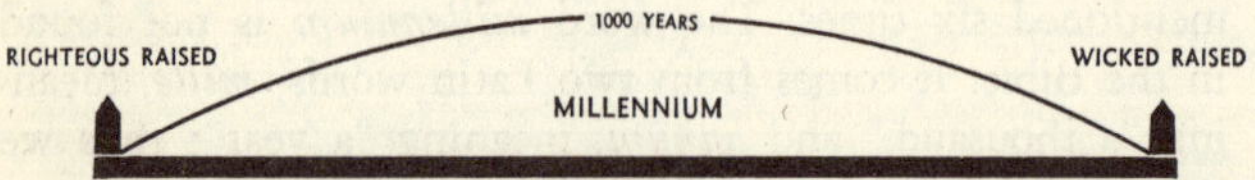

Seven Events That Mark the Beginning of the Millennium

We now know that the righteous dead are raised to life at the beginning of the one thousand years. If we can discover what other events take place in connection with the resurrection of the saints, we know that these also will be at the beginning of the millennium. Our problem is therefore simple.

The number one event that marks the millennium's start is the second coming of Christ. We read, "The Lord himself shall descend from heaven with a shout, with the voice of the archangel, and with the trump of God: and the *dead in Christ* shall rise first." 1 Thessalonians 4:16. There we have the second coming of Jesus and the resurrection of the righteous.

What else? "Then we which are *alive* and remain shall be caught up together with them [the resurrected righteous] in the clouds, to meet the Lord in the air." Verse 17.

What more? "We look for the Saviour, the Lord Jesus Christ: who shall change our vile body, that it may be fashioned like unto his glorious body." Philippians 3:20, 21.

Yes, the bodies of both the righteous living and the righteous dead will be changed, glorified, and made immortal. "We shall not all sleep [die], but we shall all be changed, in a moment, in the twinkling of an eye, at the last trump: for the trumpet shall sound, and the dead shall be raised incorruptible, and we shall be changed. . . . This mortal must put on immortality." 1 Corinthians 15:51-53. This is all at the second coming of Christ, at the beginning of the millennium.

What else occurs? Yes, the righteous are all taken to heaven. The living shall not go before ("prevent") those who have died. (1 Thessalonians 4:15.) And of the faithful dead we read that they "received not the promise [at death]: . . . that they without us should not be made perfect." Hebrews 11:39, 40. The righteous all go together to the "many mansions" Christ went to prepare, "that where I am, there ye may be also." (John 14:1-3.)

What more? The wicked shall be consumed and destroyed "with the brightness of his coming." (2 Thessalonians 2:8.) "As it was in the days of Noe, . . . the flood came, and destroyed them all. Likewise also as it was in the days of Lot; . . . it rained fire and brimstone from heaven, and destroyed them all." Luke 17:26-29. The unrepentant wicked who are alive when Christ comes will be consumed with the very glory of His coming. "The Lord thy God is a consuming fire." Deuteronomy 4:24.

Now, the final point: Satan is bound, "that he should deceive the nations no more, till the thousand years should be fulfilled." Revelation 20:3.

God has Satan bound to prevent him from deceiving anyone for one thousand years. Note how effectively this will be done. The wicked will all be dead. The righteous will all be gone to heaven. There will be no human being to deceive. Satan is bound by this chain of events at the beginning of the millennium. Until something happens he cannot work at his trade.

At this point a diagram of the millennium looks like this:

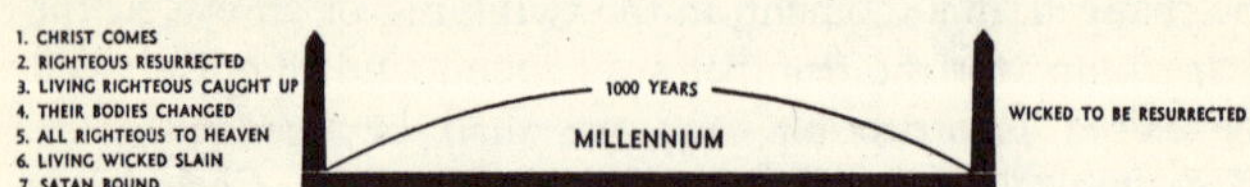
1. CHRIST COMES
2. RIGHTEOUS RESURRECTED
3. LIVING RIGHTEOUS CAUGHT UP
4. THEIR BODIES CHANGED
5. ALL RIGHTEOUS TO HEAVEN
6. LIVING WICKED SLAIN
7. SATAN BOUND
1000 YEARS
MILLENNIUM
WICKED TO BE RESURRECTED

Conditions During the Millennium

There are four things to remember about the period of the thousand years.

First of all, the earth is desolate. It is like a bottomless pit. (Revelation 20:3.)

The original Greek for bottomless pit means "abyss." From the Septuagint Greek Version it is translated "without form and void," in Jeremiah 4:23. "I beheld the earth, and, lo, it was without form and void; and the heavens, and they had no light." Reading on, we find, "I beheld the mountains, and, lo, they trembled, and all the hills moved lightly. I beheld, and, lo, there was no man, and all the birds of the heavens were fled. I beheld, and, lo, the fruitful place was a wilderness, and all the cities thereof were broken down at the presence of the Lord, and by his fierce anger." Verses 24-26.

Second, the wicked are dead. Jeremiah says in the verses just quoted that "there was no man."

Third, Satan is bound in this bottomless pit. On this desolated earth there is no one to deceive. He will have a thousand years of vacation from deception—a millennium of meditation on the long career of rebellion and the pitiful condition to which it has brought him, and plenty of time to lay plans for a final assault against God at the end of the long, long darkness, when the wicked dead shall stand on their feet once more.

Fourth, the righteous are engaged in a work of judgment in heaven.

Said John, "I saw thrones, and they sat upon them, and judgment was given unto them." Revelation 20:4.

Paul exclaims, "Do ye not know that the saints shall judge the world? . . . Know ye not that ye shall judge angels?" 1 Corinthians 6:2, 3.

After all, I would rather be in heaven than on earth during the millennium, wouldn't you? Clearly the Bible teaches that the saved will have part in the judgment. But why have a judgment after all cases have been decided?

True, when Christ comes He brings the reward with Him and takes His people to heaven. But the wicked are to be raised from the dead at the end of the thousand years to receive the punishment of the second death. Just how will God deal with these cases? Who will be beaten with many stripes, and who with few? And what about people whom we thought would be in heaven, but whom we do not find there?

How wonderfully wise is God! Suppose you had a very dear friend on earth, but in heaven he was not to be found. Well, during the millennium you will find out just how God has dealt with his case and the cases of all others. God takes one thousand years for this work. He will run no risk of having one single doubt in any mind about His work for fallen man.

During this period God allows the saved to sit, as it were, beside Him and learn how hard He tried to save every person. I think we shall understand Him better and love Him more after we have learned from the Saviour Himself His story of salvation, don't you? When it is all over we shall say, "True and righteous are thy judgments." There will be no soil in our hearts for the growth of seeds of doubt. "God shall wipe away all tears from their eyes."

At this point the millennium diagram looks like this:

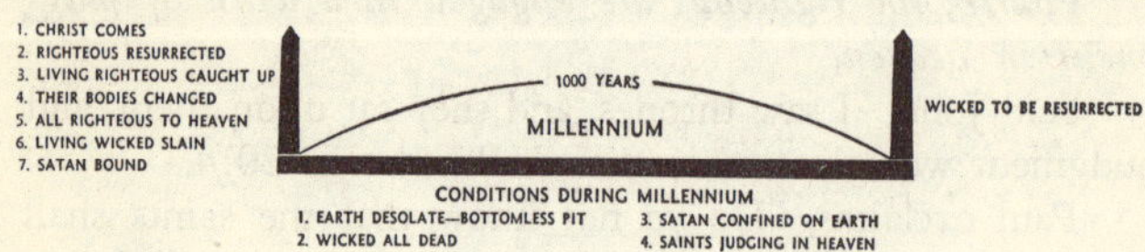
1. CHRIST COMES
2. RIGHTEOUS RESURRECTED
3. LIVING RIGHTEOUS CAUGHT UP
4. THEIR BODIES CHANGED
5. ALL RIGHTEOUS TO HEAVEN
6. LIVING WICKED SLAIN
7. SATAN BOUND
1000 YEARS
MILLENNIUM
WICKED TO BE RESURRECTED
CONDITIONS DURING MILLENNIUM
1. EARTH DESOLATE—BOTTOMLESS PIT
2. WICKED ALL DEAD
3. SATAN CONFINED ON EARTH
4. SAINTS JUDGING IN HEAVEN

Seven Events That Mark the End of the Millennium

We come now to the close of the millennium. What are the seven events which now occur?

1. *The wicked dead are resurrected.* "The rest of the dead lived not again until the thousand years were finished." Revelation 20:5. The mighty host of the wicked, in number like the sand of the sea, stand upon the earth once more. (Verse 8.)

2. *Satan is "loosed out of his prison."* Verse 7. The raising of the wicked dead from their graves gives him opportunity to deceive once more.

3. *Satan "shall go out to deceive the nations."* Verse 8.

How can he deceive them when they are already lost? Let us see.

4. *The Holy City, New Jerusalem, descends from heaven.* (Revelation 21:2.) That this takes place in close connection with the loosing of Satan is plain from what follows.

5. *Satan marshals the wicked about the holy city.* "And shall go out to deceive the nations . . . to gather them together to battle. . . . And they went up on the breadth of the earth, and compassed the camp of the saints about, and the beloved city." Revelation 20:8, 9.

Words could not be plainer. Satan will go out to the great resurrected warriors of bygone years, and convince them that under his invincible leadership and theirs the city of the saints can be taken. Billions upon billions of soldiers will be at their command.

6. *"Fire came down from God out of heaven, and devoured them."* Verse 9. Talk about atomic bombs and Hiroshima, Nagasaki, or Bikini atoll! Everlasting fire will descend and devour unnumbered billions of rebellious, unrepentant sinners. "Who shall be punished with everlasting destruction from the presence of the Lord." 2 Thessalonians 1:9.

Peter watched this fire in vision and wrote, "The heavens shall pass away with a great noise, and the elements shall *melt* with fervent heat, the earth also and the works that are therein shall be burned up." 2 Peter 3:10. So the fire of God, as it were, sets the very gases of the atmosphere aflame, and the earth itself melts. ("Seeing that all these things shall be dissolved." Verse 11.) The globe becomes a seething lake of fire, a veritable shoreless ocean of destruction.

Said the prophet Obadiah, "As ye have drunk upon my holy mountain, so shall all the heathen drink continually, yea, they shall drink, and they shall swallow down, and they shall be as though they had not been." Verse 16.

"Yet a little while, and the wicked shall not be: yea, thou shalt diligently consider his place, and it shall not be." Psalms 37:10.

"The day cometh that shall burn them up, saith the Lord of hosts, that it shall leave them neither root nor branch." Malachi 4:1.

"And the devil that deceived them was cast into the lake of fire. . . . And death and hell [the grave] delivered up the dead which were in them. . . . And death and hell were cast into the lake of fire. This is the second death. And whosoever was not found written in the book of life was cast into the lake of fire." Revelation 20:10-15.

Thus ends the fearful story of the wrath of God against sin.

Today the investigative judgment of God is in progress. During the millennium, degrees of sentence will doubtless be determined. At the end of the thousand years the sentences are executed. Some will suffer longer than others, seeming like forever, indeed, but their suffering will end in the second death.

7. *Our final picture is a new earth,* "wherein dwelleth righteousness." 2 Peter 3:13. God with His saints descends from heaven to earth with that magnificent city of God, the New Jerusalem. (Revelation 21:1-3.)

Here is the full millennium diagram:

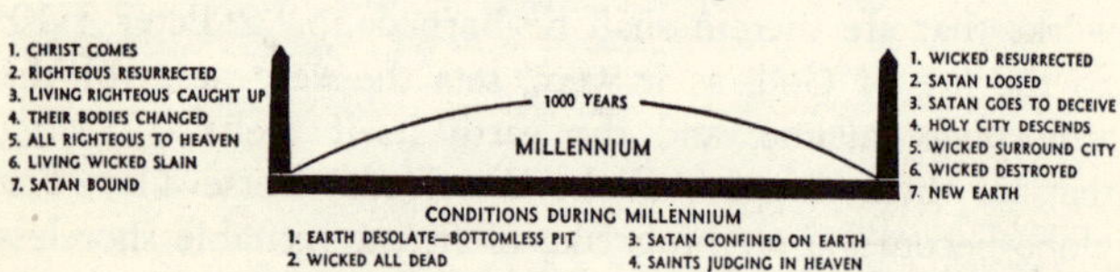
1. CHRIST COMES
2. RIGHTEOUS RESURRECTED
3. LIVING RIGHTEOUS CAUGHT UP
4. THEIR BODIES CHANGED
5. ALL RIGHTEOUS TO HEAVEN
6. LIVING WICKED SLAIN
7. SATAN BOUND
1000 YEARS
MILLENNIUM
1. WICKED RESURRECTED
2. SATAN LOOSED
3. SATAN GOES TO DECEIVE
4. HOLY CITY DESCENDS
5. WICKED SURROUND CITY
6. WICKED DESTROYED
7. NEW EARTH
CONDITIONS DURING MILLENNIUM
1. EARTH DESOLATE—BOTTOMLESS PIT
2. WICKED ALL DEAD
3. SATAN CONFINED ON EARTH
4. SAINTS JUDGING IN HEAVEN

INHERITING A PLACE IN THAT CITY

"If ye be Christ's, then are ye Abraham's seed, and heirs according to the promise." Galatians 3:29. This means complete surrender to Him. It is not merely to profess Christ, but to be Christ's—to believe in Him, to build on His words, and to walk in His steps. Then, at last, shall we inherit and come into actual possession of the realities.

There was a poor boy in London. He loved toys. He used to gaze through the glass shop windows at the many things he wished he might have, but never got. He was run over in the street and taken to a hospital. He lay on a snow-white cot. They propped him up and brought him toy soldiers to play with. He gently and fondly touched them and said, "No glass between." No more looking at toys through the glass display window! He could hold them in his hands. "Now we see through a glass, darkly; but then face to face." 1 Corinthians 13:12. The saints shall inherit the kingdom, and "the throne of God and of the Lamb shall be in it; and his servants shall serve him: and they shall see his face; and his name shall be in their foreheads. And there shall be no night there." Revelation 22:3-5.

CHAPTER 59

Where Will the Righteous Spend Eternity?

THE THOUSAND-YEAR reign of the righteous with Christ in heaven is but the first installment of their eternity. Where will eternity be spent? Will the saints remain in heaven, or will their abode be somewhere else? At the close of the thousand years we found them in the Holy City ("the camp of the saints"), which had come down from heaven to earth. What is their future to be? A brief survey of God's plan will make it plain.

GOD'S PURPOSE IN CREATION

"Thus saith the Lord that created the heavens; God himself that formed the earth and made it; . . . he created it not in vain, he formed it to be inhabited." Isaiah 45:18.

It was God's pleasure to do this. "For thy pleasure they are and were created." Revelation 4:11. Since God is holy, we know He created holy beings to dwell upon earth. And since He is unchangeable (James 1:17), we would expect Him someday, despite the problem of sin, to carry out His original purpose and pleasure. Even a human being of vision is not easily turned from his plans by obstacles.

So we read, "My counsel shall stand, and I will do all my pleasure." Isaiah 46:10. And again, "But as truly as I live, all the earth shall be filled with the glory of the Lord." Numbers 14:21. There is coming a time "of restitution of all things." Acts 3:21. "The Son of man is come to seek and to save that which was lost." Luke 19:10.

A small boy climbed high up in a tree trying to see inside an oriole's nest. He fell and broke his leg. When able to hobble about in his cast he went outside. His mother found him up the tree again, trying to reach the bird's nest. Her excited exclamations were answered by, "Mother, I just had to see inside that nest." That is the determination of a small boy.

Christ came to redeem what man had lost. As a boy of twelve he said, "I *must* be about my Father's business." Luke 2:49. He died to accomplish His purpose. Love led Him to the cross. He told His disciples that "he *must* go unto Jerusalem, and suffer . . . , and be killed." Matthew 16:21.

What God Gave to Man

In the beginning God gave man four things.

1. *He gave him life.* "God . . . breathed into his nostrils the breath of life." Genesis 2:7.

2. *He gave man a righteous character.* "God said, Let us make man in our image." Genesis 1:26. Said Solomon, "God hath made man upright." Ecclesiastes 7:29.

3. *He gave man a home in a beautiful world.* "The Lord God planted a garden eastward in Eden; and there he put the man whom he had formed." Genesis 2:8.

4. *God gave man dominion.* "Let them have dominion over . . . all the earth." Genesis 1:26.

As long as man would willingly accept the dominion of God over him he could retain and maintain his dominion over the earth.

What Man Lost

Man lost all four of the things God gave him.

1. *He lost his life.* Adam sinned. "The wages of sin is death." Romans 6:23.

"In the day that thou eatest thereof thou shalt surely die." "Dust thou art, and unto dust shalt thou return." Genesis 2:17; 3:19.

2. *He lost his righteous character.* God made man upright, but he did not remain that way. He chose the course of disobedience, or sin. "All unrighteousness is sin." 1 John 5:17. Adam sinned, and became unrighteous.

3. *He lost his home.* "Therefore the Lord God sent him forth from the garden of Eden." Genesis 3:23.

4. *He lost his dominion.* He was overcome by Satan. "Of whom a man is overcome, of the same is he brought in bondage." 2 Peter 2:19. Thus Satan became the "god of this world," the "prince of this world." He claimed rulership of it, and Christ did not dispute his claim. (Luke 4:5-7.)

Adam went forth into a world placed under the curse of sin. "Thorns also and thistles shall it bring forth to thee; . . . in the sweat of thy face shalt thou eat bread." Genesis 3:18, 19. Having cast off the dominion God placed over him, he lost the dominion God had put under him. He became the servant of sin and Satan. (John 8:34.)

What Christ Restores

Jesus came to "seek and to save" all that man lost through the fall.

1. *He restores life.* "The gift of God is eternal life." Romans 6:23.

2. *He restores character.* "Therefore if any man be in Christ, he is a new creature: old things are passed away; behold, all things are become new." 2 Corinthians 5:17. This spiritual creative process goes on in the heart of the child of God day by day. Thus we "are changed into the same image from glory to glory even as by the Spirit of the Lord." 2 Corinthians 3:18.

The Sabbath, being the sign of God's creative power,

becomes most naturally the sign of this sanctifying process in the life. (Ezekiel 20:12, 20.)

3. *Christ will restore home in a beautiful world.* He taught us to pray, "Thy will be done in earth, as it is in heaven." Matthew 6:10. The Father will send Jesus Christ at the time of the "restitution of all things." (Acts 3:21.) Said Peter after seeing in vision the earth and its elements melted by fire, "Nevertheless we, according to his promise, look for new heavens and a new earth, wherein dwelleth righteousness." 2 Peter 3:13.

4. *Christ restores man to dominion.* Satan overcame man and took his dominion. Through Christ man overcomes sin and Satan, and recovers dominion. Said Christ, "To him that overcometh will I grant to sit with me in my *throne,* even as I also overcame, and am set down with my Father in his throne." Revelation 3:21. Again He said, "Well done, thou good and faithful servant: thou hast been faithful over a few things, I will make thee ruler over many things." Matthew 25:21.

Then the curse of sin will be removed. "And there shall be no more curse." Revelation 22:3.

A Divine Picture of the New Earth

1. The New Jerusalem, capital city for the new earth, comes down from heaven. (Revelation 21, 22; Zechariah 14:4-9.)

2. God Himself dwells with men. (Revelation 21:3.)

3. Regular Sabbath worship in the city. (Isaiah 66:22, 23.)

4. Country life with homes. (Isaiah 65:17, 21.)

5. No sickness. (Isaiah 33:24.)

6. No pain, sorrow, crying, or death. (Revelation 21:4.)

7. Changed nature of animals. (Isaiah 11:6-9.)

8. Earth beautiful and fruitful. (Isaiah 35.)

9. Will know each other. (1 Corinthians 13:12.)

10. We cannot grasp all. (1 Corinthians 2:9.)

He will restore dominion and remove the curse. We do not propose undue speculation on the details of the future life. Its loveliness will surpass our fondest dreams, its beauty will excel our most enthusiastic imaginations, and its joy will soar above the flight of our highest hopes. "One pulse of harmony and gladness beats through the vast creation. . . . From the minutest atom to the greatest world, all things, animate and inanimate, in their unshadowed beauty and perfect joy, declare that God is love."—*The Great Controversy,* p. 678.

How Shall We Be Ready?

To Abraham, God promised the whole earth. Yet "he gave him none inheritance in it, no, not so much as to set his foot on: yet he promised that he would give it to him for a possession." Acts 7:5. The simple truth is that Abraham never owned a square foot of ground, save a grave, which he purchased from Ephron the Hittite, for himself and Sarah his wife.

How did Abraham understand this great promise of God that he should be "heir of the world"? Romans 4:13.

Here is the answer: "By faith Abraham, when he was called to go out into a place which he should after receive for an inheritance, obeyed; and he went out, not knowing whither he went. By faith he sojourned in the land of promise, as in a strange country, dwelling in tabernacles with Isaac and Jacob, the heirs with him of the same promise: for he looked for a city which hath foundations, whose builder and maker is God." Hebrews 11:8-10.

How do we come under this glowing promise of the future? "If ye be Christ's then are ye Abraham's seed, and heirs according to the promise." Galatians 3:29.

Someone asked a Negro slave whether his master was

going to heaven. He answered, "No! My master never goes anywhere without telling me about it, and he always takes several days to get ready. He hasn't said anything to me about it, and he hasn't been getting ready, so I know he isn't going."

A lifeboat was being loaded on a sinking ship. A woman asked the captain, "How much baggage can we take?"

"No baggage, madam," was the prompt reply. We should not plan on taking any baggage to heaven. We should lay up our treasures in heaven now by investing our means and energies in the kingdom of God.

Of the noble lineage of the faithful we read, "These all died in faith, not having received the promises. . . . But now they desire a better country, that is, an heavenly: wherefore God is not ashamed to be called their God: for he hath prepared for them a city." Hebrews 11:13-16.

The heavenly home is a country. It is this earth made new. "Affliction shall not rise up the second time." Nahum 1:9. The sordid specter of sin will never show its form again. The ugly shadow of rebellion will nevermore lurk far or near in God's widespread universe. Sin and sinners will be no more. Unshadowed beauty and perfect joy will declare that God is love.

SECTION ELEVEN

GOD SPEAKS CONCERNING THE CHURCH, CIVILIZATION, AND HAPPINESS

Lambert, Devaney, Hammond Instrument Co.

Our land is filled with churches, each claiming divine authority for its existence. would be keenly interesting to follow Christ to the pew of His choice.

CHAPTER 60

Christ's Church Today

IF JESUS should again come to earth to show men how to live, what church would He join? The Scriptures teach "Jesus Christ the same yesterday, and to day, and for ever." Hebrews 13:8. Therefore He would hold to the same principles now as He did when here nearly two thousand years ago. In a world of sinners needing redemption from sin Christ would seek a church that would teach His way of salvation.

A Church Preaching Repentance

As the Saviour went forth to save the lost, of Him it is written, "From that time Jesus began to preach, and to say, Repent: for the kingdom of heaven is at hand." Matthew 4:17.

John the Baptist was still sending forth his clarion call: "Repent ye." "Bring forth therefore fruits meet for repentance." Matthew 3:2, 8. Then came Jesus lifting His voice in ringing tones, "Except ye repent, ye shall all likewise perish." Luke 13:5.

Repentance means godly sorrow for sin (2 Corinthians 7:9.) It includes turning away from sin. "Repent, and turn yourselves from your transgressions; so iniquity shall not be your ruin." Ezekiel 18:30.

Christ calls the sinner to turn his back on sin, face a God of goodness, and thus be led to true repentance. (Romans 2:4.)

The story is told of a hardened prisoner who remained untouched by the kind deeds and attentions of any who sought to break through the barriers he had raised against all men. His face was sullen, his heart was bitter, his soul was rebellious, and his speech was blasphemous.

A woman entered the prison with a beautiful little two-year-old girl. The hardened prisoner stood apart from his fellows in the open ward. Spying him, the little girl let go the woman's hand and ran toward this wicked criminal. Even the other prisoners feared for the child's safety. But it was too late to do anything.

Stretching forth her tiny arms, the child said, "Take me up, man, take me up." Half-dazed, the stony-faced prisoner reached down and picked up the child. She stroked his wiry beard, patted his hardened face, threw her little arms around his great stubborn neck, and exclaimed, "I love you, man; I love you, man."

The heart of sin melted, and became a spring that sent forth great tears to trickle down the deep lines of his penitent face. The love of God in the face of a little child had broken a heart of stone.

From Calvary's cross the Son of God has been "exalted . . . to be a Prince and a Saviour, for to give repentance to Israel, and forgiveness of sin." Acts 5:31. Thus is brought to man "the light of the knowledge of the glory of God in the face of Jesus Christ." 2 Corinthians 4:6.

The well-known author Stanley High, in the *Christian Century,* January 19, 1949, referring to the World Council of Churches at Amsterdam, said that the "ecclesiastical leadership at Amsterdam has transferred its concern from the spiritual business of converting man to the secular business of converting man's institutions. . . . Amsterdam made it appear that the most essential measure for society's redemption is not our own *internal repentance, but the world's external reform.*" (Italics ours.)

, R&H Pub. Assn. Robert M. Eldridge, Artist

hat happens during the millennium to this earth, the people of God, the millions of sinners, and to Satan himself is clearly outlined in the Scriptures.

 Vernon Nye

Jesus' promise, "I go to prepare a place for you," will become a reality to ever faithful believer in His saving name. These will be "peaceful habitations."

Before the throne of God angels must weep as they bear the message of how the church turns from the saving gospel of Christ for the soul, to tinker with the social structure in a deluded effort to save civilization, as "time is running out." Said Jesus, "If the blind lead the blind, both shall fall into the ditch." Matthew 15:14.

To the last-day Laodicean church Christ says, "I know thy works, that thou art neither cold nor hot. . . . Because thou sayest, I am rich, and increased with goods, and have need of nothing; and knowest not that thou art wretched, and miserable, and poor, and blind, and naked: . . . be zealous therefore, and repent." Revelation 3:15-19.

Christ would seek today for a church with a message of repentance.

A Church Preaching Regeneration at Calvary

It is commonly said that the philosopher asks Why? and the scientist asks How?

Nicodemus leaned to the scientific. To him Jesus said, "Except a man be born again, he cannot see the kingdom of God." John 3:3. In reply this ruler of the Jews asked, "*How* can a man be born when he is old?" Verse 4. Again Christ spoke, "Marvel not that I said unto thee, Ye must be born again." Verse 7. To all this Nicodemus could only exclaim, "*How* can these things be?" Verse 9.

To get on familiar ground, Jesus said, "As Moses lifted up the serpent in the wilderness, even so must the Son of man be lifted up: that whosoever believeth in him should not perish, but have eternal life." Verses 14, 15. Then followed that marvelous verse, John 3:16.

Nicodemus went away. For three years and more he pondered the sayings of Jesus. Then he followed Him to His trial and to Calvary. As he saw the Son of God "lifted up" between earth and heaven like a serpent on a pole, it was then he realized that Christ was dying for the sins of Nicodemus. He must have felt as did the fervent Isaac Watts when he wrote:

"O, never till my latest breath
Can I forget that look;
It seemed to charge me with His death,
Though not a word He spoke."

From the heart of Nicodemus there went forth to God a great and earnest cry, "Lord, make me over again. Let me be born again of water and the Spirit, that I may live like Thee and for Thee." *He found true repentance and regeneration at Calvary.* They are the product of man's submission to the love of God, who gave His Son for the redemption of the world.

It is interesting to note that Jesus said, "Except a man be born of water and of the Spirit." Verse 5.

Baptism involves the water. Jesus was baptized by John the Baptist "in Jordan." (Mark 1:9.) Then Christ came up "out of the water." Verse 10. John was immersing the candidates. He baptized at Aenon, "because there was much water there." John 3:23.

After His resurrection Jesus commanded His disciples, "Go ye therefore, and teach all nations, baptizing them in the name of the Father, and of the Son, and of the Holy Ghost." Matthew 28:19. Jesus was baptized by immersion, and told His disciples to teach and baptize among all nations. The word *baptize* means to "immerse or plunge beneath the water."

Born-again Christians are to be born of water as well as of the Spirit. When Philip baptized the eunuch of Ethiopia "they went down both into the water, both Philip and the eunuch; and he baptized him. And when they were come up out of the water, the Spirit of the Lord caught away Philip." Acts 8:38, 39.

Bible baptism in water signifies the death of the old

man of sin in our nature, his burial, and our resurrection to "walk in newness of life." (Read Romans 6:1-6.) By baptism we also allege our faith in the death, burial, and resurrection of Christ.

Regeneration, Calvary, and baptism are linked together. If Christ were on earth today, He would be looking for a church which keeps together that which He put together.

Have you followed your Lord down to the watery grave and there been "buried with him by baptism into death: that like as Christ was raised up from the dead by the glory of the Father, even so we also should walk in newness of life"? Romans 6:4. Christ commanded the baptism of converts to His gospel. All those who accept His full gospel should be baptized.

A Church That Upholds the Ten Commandments

When the great preacher Dwight L. Moody said, "I have never met an honest man that found fault with the Ten Commandments," he took a stand that every honest man should think about. The reason many men find fault with the Ten Commandments is that the commandments find so much at fault in men. Sin is the transgression of God's law, and Christ came to save men from sin and to restore them "to unfeigned obedience to the holy law," as Hiscox's *Baptist Manual* rightly states it.

Said the prophet Isaiah of Jesus, "He will *magnify* the law." Isaiah 42:21. And true to the prophecy, Jesus magnified the Ten Commandments. He took the seventh commandment against adultery, and made it apply to even the lustful desires of the heart. (Matthew 5:27, 28.) He X-rayed the law of God, and showed that it was a living law whose roots ran deep into the principles of love and holiness. He X-rayed men, and revealed evil rooted deep beneath the surface of outward, letter-of-the-law behavior.

Preaching to a great multitude, He exclaimed, "Think not that I am come to destroy the law." Verse 17. Then it was that He proceeded to magnify the commandments.

Most of all, He magnified the law in His life. Coming up to Calvary, He said, "I have kept my Father's commandments." Thus He fulfilled the prophecy: "Lo, I come: in the volume of the book it is written of me, I delight to do thy will, O my God: yea, thy law is within my heart." Psalms 40:7, 8; Hebrews 10:7.

In the heart of the born-again believer this holy law is to be written. (Hebrews 8:10.) The believer then becomes "the epistle of Christ . . . written not . . . in tables of stone, but in fleshy tables of the heart," and "known and read of all men." 2 Corinthians 3:3, 2.

How many sermons have you heard on the Ten Commandments in the past ten years? Have you heard any sermons against the Ten Commandments? Moody said that no honest man would find fault with this law of God. Why should any man find fault with the Ten Commandments? (Read them in Exodus 20:3-17.)

Some find fault with the first commandment because they want to worship their own god or gods.

Others find fault with the second commandment because they wish to use images in their worship of even the one true God. So they just remove this commandment. Any Catholic catechism dealing with the Ten Commandments deletes the Bible's second commandment, which forbids "any graven image." The Lutheran catechism retains the papal law.

Many object to the third commandment because it forbids profanity, or taking the name of God in vain. Even women are becoming so profane in speech that one manufacturer put up a sign in his plant, "Ladies! Please watch your language! Men present!" And a lot of men think profanity a mark of manliness.

There are those who object to the fourth commandment because it calls the believer to keep the seventh-day Sabbath (Saturday). Many ministers would preach and observe the true Sabbath if the people would go along. The Bible says that the people prefer teachers who will teach what the people want to hear. "Itching ears," is the Bible description. That means ears that like flattery and smooth things, preferring fables to truth. (2 Timothy 4:1-4.) Others will fight the entire law of God in order to destroy the Sabbath commandment.

Who is back of this opposition to God's divine law? The same one who has always been back of it. Satan opposed the Son of God and the law of God in heaven. He has waged his campaign against God's true church for six thousand years. Today he goes forth "to make war with the remnant of her seed, which keep the commandments of God, and have the testimony of Jesus Christ." Revelation 12:17. Christ and God's commandments go together, and wherever this holy union is found Satan incites opposition to it. Christ's church is the commandment-keeping church.

If the Saviour of men came to your community, He would ask you, "Is there a church here that keeps the commandments of God and holds to My testimony?"

A Church That Preaches Bible Prophecy

When Jesus began His public ministry He stood up in His home church on the Sabbath and read from the prophecy of Isaiah. When He finished the reading and sat down, all eyes were fastened on Him. When the tension was at its height He said, "This day is this scripture fulfilled in your ears" (Luke 4:21); in other words, "I am come to do the work predicted in the prophecy I just read. This is the 'acceptable year.' This is the time. I am the Christ."

Strange as it may seem, the same people who had wondered at His gracious words as He read the Bible to them, now gnashed their teeth, thrust Him out of the synagogue, took Him to the top of a cliff, and tried to cast Him down headlong.

John the Baptist came preaching that he was "the voice of one crying in the wilderness," as predicted by Isaiah the prophet. (Matthew 3:3.) Jesus testified that John was a true prophet. Yet the church rejected both Christ and John, despite the fact that their work was based on Bible prophecy that applied to their day.

Today Jesus would look for the people who preach the prophecies that apply to our time. He would search for a church preaching His second coming; pointing out the signs of world wars, famines, pestilences, earthquakes in divers places, and abounding iniquity, and best of all, carrying the everlasting gospel to all the world for a witness. (Matthew 24:1-14.)

He would seek a church preaching the great prophetic messages of the three angels of Revelation 14:6-10. He would bend an ear to hear the words: "Fear God, and give glory to him; for the hour of his judgment is come: and worship him that made heaven, and earth, and the sea, and the fountains of waters." Revelation 14:7. Would He find a church in your city, town, or community, worshiping on the Sabbath day in honor of this Creator, and preaching a clarion, prophetic message scheduled for our day, and calling men to Calvary in true repentance?

A Church Separate From the World

When Christ was upon earth the Jewish church was interested in a Messiah who would establish His kingdom through the gateway of political control. They disowned the Son of God who came to save sinners.

Today the great professed church of Christ is moving

in the same direction as did the Jewish church. It is seeking to save the world through social and political reforms. The world would be converted en masse, and we would have a kingdom of God on earth composed of the holy church and the holy state, they think.

Jesus and the Bible paint no such picture of the true church. Said Jesus, "If the world hate you, ye know that it hated me before it hated you. If ye were of the world, the world would love his own: but because . . . I have chosen you out of the world, therefore the world hateth you." John 15:18, 19.

The world is not to become better and better. "Evil men and seducers shall wax worse and worse, deceiving, and being deceived." 2 Timothy 3:13. Wickedness will increase. Righteousness will decrease. Men will think otherwise because they are deceived.

Once in a while even a modernist seminary has a leader who will open his eyes for a moment and admit that the Bible teaches a separation of saints and sinners.

In the *Sunday School Times,* January 23, 1949, Dr. Wilbur M. Smith quotes Dr. Reinhold Niebuhr, of Union Theological Seminary, as follows:

"'It is significant that the New Testament invariably pictures human history as moving toward a climax in which evil becomes more and more naked and unashamed, pride more arrogant, and conflict more covert. These various apocalyptic visions taken seriously point to an interpretation of history in which there is no suggestion of a progressive triumph of good over evil, but rather of a gradual sharpening of the distinction between good and evil.'"

Yes, that is the Bible picture. And the book of Revelation points out that the great worldly church itself will lower her standards until she becomes, as it were, "the habitation of devils, and the hold of every foul spirit, and a cage of every unclean and hateful bird." Revelation 18:2.

The church will yoke up with the nations, and they will drink of her adulterated doctrines. Giddy with power, living under the hallucination of the glory of world leadership, the church sacrifices her purity and spiritual heritage of holiness.

"After these things I saw another angel come down from heaven, having great power; and the earth was lightened with his glory. And he cried mightily with a strong voice, saying, Babylon the great is fallen, is fallen." Revelation 18:1, 2.

This is the last-day stage of the worldly-minded church. The false doctrines of ancient Babylon are in her. Sunday, a vestige of sun worship, prayers for the dead, consultation with supposed spirits of the dead—these and other theories and practices are or will be part of the great confusion of modern Babylon, the spiritually fallen church.

"I heard another voice from heaven, saying, Come out of her, my people, that ye be not partakers of her sins." Verse 4.

If the Saviour of men were on earth today He would look for a church that is distinctly separate from the world, and separated from the worldly-minded churches that join up with the world.

A Church With Eyes Open for Light

This church of Christ will close its eyes to the allurements of sin and keep them open to the light of God.

To the Jews, Jesus said, "This people's heart is waxed gross, and their ears are dull of hearing, and their eyes they have closed; lest at any time they should see with their eyes, and hear with their ears, and should understand with their heart, and should be converted, and I should heal them." Matthew 13:15.

In His Sermon on the Mount Jesus said, "If therefore thine eye be single, thy whole body shall be full of light. But if thine eye be evil, thy whole body shall be full of darkness." Matthew 6:22, 23.

Jesus was really saying, "If your eye is open and clear and honest, you will see the light of God's will; and if you live it, your whole body shall be full of light. But if you close your eyes, or turn them away from the truth of God, your heart will become dark."

Even the light we have had will be no more than darkness to us, for "if therefore the light that is in thee be darkness, how great is that darkness!" Verse 23.

Jesus was pointing out this great truth again when He said, "Walk while ye have the light, lest darkness come upon you." John 12:35.

The way of the Christian is a lighted way. The light moves on, and we follow. "The path of the just is as the shining light, that shineth more and more unto the perfect day." Proverbs 4:18.

What will happen if a good man, a just man, who has been living up to the light he has received, refuses to accept more light, and declines to walk in advancing light? The answer is here: "Now the just shall live by faith: but if any man draw back, my soul shall have no pleasure in him." Hebrews 10:38. One dear old woman said, "Yes, it's in the Bible, but I wish we hadn't found it."

What shall we do? "We are not of them who draw back unto perdition; but of them that believe to the saving of the soul." Verse 39.

If Christ came to dwell on earth today, He would search for a church preaching repentance and regeneration at Calvary, upholding and obeying the Ten Commandments, including the Sabbath, proclaiming His coming and the prophecies which apply to our day, calling for separation from the world, and cherishing a love for truth which follows the Spirit as it guides "into all truth." (John 16:13.)

If the Saviour came to your city, your town, your community, would He join your church? If not, and if He started one of His own, would you join it?

"As Jesus passed forth from thence, he saw a man, named Matthew, sitting at the receipt of custom: and he saith unto him, Follow me. And he arose, and followed him." Matthew 9:9.

"The sweet persuasion of His voice
Respects thy sanctity of will.
He giveth day: thou hast thy choice
To walk in darkness still.
A tenderer light than moon or sun,
Than song of earth a sweeter hymn,
May shine and sound forever on,
And thou be deaf and dim.

"Forever round the mercy-seat
The guiding lights of love shall burn;
But what if, habit-bound, thy feet
Shall lack the will to turn?
What if thine eyes refuse to see,
Thine ear of heaven's free welcome fail,
And thou a willing captive be,
Thyself thine own dark jail?"

CHAPTER 61

How Can a Man Have Peace of Mind in a Troubled World?

MODERN MAN made a great mistake. Of his factories, his libraries, and his laboratories he built a temple. In this magnificent structure of human wisdom he placed his new god, the god of science. With intellectual honesty modern man might now bow in adoration, wonder, and worship.

This king of the gods was to save man from superstition, free him from drudgery, provide him with plenty, embellish his life with leisure and luxury, banish his diseases, and usher him into the golden age of civilization.

THE TWOFOLD FAILURE OF SCIENCE

But alas and alack! This new scientific god has failed man in two of his greatest needs.

First of all, he has given man no law for his life. He has revealed a thousand secrets concerning nature's laws—laws in the realms of physics, chemistry, mathematics, medicine, and astronomy. As men burn incense on his altar new wonders spring forth, and the prophets of science speak of mysteries, which when unveiled would make the world a mechanical paradise.

But the seers of science can discover no law for man. They hear no voice, saying, "This is the way, walk ye in it."

The eminent British scholar, C. E. M. Joad, in his book *Philosophy for Our Times,* says, "While our civilization hangs on the verge of destruction through its inability to control the powers which science has conferred upon it, young men and women wander aimlessly along the road of life without knowing whither they are travelling, or why indeed they travel at all. In a word, *they are without creed or code, standards or values.*"—Page 12. (Italics ours.)

"There has grown to maturity a generation which is to all intents and purposes without religious belief. To say that, as a result, life has for it no point and the universe no purpose would be true, but it would not be the most important truth. More important is the fact that, to the present generation, it is a matter of no interest whether life has a point, the universe a purpose or not. It does not care and, therefore, it does not inquire."—*Ibid.,* pp. 12, 13.

"Here, then, is an age which is without beliefs in religion, without standards in morals, without convictions in politics, without values in art. I doubt if there has ever been an age which was so completely without standards or values."—*Ibid.,* p. 24.

Sired by the god of science, suckled at the breast of the goddess of human learning, we moderns have grown up as pagans. We live but for today. We discover no law by which we may live today with reference to God's tomorrow.

Our god of science has failed us a second time. He has given us no peace for our souls. Scientific knowledge in the possession of unsanctified men but speeds us more swiftly toward possible destruction. Like an apparently irresistible mass in motion, civilization hurtles on toward an immovable object. The crash seems inevitable, and the results seem final.

Stephen King-Hall, able commentator, wrote on December 2, 1948: "Our civilization today is like a conveyance which is rushing ahead into the future at an ever-increasing speed, carrying in its disintegrating framework a little two-legged creature, rather white-faced as he pulls levers, right, left and center, hoping that he may be lucky enough to find the brakes, or at any rate to stop the acceleration before . . . the whole outfit falls apart in glowing fragments." Of the drivers he says, "They do not know where they are going; they cannot find the brakes, and they are beginning to desire to find God on earth."—Quoted in *Signs of the Times,* March 1, 1949.

The possession of knowledge does not of itself produce peace of mind. Concerning this the wise man, Solomon, wrote, "In much wisdom is much grief: and he that increaseth knowledge increaseth sorrow." Ecclesiastes 1:18.

John E. McCaw, of the United Christian Missionary Society, in an address reported in *World Call,* November, 1948, gives this graphic picture: "Higher education today is producing the immoral, or at most, amoral man riding across the earth in a cap and gown with an electronic computor in one hand and a cyclotron in the other."—Page 17.

The simple unpalatable truth is that the key of knowledge that was to open the door to unprecedented happiness has but let man into a prison house more vast, where giants of fear and despair clutch at the throats of hope and peace. Knowledge alone is not the key to happiness.

Two Things to Remember

One thing to remember is that happiness cannot be found by seeking it for ourselves. No greater guarantee of absolute failure could possibly be given.

A discerning writer has said, "You are making a mistake in searching for happiness. . . . While your thoughts are so much upon yourself, you cannot be happy."

The oft-repeated story of stubborn, crabbed grandpa is

to the point. Nothing seemed to please him. Suddenly he changed. His eyes twinkled, his words were merry, his manner was gentle, and his hands were willing. Someone asked, "Grandpa, what has happened to you?"

"Well," he said, "I've spent my whole life striving for a contented mind. It's done me no good, so I decided to be contented without it."

This is just another way of saying that grandpa had decided to think about something a great deal more important than his own happiness. Self-seeking spells unhappiness.

"The elusiveness of happiness is indicated by the fact that it cannot be sought and found for its own sake, nor as an end, but is something like a butterfly, which, when pursued, seems always just beyond our grasp, but which, if we sit down quietly, may light upon us."—*Sentinel.*

No, we do not sit down and deliberately wait for happiness, for that would be but another way of seeking for it. We simply must dismiss the whole idea of searching for it. This is another way of saying that to really live, self must die. That is what Jesus meant when He said, "Verily, verily, I say unto you, Except a corn of wheat fall into the ground and die, it abideth alone: but if it die, it bringeth forth much fruit." John 12:24.

Wise doctors of psychiatry may clothe their counsel in different words, but their fundamental advice is but the simple gospel of Christ. He came to show us how to live "more abundantly." (John 10:10.) The death of self is the beginning of life. Failing to discover this experience, we shall spend our lives, each in his own way, chasing the butterfly of happiness until our joints grow creaky and our brains senile. To make personal happiness the chief goal of life is selfish, unworthy, and disappointing.

The second thing to keep in mind is that we dare not judge the way of life by the way we feel.

One has truly said, "There are thousands who are traveling the road of darkness and error, the broad road which leads to death, who flatter themselves that they are in the path to happiness and heaven; but they will never find the one or reach the other." What is wrong with these persons? They depend upon their feelings. If they feel happy, that settles it. If they think they are going to heaven, that guarantees it. That is the way they calculate, as my father used to say.

John B. Sherrin, in an issue of *Homiletic and Pastoral Review,* struck at this fallacy of feeling as a gauge of happiness when he wrote, "Happiness is not in circumstances but in ourselves. It is not something we see like a rainbow, or feel, like the heat of a fire. Happiness is something we are."

Thousands judge their religious experience by the way they feel. Many deliberately set out to reach a certain state of what they believe to be a spiritual ecstasy. Like Indians in a war dance, they build up feeling to a given pitch. Feeling is the guide and gauge. Others concentrate in quietness, with the aim of reaching a higher plane.

Many more of us struggle on in a discouraged state, because one day we are on the mountaintop and the next day down in the valley. We get discouraged over feeling discouraged. We despair at the disparity and change we see in our experience. To ourselves we say, "I am unstable like Reuben, and I cannot excel at this business of life and happiness."

To those who seek the way of life through religion it is well to recall the words of Scripture: "Be not righteous over much." Ecclesiastes 7:16. Too much introspection, too much concern with self, too much watching and weighing of the feelings will lead to self-centered despair on the one hand or obnoxious Phariseeism on the other.

There is considerable good sense in the following

words: "Bible sanctification does not consist of strong emotion. Here is where many are led into error. They make feelings their criterion. When they feel elated or happy, they claim that they are sanctified. Happy feelings or the absence of joy is no evidence that a person is or is not sanctified. . . . True sanctification is a daily work, continuing as long as life shall last. Those who are battling with daily temptations, overcoming their own sinful tendencies, and seeking for holiness of heart and life, make no boastful claims of holiness. They are hungering and thirsting for righteousness."

These words indicate battle, conflict, effort. Someone has said, "Peace is not the absence of conflict from life but the ability to cope with it." The seaman who will sail only a calm ocean will do little shipping. Life never offers complete satisfaction. Useful life must carry some burden lest it be an empty wagon, a train without passengers, a ship turned derelict upon the ocean of time.

Feelings of peace, happiness, or satisfaction may find a large place in your life, but if allowed to determine its course, they will bring to failure the most auspicious beginning.

When our first baby came along we all had a miserable time with his colic. I had to get up at night, in the cold, to warm his milk, pat him on the back for what seemed endless hours, all the while fighting sleep. If I should live beyond the 969 years of famed Methuselah, I doubt whether I would ever come to *feel* happy over the anticipation or the experience of getting up barefoot in the cold, or patting a baby's back while myself hungry for sleep.

Why, then, did I do these things? Because I loved the child and had a responsibility to bear. My actions were not dictated or my duty prescribed by my feelings. Momentary pleasing of ourselves, measured in feeling, is not a safe guide for living.

The Son of God did not bear the scorn of sinful men because it felt good. He did not die at their hands because it felt good. Some higher, more noble purpose dominated His life, else He would have wiped the bloody sweat of agony from His brow and returned to heaven, leaving man to perish in his sins.

All will agree that the greatest joy is in heaven. Few stop to consider that the deepest sorrow is also there. The greater the love, the greater the joy at the salvation of one soul. The greater the love, the deeper the sorrow at the loss of one who might have been saved. More love means more joy and more sorrow. Less love means less joy and less sorrow.

As long as love and sin compete for supremacy there will be both joy and sorrow. When Jesus stood weeping at the tomb of His friend Lazarus, the Jews said, "Behold how he loved him." He wept because He loved. When one sinner repents there is more joy in heaven than "over ninety and nine just persons, which need no repentance." Heaven rejoices because Heaven loves.

In the conflict between good and evil, between love and sin, between Christ and Satan, we are all involved. The fitful, changeful, fluctuating feelings of the human heart are not a safe guide in making choices that determine our destiny.

Two Kinds of Peace

Christ is speaking. He is just ready to enter Gethsemane. He who was called by Isaiah, "a man of sorrows, and acquainted with grief," was shortly to say, "My soul is exceeding sorrowful, even unto death." Matthew 26:38. In such an hour He said to His disciples, "Peace I leave with you, my peace I give unto you: not as the world giveth, give I unto you. Let not your heart be troubled, neither let it be afraid." John 14:27.

Here are two kinds of peace—the peace of Christ and the peace of the world. As a matter of fact, the peace of the world is not considered by Heaven as real peace at all. "The wicked are like the troubled sea, when it cannot rest, whose waters cast up mire and dirt. There is no peace, saith my God, to the wicked." Isaiah 57:20, 21. How true are the words of the prophet: "They have healed also the hurt of the daughter of my people slightly, saying, Peace, peace; when there is no peace." Jeremiah 6:14.

Money stands for many of the things the world offers us because it may be used to purchase them. It has been said that if all the gold in the world were melted into the form of a cube, it would be the size of an eight-room house. If you suddenly became the owner of that cube of precious metal, would you find peace? The chances are that you would soon have less peace than you ever had, and millions of others would be less happy. As Charles F. Banning put it, you "could not buy a friend, character, peace of mind, a clear conscience, or a sense of eternity."

Modern science may give us more money and more things, but it cannot give us peace.

God's Way of Peace

Where science fails God succeeds. Science, whose every step of progress is based upon discovery and application of nature's laws, gives man no moral law.

God has given us His perfect law. He spoke these commandments and "added no more. And he wrote them in two tables of stone." Deuteronomy 5:22.

Then He promises us the peace of obedience. "Great peace have they which love thy law: and nothing shall offend them." Psalms 119:165. Again He exclaims, "O that thou hadst hearkened to my commandments! then had thy peace been as a river, and thy righteousness as the waves of the sea." Isaiah 48:18.

Of what value is the peace of obedience to us when we have been disobedient? "Now we know that what things soever the law saith, it saith to them who are under the law: that every mouth may be stopped, and all the world may become guilty before God." Romans 3:19.

There can be no true peace in the presence of a guilty conscience. No lash has more or sharper tails of steel than the whip of conscience.

Up to the Temple went a publican to pray. Ashamed to look up, beating his breast with his hands, he cried, "God be merciful to me a sinner." Luke 18:13. The law was holy, but he was unholy. The law was just, but he was unjust.

Of this suffering man Jesus declared, "I tell you, this man went down to his house justified" (verse 14); that is, he was forgiven. His past life was accounted just although it had been unjust.

What else did the publican have besides or with forgiveness? "Therefore being justified by faith, we have peace with God through our Lord Jesus Christ." Romans 5:1. From a guilty conscience we escape by confession and faith to the cross of Christ, where we find peace. "Having made peace through the blood of his cross." Colossians 1:20.

The drowning man in his last moments of conscious terror grasps at a floating straw upon the surface of the water. But he goes down for the last time, taking the straw with him.

Upon the deep and troubled waters that swirl about our unworthy and guilty lives is borne a floating piece of wood. In desperation, with our last ounce of strength, we fling ourselves upon it—and lo! it is a cross. Clinging steadfastly to it, we make our way to shore, to safety, to life. Once it was a cross of shame. Now it is the cross of salvation.

"Upon the cross of Jesus,
Mine eye at times can see
The very dying form of one
Who suffered there for me.
And from my smitten heart with tears,
Two wonders I confess,—
The wonders of his glorious love,
And my own worthlessness."

David cried out, "My sin is ever before me," "neither is there any rest ["peace," margin] in my bones." Psalms 51:3; 38:3. Delivered from this state of remorse, he exclaimed, "Blessed [happy] is he whose transgression is forgiven, whose sin is covered." Psalms 32:1. This is the peace of reconciliation, of justification, of forgiveness. The greater the sense of guilt, the greater the joy at deliverance from it.

Next comes the peace of fellowship. "What the law could not do, in that it was weak through the flesh, God sending his own Son in the likeness of sinful flesh, and for sin, condemned sin in the flesh: that the righteousness of the law might be fulfilled in us, who walk not after the flesh, but after the Spirit. . . . To be spiritually minded is life and peace." Romans 8:3-6.

To keep the law of God brings peace. To break its commandments brings guilt. The cross of Jesus brings the peace of forgiveness. Then the Spirit of God gives us power to obey the law. We are restored to fellowship with God. "The Spirit itself beareth witness with our spirit, that we are the children of God." Verse 16.

Will our sorrows and troubles now end? The next verses give the answer. "If children, then heirs; heirs of God, and joint-heirs with Christ; if so be that we suffer with him, that we may be also glorified together. For I reckon that the sufferings of this present time are not worthy to be compared with the glory which shall be revealed in us." Verses 17, 18.

Not peace without pain, but peace despite pain, and sometimes through pain. Not peace without trouble, but peace *in* trouble. Not peace without tempest, but peace *in* the tempest. As has been so wisely said, "At the heart of the cyclone tearing through the sky is a place of central calm."

In this whirling tornado of life there is a calm at the center with God. "Clouds and darkness are round about him." Psalms 97:2. Fear not the storm. Fellowship with God at its center.

He "maketh the clouds his chariot: who walketh upon the wings of the wind." Psalms 104:3.

God drew near to Abraham in the "horror of great darkness. . . . And he said unto Abraham, Know of a surety." Genesis 15:12, 13.

"Moses drew near unto the thick darkness where God was." Exodus 20:21.

Job cried out, "He hath set darkness in my path." "Then the Lord answered Job out of the whirlwind." Job 19:8; 38:1.

Does your life seem often surrounded by clouds and darkness and whirlwinds? Let God speak to you. He will bring to you treasures of peace as bright as any you ever enjoyed in days of light.

"The clouds but cover the sunshine,
They cannot banish the sun:
And the earth shines out the brighter
When the weary rain is done.
We must stand in the deepest shadow
To see the clearest light
And often from wrong's own darkness
Comes the very strength of right."

—G. M. REA.

A pilot flying the cyclone area of the Caribbean Sea said, "We use the cyclones. We get on one edge and ride a one-hundred-mile-an-hour tail wind. Coming back, we get on the other side with the same advantage."

"If fate throws a dagger at you, there are two places to take hold of it—by the blade or by the handle." Self-pity cuts itself on the blade. Faith grasps the handle.

The ways of sin are mysterious. The ways of God are sometimes so. Let not feeling be our guide. Let God be our guide. Let faith follow and fellowship, and let God explain in His own good time and way.

"Judge not the Lord by feeble sense,
But trust him for his grace;
Behind a frowning providence
He hides a smiling face.

"Blind unbelief is sure to err,
And scan his work in vain;
God is his own interpreter,
And he will make it plain."

—WILLIAM COWPER.

Our last step is the peace of purpose—the purpose to serve. Said Jesus, "Take my yoke upon you, . . . and ye shall find rest unto your souls." Matthew 11:29.

We may know the commandments of God, the forgiveness of God, and the fellowship of His Spirit in holiness of a kind. But this is but the half of life. The whole of life has another half, and that half is the yoke of Christ. It is unselfish service.

"Happiness that is sought from selfish motives, outside of the path of duty, is ill-balanced, fitful, and transitory; it passes away, and the soul is filled with loneliness and sorrow; but there is joy and satisfaction in the service of God."—*Steps to Christ,* p. 130.

A woman broke her spine and severed the spinal cord in an accident. For ten years she lay in a hospital. To her minister she said:

"They say life begins at forty. I was forty the day after my accident. Life began for me then."

That day this woman took up her cross of suffering and her yoke of service. People flocked to her bedside. They went away with a new radiance in their hearts, given to them by one who might have given up and said, "I have no work to do."

It was the great Albert Schweitzer who said, "I don't know what your destiny will be, but one thing I know: the only ones among you who will be really happy are those who will have sought and found how to serve."

Bess Cochrane, in *Without Halos,* tells of how radiant Mandy went to church. The minister said to her, "You have found happiness, haven't you, Mandy?" To which she replied, "No, suh! I ain't found it. I'se made it."

Put it this way: Half our happiness we receive. The other half we make by serving our best in love and sincerity. That is something of what is meant by the saying, "Happiness is not given; it's exchanged." The more people who serve more, the more happiness is literally manufactured and exchanged. It is axiomatic that society can have more of any product only if more is produced and made available. And "it is more blessed to give than to receive." Acts 20:35. He who gives most of himself in service always has the edge in happiness over the receiver.

The Greatest Service and the Greatest Joy

"Even as the Son of man came not to be ministered unto, but to minister, and to give his life a ransom for many." Matthew 20:28.

When we stand before Calvary, where the ministry of Christ's life was poured out in the fullness of sacrifice, we receive salvation. We experience the joy of salvation. Heaven's joy is yet greater than ours, for Heaven gave salvation. This is the "more joy" in heaven over a sinner that repenteth. Christ sees of the "travail of his soul, and shall be satisfied." Isaiah 53:11.

Likewise when a sinner saved by grace becomes the channel of salvation to another, he experiences this greater joy of giving, of serving.

Said Paul, "What is our hope, or joy, or crown of rejoicing? Are not even ye in the presence of our Lord Jesus Christ at his coming? For ye are our glory and joy." 1 Thessalonians 2:19, 20.

Dr. Charles R. Brown mentions an old legend that tells how the gate of heaven was so narrow that one man walking alone could not get through. Two men, one of whom had helped the other, found the gate wide enough for them. When ten men came, all of whom had been serving one another in love, they found the gate so wide that they could see no post on either side.

At the age of eighty-one Evangeline Booth said, "The more I saw of the darkness of the world, the more I wanted to tell about the light of the world." This is the "more joy" of being a channel of the saving grace of God.

Closing Summary

True happiness is a by-product of the life we live.

First, we subscribe to the commandments of God. "He that keepeth the law, happy is he." Proverbs 29:18. "Blessed are they that do his commandments, that they may have right to the tree of life, and may enter in through the gates into the city." Revelation 22:14.

Second, we confess our guilt in that we have all sinned. We have transgressed the law of God. "Blessed is he whose transgression is forgiven." Psalms 32:1.

Third, through the reception of the Holy Spirit we become spiritually minded, no longer minding the things of the flesh, but having the "righteousness of the law . . . fulfilled in us." Romans 8:4.

"To be spiritually minded is life and peace." Verse 6. This is fellowship.

All these things we do whether we feel like doing them or not. We confess our sins whether we feel like confessing or not. We receive forgiveness by faith, not by feeling. We submit to the law of God and the Spirit of God, whether we feel like submitting or not. "The carnal mind . . . is not subject to the law of God." Verse 7. We obey God's commandments because we choose to let the Spirit control our minds and hearts. We become spiritually minded.

And finally we go forth in our sphere to the service of God, whether we always feel like it or not.

On a cold wintry night a lighthouse keeper lay sleeping. Just before dawn his wife awoke at the raging of a terrible storm. Violent waves pounded the rocky shore. As the faint light of morning came she saw a ship breaking on the reef. Three men, almost frozen to death, still clung to the broken masts. To herself she said, "What shall I do? Shall I call my husband? If I wake him, and he puts out in this storm, he may perish!" But the call of duty came before the voice of feeling. She roused her husband from slumber and helped put him forth on the raging waters in a boat that seemed like an eggshell in a tempest. She waited, prayed, watched, and agonized. The three men were saved, because a woman and a man were dedicated to service.

The disciples of Jesus very often contended among themselves as to which should be accounted the greatest. Said Jesus to them, "I am among you as he that serveth." Luke 22:27.

In the very shadow of Calvary, when the pride of the disciples stood erect and stiff, Jesus girded Himself with a towel and bent to wash their feet in preparation for the Passover, at which He was to be the sacrifice.

Was this mock humility, a mere means of showing up the selfishness of His disciples? Read the following words from His lips, and draw your own conclusion:

"Let your loins be girded about, and your lights burning; and ye yourselves like unto men that wait for their lord, when he will return from the wedding; that when he cometh and knocketh, they may open unto him immediately. Blessed are those servants, whom the lord when he cometh shall find watching: verily I say unto you, that he shall gird himself, and make them to sit down to meat, and will come forth and serve them. . . . Be ye therefore ready also: for the Son of man cometh at an hour when ye think not." Luke 12:35-40.

When Christ comes the second time He will gather His servants. All the redeemed from Adam down through the ages will be led through the gates of pearl over the streets of gold to the throne of God. Then wonder of love, they sit down to eat, and the Saviour of Calvary girds Himself and comes forth to serve them. Thus begins the eternity of the servants of the Christ who serves. Heaven is the place where love serves.

If we are to serve with Christ there, we must begin here. If we are to confess Him there, we must do so here. If we are to obey God then, we must keep His commandments now. If we are to dwell with God in heaven, we must have fellowship with Him here. So doing, we shall have peace.

"And the peace of God, which passeth all understanding, shall keep your hearts and minds through Christ Jesus." Philippians 4:7.

"Now the God of peace, that brought again from the dead our Lord Jesus, that great shepherd of the sheep, through the blood of the everlasting covenant, make you perfect in every good work to do his will, working in you that which is wellpleasing in his sight, through Jesus

Christ: to whom be glory for ever and ever. Amen." Hebrews 13:20, 21.

"What a treasure I have in this wonderful peace,
Buried deep in my innermost soul;
So secure that no power can mine it away,
While the years of eternity roll!

"Peace! peace! wonderful peace,
Coming down from the Father above;
Sweep over my spirit forever, I pray,
In fathomless billows of love."

—W. D. CORNELL.

Date Due